LENNON ON LENNON

CONVERSATIONS WITH JOHN LENNON

EDITED BY JEFF BURGER

CHICAGO
REVIEW
PRESS

An A Cappella Book

Copyright © 2017 by Jeff Burger
All rights reserved.
Published by Chicago Review Press Incorporated
814 North Franklin Street
Chicago, Illinois 60610

ISBN 978-1-61374-824-4

Library of Congress Cataloging-In-Publication Data
Names: Lennon, John, 1940–1980. | Burger, Jeff, 1949– editor.
Title: Lennon on Lennon : conversations with John Lennon / edited by Jeff
    Burger.
Description: Chicago : Chicago Review Press, 2016. | Includes index.
Identifiers: LCCN 2016008158 (print) | LCCN 2016010359 (ebook) | ISBN
    9781613748244 (cloth) | ISBN 9781613748251 (adobe pdf) | ISBN
    9781613748275 (epub) | ISBN 9781613748268 (kindle)
Subjects: LCSH: Lennon, John, 1940–1980—Interviews. | Rock
    musicians—Interviews. | Beatles.
Classification: LCC ML420.L38 A5 2016 (print) | LCC ML420.L38 (ebook) | DDC
    782.42166092—dc23
LC record available at http://lccn.loc.gov/2016008158

A list of credits and copyright notices for the individual pieces in this collection can
be found on pages 449–450.

Typesetting: Nord Compo

Printed in the United States of America
5 4 3 2 1

For Madeleine, Andre, and Myriam.
You made my biggest dreams come true.

CONTENTS

PREFACE

John Lennon spent only about thirteen years in the public spotlight—from 1963 until mid-1975 and, following a period of seclusion, during the fall of 1980—and he has been gone for nearly three times as long. Yet he remains omnipresent more than thirty-five years after his death. Rarely does a day go by when I don't hear one of his songs, read an item about him in a newspaper or magazine, see his image on a T-shirt, or hear his influence in the work of other artists. We'll likely be listening to and talking about this man for many years to come.

His music is only one of several reasons why he remains fascinating. He developed during his years of prominence into a highly opinionated and controversial figure with a commanding personality and quick wit. And for many of the years after he achieved fame, he made a point of living his adventurous life as openly as possible. Whether he was experimenting with LSD, Transcendental Meditation, primal therapy, macrobiotic diets, or recording techniques, the public was on board every step of the way. He spoke candidly about his intense, sometimes tumultuous relationship with Yoko Ono, his split with the Beatles, his squabbles with Paul McCartney, and just about everything else, baring his emotional ups and downs for all to see. He even literally bared himself, on the jacket of his *Two Virgins* LP and in the iconic photograph of him and Ono that Annie Leibovitz took just hours before he died.

Like the Beatles—who covered the vast distance between "I Want to Hold Your Hand" and "Strawberry Fields Forever" in an astonishing three years—Lennon transformed himself during his years in the public eye. He struggles to find words during much of this book's first interview, which he gave to a New Zealand radio station on June 21, 1964. But he seems increasingly well spoken—and often outspoken—in subsequent Beatles interviews; and, by the late 1960s, he evidences not only a keen sense of humor but also strong views on a wide range of issues.

By the time he granted this book's, and his, final interview—on December 8, 1980, only hours before his death—he had become one of the most famous people on the planet and an articulate commentator on politics, human relations, and world peace. The once tongue-tied young man had evolved into someone whose words and music affected millions around the world.

Lennon pushed the limits at every turn, whether he was performing "Woman Is the Nigger of the World" on *The Dick Cavett Show*, talking left-wing politics on the mainstream *Mike Douglas Show*, conducting interviews with Ono from their bed, or holding a press conference with his head covered by a bag. (The couple called this "bagism" and claimed that it promoted "total communication.")

"You may say I'm a dreamer," Lennon sang in his anthemic 1971 hit "Imagine," and he certainly was that. Some of his dreams, opinions, and other pronouncements now sound ahead of their time, or even ahead of ours; others today seem dated, naive, or even ridiculous. During a 1971 conversation with New York radio personality Howard Smith, he appeared to plead poverty, saying, "Most of it [the money] never got to us [the Beatles]. . . . We ain't got any millions in the bank, I'll tell ya that." At another point, asked to reconcile his penchant for healthy foods with his cigarette smoking, he told Smith, "Smoking doesn't harm you as much as all the chemical crap you eat every morning. . . . I think in the old days the government used to keep you down by not educating you. Now they keep you down by poisoning you."

To borrow an album title from the late rock great Lou Reed, Lennon was "growing up in public," which may help to explain why we witnessed such dramatic shifts in his views over time. In 1971 he dismissed his Beatles years in a conversation with left-wing activist Tariq Ali, saying, "It was complete oppression. I mean, we had to go through humiliation upon humiliation with the middle classes. . . . I found I was having continually to please the sort of people I'd always hated when I was a child." But a few years later, he was looking back fondly on the Beatles era and speaking critically of Ali and other political activists.

"That radicalism was phony, really, because it was out of guilt," he told *Newsweek*'s Barbara Graustark a few months before his death. "Being a chameleon, I became whoever I was with. When you stop and think, what the hell was I doing fighting the American government just because [Yippie leader] Jerry Rubin couldn't get what he always wanted—a nice cushy job?"

While Lennon changed over the years and sometimes mixed silliness with wisdom, he always sounded sincere. And he was never, ever boring. There's no question in my mind that the world is better off for having dreamers like Lennon, imperfect as they may be. Besides, he was prescient regarding the women's movement and right about a lot of other things, including the Vietnam War, Richard Nixon, and maybe even Ono's music, which was widely derided in earlier years but is today cited as a major influence by more than a few artists.

As for the Lennon quotes that now sound puerile, pointless, or anachronistic, well, consider his comment in 1968 that some of his published statements simply "said how I felt that day. But do I have to stand by that for the rest of me life just because it's in print?" Or, as he told talk-show host Dick Cavett in 1971: "If . . . you're in a certain mood, you'll say certain things to them [reporters]. And then people bring it back five years later: 'So you said this, did ya?' But you've forgotten all about it. You've changed your mood, it's a different day, it's a different year, you know, and you're feeling entirely different. . . . If everybody's words were recorded as they were saying it, there's lots of things you say that either turn out to be silly or you didn't mean it or it's spur-of-the-moment or you meant it or you had foresight or didn't."

Lennon talked often with the media, frequently at great length, and a complete collection of his hundreds of print and broadcast interviews would fill many volumes. In fact, entire books have been devoted to single interviews, most notably *Lennon Remembers*, a 1970 conversation with *Rolling Stone* editor Jann Wenner, and *The Playboy Interviews with John Lennon & Yoko Ono*, which resulted from about twenty hours of talk with journalist David Sheff in September 1980. There is also so much material online that I initially questioned the necessity of this book.

But as I explored Lennon's conversations and tracked down information—a task complicated by the fact that many of the interviewers have long since died, as have many of the media outlets—I became convinced that this project made sense. The most engrossing discussions were not in one place and many had never appeared in print or even been transcribed. Some—including conversations that represent more than a third of the material anthologized here—have long been difficult or impossible to find in any form. As for the Q&As that have previously been obtainable, I found countless instances of poorly or incompletely transcribed conversations, inaccurately listed dates and places, misspelled names, and incorrectly attributed comments.

Here, then, is an annotated, fact-checked, chronologically arranged anthology of some of Lennon's most illuminating and representative interviews. Interspersed throughout the book, also, are key quotes from dozens of additional Q&As. Together, this material paints a revealing picture of the artist in his own words. It also suggests some of the directions his life might have taken if it hadn't been cut short. And it offers a window into the late 1960s and '70s, which, as these interviews make clear, was a very different time in America and the world.

———————

This is my third book for Chicago Review Press's Musicians in Their Own Words series, following volumes on Bruce Springsteen and Leonard Cohen. Most of the response to those collections was gratifyingly positive, but one occasional criticism concerned repetition. There was some of that in the earlier books, and there's a little of it here, because it's inherent in the format. Interviewers do sometimes ask similar questions, and interviewees do sometimes recycle responses.

As in the earlier books, I have attempted to select interviews that largely cover territory not explored elsewhere, but there are only two ways I could have avoided all repetition. One would have been to exclude pieces that introduced any redundancy, which would have eliminated many conversations that contain important commentary not found in other Q&As. Another would have been to edit out portions of interviews that touch on subjects addressed similarly elsewhere.

I suspect most fans will prefer unadulterated conversations to ones that have been expunged of all repetition, so I've opted to present full interviews. (The one exception is a lengthy Q&A with Maurice Hindle and his companions, which for several reasons is excerpted from the even longer original.) Besides, I kind of like the occasional return to previously covered turf. It suggests that a subject was particularly important to Lennon and/or to his questioners, and when the same subject or idea is addressed in two or more discussions, the varying statements often shed additional light.

A word about style. Most of the chapters in this book resulted from my transcriptions of audio and video recordings. I have edited them slightly for readability and have formatted them to conform to the guidelines in the *Chicago Manual of Style*. The three pieces here that have previously been published in print have not been altered to fit that style, however; those appear as they originally ran in *Rolling Stone*, *Spin*, and *Newsweek*.

Many of these conversations involve more than Lennon and an interviewer. During the Beatles' years together, he rarely spoke to the press without his bandmates in tow, and the group often tried to deal with incessant requests for interviews by talking to multiple reporters at once in press conferences. Because Lennon and Yoko Ono remained inseparable during most of the years they knew each other, there's also lots of her in these pages. And you'll find an assortment of other characters here as well—everyone from the aforementioned Jerry Rubin and LSD advocate Timothy Leary to actresses Shirley MacLaine and Tallulah Bankhead, all of whom add color to already colorful conversations.

As you'll see, some of these discussions don't even feel like interviews. Lennon did do his share of formal Q&As. But he was just as likely to be found lying on his bed with Ono and journalist Howard Smith, eating tempura shrimp, listening to the radio, and chatting for hours—all while a tape recorder ran. In another case, he passed the better part of an afternoon talking and nibbling macrobiotic bread with a trio of college students, again with the tape rolling. On other occasions—including this book's encounter with New York radio personality Dennis Elsas—he took on the role of DJ, playing records, reporting the latest weather, and even reading commercials.

One thing you won't discover here are any lengthy conversations from the early and mid-1960s or anything from 1976 through 1979. I have included a few pieces from the former period, but Lennon didn't give many in-depth interviews during that time. His comments to the press in that era tended to be limited to clever one-liners, often during group press conferences.

Fortunately, he opened up much more beginning around 1968, but then, seven years later, he closed the door to the media and opted for a private life as a househusband and father to his son Sean, who was born in October 1975. The following January, when *Melody Maker*'s Chris Charlesworth telegrammed the singer to request an interview, Lennon replied with a postcard that read, "No comment . . . am invisible."

And indeed he was, until the fall of 1980. That's when he and Ono again began granting interviews, to promote *Double Fantasy*, their first new album in five years, which appeared less than a month before Lennon was killed outside his Upper West Side New York apartment.

———

My thanks to the folks at Chicago Review Press, especially senior editor Yuval Taylor, who proposed and oversaw this project, and editor Ellen Hornor. Thanks, also, to everyone who contributed to or otherwise helped with this volume, particularly Tariq Ali, Jennifer Ballantyne at Universal Music, Denis Berry at the Futique Trust, Bill Bernstein, Ezra Bookstein at the Smith Tapes, Dick Cavett, Dennis Elsas, Melissa Garza at Westwood One, Maurice Hindle, Michael Horowitz, Jeff Nolan at Hard Rock, Lorelei Robbins, and Frances Schoenberger.

Special thanks to my good friend Ken Terry, who jumped with me into the wild world of journalism more than forty years ago and has shared its ups and downs with me ever since; and to Julien Beresford, Kathy Brunjes, Todd and Deborah Burger, Carl and Ann Hartog, and Jeannie Shaw. Thanks, also, to Jennifer Leach English, my valued friend and partner in crime at AIN Publications, and to all my other coworkers at AIN, especially the folks I work with most closely: Charlie and Susie Alcock, Mona Brown, Mike and Colleen Giaimo, Tom Hurley, Martha Jercinovich, David Leach, Wilson Leach, John Manfredo, Lysbeth McAleer, Mark Phelps, Greg Rzekos, Ian Whelan, and Annmarie Yannaco.

Greatest thanks always to my amazing wife and best friend, Madeleine Beresford, and to our two wonderful children, Andre and Myriam. We can debate whether "all you need is love," but it sure does help.

—Jeff Burger
Ridgewood, New Jersey, 2016

RADIO INTERVIEW

Doreen Kelso | June 21, 1964, St. George Hotel, Wellington, New Zealand |
Broadcast date unknown, 2ZB (Wellington, New Zealand)

The Beatles' earliest meetings with the press were manic affairs, with teenage girls screaming, multiple reporters shouting often ridiculous questions, and the Fab Four shooting back
funny, lightweight replies. Typical was the press conference they gave when they arrived
at JFK International Airport on February 7, 1964, at the beginning of their first visit to the
United States. The event started with an MC pleading, "Could we please have quiet? Could
we please have quiet? Quiet, please! Unless you keep quiet, we won't have a press conference." And finally: "Will you please shut up?"

Then came questions about whether the Beatles' haircuts helped them perform and
whether they were "afraid of what the American Barbers' Association is going to think of
you." We got an early taste of John Lennon's wit—and candor—when someone asked the
group to sing and he replied, "No, we need money first." Mostly, though, the JFK Q&A and
other Beatles press encounters of the period serve just to remind us of the sort of inane
questions they had to put up with in the early days.

The following brief interview with New Zealand radio personality Doreen Kelso, which
took place a little more than four months after the press conference at JFK, is one of the
exceptions to the rule. The mood is more subdued than usual, because no fans are present and because the participants include only one reporter and—fairly unusual for those
days—just one Beatle. And while the interviewer does ask the inevitable haircut question,
she also throws in a few serious queries.

Beatlemania was in full swing at the time of this conversation. The group had released
several exuberant, addictively upbeat hit albums in short succession, including *Please Please
Me, With the Beatles,* and *Beatles for Sale.* They had also taken the States by storm,

performing on a February 9, 1964, broadcast of *The Ed Sullivan Show* that attracted an estimated seventy-three million viewers, the largest American television audience up to that point. *A Hard Day's Night*, their first all-originals collection, would appear in the United States just five days after this interview and would spend fourteen weeks at the top of the charts. Its music—including such classics as "If I Fell," "And I Love Her," and "Things We Said Today"—would help turn their shoestring-budget first film into a major hit.

On their summer tour of Australia and New Zealand, their popularity proved as strong there as it was in the United States and United Kingdom. The Beatles attracted the usual screaming crowds, and kids scooped up their records in unprecedented numbers. On the Australian pop charts for 1964, they held nine of the top twenty-five positions, including the top six. They also managed to have fourteen songs on the list, because most of their records were two-sided hits.

But as this Q&A suggests, these were still early days indeed when it came to Lennon's dealings with the press. Perhaps somewhat less at ease than usual without his bandmates by his side, the twenty-three-year-old singer appears to struggle at times to express himself. The program's announcer, meanwhile, underscores the fact that at least a few people remain uninitiated to the Beatles by getting Lennon's name wrong in his introduction. —Ed.

Announcer: The interviewer then spoke with John Lemon [*sic*].

Doreen Kelso: You do have fans from all age groups, don't you?

John Lennon: Yes. Some people say it's a . . . that when you get older fans, the kids don't like you. It's true with a pocket of kids, but it's much more satisfying to have a good, you know, sort of, I can't think of the word, coverage of, and y'know, what's the word? I can't, y'know . . . oh, it doesn't matter anyway, more different types than just one packet of, pocket of, sort of [*laughs*] one packet of little fans in one corner, y'know.

Kelso: Your book, *In My Own Write* [*Correct title is* In His Own Write. —*Ed.*] . . . what's it all about, John?

Lennon: It's about nothing. If you like it, you like it; if you don't, you don't. That's all there is to it. There's nothing deep or anything in it. It's just meant to be funny.

Kelso: Entertainment.

Lennon: I hope.

Kelso: What about the next one you're writing?

Lennon: I don't know. I'm just, y'know . . . I don't know whether I'll ever write one if I get . . . it just depends how I feel. I'm just writing now and then when I feel like it. I only do it when I feel in a funny mood.

Kelso: You mentioned art school. Were you going to be an artist of some kind?

Lennon: I went to art school because there didn't seem to be any hope for me in any other field. It was about the only thing I could do, possibly, but I didn't do very well there either 'cause I'm lazy, you see. So that's the way it goes.

Kelso: Did you use your art at all? Have you done any drawings?

Lennon: I did the drawings for the book. That's the most amount of drawing I've done since I left college.

Kelso: John, what was your group called originally?

Lennon: We had one or two names. I had a group before I met the others called the Quarrymen, and then Paul joined it, and then George joined it. Then we began to change the names for different bookings, you know, and then we finally hit upon the Beatles.

Kelso: And what about the haircut?

Lennon: That just, ah, it's so long ago we can hardly remember. It was something to do with Paris and something to do with Hamburg, and we were not quite sure now 'cause there's so much been written about it. Even we've forgotten. That's true.

Kelso: Have to read it up to find out.

Lennon: Yeah, well, you know, they just make it up about the hair now, but it was something that happened between Hamburg and Paris.

Kelso: How do you feel about all the manufacturers sort of jumping on the bandwagon with all the Beatles shoes and bags and clothes?

Lennon: Well, most of them spelling it *B-E-A-T-L-E-S*, we've got some sort of thing in it. I don't know how it works; our accountants do it. So I don't mind it as long as we're in on it. And the ones that aren't are usually tracked down, if you're listening, and the clever ones try and use B double-E, but it doesn't often help, you know.

Kelso: Is there anything you want to do and see while you're in New Zealand?

Lennon: I want to see this stuff steaming out of the ground.

Kelso: Rotorua. [*A town on New Zealand's North Island, known for geysers and thermal mud pools fueled by geothermal activity. —Ed.*] Will you get up there?

Lennon: I don't know. We'll try.

LENNON ON . . .

Forming the Beatles

"About the time of rock 'n' roll in Britain—I think I was about fifteen, so it would be 1955—there was a big thing called skiffle, which was a kind of folk music, American folk music, only . . . with washboards. And all the kids, fifteen onwards, used to have these groups, and I formed one at school. And then I met Paul . . . and then I met George, and that's the way it went. We changed to rock, and that was all there was to it."

—from interview with the late KRLA disc jockey Jim Steck, *Hear the Beatles Tell All* album, released 1964

LENNON ON . . .

A Way to End Wars

"I don't think there is one, you know. Not if everybody was all rich and happy, and each country had all they wanted, they'd still want the next bit. I don't think there'll ever be any solution . . . only, just, you know, a sort of power block where everybody's got the same weapons."

—from interview with Larry Kane, Baltimore, Maryland, September 13, 1964

LENNON ON . . .

Making It in America

"America, it just seemed ridiculous . . . I mean, the idea of having a hit record over there. It was just, you know, something you could never do. That's what I thought, anyhow. But then I realized that it's just the same as here—that kids everywhere all go for the same stuff. And seeing we'd done it in England and all, there's no reason why we couldn't do it in America, too. But the American disc jockeys didn't know about British records; they didn't play them; nobody promoted them, and so you didn't have hits. . . . It wasn't until *Time* and *Life* and *Newsweek* came over and wrote articles and created an interest in us that American disc jockeys started playing our records. And Capitol said, 'Well, can we have their records?' You know, they had been offered our records years ago, and they didn't want them. But when they heard we were big over here they said, 'Can we have 'em now?' So we said, 'As long as you promote them.'"

—from interview with Jean Shepherd, Torquay, England, October 28, 1964, published in *Playboy* (US), February 1965

LENNON ON . . .

His Potential as a Book Author

"If I hadn't been a Beatle, I just wouldn't have thought of having the stuff published 'cause I would've been crawling around, broke, and just writing it and throwing it away. I might've been a Beat poet."

—from interview with Cliff Michelmore, broadcast on BBC's *Tonight*, June 18, 1965

LENNON ON . . .

Whether the Beatles Would Record with Elvis

"None of us have ever liked those albums where they put two people together who are either similar or, you know . . . I don't know. Like Sinatra and somebody else, you know. But I don't like that. Anyway, I'd hate an album like that."

—from interview with Chicago disc jockey Jerry G. Bishop, San Diego, August 28, 1965

PRESS CONFERENCE

August 11, 1966, Astor Towers, Chicago

From the time the Beatles arrived in America in February 1964 until shortly after this press conference, it seemed as if they ruled the world and could do no wrong. Their singles dominated the charts, their films drew large crowds, and their hit albums—each better and more sophisticated than the one before—arrived at a dizzying pace. In a period of approximately twelve months leading up to this press conference, for example, their releases included *Help!*, *Rubber Soul*, *Yesterday and Today*, and *Revolver*.

But then, for a brief time, the whole business appeared at risk of collapse, all because of something John Lennon had said to British journalist Maureen Cleave. "Christianity will go," he told her. "It will vanish and shrink. I needn't argue about that; I'm right, and I will be proved right. We're more popular than Jesus now; I don't know which will go first—rock 'n' roll or Christianity. Jesus was all right, but his disciples were thick and ordinary. It's them twisting it that ruins it for me."

It would be difficult to overstate the furor that followed that comment—particularly the line about the Beatles' popularity exceeding Christ's. Reaction was relatively light when the *London Evening Standard* published the quote on March 4, 1966, but the response intensified, particularly in the southern United States, after an American teen magazine picked up the lines a few months later.

Birmingham, Alabama, DJ Tommy Charles, of WAQY-AM (known as "Wacky 1220"), told his listeners: "If you as an American teenager are offended by statements from a group of foreign singers which strike at the very basis of our existence as God-fearing, patriotic citizens, then we urge you to take your Beatle records, pictures, and souvenirs to any of the collection points about to be named, and on the night of the Beatle appearance in Memphis, August 19, they will be destroyed in a huge public bonfire at a place to be named soon."

As it turned out, the controversy didn't last much longer than the bonfire, but records were indeed destroyed, and the Beatles convened press conferences in multiple US cities at which Lennon variously tried to explain and apologize for his comments. During this Chicago meeting with reporters, which took place six days after the UK release of *Revolver*, he attempted to do both. —Ed.

Reporter: Mr. Lennon, we've been hearing a great deal of interpretations of your comment regarding the Beatles and Jesus. Could you tell us what you really meant by that statement?

John Lennon: I'll try and tell ya. I was sort of deploring the attitude that . . . I wasn't saying whatever they were saying I was saying, anyway. That's the main thing about it. And I was just talking to a reporter [Maureen Cleave], but she also happens to be a friend of mine and the rest of us, at home. It was a sort of in-depth series she was doing. And so I wasn't really thinking in terms of PR or translating what I was saying. It was going on for a couple of hours, and I just said it as, just to cover the subject, you know. And it really meant what, you know . . . I didn't mean it the way they said it.

It's amazing. It's just so complicated. It's got out of hand, you know. But I just meant it as that—I wasn't saying the Beatles are better than Jesus or God or Christianity. I was using the name *Beatles* because I can use them easier, 'cause I can talk about Beatles as a separate thing and use them as an example, especially to a close friend. But I could have said "TV" or "cinema" or anything else that's popular, or "motorcars are bigger than Jesus." But I just said "Beatles" because, you know, that's the easiest one for me. I just never thought of repercussions. I never really thought of it. . . . I wasn't even thinking, even though I knew she was interviewing me, you know, that it meant anything.

Reporter: What's your reaction to the repercussions?

Lennon: Well, when I first heard it, I thought, *It can't be true.* It's just one of those things like bad eggs in Adelaide, but when I realized it was serious, I was worried stiff because I knew how it would go on. All the nasty things that would get said about it and all those miserable-looking pictures of me looking like a cynic. And they'd go on and on and on until it would get out of hand and I couldn't control it. I really can't answer for it when it gets this big. It's nothing to do with me now.

Reporter: A disc jockey from Birmingham, Alabama [*the aforementioned Tommy Charles —Ed.*], who actually started most of the repercussions, has demanded an apology from you.

Lennon: He can have it. I apologize to him. If he's upset and he really means it, you know, then I'm sorry. I'm sorry I said it for the mess it's made, but I never meant it as an antireligious thing or anything. You know, I can't say anything more than that. There's nothing else to say, really, no more words. I apologize to him.

Reporter: Mr. Lennon, are you a Christian?

Lennon: Well, we were all brought up to be. I don't profess to be a practicing Christian, and Christ was what he was, and anything anybody says great about him I believe. I'm not a practicing Christian, but I don't have any unchristian thoughts.

Reporter: Was there as much of a reaction to your statements through-out Europe and other countries around the world as there was here in America?

Lennon: I don't think Europe heard about it, but they will now. It was just England, and I sort of got away with it there, inasmuch as nobody took offense and saw through me. Over here, it's just as I said: it went this way.

Reporter: Some of the wires this morning said that Pan American Air-lines had provided each of you with free Bibles.

Lennon: We never saw that.

Reporter: If Jesus were alive today in a physical form, not a metaphysical one, he would find "Eleanor Rigby" a very religious song, a song of concern with human experience and need. I'm curious about your expression of that.

Lennon: Well, I don't like supposing that if Jesus were alive now, knowing what he'd like to say or do. But if he were the real Jesus, the Jesus as he was before, "Eleanor Rigby" wouldn't mean much to him. But if it did come across his mind, he'd think that, probably.

Paul McCartney: It was written because there are lonely people, and uh, it was just a song about—

George Harrison: And we had to have another track to fill up the LP.

McCartney: Anyway, what you said is right.

Reporter: Do you think the Americans lack a sense of humor?

Lennon, McCartney, Harrison, and Ringo Starr [*in unison*]: No.

McCartney: The thing is, you know, when we talk about all these things you say . . . "the Americans," but as you said, the Americans can't all be the same person. They can't all think the same way, you know. Some Americans lack humor and some Britons lack humor. Everybody lacks it somewhere. But there are just more people in the States, so you can probably pick on the minority classes more, you know.

Reporter: I read something recently that you were—

Lennon: Never said it!

Reporter: —worrying about the Beatles being brought down, that certain people were interested in getting the Beatles over with.

Lennon: Oh, I don't know. I think that's a bit of one that's . . . you know, I don't really know about that story, honestly.

Harrison: Sounds like a homemade one.

Lennon: There's nobody pulling us down. I'd agree that if we were slipping, there's lots of people that'd clap hands daddy-come-home.

Reporter: What kind of people do you think would be interested in—

Lennon: I don't know, because they never show themselves until that time arises when it's right for them.

Reporter: Do you feel you are slipping?

Lennon: We don't feel we're slipping. Our music's better—our sales might be less—so in our view we're not slipping, you know.

Reporter: How many years do you think you can go on? Have you thought about that?

Harrison: It doesn't matter, you know.

McCartney: We just try and go forward and—

Harrison: The thing is, if we do slip, it doesn't matter. You know, I mean, so what? We slip, and so we're not popular anymore. So we'll be us unpopular, won't we? You know, we'll be like we were before, maybe.

Lennon: And we can't invent a new gimmick to keep us going like people imagine we do.

Reporter: Do you think this current controversy is hurting your career?

Lennon: It's not helping it. I don't know about hurting it. You can't tell if a thing's hurt a career . . . until months after, really.

Reporter: You were also quoted as saying that you were not looking forward to the American tour, and that the only part of the tour that you really wanted to get to was the California part of the tour.

Harrison: I think I said that.

Lennon: Well, somebody probably said, "Which place do you like best in America?" and we probably said, "We enjoy L.A. most because we know a lot of people there." And that's how that comes to be, "We only want to be in L.A." You know, it just so happens we know a few people there, and we usually get a couple of days off, so we usually say L.A.

Harrison: We usually eat different food from hotel food. Not that there's anything wrong with hotel food! But, you know, it's a break from hotels because we get a house.

Reporter: Are there any southern cities included in your tour this trip?

McCartney: Yeah.

Lennon: Memphis. We're going there. Yeah.

Reporter: What is your feeling about going down South where most of this controversy has arisen?

Lennon: Well, I hope that if we sort of try and talk to the press and people and that . . . you know, you can judge for yourselves what it meant, I think, better by seeing us.

McCartney: The thing is, if you believe us now, what we're saying, you know, and we can get it straight, then . . .

Lennon: It might get through.

McCartney: 'Cause, I mean, we're only trying to straighten it up, you know.

Lennon: 'Cause we could've just sort of hidden in England and said, "We're not going, we're not going!" You know, that occurred to me when I heard it all. I couldn't remember saying it. I couldn't remember the article. I was panicking, saying, "I'm not going at all," you know. But if they sort of straighten it out, it will be worth it, and good. Isn't that right, Ringo?

Reporter: Do you ever get tired of one another's company?

Lennon: We only see each other on tour. All together as four at once, you see.

Reporter: To what do you ascribe your immense popularity?

Lennon: [*To McCartney.*] You answer that one, don't you?

Starr: I thought [Beatles press officer] Tony Barrow answers that one.

McCartney: Really, if you want an honest answer, none of us know at all.

Reporter: This is your third trip to Chicago. Have you had a chance to *see* Chicago yet?

McCartney: No, we . . . it looks nice out the window!

Harrison: This is the first time we've actually stayed here, I think.

Reporter: Do you hope to someday see some of these places that you've just flown in and out of?

Harrison: We can go to everywhere, really, I suppose. Everywhere we want to go when . . . when the bubbles burst.

Reporter: John, your music has changed immensely since you first started out. Is this because you've become more professional, or is it that you're trying to show the public—

Lennon: It's not trying, or being professional. It's just, you know, a progression.

Harrison: It's trying to satisfy ourselves, in a way. But you know, that's why we try and do things better, because we never get satisfied.

Lennon: It's only that, you know. It's not sitting 'round thinking, *Next week we'll do so and so and we'll record like that.* It just sort of happens.

Tony Barrow: Can we make this the last question, please?

Reporter: Yeah. A short one for Ringo.

Starr: Oh, no!

Reporter: Two weeks ago, we had a World Teenage Show here in Chicago.

Starr: And you won.

Reporter: There was a set of drums there on the floor, cordoned off, that said, "These are the drums that Ringo Starr will play when he's in Chicago." Now today at the airport, I saw some girls screaming when they saw an instrument case, apparently containing your drums, being loaded into a truck. Which drums are yours? Where are they?

Starr: Well, I hope they're both mine. I don't know. [Road manager] Malcolm [Evans] will tell you about that, you know. He just puts 'em in front of me. I just play them. He's the one who . . . have we got two kits? No? Oh, don't tell 'em that.

Reporter: One more question regarding your marital status. Has there been any change that you could tell us about?

McCartney: No, it's still three down and one to go.

RADIO INTERVIEW

Fred Robbins | October 29, 1966, Carboneras, Spain | Broadcast date unknown,
Assignment: Hollywood, syndicated (US)

As noted earlier, the mid-'60s found the Beatles racking up triumphs in rapid succession. *Help!* proved a big success in the summer of 1965, both cinematically and on record, and the group waited less than four months to follow it with *Rubber Soul*, a quantum leap musically that featured such classics as "In My Life," which Lennon largely wrote, and "Michelle," which McCartney primarily composed. (Like all of their songs on Beatles albums, these tracks are credited on the record label to both of them.)

Then came the US-only *Yesterday and Today* in June 1966, a collection of single tracks and UK album material, and *Revolver*, which appeared in the United Kingdom in August and featured such numbers as McCartney's "Eleanor Rigby," Harrison's sitar-spiced "Love You To," and Lennon's "I'm Only Sleeping." (The American edition, which came out four months later, omitted the last of these songs, as it had already surfaced on *Yesterday and Today*.)

But Lennon was restless. With *Revolver* finished, he decided the time had come to slip off on his own and try something new. So when Richard Lester—director of both *A Hard Day's Night* and *Help!*—invited him to appear in the movie *How I Won the War*, Lennon said yes.

When American journalist Fred Robbins interviewed Lennon on the film set in Carboneras, Spain, he found the Beatle immersed in the movie project, sporting a new haircut, and talking repeatedly about a need to test his wings and "try something for a change."

Lennon didn't know it at the time, but he was only days away from a much bigger change than the film role represented: at London's Indica Gallery on November 9, less than two weeks after this conversation took place, he would meet an avant-garde artist named Yoko Ono. —Ed.

Fred Robbins: Well, so our good friend John Lennon has been shorn.

John Lennon: Yes.

Robbins: How does it feel?

Lennon: It feels quite comfortable out here, you know. It's not too short.

Robbins: I was telling Michael [*Probably a reference to Michael Crawford, the film's star. —Ed.*] that you look a little like Bob Dylan this way. Have you noticed it? Anybody else say that?

Lennon: I dunno. Lots of people have said it. It's because me hair's standing on end. [*Laughs.*]

Robbins: It's very becoming, John. Honestly. I think it's easy to get used to, eh?

Lennon: It's quite easy to get used to. It's full of sand and old rubbish, you know.

Robbins: Think it'll take long to grow it back?

Lennon: No. It looks quite normal at night when I comb it, if I can get my comb through it. You wouldn't know it wasn't just the back's short and no sideboards.

Robbins: This must surely be one of the most unusual locations in the world, John. I wonder if you could describe it and tell us exactly where we are and what's going on here.

Lennon: You're asking me where we are! [*Giggles.*] Well, as far as I know, we're somewhere in Spain. It could be anywhere for all I know, actually. And it's just like . . . I dunno. It's like a dump, really. It's like the moon, you know—just desert and sand and hills and mountains. They're not very nice to look at, but the weather's OK now and then.

Robbins: Beautiful weather. What a perfect spot for this picture. This is supposed to represent what?

Lennon: North Africa, and I believe it's pretty similar.

Robbins: First dramatic role, huh, John?

Lennon: Well, *dramatic*'s a good word. [*Laughs.*] First *role*, really. The others were just messing about.

Robbins: How do you take to it? How does it come to you?

Lennon: Well, sometimes it comes hard [*laughs*] and sometimes it comes easy. It depends on the day.

Robbins: Do you like it? Do you find it's natural to be an actor?

Lennon: Well, some of it is natural. The most unnatural bits are hard, you know—the ones that are *really* out of character for me. It's all right, but it's not the be-all and end-all for me.

Robbins: But you do like it? You'd like to do more of it?

Lennon: I think I'd do limited amounts of stuff, because I *am* limited in what I could do.

Robbins: Really? You don't know until you try.

Lennon: No, I don't. But I don't want to be trying meself out in films. It's too public.

Robbins: It's true. John, did you know you could write before you wrote?

Lennon: I didn't think about it, because I was always writing, you see, just sort of naturally.

Robbins: In other words, the acting thing is still a new thing for you . . . just trying your wings.

Lennon: Yes, it's really trying me wings.

Robbins: It'll be fascinating to see what happens. Can you tell me about your character? Who do you play?

Lennon: It's a private soldier called Gripweed. He's not particularly nice. He's not *too* horrible. He's just looking after himself all the time. That's the main thing.

Robbins: And what relationship do you have to the other people in the film?

Lennon: Well, none really. We don't really have much of a relationship. We're not fighting or anything. We don't have a lot to say directly to each other. And . . . well, I'm [actor] Michael Crawford's batman. He's Officer Goodbody, and I'm meant to look after him, you know. But I spend most of the time not looking after him and trying to dodge it.

Robbins: Kind of mess things up a little bit, huh?

Lennon: Uh, it's a bit like that.

Robbins: That's a different connotation of the word *batman*. You know, in America we have a television series . . .

Lennon: [*Giggling.*] Oh, I know. We got it in Britain, too.

Robbins: You've got it here, too. But it really means an aide here, or helper, a batman.

Lennon: Oh, yeah. That's just the usual army term for the fella that crawls about, looking after the officer. You know, "Yes, sir. No, sir. Certainly, sir."

Robbins: And you got who else in this cast?

Lennon: There's Lee Montague, Jack Hedley, Roy Kinnear. Now let me think. Michael Hordern, of course, and Ronny Lacey—he's a great lad. They're all great lads.

Robbins: And you're right here with your old buddy [director] Dick Lester again.

Lennon: Yes, yes. He's all right. [*Laughs.*]

Robbins: He certainly established a style, John, with you fellas.

Lennon: I think . . . he has, hasn't he?

Robbins: I mean, the individuality of you guys, as well as his uniqueness as a director. . . . It was a great marriage in both pictures so far, you know. I think it's exciting that he's directing you in your first role away from the group.

Lennon: Well, I wouldn't have accepted, probably, if it hadn't been him. I would've been too nervous, you know. I can make a fool of meself in front of him because I know him. If it had been some other director saying "Do this and do that," I would have fallen apart.

Robbins: What does this character give you a chance to do, and in what light does it show you, as opposed to anything you've done in the past?

Lennon: It just *is* completely opposed to anything I've done in the past. I'm just a different person in it, and I'm just nothing like people have seen me before, really.

Robbins: Is that why you took the part?

Lennon: I took it because I was interested in the film and interested in trying me wings at something else. And I felt like doing something for a change, and this just happened to come up at a time when I felt in that mood.

Robbins: What generally does the film deal with, I wonder, without giving away any of the plot?

Lennon: It's very hard to generalize. [*Giggles.*] It's a strange film. It's just . . . I can't really say. . . . It's just about these people in the war, together and not together. That's all.

Robbins: A British squadron.

Lennon: Yes. It could be *any* squadron. It could be any soldiers, anywhere.

Robbins: Where have you been filming so far?

Lennon: We've been to Germany. We were there two weeks, filming on the NATO grounds. Whoopee. [*Giggles.*] And then we came out here.

Robbins: Does this mean that all of the boys are going to be trying different things as you go along, John?

Lennon: Well, I can't speak for the others, you know, but George has just got back from India—*trying* India. [*Giggles.*]

Robbins: I saw a picture of him with a mustache the other day, picking up that teacher of the sitar [Ravi Shankar] at [the] London airport.

Lennon: Oh, yeah. He traveled with him from India. That's his teacher.

Robbins: He flipped over that instrument, didn't he?

Lennon: Oh, yeah. Well, that fellow that teaches him is one of the all-time greats, so he's lucky that the fella would accept him as a pupil. He doesn't just have anybody.

Robbins: Will you be using the sitar as a regular sound? As a regular part of the—

Lennon: The sitar just happens to have come in useful on a couple of tracks, but it's really nothing to do with it. That's George's own scene.

Robbins: It won't be a part of the regular albums or records necessarily?

Lennon: No, unless it's called for.

Robbins: When is it called for?

Lennon: I don't know. When you suddenly think, *A sitar would be nice here.* George will obviously write more numbers with the sitars involved if he feels like it.

Robbins: You know what's marvelous, John, the last couple of years? The wonderful, wonderful songs that have come out of you and Paul and that really have established you in the complete universal audience as what you always were—great songwriters. "Michelle," "Yesterday," and all. It's just wonderful standards. And as you know, everybody's done 'em, from Count Basie to Ella Fitzgerald, which must be a great satisfaction for you.

Lennon: It is, yeah. It's great to see how they do 'em, too.

Robbins: Because you know, I remember the first time we met . . . and as always, when a new group cracks through, the skeptics, the doubters, and so on . . . but to finally prove what was always there . . . everybody realizes, "Hey, wow, these guys really are great songwriters!" Something that you knew all the time—

Lennon: We didn't really know. You don't know until it happens.

Robbins: But nobody thought you could write songs like "Michelle" and "Yesterday."

Lennon: No, because they were too busy just looking at the Beatle image.

Robbins: Are there more ballads like that coming out, you think?

Lennon: They're always there. They just come out.

Robbins: You like the soft things like that?

Lennon: Yeah.

Robbins: Getting romantic in your old age, huh?

Lennon: I've always had a bit of romantic in me.

Robbins: They're so haunting. And I believe it's only the beginning. Isn't it, John? The songwriting . . .

Lennon: I hope so. We're still fairly young, especially as musicians or songwriters.

Robbins: Where does the inspiration come from, or is it just craftsman-ship? Can you just sit down at a given time and say, "We have to write now," and out it comes?

Lennon: Well, sometimes it comes like that. Sometimes they say, "Now you must write," and now we write. But it doesn't come some days. We sit there for days just talking to each other, messing 'round, not doing anything.

Robbins: How was "Michelle" written?

Lennon: Paul had had this idea about writing a bit with some other language, with French in it. And he just sort of had a bit of a verse, and a couple of words, and the idea. I think he had some other name or something. Oh, he used to talk double-Dutch French, you see, just to sing the bit. [*Imitates singing in mock French.*] So he had that. And he just brought it along and just sort of started fiddling around, trying to get a middle eight. We pinched a little bit from somewhere and stuck it in the middle eight, and off we went.

Robbins: What about "Yesterday"?

Lennon: "Yesterday" is Paul completely on his own, really. We just helped finishing off the ribbons 'round it, you know—tying it up.

Robbins: I'm delighted to see that your last tour was such a smash for you, in view of the pressure that you were under. I was thrilled that it came out as well as it did.

Lennon: [*Giggling.*] I was pleased meself.

Robbins: Such a ridiculous thing that happened on this experience that you had. [*A reference to the Beatles-are-bigger-than-Christ controversy. —Ed.*] I want to know, just to wrap this thing up, what kind of reflections you had on that whole thing, John.

Lennon: Well, now it's just like a bad dream. It's just way in the back of my mind somewhere, and it just comes back when you read things, just odd things that crop up now and then—"Cardinal so-and-so says it's OK," or things like that. But it's really *way* in the back of my mind.

Robbins: What frightening implications, a thing like that. It could happen to anybody, you know, not just famous people.

Lennon: Yeah.

Robbins: But what a frightening implication, when things like that can be used to hurt a person.

Lennon: Yes, a pretty amazing scene that was. It was very frightening.

Robbins: It's really, you know, like the McCarthy era or any kind of wildly out-of-context . . .

Lennon: Mmm. It's just certain things seem to whip up certain emotions, and at certain times as well.

Robbins: When are you going to be doing another tour? Do you know?

Lennon: No idea. I know we've got music to write, soon as we get back. And Paul's just signed up to write the music for a film. So I suppose it's off the plane and into bed. Knock, knock, knock, "Get up and write some songs."

Robbins: A film that's not your own?

Lennon: Yes.

Robbins: Very exciting.

Lennon: *All in Good Time* [*Actually* The Family Way, *based on a play called* All in Good Time. —*Ed.*] with . . . what's the name?

Voice [*off mic*]: Hayley Mills.

Lennon: Hayley Mills is in it.

Robbins: So Burt Bacharach is going to have a little competition, huh?

Lennon: It's about time, you know.

Robbins: [*Laughs.*] I think you're right, John. Just finally now, what do you think the audience can expect now from *How I Won the War*? What have we got to look forward to? Aside from seeing John Lennon in his first dramatic role?

Lennon: Well, I mean, I'm incidental. The thing you've got to look forward to is seeing a great film, I hope. The way it's going, it seems to be fine. And if it gets out and on the road, you know, it should be a great film.

Robbins: One thing, they'll be able to see you with a peeled nose for the first time.

Lennon: [*Giggling.*] Yeah, they'll get to see a lot of things for the first time.

Robbins: It's exciting, John, and I'm delighted to talk to you again, in such a place that really does look like the moon. I guess this is what it must be like. They told us it was dusty, and it is dusty.

Lennon: It is. You've come on a good day.

Robbins: It's always good to see you, John.

Lennon: OK, Fred. See you soon.

Robbins: We'll see you again. I hope next time you'll have a smash movie score to your credit.

Lennon: Well, that'll be nice.

Robbins: I don't know where the new challenges can come from, though.

Lennon: They're always there, believe me. There's always something going on.

Robbins: It's important to have a new challenge, though, isn't it, when you've made it like this, for example? To see if you can conquer it, I guess. There'll be many more. If this turns out the way you want it, will you do other acting roles, you think, John?

Lennon: Well, I don't know if I'll sit back and . . . I don't know what I'll do. I didn't know I was gonna do this, really, till I did it. I don't think too far ahead or plan.

Robbins: Will all the guys go out and do things on their own now, do you think?

Lennon: Well, if they feel like it, if there's something to do.

Robbins: I think it's time to spread your wings. Why not?

Lennon: Yeah, there's lots to be done.

Robbins: You've got the store going for you all the time, and whatever else you want to do on the side.

Lennon: Yeah. We'll just try our best at whatever we're doing. That's the main thing.

Robbins: It's always great to see you, Johnny.

Lennon: And yourself, Fred. See ya. This is John Lennon saying goodbye from the set in [Carboneras in the province of] Almeria, Spain, of *How I Won the War*.

[*They continue talking after the ostensible sign-off. —Ed.*]

Robbins: John, this new guise of yours, with the shorter hair . . . has it given you some kind of joy, some sadistic joy, in the privacy you've been able to enjoy?

Lennon: Well, you know, I went 'round [the] palace, the flea market, and went on a bus. Did all [the] things I haven't done for a long time. It was great.

Robbins: Nobody recognized you?

Lennon: One or two people did double takes, you know, but nobody knew at all. It was shorter than this then.

Robbins: They thought, *What's Bob Dylan doing over here?*

Lennon: No, I didn't look like him then, 'cause I had it plastered down.

Robbins: That's a sweet joy, isn't it, John, to be able to have a little privacy once in a while?

Lennon: Yeah, it was great. I was knocked out.

Robbins: Especially being here, being so far away, nobody to bother you, except guys like myself occasionally, but nobody's gonna dare come down here and talk to you.

Lennon: There's nobody around here. Nobody knows. Can't go into town here, though . . .

Robbins: Have any of the guys ever resorted to disguises to be able to go someplace?

Lennon: Well, I just heard the other day that Paul was at someplace in London disguised as an Arab. [*Robbins laughs.*] I don't know whether it's true or not. But he used to say that was the only way he could really disguise himself, was as an Arab. But if he did, he got caught.

Robbins: I don't think anybody will recognize George with his mustache now.

Lennon: No, they got him, because they got him in India. There's one of those shots you can see—they caught it going out of a door, and he had a mustache. And it just said, "George Harrison in Disguise."

Robbins: Well, all you have to do now is put maybe a little babushka on or a neckerchief and keep your head the way it is, and you can go around like an ordinary human being.

Lennon: Well, to an extent.

Robbins: You know, go into the record stores and see what the reaction is to the new records and things.

Lennon: It's not that easy now. I mean, they still know your face. People that do know spot your face even if you're wearing a pith helmet.

Robbins: That's what happens, I guess.

Lennon: Mmm.

Robbins: You'll never get away from it, John.

Lennon: I'll smash me face in.

Robbins: God forbid.

LENNON ON . . .

Escaping from the Working Class

"The class thing is just as snobby as it ever was. People like us can break through a little—but only a little. Once, we went into this restaurant and nearly got thrown out for looking like we looked until they saw who it was. 'What do you want? What do you want?' the headwaiter said. 'We've come to bloody eat, that's what we want,' we said. The owner spotted us and said, 'Ah, a table, sir, over here, sir.' It just took me back to when I was nineteen, and I couldn't get anywhere without being stared at or remarked about. It's only since I've been a Beatle that people have said, 'Oh, wonderful, come in, come in,' and I've forgotten a bit about what they're really thinking. They see the shining star, but when there's no glow about you, they only see the clothes and the haircut again."

—from interview with Leonard Gross, fall 1966, published in *Look* magazine (US), December 13, 1966

LENNON ON . . .

How Meditation Changed Him

"Before I wouldn't have been here. I've got more energy and more happiness. I don't know about intelligence. I'm just happier. I'm just a better person. And I wasn't bad before. I'm better now."

—from interview with David Frost, broadcast on *The Frost Programme* (UK), September 29, 1967

LENNON ON . . .

The Beatles as Role Models

"We don't give instructions on how to live your life. The only thing we can do, because we're in the public eye, is to reflect what we do. And they can judge for themselves what happens to us—with maharishi, with drugs, with whatever we go on—if they're using us as a guideline. And we can only try and do what's right for us, and therefore, we hope right for them."

—from interview with Mitchell Krause, May 14, 1968, broadcast on *Newsfront*, WNDT-TV (now WNET), New York, May 14, 1968

TV INTERVIEW

Joe Garagiola | May 14, 1968, NBC Studios, New York | Broadcast May 14, 1968,
The Tonight Show, **NBC (US)**

The Beatles released *Sgt. Pepper's Lonely Hearts Club Band*—the best rock album by any artist up to that point, according to some critics—on June 1, 1967. Less than three months later, on August 27, manager Brian Epstein died of an apparently accidental overdose of barbiturates. Exactly three months after that, on November 27, came the US release of *Magical Mystery Tour*, which combined the six-song soundtrack of the film of the same name with some of the group's most sophisticated singles, including one of the finest two-sided hits of all time: Lennon's trippy "Strawberry Fields Forever" backed with McCartney's irresistibly tuneful "Penny Lane."

With these and other records riding the charts, Lennon and his wife, Cynthia, took off for India on February 15, 1968, accompanied by George Harrison and his wife, Pattie Boyd. They were going to see the Maharishi Mahesh Yogi, whom they'd first met in London the previous August, and to learn more about his Transcendental Meditation.

Lennon stayed about a month and a half before allegations of inappropriate behavior by the maharishi disillusioned him and prompted him to return home. At the time, the Beatles were in the process of setting up Apple Corps and preparing to record *The Beatles*, the double LP better known as *The White Album*.

Taking a break from all this, Lennon and Paul McCartney accepted an invitation to appear on America's hugely popular *Tonight Show*, which was being guest-hosted by radio and TV personality and former football star Joe Garagiola. Actress Tallulah Bankhead, who died just seven months after this interview took place, injects considerable spice into portions of the conversation, which includes chitchat but also frank talk about the maharishi and details of the Beatles' ambitious plans for Apple. —Ed.

Joe Garagiola: Ladies and gentlemen, from the Beatles, John Lennon and Paul McCartney. [*Screams and applause.*] Good evening, good evening. Can I ask you something? How did you get here? Not from England but from the hotel, with all the people out there?

John Lennon: Uh, car.

Garagiola: Car. Did you have any problems?

Paul McCartney: No, no.

Lennon: All under control.

Garagiola: Everything's always under control, huh?

Lennon: Officer Krupke [*a reference to* West Side Story —*Ed.*] got us through.

Garagiola: Officer Krupke? Is he a friend of yours?

Lennon: Yes, yes.

Garagiola: So anyway . . .

Lennon: So how are you, Johnny [*sic*]?

Garagiola: Well, I figure you've been interviewed all day. If there's any questions you'd like to ask us . . .

Lennon: What are you doing?

Garagiola: Watching you.

McCartney: Mmm, where's [regular host] Johnny [Carson]?

Garagiola: He's touring. We get another plug in here. Where is he? Gaithersburg [Maryland]!

Ed McMahon [Carson's sidekick]**:** Gaithersburg!

Garagiola: A wonderful town.

Tallulah Bankhead: May I ask you two—a big favorite all over the world—a question? I'm not . . . this is the star of the show and you two kids. But I want to ask you guys: Are the other two gentlemen . . . of the four of you . . . are they still in India?

Lennon: No, they're in England.

Bankhead: In England. Well, I want to ask you something, because people have said to me . . . they wish I'd learned to meditate; then I'd give them a chance to get a word in edgewise. . . . And I can't . . . I don't know how you do it. I would love to.

Lennon: Well, you gotta go [to India] and find out, haven't you?

Bankhead: Well, I'm not going that far.

Lennon: Oh, well.

[*Laughter.*]

McCartney: Forget it.

Bankhead: If it's taken me this long and I can't do it, I couldn't learn there.

Lennon: Well, you can't learn to swim if you keep inland, can you?

Bankhead: Can't learn to swim?

Lennon: Unless you've got a pool around you.

Bankhead: Oh, honey, I can float sitting up. Don't be silly.

[*Laughter.*]

Garagiola: I get the feeling there are two different conversations here.

McCartney: Yeah, right, yeah. We had a bit of trouble today. . . . This fella . . . we did an interview for the educational program [*an appearance on New York educational TV station WNDT, now called WNET —Ed.*]. And he [host Mitchell Krause] started asking us questions, and they were quite sort of serious questions, you know. So it was a choice between just laughing it up or answering seriously.

Garagiola: So what did you do?

McCartney: We were a bit serious.

Garagiola: You? Serious?

McCartney: Yeah. We were just sort of not too serious, you know, just sort of . . .

Garagiola: Listen, of all the . . .

McCartney: So tell us a joke!

[*Laughter.*]

Garagiola: I don't really hear that many jokes. You tell me a joke.

Lennon: We don't know any.

Bankhead: I think they're very serious fellows.

McCartney: That's it. We are, you know.

Garagiola: Listen, that's the only thing you haven't really done is tell jokes.

Lennon: We can never remember 'em, you see.

Garagiola: Would you like to be a comedian?

Lennon: No.

Bankhead: In many ways you are.

Lennon: Well . . .

[*Laughter.*]

Garagiola: Listen, if music hadn't—

Lennon: [*To Bankhead.*] I heard about you . . .

Bankhead: I got a phone call from London today from . . . his name is Antar Andrews. [*An apparent reference to Irish radio and TV personality Eamonn Andrews. —Ed.*] . . . I knew I'd say the wrong word, I've never had anything to help me, and I didn't know how to pronounce your last name.

Garagiola: You're hittin' harder.

Bankhead: [*Badly mispronounces Garagiola.*] I mean, Joe to me and to everyone else who's had the pleasure and privilege . . .

Garagiola: And John.

Bankhead: Oh, these two kids I adore. The other two, too.

Lennon: Eamonn Andrews, is it?

Bankhead: Which of you is the father? I mean, how many kids have you all got?

Lennon: I've got one.

Garagiola: Paul, you're not married?

McCartney: No, I'm not married.

Bankhead: You're the only one who is not married, are you not?

McCartney: It's true.

Garagiola: Do you . . . the four of you, socially, are you that close, or are you . . .?

McCartney: Yeah.

Lennon: We're close friends, you know.

Garagiola: Sometimes when you work together . . . I've been with groups that when the job's over, that's it. Do you have houses pretty much together?

Lennon: Within twenty miles all together.

Garagiola: And socially, it's . . .

Lennon: Well, yeah.

Garagiola: If you couldn't have done it in music—if it hadn't happened for you—what do you think you would like to do?

Lennon: Ah, I don't know. Films.

Garagiola: Films? How about you, Paul? I'm not breaking your mood, am I?

McCartney: No. No, you're doing great, you know. But, umm . . . [*Laughter.*] So, what would I like to have been?

Lennon: A policeman.

McCartney: [*To Lennon.*] No, not a policeman. [*Laughter.*] Uh, I don't know, you know. I was nearly gonna be a teacher, but that fell through, luckily. So I don't know, you know.

[*Music begins, to segue into commercial break. McCartney hums along.*]

Garagiola: [*To Lennon.*] Why don't you read that [cue card] and see what the reaction is.

Lennon: And now a word from your local stallion.

[*Laughter.*]

Garagiola: A word from your local *station*!

[*Commercial break.*]

Garagiola: OK, Tallulah, it's all right. Listen, Paul, you said something that's hard for me to believe. You were in Central Park and no one recognized you Sunday?

McCartney: Yes, that's true. Yes.

Lennon: We were very pleased, you know.

Garagiola: You just kind of wandered around? [*Music starts.*] That means . . . now a word from your local station again!

[*Commercial break.*]

Garagiola: You know we're on the air right now?

Lennon: Oh, great. How are we doing?

Garagiola: To get back to the Central Park thing, you just walked around? The police weren't with you?

Lennon: No, we just walked out, you know. We often do it. If people don't know . . . expect us, what are they gonna do but see a bit of long hair walking around like all the other long hair?

Garagiola: And just two go right along.

Bankhead: Well, everyone copies them. How can they know?

Lennon: How can you tell one from the other?

[*Laughter.*]

Garagiola: Well, how long have you been in New York now? We just found out about it.

McCartney: Three days.

Lennon: Is it three now?

McCartney: Three days.

Garagiola: Three days.

Lennon: And we still haven't got a tan.

McCartney: And it's been enough, you know, actually. [*Laughs.*]

Garagiola: Listen, when you get to a city . . . Now, you were on tour, and you got to a lot of cities. How much of it do you really see? It's ballpark to a hotel, I guess.

Lennon: You just pick up the vibrations.

Bankhead: I was eight years in England and never saw a cricket game, didn't understand one word of it. So how do you expect them to understand baseball?

Garagiola: No, no, I don't mean that. I mean when they did their concerts, they went from the hotel—

Lennon: We never saw it.

Garagiola: They never saw the city.

McCartney: The room.

Lennon: A hostel full of rooms all over the place.

Garagiola: What kind of . . .

Lennon: Hostel.

Bankhead: I was very surprised: in the press you were so polite and gracious, and I thought they were wonderful to you. And I didn't know, you know, because one hears these mad things. . . . I thought you were perfectly divine, and I said so in England. That's where they misquoted me.

Garagiola: In England?

Bankhead: Yes. They covered all the bad things from our papers.

Lennon: Yeah, yeah. It's a club they've formed.

Garagiola: A misquote club, huh? How about this new organization, Apple?

Lennon: Oh, yeah. Well, you see, our accountant came up with it. "We've got this amount of money. Do you want to give it to the government or do something with it?" So we thought—

Garagiola: Which government, first?

Lennon: Oh . . . any old government. [*Laughter.*] So we decided to play businessmen for a bit, because we've got to run our own affairs now. So we've got this thing called Apple, which is going to be records, films, and electronics, which all tie up. And to make a sort of an umbrella or something so people who want to make films about . . . grass . . . don't have to go on their knees in an office, you know, begging for a break. We'll try and do it like that. That's the idea. I mean, we'll find out what happens, but that's what we're trying to do.

McCartney: If you want to do something, normally you've got to go to big business and you've gotta go to them, the big people, you know.

Lennon: You don't even get there. Because you can't get through the door 'cause of the color of your shoes.

McCartney: [*Laughs.*] But you know, people are normally . . . big companies are so big that if you're little and good, it takes you like sixty years to make it. And so people miss out on these little good people.

Lennon: It just takes 'em longer.

McCartney: So we're trying to find a few.

Garagiola: Paul, is that because of your background? You came from a poor background.

Lennon: No, it's no sort of . . . it's just a common thing.

McCartney: There's a bit of that.

Garagiola: If you didn't feel it as a youngster, you wouldn't feel it now.

Lennon: Yeah.

McCartney: Yeah, that's right, you know. It's just 'cause we know what we had to fight to sort of . . .

Garagiola: Was it tough for you to get started?

Lennon: Well, no tougher than for anybody else, you see, but George said, "I'm sick of being told to keep out of the park." Central Park, et cetera. That's what it's about, you know. We're trying to make a park for people to come in and do what they want.

McCartney: Symbolically speaking.

[*Laughter.*]

Lennon: Right, Paul.

Garagiola: Is he the spokesman, would you say, John?

Lennon: Well, if his spokes are working, he is. And if mine are . . .

[*Laughter.*]

Garagiola: Do you have the privacy that you're leading me to believe you have, or is it a tough job?

Lennon: We have enough to keep us sane, you know. If we are sane, we have enough. [*Laughter.*] Because it's not like touring. Our life isn't like a tour, or like [the film] *Hard Day's Night* or any of those things. That's only when we're doing that we create that, or that is created. But when we're just living, it's calm.

Garagiola: Is it calm, Paul?

McCartney: Yeah. Not at the moment, you know. It's very hectic, New York. Very hectic place. 'Cause we came over from England, and it's a very sort of quiet place, you know.

Garagiola: What's so different about New York?

Lennon: Louder.

McCartney: It's very . . . [*imitates cars honking and police sirens*], you know.

[*Laughter.*]

Garagiola: You've got a hit record on your hands already.

McCartney: You know, that happens a lot here.

Garagiola: Don't you like that kind of life?

Lennon: It's all right. You get into it. I mean, three days isn't enough to get used to that.

Garagiola: Would you like to get into it?

Lennon: Ah, not today.

Bankhead: Are you nervous on a show like this? Because it scares me to death.

McCartney: Always nervous.

Lennon: Yeah, sure. Sure.

Garagiola: Why would you be nervous?"

Lennon: Because, uh . . . it's not natural.

[*Laughter.*]

Garagiola: I don't know, I'm just kind of visiting with you. . . . I would feel it's natural. I feel like I've heard about you and I want to meet you.

Lennon: I mean, this situation isn't natural to a human being . . .

McCartney: If we meet you and talk at your house, then that's all right, you know, because we can actually talk naturally. It's a bit difficult when you know you're going out into a million homes.

Garagiola: So you're guarded pretty well in what you say, then?

Lennon: No, not guarded.

McCartney: No, but it's still difficult, you know. [*Gestures to camera crew.*] There it is! Look! It's going out!

[*Laughter.*]

Lennon: Well, aren't you nervous at all?

Garagiola: I am nervous because of the . . . uh . . .

Lennon: Well, because . . . because . . . because! It's the same thing!

[*Laughter.*]

Garagiola: Except that you are very successful in what you do.

Lennon: It doesn't make any difference.

Garagiola: So what you're telling me is that you have fears and anxieties like everybody else?

Lennon: Sure! We're human, man!

McCartney: You know that old showbiz thing everybody says: "Well, you know, you always get nervous before you go on the stage"? Uh, I think we get 'em all the way. When you go onstage it's just one of those things.

Garagiola: But you get over that all right.

Lennon: Oh, sure. It's part of the game.

Garagiola: Here's what'll really settle you down.

Lennon: Oh, great.

[*Commercial break.*]

Garagiola: Five million homes [are watching the program]. We were corrected, Paul. I can tell the whole world I made a mistake with the Beatles . . . four million. Listen now, I have something in common with both of you. I met the guru, the maharishi. And I noticed that he went out with an act—the Beach Boys. And it folded. [*The tour was abandoned after seven dates due to poor attendance. —Ed.*]

Lennon: Yeah. Right.

Garagiola: What do you think of the yogi as an act?

Lennon: Yeah. Well, we found out that we made a mistake there.

McCartney: We tried to persuade him against that, you know.

Garagiola: To go out?

McCartney: Yeah. I thought it was a terrible idea.

Lennon: We believe in meditation, but not the maharishi and his scene. But that's a personal mistake we made in public. So we're saying that for these five million and ten people . . .

Garagiola: When did you find out it was a mistake?

Lennon: Well, I can't remember the date, you know, but it was in India. And meditation is good, and it does what they say. It's like exercise or cleaning your teeth, you know. It works, but we're finished with that bit of it.

McMahon: Has he [the maharishi] changed? Is that why . . .

Lennon: Well, no. I think it's just that we're seeing him a bit more in perspective, you know, 'cause we're as naive as the next person about a lot of things.

McCartney: We get carried away with things like that, you know. I mean, we thought he was magic, you know—just floating around and everything. Flying.

Garagiola: Do you think that the kids in America have turned him off?

Lennon: Well, it could be something to do with it. But I wouldn't say "Don't meditate" to them, because a lot of them would get a great deal from it.

McCartney: You know, the system is more important than all those things.

Lennon: He's surrounded with . . . it seems like, the old establishment that we know so well.

Garagiola: Are you saying, "Meditate, but not with the yogi"?

McCartney: Yeah. I mean, he's good. There's nothing wrong with him. But we think the system is more important than all the big personality bit. You know, he gets sort of treated like a big star. He's on the road with the Beach Boys, and it's all that scene. And it's a bit strange, and also it [the tour with the Beach Boys] folds, you know. That's the silly thing.

[*Laughter.*]

Bankhead: Does he giggle as much as . . .

Lennon: Yes. It's his natural asset. [*Laughter.*] Well, you see, it depends on what way you're looking at it at the time. If it's not getting on your nerves, it's "Oh, what a happy fellow." It depends how you feel when you look at him.

Garagiola: I had him on the show, and he just giggled and giggled the whole time. I figured there was something . . . maybe my tie was loose. That kind of a feeling. Who was the first one that met the yogi?

Lennon: We all met him at the same time.

Garagiola: Can you tell us the circumstances?

Lennon: Well, he was just doing a lecture in London at the Hilton. . . . So we all went, and we thought, *What a nice man.* And we were looking for that. You know, everybody's looking for it, but we were looking for it that day as well. And then we met him, and he was good, you know. He's got a good thing in him. And we went along with it.

Garagiola: But now you just got off the train, huh?

Lennon: Right. Nice trip, thank you very much.

[*Laughter.*]

Garagiola: You know, you seem to have . . . your own careers have kind of switched to where . . . not that you lose a group, but you seem to be changing your audience.

Lennon: See, everything changes. So we change as well. And our audience changes, too, all the time. We can't put our finger on what age group or why. But we know everything changes, and us, too.

McCartney: When we first started, we had leather jackets on. Little caps and the big cowboy boots. But then we changed to suits, you know.

Lennon: We thought, *That'll get 'em.*

[*Laughter.*]

McCartney: And we lost a whole lot of fans. They all said, "You've gone posh." They didn't like it, you know, because we were all clean. [*Laughter.*] So we lost that crowd, but we gained all the ones that liked suits. It happens like that. That's what keeps happening. And we lost a lot of people with *Sgt. Pepper*, but I think we gained more.

[*Applause.*]

Garagiola: Do you think you're going to be able to top *Sgt. Pepper*?

Lennon: Well, you know, it's the next move, and I can't say yes or no, but I think so. Why not? 'Cause it's only another LP, really. It's not that important.

Bankhead: I have a godson who's got my middle name, which is Brockman. And he was playing . . . I thought it was Bach. It turned out to be one of your new-style things, and I adored it. I thought it was lovely. Just on the piano . . .

Lennon: It depends how you play 'em, because it's only a melody.

Bankhead: He's sixteen and he loves music, and he's been playing for a few years, that's all. But he had a real feeling for it, you know. He loved you before, too. But I just couldn't believe it was by the Beatles. It was so different.

Garagiola: Well, you have to be the most imitated group.

Lennon: Well, maybe. Yeah.

[*Laughter.*]

Garagiola: When you talk about Lennon/McCartney songs, do you work together, or one writes one, or . . .

Lennon: It's all those combinations you can think of. Every combination of two people writing a song . . . inasmuch as we can both write them completely separately, and together, and not together. But we obviously influence each other, like groups and people do.

Garagiola: I have a big list here, which I can't find, but I can think of my favorite—"Yesterday." [*Applause.*] What were the circumstances behind that, Paul, for example? How does that happen?

McCartney: I don't know. I woke up one morning with a piano . . .

Lennon: [*Sings.*] I woke up one morning . . .

[*Laughter.*]

McCartney: Piano by my bed . . .

Lennon: [*Sings.*] Duh-dut, duh dut-a-la-dut!

[*Laughter.*]

McCartney: Went to the piano . . .

Lennon: Yeah?

McCartney: And this is what I said! You know, I just started playing it and this tune came. 'Cause that's what happens. They just sort of . . . they come, you know. It just came, and I couldn't think of any words to it, so originally it was just "Scrambled Egg." So it was called "Scrambled Egg" for a couple of months . . . [*laughter*] . . . until I thought of "Yesterday." So then that's it.

Garagiola: Are you putting me on?

McCartney: No, that's true.

Garagiola: Scrambled eggs? You wrote a song about scrambled eggs?

McCartney: True story.

Lennon: "Scrambled Egg" was over here as an instrumental first.

McCartney: That's true, you know.

Lennon: Didn't do so well with that title, you know.

[*Laughter.*]

Garagiola: So you wrote a song, start out to call it "Scrambled Egg," ended up "Yesterday."

Bankhead: Oh, the story of my life, huh?

Garagiola: How long are you gonna be here? How long are you gonna stay here?

Lennon: Uh, it could be any minute now.

[*Laughter.*]

Bankhead: Oh, please! Don't leave me here!

Garagiola: I know we've probably kept you out here longer than we should have, but I'm going to take a . . . I have a reverse question I'm going to ask you, and feel free not to answer it. What is the one question that bugs you the most? About your hair?

Lennon: No. We're past being bugged by questions, unless they're very personal. I mean, you just get normal human reactions to a question. You know, but there used to be one about, "What are you going to do when the bubble bursts?" We'd have hysterics, because somebody always asked it.

Garagiola: Let's go down the list of the questions. What are you going to do when the bubble bursts?

Lennon: I haven't a clue, you know. I'm still looking for the bubble.

[*Laughter.*]

Garagiola: [*To McCartney.*] I've heard you on interviews. You have fun with reporters. You just play right with them.

McCartney: No, no. I'm serious. Serious.

Garagiola: You are? I think you're the kind of a guy that would say, "Here's a match . . . see how much gas is in the tank." Would you be that kind of a guy?

McCartney: Yeah, sure.

[*Laughter.*]

Garagiola: Paul, John, I know that you've got a busy, busy schedule.

[*Groans from the audience.*]

Lennon: That's the way it goes, folks!

[*Laughter.*]

Garagiola: And I want to thank you all. But you've got to stay here. . . . Before you go we have a commercial. . . . Do you want to give it a John Lennon reading? We have to say good-bye. Does that make you sad to have to leave me, John?

Lennon: All good-byes are sad, aren't they, Joe?

Garagiola: Why don't you write a song. Call it, "Say Good-bye to Joe."

Lennon: "Good-bye, Joe. See you in the morning . . ." Oh, that's some other line.

[*Laughter.*]

Garagiola: Paul, you got any ideas?

McCartney: Uh . . . no . . . Joe . . . [*Laughter.*] OK, um . . . no, I can't think of a song.

Garagiola: When you get home and you start to write "Scrambled Eggs Number Two," will you think about me?

McCartney: OK.

Lennon: And I'll join you somehow.

Garagiola: Thank you very much.

LENNON ON . . .

Apple Records' Goal

"The aim of this company isn't really a stack of gold teeth in the bank. We've *done* that bit. It's more of a trick to see if we can actually get artistic freedom within a business structure."

—from press conference at the Americana Hotel, New York, May 14, 1968

LENNON ON . . .

His 1968 Art Show

"Like the street maps or things that say where a place is—You Are Here on those street-map things—you seen 'em? I thought that'd be a good idea to have a show where you actually have the street map in the gallery and you went in and saw that. So I thought, *Now if I did that . . . I'll put it on canvas so that makes it 'art.'* I mean, it is or it isn't, however you like it. So I put up a big white, round canvas and it just said You Are Here that I'd written on it. And the point of the show was people went through various things to get to the canvas, and then they reacted to it . . . I had a hat saying For The Artist, which they put money in or chewing gum or all sorts of rubbish."

—from interview with David Frost, *Frost on Saturday*, ITV (UK), August 24, 1968

LENNON ON . . .

The Beatles' "A Day in the Life"

"'A Day in the Life'—that was something. I dug it. It was a good piece of work between Paul and me. I had the 'I read the news today' bit, and it turned Paul on. Now and then we really turn each other on with a bit of song, and he just said 'yeah'—bang, bang, like that. It just sort of happened beautifully, and we arranged it and rehearsed it, which we don't often do, the afternoon before. So we all knew what we were playing. We all got into it. It was a real groove, the whole scene on that one. Paul sang half of it and I sang half. I needed a middle eight for it, but that would have been forcing it. All the rest had come out smooth, flowing, no trouble, and to write a middle eight would have been to write a middle eight, but instead Paul already had one there. It's a bit of *2001*, you know." [*An apparent reference to the Stanley Kubrick film. —Ed.*]

—from interview with Jonathan Cott, September 17-18, 1968, London, published November 23, 1968, *Rolling Stone* (US)

CONVERSATION

**Maurice Hindle & Friends | December 2, 1968, Kenwood (Lennon's home), Surrey, UK |
Brief excerpts published January 1969, *Unit* (UK)**

This conversation—one of the first in which John Lennon emerges from his Fab Four persona to discuss politics, class, and other subjects in depth—resulted from an improbable sequence of events. Maurice Hindle, a twenty-three-year-old first-term student at England's Keele University, had joined *Unit*, the school's contemporary-arts magazine, and decided to try to secure an interview with the musician.

Hindle wrote to Lennon via the Beatles Fan Club address he'd found in *Beatles Monthly* magazine and asked that his letter be forwarded. Realizing how easily his communication could go astray, he was taken aback when Lennon replied, saying he would be interested in an interview and suggesting that Hindle phone him.

When they spoke on the telephone, on Friday, November 29, 1968, Hindle proposed meeting in a week. But Lennon—who was now living with his Japanese girlfriend—said that he and Ono never planned that far ahead. So Hindle agreed to meet the couple the following Monday. He was to go to Weybridge, then call Lennon from the rail station there.

On the appointed day, Hindle told me, he arrived at the station along with two fellow Keele University students: Daniel Wiles, who wound up playing a large role in the conversation, and Bob Cross. Hindle called Lennon, who drove to the station with Ono in his Mini Cooper to pick up the trio. They then went back to the couple's home for a long and discursive taped conversation. (The recording would sell at auction to Hard Rock Cafe International nearly twenty years later for more than $37,000.)

The Beatles had just released their instantly successful and much-talked-about eponymous double LP, also known as *The White Album*. But Hindle was more interested in discussing "his ideas on life, the universe, and everything," he recalled decades later. "Especially in the year of unprecedented social and political ferment."

Lennon was beginning to speak out about that ferment, and also about his own life, which was changing rapidly. The previous month, on November 8, his divorce from first wife Cynthia had been finalized; three days after that, he and Ono had released *Unfinished Music No. 1: Two Virgins*, which featured a nude cover shot of the couple.

"What lay behind my stated interest in their current ideas and activities," Hindle told me, "was a concern to find out in a face-to-face interview the way John's life, ideas, and attitudes might be changing at this time."

One major topic of the conversation was "An Open Letter to John Lennon," which had been published in the October 27, 1968, issue of *Black Dwarf*, a left-wing UK newspaper edited by activist Tariq Ali. Hindle showed Lennon the letter, from the publication's music critic, John Hoyland, which suggested that the singer's music was losing its bite. "What we're confronted with is a repressive, vicious, authoritarian system," Hoyland had written, adding, "Now do you see what was wrong with 'Revolution'? That record was no more revolutionary than *Mrs. Dale's Diary*," a reference to a BBC radio serial drama.

After meeting with Hindle, Lennon wrote a reply to Hoyland that appeared in *Black Dwarf*'s January 10, 1969, issue: "You say, 'In order to change the world we've got to understand what's wrong with the world. And then destroy it. Ruthlessly.' I'll tell you what's wrong with the world—people—so do you want to destroy them? What kind of system do you propose and who would run it?"

As Hoyland would point out in a 2008 article in the *Guardian*, Lennon subsequently shifted some of his views, invited Tariq Ali to his home for a discussion (see page 153), and wrote such songs as "Power to the People." Also, on November 26, 1969, he returned his MBE (a medal awarded by the Queen of England to each of the Beatles, in honor of their artistic contributions), saying he was doing so "in protest against Britain's involvement in the Nigeria-Biafra thing, against our support of America in Vietnam, and against 'Cold Turkey' [then his latest single] slipping down the charts."

Meanwhile, wrote Hoyland, "I shifted my position as well to one that was a little less naively and narrowly political. . . . I valued the emotional honesty of Lennon's post-Beatles music much more than I might have done earlier."

Here's an extended excerpt from Lennon and Ono's hours-long conversation with Hindle and his fellow students. The discussion took place only a little more than six months after the US television appearance with McCartney on *The Tonight Show*, which is hard to believe, given how much Lennon appears to have changed. —Ed.

Daniel Wiles: Why do people want to be rich? Is it just because of the telly or adverts or the system?

John Lennon: Well, I wanted to be rich because I was relatively poor and I thought rich would sort of get you out. It did get me out, but it only got me out of Liverpool, y'know. It didn't get me out of me mind or out of me body. And whether I would've started meditating and eating macrobiotic food, et cetera, et cetera, acid, all the trips that I've been through this last two years . . . I probably would've done it rich or poor, you see? And then wouldn't have bothered to try and make money.

But I didn't try too hard. It just so happened my gimmick was the one that earned money, y'know. I used to think, *Oh, anybody can write songs and be a pop star.* I think we even said it in the Beatles book. [*A reference to* The Beatles, *an authorized 1968 biography. —Ed.*] It was only last year when we were talking to [the book's author] Hunter Davies. I've changed that much since then. I don't believe it [that anybody can succeed as a pop star], no. I made it 'cause of me, and I have that thing that makes that music and makes those songs up.

I believe everybody's got something. It's just they've got to bring it out.

Wiles: Yeah, that struck me, that business about—

Lennon: Because it was always people saying, y'know, just all the time or whatever, "What have you got? What have you got that . . . ?" Y'know, I can't . . . Christ knows what it is, y'know. So it was really a reaction [when I said], "Look, man, anybody can do it. For Christ's sake, we were just ordinary lads." I can come from any society. Yoko and I are like that [close] mentally. And she comes from some kind of high-class Japanese banking family that wouldn't even let me sweep the floor. And I come from Liverpool . . . and she comes from the East . . . y'know?

And . . . [she's] the nearest thing to me I've ever come across in me life, y'know. And, I mean, I believed intellectually before that you could come from working class or you could be born royal and still make it, y'know. Even though I think that it's harder to be born into that situation and taught that you are above all. Shit, her [Ono's] hardest thing was being brought up to believe she was special and that her class was special and that you don't have to communicate or worry.

At least if you're born at the bottom, you've told that you're nothing, and you either accept it or you try and set out to do something about it. And that choice you've got. But if you're up there, born royal, you're told that you're great. You're told that you don't need to do anything to justify living. And they've got to get over that.

That's why I'm always cracking about royalty. . . . The ones that accept it, well, y'know, piss on 'em. But the ones that try and do anything . . . it must be bloody hard for 'em to be brought up and told you are unhuman, that you're almost the son of God and brought up in that atmosphere. It's incredible that any of them have done anything, but I don't know whether any of them have, except for set up Boy Scout funds and all that. But y'know, whatever they're trying to do . . . it's difficult.

Wiles: Has success and money brought any of the other Beatles happiness?

Lennon: No, no, they're all in the same boat.

Wiles: Have you met any people that are rich and happy?

Lennon: No, no. No, no. The rich people I've met . . . the ones that are so-called happy with it are happy in that sort of way that the woman in the semidetached [house] is happy. Like we used to live in a row of about twenty, and the ones at that end who had two cars or something were supposed to be happier than those that had no car or no phone or whatever. So the rich people are supposedly happy like that. But I've met no happy people in bags, in one bag or another. Like rich or poor, y'know? And I've never met anybody completely happy. 'Cause I don't believe it exists. There's always got to be the positive-negative, yin-yang bit.

Wiles: Yeah.

Lennon: And there's no such thing as just happiness. Pure, like that. I think you can reach a state of consciousness. I don't know whether you can make it in this life. All the Buddhas and the Jesuses, all the great ones that were pretty hip, conscious-wise . . . I don't think they had complete happiness. But I reckon that you might get that; I think complete happiness is when you are a bit of electricity . . . when you've made the absolute, as the Buddhists say . . .

And I've had that through meditation—just a state where you are not aware of anything. So there you've been, and that's complete happiness. You just are. And that is what happiness is . . . the peace we're looking for. It's just to be, and nothing affects you and you affect nothing, literally. . . . The happiest people are the people that are "being" more times a week than anybody else. . . . It's just down to that.

Wiles: Ravi Shankar, he's a very happy chap.

Lennon: He's fairly happy, but he hasn't got it made by any means. He's just a guy, y'know?

Wiles: Yeah, but when he plays . . .

Lennon: Yeah, but when you play . . . I've had that [feeling] playing. Anybody that paints, draws, or anything . . . The bit about being is the same, or almost the same, I'm not really sure, as when you're playing a groove, and Ravi does it. As soon as he hits it, he cuts out.

Wiles: Yeah.

Lennon: And we did, we had it playing. Every time there's a good session—you're watching musicians and they're really playing well—they're out of it. And that's when you just are being. There's nothing hassling you, or not hassling; it's just . . . you know, and that's it. And you get it from writing, or you can get it daydreaming, or idling about as a kid on a desk just sort of . . . or in the grass in the sun just for a moment, you go [makes noise].

And you always fight back, you know . . . That's the whole bit. Even when you're meditating and doing these things with the whole express purpose of getting into that state, you've got to practice it like you'd practice anything to stop being frightened when you get the state. The different levels you get to on meditation, you get to a plane . . . and you're fighting it all the time. It's just the whole time is spent to stop being frightened of nothing.

Maurice Hindle: Don't you think . . . you've got more fighting against it ever since the inception of what we call civilization?

Lennon: I think we've got a lot further away from it since we got civilized, you know. And since Christianity became Christianity with a capital *C* and nothing to do with Jesus Christ.

Hindle: But in my mind, the difference is what [Canadian philosopher of communication theory Marshall] McLuhan says—that, for once, everyone's become self-conscious in a position where the tribal group who weren't self-conscious but acted totally without ego—

Lennon: Yeah, but I think the world is on a trip, you know, and like on record—I must relate to our records, because that's the thing I've done most—our records, we went through the childish, tribal bit, which is the early records; the self-conscious bit, which is *Rubber Soul*, say pre-*Pepper*, coming out of *Pepper*; and now [our records are as] un-self-conscious, I think, as you can get, relatively speaking . . .

And then, we're suddenly becoming aware of something and becoming self-conscious and going through all the hassles you go through being self-conscious where you're so self-conscious you can't do anything. And then to come out of that is the next stage, which I think we're going into: being self-conscious but realizing that you can handle it, you know?

And that's the breakthrough. It's the end of the trip, if it was a good trip. [*Laughs.*] [Understanding that] you can handle it and that we're just going through a big trip. The whole world, the whole universe, is just one big trip, and we're just going through a bit of it. We've got to get hung up about what we're going through now and how we arrived at it. How they coughed up Christianity, Buddhism, how they did all that.

They, they . . . but *we* do it. We did it, if you believe in reincarnation. It was us then, anyway. We've all done it. We've been them all. We've been the fascists, and we've been everything. And we're just tripping out while we're going through that bit now, so we're becoming self-conscious of what we did with the basic thing we had. We've become too self-conscious of it, and now we've got to put it in perspective. And we can have cars and tellies and that but still get back to the spiritual bit, which is the bit we've missed out on.

Wiles: There are some things which seem sort of inconsistent with your last few [albums]. . . . I don't know what the other three think, but in the Hunter Davies thing you said that you'd often sort of write three draggy songs, which you didn't enjoy doing, just to finish an LP, but also this Apple business . . . I don't know if it's going into production, but this machine to stop people recording records . . . [*This is a reference to an invention by Yanni (later John) Alexis Mardis, an early Apple Corps employee dubbed "Magic Alex" by Lennon. "He had an idea to stop people taping our records off the radio," recalled Ringo Starr in* The Beatles Anthology. *"You'd have to have a decoder to get the signal. . . . We brought EMI and Capitol in from America to look at it, but they weren't interested at all." —Ed.*]

Lennon: No, no. I mean, the guy came up with that invention. So the thing is, obviously we're not going to sell that to people to jam the records, man. I mean, even just as a public-relations job, it'd be the dumbest thing on earth. But the invention's out, word-wise. Even the dumbest fascist is not going to do it if it's going to spoil his image. And we wouldn't put that out, but the thing we will do is to sell it to the tape-recording people to prevent us putting it out to the record people; 'cause it would spoil the tape, just like that.

We're playing that game, and we're playing the game on their terms. Let's copy it and change it. And why not have a go at that? And that's what we'll do with it, 'cause somebody's going to do it soon. It's a feasible thing. Even if we'd done it, somebody'd come up with something that'd change it. There's no getting out of that. You can't beat it. You can't do that. You know, that's why they keep changing. You can always get around it. And obviously we wouldn't do that, y'know, for any reason on earth. Just morally I wouldn't put me name . . . I wouldn't do it. I know the others wouldn't do it. Even if any advice we got was, "Come on, man, come on."

Wiles: What about the records and doing draggy tracks?

Lennon: It's not draggy tracks. It's like draggy tracks as opposed to just completely enjoying it. And that's the job I've chosen to do, is to record and write songs. . . . If I'm feeling draggy . . . I mean, when I say I wrote "Good Morning Good Morning" or something like that, and I didn't like it and I didn't enjoy it, I mean I didn't enjoy it as a whole; it was a job of work. But I got enjoyment from doing it.

But you can't pin people like me down on every literal thing that's said in print like that. Like this guy [John Hoyland in *Black Dwarf*] said it was a con job. Now, I say it is a con job and in the terms of reference that I mean by *con*, I say Picasso was conning them and so was Beethoven, and having a laugh up their sleeve, because they were. Anybody that's as great as they were knows where it's at, and they know that all this drivel that's written about our songs and the Stones and Dylan and all that . . . Dylan knows where it's at. We know where it's at in regards to our songs and what people write about them. And that is the con job.

If somebody gets uptight about me putting "wobble of a grapefruit" in the middle of a song just for a laugh, or because I like the sound of "wobble of a grapefruit" . . . and to me that's a con, because I know Thomas Mann [*actually a reference to music critic William Mann. —Ed.*] or somebody will write something about the great sense of rhythm of that line, "wobble of a grapefruit." And he's right, but I put it in for a laugh, and that's a con job. But so I don't think *con* is a derogative word. . . .

So I'm not answerable to everything I said to Hunter Davies. There's a few bits in there that I said how I felt that day. But do I have to stand by that for the rest of me life just because it's in print?

Wiles: Why did you agree to it [the authorized biography], then?

Lennon: Because it was done. It was agreed to a long time ago when Brian [Epstein] was alive, and he said, "This guy wants to write a book on you, and why not?" So it was "why not?" The idea was to try and get some kind of vaguely [accurate] version of what was going on . . . that had some connection with what we thought was going on as well. 'Cause people were going to do it, anyway. But even that book is so nothing to do with what we are. It's so outdated, like he says at the end of it.

Wiles: Yeah.

Lennon: You know, you can't do it. But people are going to be writing about us for the rest of our lives probably, and after we're dead, so I tend to either confuse the issue so much they never knew what was going on or to try and keep shoving out bits and bits of what I think is my version of how it happened, and how Beatles happened, and how the different things happened as a result of this or that or how I was influenced or not influenced. So whoever is bothered to be looking at it in the future, if they ever do . . . But people that really know will sort out . . . they'll know what was going on with it, and they won't have to go through a million, million things, y'know? Just like that.

And it's nice to be written about, man. It's just a sense of history, and it's good for your ego, and we enjoyed it. And it was a bit of a drag having to keep talking about things, but it was nice talking about your childhood, remembering the gags and all the things that happened.

Hindle: As far as the music is concerned, do you personally think that in the record media, the potential has fallen? Do you feel as if you've come to an end?

Lennon: No, and we haven't even started. We keep saying this. There's no end to it. There is no end and there's no beginning, y'know. It's infinite, and there's just no end to it. There's just every possibility, combination of sound on earth, is open to us and anybody else who cares to listen. Just what's going on now, that's a record. To me, that's a record, this whole bit. And we've got all that to work on. There's no end to it, and there's no bag to put it in, and it just goes on and on and on. And the only end I can see is if I get fed up with doing it or wanna do something else.

Wiles: God help you.

Lennon: Well, why God help me?

Wiles: Well, because it's just if you get fed up with doing it . . .

Lennon: There's plenty to do, man.

Wiles: Oh, you mean find something else instead?

Lennon: Yes, yes. I couldn't not produce or create. I'm creating a lot more than just the records, just with Yoko, just all the time. I can't stop. That's my gig, and I've always done it. As a kid, it was making puppets or drawing or writing poetry. That's my gig on earth is to turn out all this stuff. And I'll turn it out, regardless of what anybody says or thinks about it, you know?

Wiles: "Revolution 9"—is it about death?

Lennon: [*Reaches to check tape recorder.*] Just checking we're not wasting our time. [*Laughter.*] How can it be about just death?

Wiles: Well, it seems to me to be about death.

Lennon: Well, then it is, then. Right? When you heard it. How many times have you heard it?

Wiles: About four.

Lennon: Four, so it's about death. Well, listen to it on another day. In the sun. Outside. And see if it's about death then. It's about everything. I mean, it's not specifically about anything. It's a set of sounds like walking down the street is a set of sounds. And I just captured a moment of time, put it on disc, and it's about that.

Wiles: I thought it might have some specific meaning that you meant it to have.

Lennon: No, no. Nothing does, y'know.

Hindle: Just sound going on every which way?

Lennon: Yeah, you know. It was maybe to do with the sounds of a revolution, y'know? There was some shooting, and there was some babies crying, and there was some peace . . . so that's the sort of vague story behind it. But apart from that, it's just a set of sounds.

Wiles: I think it's the best track, actually.

Lennon: Thank you. That means a few people are getting it.

Hindle: You've said do what you can with what's going on. . . . You're going to get it all again if you revolt and go smashing things up. You can't get away from that.

Lennon: Yeah. There's no way out. Smashing it up or whatever, there isn't any way out. We've all just gotta go chugging along, doing what we can. You know, but all the words on "Revolution 9" were just random talking. There was nothing written down, bits of film script, this and that. I think it was just George, Yoko, and I. I did a lot of it with loops and chopped-up old Beethoven that was lying around EMI or any bits and pieces, stuck them together . . . and we did songs sort of like priming the canvas . . . tracks that I didn't know if they were going to be for ["Revolution 9"] or not. Just where we had the tape on, a bit of echo on, and a cup of tea or something, and George and I just talked for about twenty minutes.

Just anything. I mean, we've been doing it for years on tape around the world. Just, "And so, brother, we'd like to say to you, welcome. . . ." Y'know just any rambling. And I got all the tapes on the different machines, all the loops on different machines, and all the basic tracks. So it was like a big organ or something where I knew vaguely which track would come up if I did that. And I just tried to get the bits of conversation in that I liked, that seemed to say something like "Do what you can, brother" or anything like that and tried to pull out the ones I didn't like. So I think I did it in one go. I just got it, and then I did some slight editing after that. And so most of it is completely random in that respect and all the words.

But you see, it's like throwing the dice or the I Ching or whatever it is. There's no such thing as random, really. It's random compared with sitting down and saying, "It's been a hard day's night, it's been a hard day's night, working like a dog." But even that's random. [*Makes sound like rolling dice.*] And it was a couple of sixes, and I'm not about to do it again and settle for an eleven. It probably was an eleven, rather than . . . You very seldom get a double six in whatever you're doing on that buzz, 'cause when you're on the buzz where you're actually doing the thing where you're not aware, very seldom is the tape recorder on or everybody's got it at the same bit. So most things are nine out of twelve or things like that.

Hindle: Do you think it has changed since you first started?

Lennon: How do you mean?

Hindle: [*Inaudible.*] . . . where you weren't self-conscious.

Lennon: Yeah, but on this album [*The Beatles* a.k.a. *The White Album*] we had rid ourselves of the self-consciousness, so we were doing what we were doing earlier on but with a better knowledge of technique of recording. Quite a few of the tracks are just straight takes of us playing. "Yer Blues," we were just in a room half the size of this, just to have a change from the big studio, and we just did it. And "I Will" and "Julia" and all them is just us singing like that, but the technique makes it a bit better than one of us just singing in the early days.

It's just we know the technique of recording better. If we did the first album again with "Twist and Shout" and all those things on, it'd be the same. We sounded more like us on this record then than we do on that record. People who heard us in Liverpool and Hamburg and the early days, before we turned into just a mass scream . . . that's how we played—heavy rock. But when it was put down on the early records, there was never enough bass in it, the guitar solo never came through, and generally we didn't know about recording then. So now we know how to record a bit.

Hindle: Do you like some forms of art better than others?

Lennon: I think it's just a matter of choice, y'know? I think that's a snob attitude to say something's better than something else. You can prefer something, y'know? And something might give you a better buzz. The only art I really dig is Yoko's and a few people like Richard Hamilton. [*A British pop-art painter and collagist, who designed the Beatles' White Album cover. —Ed.*]

Wiles: Have you ever seen Steve Dwoskin's films?

Lennon: No, no. But there's very few of them [artists] that I prefer to the others. The others are just OK, y'know. And there's some greats in the past. But there's very few people today that . . . I mean there was very little art that turned me on. It was only discovering Yoko at [London's] Indica Gallery that really turned me back on to art. I'd been fishing around, looking at what was going on. And there was no turn-on—there was the same old rubbish coming out over and over again. It was like pre–rock 'n' roll, pop-music art, until people like Andy Warhol, Yoko, and [avant-garde composer and artist John] Cage and all those people did what they did. And that concept art is the only one worth bothering about, for me. It's the only turn-on I've had since Elvis and rock 'n' roll.

Wiles: But do you get as much satisfaction from watching it as actually doing it?

Lennon: Watching what?

Wiles: Well . . .

Lennon: Oh, no, no. That's why I'm doing it, y'know? I mean, the same as I heard Elvis and then I had to do it. I got great joy listening to his records, which I'll never forget, and which I can re-create playing them. But *doing* it is something else, y'know? And I've had great joy from [British cartoonist] Ronald Searle when I was a kid. But I had to draw it meself to get the real buzz. And the same goes for Dylan and all the people that have influenced me and Yoko. I've got to do it, man. And if I—

Yoko Ono [*To Lennon.*]: Is there anything else for him to take? [*Ono is referring to Lennon's driver, who is about to drive to Apple headquarters on an errand. —Ed.*]

Lennon: No, just . . . will you wrap the film up? Oh, can you just bring the two films in here I want him to take in—the one we watched?

Hindle: The thing about art, then . . . I mean, there are sort of two concepts of art as something different from life. Like in the past, say, and art as . . . what you're doing, what everybody's doing. I mean, a conscious effort to try and create things that other people are going to get . . .

Lennon: Yeah, well, it's like Andy Warhol and those people sort of said: "Everything's art." Like, "Here's your can of soup," y'know. To just sort of show people that it's all art if you look at it with an artist's eye or an open mind.

Hindle: But you must still see it as a transitional period to the point where everyone says, "All right, everybody's got it." You don't have to show it to everybody else, because everybody's there.

Lennon: Ah, yeah, but there'll always be people that will be showing some other viewpoint to it.

Hindle: Do you think so?

Lennon: Yeah, I mean, that's when everybody's sort of hip to that in the year of whenever . . . and which won't be too long, because there won't be much else to do, you know.

Hindle: Yeah, that's what I was thinking . . .

Lennon: Yeah, right, right. So that's going to be great. But if I'm with some ordinary guy that can't create the way I create, but he can appreciate it in the year two million when I'm reborn or not, I'll be creating some other viewpoint of what's going on, y'know. There'll be something for artists or musicians and all the people like me to do. Even when everybody's hip to what's going on all around, y'know. There'll still be the performers and the singers and the equivalent of whatever's going on then.

Hindle: What makes you think that?

Lennon: Because . . . people are never going to be the same. There'll always be people like me doing something like I do. . . . Even if it'll all be pretty conceptual and spiritual and "mind music" and like that. But even if I didn't have to sing to you, to sing my songs—presuming none of you can play or sing—and I was giving you a performance in the year 2012, the stuff I create still comes from inside, like the language. I've still got to translate it onto this [guitar] to sing to you. But if we had direct communication, I'd still be communicating those songs to you. Now, you can probably do it yourselves. But if I'm a sort of natural musician, I'll be able to sing to you songs that you wouldn't be able to create yourself, y'know.

Hindle: But what I'm saying is, you get to that point where you get to the essence. Y'know, I mean, the whole working towards everything by externalizing things and showing people . . . In the end, you get to the essence, where everybody's got it, and there's no need to externalize it, so—

Lennon: Well, externalize it, no, but it'll still be . . .

Hindle: But to say it's music and it's films and that . . . I mean, that presupposes some sort of thing that you have to go through to get to it, but you won't have to.

Lennon: Yeah, I see what you're getting at. But I still think there'll be people sort of . . . I can't think of an example to show how I mean it.

Wiles: Though I think it's being incredibly optimistic, y'know. I can't help feeling that—

Lennon: I am optimistic, you know, and—

Wiles: Yeah, but I can't help feeling that you're sort of . . . I don't know, in your last three years, you've got out of touch with the masses.

Lennon: Yeah, but what's the masses, man? What do you mean by that? Out of touch with what, y'know? With nine-to-five and all that? I've never been in touch with—

Wiles: No, with people's attitudes and sensibilities. I mean, your friends are presumably sort of enlightened people—

Lennon: No, they're not. My friends are just ordinary people, y'know? There's a friend of mine, now . . . he's neither enlightened or not enlightened. He is the masses, y'know. See, I'm the masses, man. I've *been* the masses, I *am* the masses. Nothing's changed.

Wiles: Well, you're not, you see, because if you're—

Lennon: But because I'm not living on Old Compton Street or something doesn't mean a shit, y'know! So I've never been in contact with the masses, according to the way you're talking. I've never been there, man! I was never there mentally all me life! Why do you think I'm me? The whole point about *me* is that I've never been there!

Physically, right, I went through it all. And mentally I went through all the things that all the other guys at school did. [*To Ono, regarding film being taken to Apple.*] I'd like you to get me some Cellotape to stick it down before it all unreels. [*To Wiles.*] Y'know? So using your term of reference, I've never been there, in contact with the masses, 'cause I've always been outside of it. Whether I knew it or not, y'know? That's why I'm me and not doing some gig in Liverpool at nine-to-five, or even bumming around the coffee bars.

Wiles: But that's why I think you're being terribly optimistic to think that people can ever become as you'd like them to be . . . everybody to be, y'know, turned on.

Lennon: *Relatively* turned on! That's why I'm saying to him [Hindle] that there'll always be people . . . If this scene is 2012, or whenever—that may be early—whenever it is when people are doing . . . it'll still be relative. But the masses will be where I am today, and me, I should be somewhere else. . . . I should be as groovy as Jesus by *then*—

Wiles: Yeah.

Lennon: —and the masses should be as groovy as the grooviest people around now!

Wiles: But when you look back, do you think there's been this advance over the last few hundred years?

Lennon: I think it goes and comes, y'know. Cycles. Like all the astrologers and all those people say. We've been, and fallen back. And I think it continues on that, and that when the earth as a whole evolves to its full state of consciousness, there's a good chance it will just fall back into the crap again, y'know. So, I mean it's all, ah, what's the use of it? But if you believe in reincarnation, the point is that you're going to be around in the future, so you may as well, even for selfish reasons, fix it up for when you come back.

Wiles: Yeah.

Ono: [*Laughs.*] Are you buzzing?

Lennon: Yeah, a bit, yeah!

Hindle: So you are seeing it [the thing about cyclic change] as a vertical rather than a horizontal.

Lennon: I just see it as a loop, y'know.

Hindle: Going 'round?

Lennon: Yeah. And you get up to the top . . . and [*begins singing verse from the Beatles' "Helter Skelter"*] down to the bottom of the hill and you do it again . . .

Hindle: Yeah, but I mean, saying . . .

Bob Cross: Possibly every loop gets a bit higher . . .

Lennon: Yeah.

Hindle: I don't personally see it as a sequential thing, upward or downward—

Lennon: No, no, no, well . . . I mean, that's only a way of describing it.

Hindle: Yeah.

Lennon: Like in meditation, they used to say you "go within yourself," like "The kingdom of heaven is within you"—all that. You're not actually going in, out, or anywhere. And the whole place isn't actually going up, down, or anything. But that's the only language we've got, y'know? We can't *conceive* of what's happening. And when Jesus or any of the master types try and tell you, they've got to put it in language like "up," "down," "'round."

Ono: No, but that's one thing that whenever [*inaudible*] we're not in that state and all that, we never really [*inaudible*].

Lennon: What . . . was that?

Ono: That's the only time that I felt a kind of snobbery in the vertical idea . . . you know, going to the next stage.

Wiles: Yeah.

Lennon: Yeah, but it's only a language of describing a state of consciousness, isn't it?

Ono: No, but—

Lennon: So it's not up, down, 'round, and about. But the way they describe it in all the good old books is you go up and you go down, you know? And you say you're up when you're high and you're down when you're depressed. But you're not. And it's as valid as that.

Wiles: Did you think *Yellow Submarine* was good, the film? And how much did you have to do with it?

Lennon: Very little.

Wiles: Did you like it?

Lennon: I enjoyed it, y'know. I thought it was all right.

Wiles: It was brilliant, I thought. I thought "Nowhere Man"—

Lennon: Yeah, I liked the guy's drawing, you know? And I liked some of the things they did. I thought it was all right.

Wiles: Did you like the vacuum man that sucks things up?

Lennon: Oh, yeah. They pinched that from an idea I had about the sweeper in the garden, in the pool. But I mean, they didn't pinch it because I was writing a song about it for them, but I never did it—about Horace, the vacuum.

Ono: You mean you had a song about Horace, the vacuum?

Lennon: Well, they were saying, "Have you got any more songs for the cartoon?" And I said I'd write one. They wanted one about a monster. I said, "I'll write you one about Horace," the thing that goes around the swimming pool sucking up the dirt. I was going to write about Horace, who sucked up, but I never did it. So they just took that, obviously, and made a vacuum thing out of it. [*To Ono.*] That's for Anthony [Fawcett, Lennon's new personal assistant] to give to Tony Bramwell [senior Apple assistant and later CEO of Apple Records]. Has he gone?

Ono: No.

Lennon: Can you tell him that he's got to hand it to Tony Bramwell personally? Otherwise it'll vanish.

Wiles: Is it an underground film? [*Wiles is referring to the film that Lennon is asking Ono to have delivered to Bramwell. —Ed.*]

Lennon: Well, I suppose so. It's a film of [the] *You Are Here* show [Lennon's first art exhibition, held in July 1968 at London's Robert Fraser Gallery]. Of all the people reacting to it. I had a candid-camera team hidden behind the door, watching all the people doing it. Sort of looking at the picture and, you know, not knowing how to take it, and all the art critics and the artists are all— [*Shouts to personal assistant Pete Shotton about the Bramwell errand.*] What? Yeah. There might be something for him to bring back, too.

Hindle: Something else I want to ask about is the LP *Two Virgins*. [*The record, whose full title is* Unfinished Music No. 1: Two Virgins, *came out in November 1968 and was Lennon and Ono's first album release together. It barely made a dent in the charts but drew attention for its cover, which featured a nude photo of the couple. —Ed.*]

Lennon: [*To Pete Shotton.*] Oh, yeah, tell him to get *Two Virgins* and bring that back. Yeah, they should be bringing me some back today. Yeah?

Hindle: Where do we get it [a copy of the album]?

Lennon: No, it's not out yet. There's such a lot of fighting and hassling trying to stop it, y'know, and EMI is putting it [the message] 'round the world—"don't touch it"—to all their companies. And they're meant to be helping us. And I think it's coming out this week. They're sending out the thing to the retailers for them to place the orders, so the thing is to go and keep asking for it, till the retailers say, "Oh, they want it." But it'll come out even if we have to send it 'round in a van, you know?

Wiles: Have you heard about this ridiculous Hendrix thing where they put it in a brown paper bag? [*A reference to the UK version of the Jimi Hendrix Experience's* Electric Ladyland *album, which some retailers sold* *in a paper bag to hide the cover image of nineteen naked women.* Two Virgins *was destined to suffer the same fate. —Ed.*]

Lennon: Oh, yeah, yeah.

Wiles: Oh, Christ.

Lennon: I don't care even if they put it out in a brown paper bag, as long as it goes out, you know?

Help yourselves to some nice bread she [Ono] made. Macrobiotic bread, as they say. I'll just get a chunk before it vanishes.

[*The tape is stopped while everyone eats. It restarts during a discussion of the Beatles' contractual obligations. —Ed.*]

Lennon: Because our output's been so much, I think we've covered any contract they have. But they do have a thing saying so many songs a year . . .

Wiles: Really?

Lennon: Oh, yeah. But I mean, when you do sign up originally, you sign up 'cause you're glad to sign up, y'know? And then you go on and on, trying to get a bit better deal all the time. But just the last deal Brian [Epstein] made, we signed up for nine years, so there you go . . .

Ono: Here's some macrobiotic bread.

Lennon: Yeah, I've explained the philosophical content behind the bread.

Wiles: If I can stay [on the diet] for three days, maybe I'll become a—

Lennon: Ten days.

Wiles: Ten days?

Cross: What do you do after that?

Lennon: Well, then you eat macrobiotic food, y'know, which is quite easy to get. You get some from the health [food] shop, some from your local farmer. You can always find it. It's mainly untouched by human chemicals is the joke. But it's no meat, no milk, no sugar. It sounds impossible, but it's easy. Once you've got the buzz, you don't want to lose it.

Hindle: Where I live there's nothing macrobiotic.

Lennon: They've got . . . it's that "Free food and meals. One meal or soup, bread and spread." They'll always give you something to eat. But it costs them so much to get, because it's hard to get it, and there's so few people eating it, y'know.

Wiles: You know the Dragon in [inaudible]? That's fantastically expensive . . .

Lennon: Well, that's not macrobiotic.

[*The tape is turned off again. It resumes with Lennon talking about the press being relentlessly negative about his relationship with Ono and their art projects.*]

Lennon: [Responses came] from the balloons that were sent out. [*At the July 1, 1968, opening of Lennon and Ono's* You Are Here *art show at London's Robert Fraser Gallery, 360 helium balloons were released. Each balloon had a label inviting its finder to send a written reply to Lennon at the gallery, and many of the ones he received made racist comments about Ono. —Ed.*] "You and your Jap bastard" and all that. [*Ono laughs.*]

Hindle: Did you get much response from it [the show]?

Lennon: Oh, yeah. And from the gentlemen of the press and all that: "He should stick to yodeling." [*Hindle laughs.*]

[*Inaudible conversation.*]

Lennon: Nigel. [*Replying to question about a poem, "Good Dog Nigel," in Lennon's first poetry collection,* In His Own Write.]

Wiles: Yeah, Nigel . . . "we're putting you to sleep at three o'clock"—my God, that was horrible. . . . You must have been in a bad mood then!

Lennon: No, no. I just write 'em. And then they all sort of end up like that, y'know. I don't have to be in a bad mood to write like that . . .

Hindle: Kakky Hargreaves is another one [character from "I Remember Arnold," in Lennon's *In His Own Write*].

Lennon: That's a very early one.

Wiles: But you seem to be . . . well, I don't know which songs you write, but a lot of the writing seems to be very bitter.

Lennon: Yeah, well . . .

Ono: [*Laughs.*] You've had that period, don't you?

Lennon: I've still got it . . .

Hindle: The chip . . .

Lennon: Mmm?

Ono: Chip on your shoulder . . .

Lennon: It's the chip we've all got, the thing we've been talking about all day, you know, is what I'm talking about. Whether it's just in a man-woman relationship or man-establishment relationship. It's that, you know. That's what the chip is. [*In mock formal voice.*] Manifests itself in many different forms. [*Ono laughs.*] But it's the same old chip.

Wiles: But if anyone should have escaped from it, or could have escaped from it—

Lennon: Let us know . . .

Wiles: —it's you . . .

[*Ono laughs.*]

Lennon: Yeah, but I mean, I can escape from bringing out *Two Virgins* and getting ostracized for it and just live on the income from "Yesterday" for the rest of me life, y'know. But I don't want to do that. It wouldn't satisfy me in any way. I'm still fighting for the same things I was fighting about as a kid.

Wiles: What do the others do?

Lennon: They're all doing their bit, y'know. George is out in the States, just reconnecting with Dylan and a few people out there that we sort of lost touch with. Seeing who he can pick up for the label [Apple Records].

There's a great record he's got. God knows how we'll release it: "The King of Fuh" [issued by Apple in 1969]. [*Laughter.*] And it's just fantastic, by a fella called Brute Force [an American singer/songwriter whose real name is Stephen Friedland]. And it's . . . [*sings*] "Hail the Fuh-king," y'know. [*Laughter.*] Just very good bit. Very good. So we're hoping to put that out one way or another. [*Sings.*] "All hail the king of Fuh-king . . ."

Wiles: Do you think you got busted for drugs because you offended the establishment?

Lennon: Oh, that was in the *Black Dwarf* thing. Well, he's [John Hoyland] probably right. Earlier on, the mop-top thing was preventing us getting busted. Because we were open about it years ago. I mean, it was common knowledge. And then, I don't really know the reason why they suddenly busted me now. Probably because I've been waving me flag a bit, that's all. Like *Two Virgins* and various other things. But you see, this guy's one of those [who says], "The Stones are changing it, you're not." One of them . . .

You know, the Stones and I are great mates. But the Stones did pull back their album cover, you know, so tell him that. . . . I'm sick of this sort of petty thing. It's been going on for years. It used to be, "The Stones do that, and you do this," with the fans and that. But now it's all down to these revolutionaries, y'know. And the thing is, the Stones and I are close, and where's he?

Ono: I haven't seen that [letter in *Black Dwarf*], have I?

Lennon: Oh, this is the one from the *Black Dwarf*. It'll get you going.

Hindle: It's another thing you have to be talking about . . . street-fighting groups versus the capitalistic Beatles.

Lennon: Yeah, well, they'll see, y'know. See, I'm not here to change them. They can get on with it. Let them straighten out a few people's faces and see where it gets them. But I'll tell you what: if those people start the revolution, me and the Stones are probably the first ones that they'll shoot. You know, I mean that. It's just the kind of thing they do. . . . The ones who are really doing it get shot, y'know. It's the guy that wrote the letter that'll do it. He'll shoot me just for living here. I mean, that's the kind of Christian communist attitude they've got, y'know. We're all one, brother, but you can't live here.

Wiles: Yeah.

[*The tape recorder is turned off briefly. It resumes with Lennon continuing to read and comment on the* Black Dwarf *letter from John Hoyland.*]

Lennon: He's talking about the Stones and the Who, and how they came bursting out. He's forgotten to mention that if it wasn't for us [the Beatles], the Stones and the Who would never have been *allowed* out. Amazing. These people are so bitter, all of them, and they're holding the whole thing back by their quibbling about. They're already showing with what they write, and how they say it, how they can never run a new scene. Because they're already quibbling about. Before we've even done anything, they're quibbling about who's doing what, and who's the ethnic one, and who isn't.

And let them go and talk to the Stones, the Who, Dylan, me, Yoko, Andy Warhol. Anybody that's doing anything doesn't think like this. And that's what none of them can understand, is that they're the ones that are holding it back by breaking it up in the ranks, already. Before anything has even moved forward half an inch, there's some fools like this [who] are trying to get it into another bag, before we've even burst the old bag.

Wiles: Yeah. The problem is that the people who have the ideas, like you and Marx and Jesus and God knows what, and then you have—

Lennon: [*Lennon and Ono chuckle.*] Me, Marx, Jesus . . . great. Yeah . . . OK!

Wiles: Then you have the people who push these ideas. Now, Jesus's and Marx's ideas lent themselves to being pushed. But you say, right, you don't push them, except by gently spreading them. And this is why yours has more chance of success. Christianity, I mean, it was a good idea once, but look at the buggers who are in charge. You know, it's ridiculous. And the same with communism, and the same with this business [the *Black Dwarf* letter from John Hoyland]. I mean . . .

Lennon: The same goes for capitalism, probably. I don't know who thought of it, but the idea, I don't see what . . . what is capitalism? Like, y'know, I don't really know what the definition is. I can get communism and Christianity. But capitalism seems to cover everything else, y'know.

Wiles: It's not an ideology; it's just a method of economic—

Hindle: But some of the conservatives would have it that it is an ideology. I mean, they all sort of revere it as something unknown, y'know, trying to see the whole thing as just natural for men to do to each other—

Lennon: Yeah, I'm not sure, y'know, 'cause I'm anti them all. I don't believe any of them are doing it. But I don't want to get in any bag about capitalism, communism.

Wiles: But even the little ones, y'know, Tariq Ali and [such] people, they're all just self-seeking, sort of . . . y'know, they haven't got anything to offer. They just sort of get well known and get—

Cross: Well, I think some of them must have some—

Lennon: Well, some of them, they believe . . . like Saint Paul, he cocked up Christianity a lot, I believe. He *thought* he was doing it right. Like all these sort of mad Tories and the mad Socialists. They *think* they're doing it right, and that's the frightening bit. It's all right if you're up against somebody who knows he's a bastard, and he's doing it because he's a bastard, y'know, but he's out to get you.

But it's these sort of fanatics like [Reverend Ian] Paisley in Ireland [Ulster fundamentalist religious leader and politician] and the ones here—[Enoch] Powell [prominent Tory politician who made what came to be known as a racist speech in April 1968] or whoever the equivalents are over here—who believe they're doing right. And they're the frightening ones. And the same housewives and everything who are booing and shouting at the murderess in the case and would kill her on the spot . . . all the different things. And all those people that don't *know* what they're doing. That's what's frightening . . . the people that don't realize what they're up to. If you just know where they're at, well, you know what to do about it.

Hindle: This brings up the question of . . . the passing of information. What would you term art now? There seem to be two ways of going about describing what people think as artists in the past. Like saying what's wrong with the society at the time. And the other part is just analyzing the great things about life. Y'know, just holding out and saying, "This is the thing that comes out of a large montage of what they behold."

Lennon: Yeah.

Hindle: But there seems to be a tendency of just knocking what everything is and telling people what's wrong. And out of that will come nothing but just the apprehension of what's wrong.

Lennon: Yeah, and I think that's what this guy [*Black Dwarf* letter writer John Hoyland] is doing.

Hindle: Yeah, but you don't see that you—

Lennon: I don't think I'm doing that. Because I'm not saying what's going wrong, y'know. I'm doing the montage bit, just reflecting as fast as I can. You know, reflecting what happens to me.

Hindle: This is what you get from "[Revolution] 9," yeah.

Lennon: And, like the *You Are Here* film and the press cuttings, anything like that . . . I'm trying to get them out, to show people what's coming at me. That's one little piece of the montage. And I'm trying to put that out all the time, to show them my relationship with all these people. And art's a bag you can get it out in. There's no such thing as art, either, but we've just got to use the word. If only we *were* in with the establishment, we would have had it a damn sight easier, Roland Muldoon. [*A reference to a British actor and producer of antiestablishment political theater. —Ed.*]

Hindle: What about the question of Apple?

Lennon: What do you mean?

Hindle: Do you think there is anything to be answered at all about what he [the *Black Dwarf* writer] accuses you of?

Lennon: I've forgotten what he said. What's he say?

Hindle: Well, you know, in that letter, about creating a hierarchy again in the organization . . .

Lennon: Well, there's a danger of creating that.

Hindle: Alienation, you know . . .

Lennon: Yeah, there's a danger. So we're not gonna just not do it. The thing that Apple basically was originally was so we could control our own records completely. And then we got this idea, "Oh, if we could do this, if we could do this . . ." And we tried to do a million things at once, y'know. And it was all idealism. And now we're getting back to we've just got to get a record company, and possibly electronics, so we just happen to know this guy who seems to be turning out this mad stuff ["Magic Alex" Mardas]. And it's down to that.

At first it was going to be everything, you know. And if we're going to lose, y'know, it'll give the guy a laugh, because we either make or break in the next three months. It'll either just all collapse, and we'll all be broke, and it'll make 'em all happy, and they'll think we're ethnic again.

Hindle: Be acceptable.

Lennon: Yeah, we'll be acceptable. Or it'll break even, and it'll be a record company that he'll be getting all the records he wants from America through, because all those people want to be with us.

Cross: It'll help you there, won't it, because you'll be able to issue virtually what you want, or—

Lennon: Yeah, just to have control of our own records was the bit, but we still have the tie-up with EMI so we have to do that, anyway. But just to channel some things through, y'know. To have some kind of . . . just for the workers. And we are the workers. To control what we put out—that's all we're trying to do. And at first we were trying to do a big conceptual, idealistic thing, which we found impossible. And Apple hasn't made any money yet. You know, it's just a complete loss. And it's one of the biggest laughs to the establishment. Y'know, the real establishment are dying for it to break! They don't want anybody like us in the scene, y'know.

Wiles: Do you care if it breaks?

Lennon: I care that it breaks, because our idealism is real. And we'd *like* it to be something that helps other people as well as helping ourselves, and that brought out records that people want. But . . . if it breaks, it breaks, y'know. Ob-la-di, ob-la-da. And it's just that. That's my attitude all down the line. Whatever will be. But don't just be about sitting in the shit and hoping, y'know, accepting the will of Allah. Because you do have a choice of some kind. But if it breaks, it breaks. If it doesn't, it doesn't. It's not going to break me, y'know. I'm not Apple.

Hindle: We've got through quite a lot now, haven't we?

Lennon: Hmm. [*Reading* Black Dwarf *letter again.*] He might get his wish here: "I hope they get so fucked up with their money." [*Chuckles.*] He might be right.

Hindle: What would happen?

Lennon: Hmm?

Hindle: You'd be just the same? I mean, the fact—

Lennon: Sure, I would! I mean, I've lost a fortune this year on friends, relatives, and divorces. Compared to the other Beatles I'm, like, broke. [*Laughter.*] You know, that's true—it's just a laugh, y'know. I don't give a shit!

Wiles: You would if you didn't have it.

Lennon: I will. I have not had it. How many years have I had it? Twenty-three years without it and four years with it, right? I've got the ability to earn me living, anyway. I don't need Beatles or Apple. I don't rely on them to provide me with a living. I can live. I've lived all me life without being in any bag, y'know. And I'll continue, whatever happens to Beatles or Apple, y'know?

That's what the trouble is with these people, and anybody that's putting us down on that level, y'know? The Beatles is a nonexistent concept.

A few people who got together to do something . . . and *Black Dwarf* doesn't exist, either. It's just a few people y'know, and that's what the Beatles is. But I'm not going to live or die by whatever happens to the Beatles, England, the world, or anything. It makes no odds. I believe in the inside bit.

Wiles: Do you ever sort of lie in bed at night and think, *Christ, what the hell's going on?*

Lennon: Oh, yeah. Yeah, about once a week! [*Laughs.*]

Wiles: No, I mean about your success and about—

Lennon: I don't think about my success. I think that the success I've had is to enable me to do what I'm going to do from now on.

Wiles: What, do you think you're predestined?

Lennon: I don't know about predestined. That's what I was saying about the luck and that bit. I think you get a choice of which path you're gonna take, but there's only like a couple of paths. And I think the path that I took through music was the path that took me here. And until I was fourteen, the path was going to be art or writing. But there was just that choice, at about eighteen, twenty, or something. And it was music, and music brought me here. But it's only to enable me to do whatever I'm doing now.

Wiles: Were you ever really unhappy when you were rushing around making money?

Lennon: Oh, that was the most miserable time of our lives, was the mop-top, MBE, cop-out period. . . . That was the torture, and that's why we dropped touring. It just wasn't even the physical fact. It was the thing that we were put through to get what we earned, y'know?

Hindle: But it's what brought you here . . .

Lennon: Oh, yeah, yeah, but it's put me back where I started, y'know. That's why I'm saying that it wasn't worth the drum. It wasn't worth the MBE and that.

Yeah, but it was in retrospect. But it wasn't . . . anybody listening, or gonna read it . . . don't bother, y'know. 'Cause you're back where you started. Just play it by ear, but forget about making it, y'know. There's nothing to make. I could never have done it alone, that. There always had to be one of us carrying it at the time, to do the compromise, and everybody else was just, "Fuck off!" Everyone else was in such a state that we had to take it in shifts to be the mop-top. Y'know, and you look back on all them old photos, there's usually three faces, or two . . . [*Laughter.*]

And it was a really hard grind. And it was a joke. I mean, we dropped it as soon as we got a moment to think about it. It was [*makes a whirring noise like a machine under load*]. And then we just stopped it for a second, got off, and stayed off. And that was about two or three years ago.

Wiles: People were very upset about that, though?

Lennon: Yeah, but I mean, they'd want us to carry on like Flanagan and Allen [long-lived traditional English music-hall act], the wheeling-'em-on-at-eighty-one, you know. I mean, but that's what they don't . . . they still think we're that, y'know. [*Laughter.*] Those are the people that haven't realized that we're not your all-'round, boy-next-door entertainer. Never have been, y'know. I mean, that's what they want—the Crazy Gang [a group of British entertainers that formed in the 1930s] or the Marx Brothers or something.

Wiles: Do you like entertainment films?

Lennon: Yeah, I like all sorts. I can watch anything. Depends what mood I'm in. I don't go and see many films. I prefer to go and see something that I go specially to see.

Wiles: Don't you get worked up about pretentious films?

Lennon: I try not to get worked up about it, because it's a waste of energy. I believe in conserving your energy. Why waste your time on it? There's always going to be Engelbert Humperdinck, and it doesn't matter, y'know. I don't agree with the people that knock Engelbert Humperdinck just because he's doing that. Or just because he's not singing "Street Fighting Man," y'know. It's a narrow concept of life. It's fascism.

Wiles: Yeah, yeah.

Lennon: That is complete fascism. And what's wrong with the house-wives and Engelbert Humperdinck? *I don't want to listen to it, I don't want to hear it, I don't want anything to do with it.* But I'm not going to denigrate the people. I'm not such a snob as to denigrate the people that want to listen to that, or George Formby [English comedic singer and actor popular in the 1940s and '50s] or anything, y'know.

Wiles: I like George Formby. [*Decades later, in 2011, Wiles directed a BBC documentary on the singer called* Frank Skinner on George Formby. —Ed.]

Lennon: And here's this guy'll be listening to Engelbert Humperdinck when he's sixty as a bit of camp, y'know, and he'll think it's "in." Or maybe it'll be [prominent English theater critic and writer] Ken Tynan. I don't know. But you know, the whole thing'll evolve in that circle. Who is anybody to say that Engelbert Humperdinck isn't as valid as anything else, y'know? Why go on about him and waste your energy? Just dig what you like, dig what you dig, and let other people dig what they dig. They're all just snobs about it. And most of the snobs are the uncreative snobs, y'know. The ones that just listen and form their little clubs.

Wiles: That's the vast majority of people . . .

Lennon: Yeah, yeah.

Hindle: So you believe it'd come out in the end? You know, the good things would come out as a natural thing?

Lennon: Well, I go through despair and hopefulness. I try and hang on to the hopeful bit. Otherwise, there's just no point at all, y'know? I mean . . . there's really no point to our music, or Yoko's art, or my art, or anything when I get down to it, on one hand. It's just all . . . what's the use? You know, what are we up against? But there is a point, because the Blue Meanies *are* working at it like mad. And that's the only point, y'know.

Wiles: So long as you enjoy it, that's the main thing . . .

Lennon: Yeah, yeah.

Cross: How do you go about writing your songs for the group?

Lennon: Well, we haven't written together since *Pepper*, really.

Cross: Oh.

Lennon: In India we were writing a bit together. But this album [the so-called *White Album*] we wrote least of all together. Just 'cause of circumstances and all that, y'know. Or maybe we didn't feel like it. I don't know what. But we do it any way, any combination you can think of, we do it, y'know. From a line, from nothing—like "Birthday" was written in the studio from nothing. "Let's do one like that." And we did it.

There's no way of describing it unless I'm going into, sort of, "And when we wrote this, I was on piano and he was on the guitar." And then it's all right, that kind of talk, but I've said it all, y'know, somewhere or other. It's just a bit of a hassle to say it. You know, I can have a verse of a song, and we write it from then. Actually, just read the *Rolling Stone* article. [*Lennon is referring to an interview with him by Jonathan Cott that took place on September 17 and 18, 1968, and was published a little more than two months later, on November 23. —Ed.*] There's quite a lot about it in there. 'Cause I went through it a bit, just about the album and different things.

Cross: What's that in?

Lennon: *Rolling Stone*. Have you heard of it? It's a good paper.

Hindle: Oh, *Rolling Stone* magazine? Yeah.

Lennon: Yeah, yeah. That's the one that's carried our *Two Virgins* ad. [*Hindle looks at the* Rolling Stone, *sees the price, and laughs; Lennon notices.*] What, is it expensive?

Hindle: That's it, you see? You say it's no good . . .

Lennon: Well, I mean, you can steal something like this. I mean, when I didn't have it, I just took it, y'know. Especially papers and anything like that. How much is it? Three and six? [Three shillings and sixpence, or the equivalent of about four US dollars in 2016.] Oh, that is dear, isn't it? Here you are. You can have this one then. I suppose I've got another somewhere. I think the inside's missing.

Hindle: Oh, yeah, I saw the *Two Virgins* advert, that picture on the back cover . . .

Lennon: Yeah, *International Times* wouldn't take the [full-frontal nude] front-cover photo [of Lennon and Ono] unless we gave them an indemnity against it, y'know. They're so established. Amazing. But this paper just took it, and this paper was cool by it, 'cause they've had the biggest circulation they ever had. So that's where they [*International Times*] missed out. If you wanna sort of get into [writing about] the song business, you can . . . they won't care if you pinch their article, or pinch bits out of it, y'know. . . . There's a lot about the songs and different things like that in it.

Hindle: Can I take a few pictures while we're talking?

Lennon: Yeah, sure. Yes.

Hindle: Carry on talking.

Lennon: No, it's OK.

Wiles: [*Discovering he's out of cigarettes.*] Oh, Christ!

Lennon: It's all right, y'know. I'm rich with ciggies, yeah.

Hindle: Does Ringo still take photos?

Lennon: Yeah, yeah.

Wiles: Does he live 'round here?

Lennon: No, he's moved.

Wiles: How many cats have you got?

Lennon: Seven or eight. They breed like cats, some of them . . .

Ono: They do, don't they?

Lennon: Mmm, all over the landing.

Wiles: Do you ever use the swimming pool for swimming?

Lennon: I did when it's sunny, you know. But I'm hoping some established pop star'll buy it, but they're all buying the other ones. Engelbert and Tom Jones are all moving up here, and they won't buy it. I don't know what's the matter. I had it specially designed for Hollywood-style living, and I can't get rid of it! [*Laughter.*]

Wiles: Is that just the swimming pool or the whole house?

Lennon: No, no, the pool, y'know. I was conned by some firm, said they were gonna build me a covered one. But after they built it, they said, "We can't build a cover." Amazing. Conning people with a capital *C*. We've got more of this, haven't we? [*To Ono, referring to the* Rolling Stone *issue.*]

Ono: Um, well, we can get more . . .

Lennon: Yeah, OK. Three and six, y'know. It's a bit expensive. [*Laughs.*]

Ono: Oh, and also, I'll give you this one. It's some last copies of handouts for our *Film No. 5* and *Two Virgins*. There's some writing by John and me. That's the only copy I have now here, so . . .

Hindle: Great, thank you.

Lennon: [*Referring to the* Black Dwarf *letter writer.*] I wonder what that guy'll say when the Stones' record company comes out? Really throw him . . .

Wiles: Record company?

Lennon: Yeah, they're bringing out Mother Earth [American band, which in fact did not sign with the Stones' label]. They've got an "Apple" 'round the corner for their publicity. Big offices and all that.

Wiles: That was fantastic when you gave away all that stuff [from the Apple Boutique in London].

Lennon: It was a happening, but it was written up as a kind of madness, y'know. But it was a great happening. If Yoko had done it, it would've been a piece of artwork. But we did it, and they said we were daft.

That was one . . . closing down of one section [of Apple]. We just couldn't handle all that. It was just turning into a moneymaking thing, and we aren't in it to make money. As long as it breaks even, y'know, and that'll do. But it's not even breaking even. I should think [Apple recording artist] Mary Hopkin should sew it up, though. Records all over the place.

Wiles: Did you bring [singer] Tiny Tim over to England?

Lennon: Well, Derek [Taylor] did, our sort of press guy, y'know. Oh, I'll play you the Christmas record, 'cause Tiny Tim's on it. George was with him in the States.

[*The tape is stopped here while Lennon plays the Beatles' latest fan club Christmas record.*]

Wiles: Is that for release at Christmas?

Lennon: The fan club thing, yeah. We do one every year.

Wiles: Is there another side to it?

Lennon: No, no. They put it on little loose plastic discs.

Wiles: Oh, like the *Private Eye* ones [English satirical magazine].

Lennon: Yeah.

Hindle: Be good to release an album of them.

Lennon: Yeah, we might do it one day.

Wiles: Be really good, actually, because then . . .

Lennon: Yeah, well, it's good for the fans, too, y'know. That's special content for them that they get exclusive, that nobody else gets, [for] the ones that are sort of still into that . . . being in the fan club groove. But in America, they just broadcast it like a normal record, y'know.

Ono: They did?

Lennon: Yeah, yeah.

Hindle: Do they print it like a normal record?

Lennon: No, no, we didn't used to release it in the States 'cause it was too expensive, giving it away and that. Millions in the States. But we're doing it this year. I don't know how it got less expensive, but they're doing it.

Wiles: What do you think of your fans? Do you think it's sort of old-fashioned to be in a fan club?

Lennon: I think it's up to them, y'know, if they get anything out of it. I never joined any fan clubs. [*Ono laughs.*] But if they want to, y'know . . .

if they want to get Beatles pics and all that stuff that the fan club gives out. I mean, we just can't control the fan club, y'know. It'd be too much for us to put out what we'd like them to really get. I mean, we try a bit and try and change *Beatles Book* [a monthly fan magazine] a little, and things like that, but we can't do it all, y'know. They're all by-products of what we are.

Hindle: Do you see that as something separate?

Lennon: No, no. It's just a by-product, and it's not harmful, and nobody's conned by it. We just check out and hope that they're all getting the right . . . the letters they wrote in and getting an answer. And they're getting what they want from it. That's about all we can do.

Hindle: Do you ever answer the fan mail?

Lennon: No, no, we couldn't handle them. A lot of them just write straight to us, anyway. I answer any if they've got a stamped, addressed envelope. They usually only want an autograph. Otherwise, you'd spend all your life answering, y'know, still, "Where'd you get the name Beatles?" and all that.

Ono: [*Laughs.*] And about the hair . . .

Lennon: Well, we have a girl working for the two of us, but . . . if I get a stack of fan letters, I'll send them to the fan club. But I don't get many to the house. 'Cause they never know where I am these days. Hospital or prison.

Ono: [*Laughs.*] Yeah.

Hindle: There's something in that *Rolling Stone* about you doing some preproduction . . .

Lennon: I think we might make a live album next, about January or something. And then we just let whoever gets there in free, probably. It'll just be that. It's built up [in the press] into a tour of the States, free with charity . . . and they're all writing already, saying, "I'm an old-age pensioner with fifty-stone legs, and my husband died and he was a musician." And that, y'know. It gets into all that. So . . .

Wiles: Do you ever feel any obligations to the society for putting you where you are?

Lennon: No, no, I put me where I am. [*Ono laughs.*] I've only got myself to blame.

Wiles: [*Inaudible.*]

Lennon: Well, you say it . . . I mean, those people *do* owe them their life 'cause that is their life, y'know. And they'll revolve 'round it probably for the rest of their life in one form or another. So to them, the public is that. And even though a lot of it is just a lot of PR whitewash, y'know, "my great public" and that . . . We did a lot of that when we were *hating* the public, in the madhouse days. We were under such pressure, we didn't give a damn about anybody—just surviving, y'know. But we'd say, "Oh, this is great, we love our fans! Just get them off my roof, or my garden, or my back!" or anything. "Get away from me!" Like that.

But there's a lot of those people—like [English pop music singer] Frankie Vaughan's one—that mean it, y'know. And they try and do their bit, and good luck to them, y'know. They mean it. But I've never owed anything to the public. I mean, I bring out a product, and they buy it. It's like that. I never expected Mr. Rolls-Royce or Mr. Mini to allow me to sleep in his garden or have anything else. You know, I don't expect anything from anybody but the product he puts out. And I'm not for sale. My products are.

Wiles: Do you get any trouble from fans?

Lennon: Now and then, y'know. There was some bird here last night. [*To Ono.*] There was a bit of trouble, wasn't it?

Ono: Yes, we had to . . .

Lennon: Just some bird suddenly turned up. She said she's out of a mental home in Holland or something, and . . . at first I said, "Well, come on, what do you want?" She said, "I've come all the way from Holland"—which a lot of them do as justification, y'know—"and now I'm your responsibility." So I was saying, "OK, you've come from Holland. What are you going to do now?" She just sort of . . . I thought she was on a trip or something was wrong with her.

Ono: She was sitting here . . .

Lennon: So we just fed her, and I got my driver to take her to the embassy, or to the macro restaurant, or wherever she wanted to go to.

Ono: We tried to turn her on to the macrobiotic diet.

Lennon: 'Cause she said she's had mental trouble and that, which is probably true, but you know, the macro thing would cure that. I believe that, so maybe she could try it. We gave her a few bags of rice and sent her off with a few addresses in Holland or Belgium to get in touch with.

Hindle: You don't sort of feel that you're doing the same sort of thing as Engelbert Humperdinck with the fan club by sustaining that sort of obsessive behavior?

Lennon: Yeah, well, we had the decision of whether to keep the fan club or not, y'know, since we stopped being mop-tops, as it were, two years ago. It would've been suitable for us not to have the fan club. It doesn't give us anything. We don't earn from it, we don't get anything creative from it. But the point was to stop it just because we didn't really have anything to do with it or . . . if they want a fan club to let 'em have it. And we thought of just packing it in, you know.

We don't need the fan club, *Beatles Book*, or anything. But the thing is, I think they want it, and until they don't want it, we'll let it run. It's just like that. I can't see the point of stopping it just because we're not to do with it, which we never were, y'know. I mean, it was a good thing to have fan clubs. It was part of the deal. It was a bag. It was them getting a flag to wave—you each had your fan club and that. It was the point of whether to just stop it because it didn't mean anything to us as people. Only that, y'know, it's nice for people to be in your fan club. Apart from that, it's nothing.

So I think if you just tried to just stop it if they want it, if there's still twenty thousand or so waiting for news from [Beatles press agent] Tony Barrow, or whoever it is . . . It just tells them what we're doing, or where we are. And we just make sure they get the first information on what we're doing. So it gives them that. So . . . why stop it? We don't owe them a fan club . . . but it's no skin off our nose to have it.

Ono: It's convenient, too, to have it, because otherwise there'll be letters pouring in and all that, or . . .

Lennon: Yeah, well, there's that, too, I suppose, but then—

Ono: And that takes care of it, too.

Lennon: —then we'd have to either dispose of the letters or try and answer them all. Or maybe there wouldn't be any letters if there wasn't a fan club. Or less of them. It's just that choice, y'know. As long as it's wanted and it doesn't do anything, let them have a fan club.

Hindle: You mean you sort of don't care as long as people are enjoying it?

Lennon: Yeah, yeah, y'know. I believe in that . . . just for the sake of enjoyment, apart from any messages and changing the world. Just pure circus, y'know.

Wiles: Does it matter to you that your fame has made it impossible to walk around with anonymity?

Lennon: It does a bit, y'know. But it is, like they say, the price of fame. And it matters a lot to me not to be able to go around. And I keep dreaming of the time I might be able to get out. Now, I could cut all me hair off and get around for a few weeks, till they spotted me. Or I could disguise meself, but I don't want to. I'm me, and I look like this 'cause I like being like this. And so I've been through all the reasons of how I could do it. And I don't enjoy it at all, y'know, not being able to do things. Well, that's the price. It's too late to change it.

Wiles: But I shouldn't think you would, would you?

Lennon: I don't know what I'd do if I had to do it again. I don't know. To do it again would mean I'd have the experience I've had now, so obviously I'd do it differently, so as I wasn't so well known as a person, y'know. I'd do it . . .

Wiles: Would you spend less time as a mop-top?

Lennon: Oh, yeah, I would've skipped the mop-top bit altogether, retrospectively speaking.

LENNON ON . . .

His Finances

"A few divorces [*in fact, Lennon had been divorced only once —Ed.*] and suddenly I'm like the poorest Beatle. . . . I don't care if I have no money or a lot of money. I'm not out to make more money. But I'm out to break even. I've earned it, the money I've got. But a lot of other people who shall be nameless have carved us up in the usual way that pop stars and people are carved up. And my main concern about money . . . I never bother about it, only the thought that there's quite a few people sitting comfortably, having done nothing but trick us to get our money. And I'd sooner throw it down the drain or give it away to the fascists or the Tories or the left wing or anybody, rather than just be conned."

—from interview with Dutch sociologist Abram De Swaan, broadcast on *Rood Wit Blauw* (TV show), December 12, 1968

PRESS CONFERENCE

March 31, 1969, Hotel Sacher, Vienna, Austria

On January 30, 1969, the Beatles gave their final public performance on a London roof-top. Less than two months later, on March 20, Lennon and Ono married on the island of Gibraltar. And eleven days after that, the couple conducted a press conference in Vienna while wearing bags over their heads.

As Lennon later sang in "The Ballad of John and Yoko": "Made a lightning trip to Vienna, eating chocolate cake in a bag / The newspapers said, 'She's gone to his head, they look just like two gurus in drag.'" But he wasn't fazed by the questions from the reporters, who seemed not to take the event seriously. In fact, as Lennon subsequently told *Rolling Stone* editor Jann Wenner, the Vienna press conference was "the best thing we did in a bag together."

"It was like a hotel press conference," Lennon recalled. "We kept them out of the room. We came down the elevator in the bag, and we went in and we got comfortable, and they were all ushered in. It was a very strange scene because they'd never seen us before, or heard . . . Vienna is a pretty square place. A few people were saying, 'C'mon, get out of the bags.' And we wouldn't let 'em see us. They all stood back, saying, 'Is it really John and Yoko?' and 'What are you wearing, and why are you doing this?' We said, 'This is total communication with no prejudice.' It was just great. . . . And they never did see us."

Lennon and Ono can be heard humming a waltz as the proceedings begin. –Ed.

Unidentified Man: Everybody in, please.

John Lennon: Yes, [the questioning can start] as soon as they like. Normal procedure.

Yoko Ono: Any questions, please?

Unidentified Man: OK, could you please be so kind . . . when you have questions, ask them in English. John has been in Hamburg and he knows German a little but not too much.

Reporter: Will you come out?

Lennon: No.

Reporter: Why not?

Lennon: Because this is a bag event. Total communication.

Reporter: What is it?

Lennon: It's total communication.

Reporter: Don't you think it's a little bit out of fashion, what you do?

Lennon: Do you think it's a fashion to stay in a bag?

Reporter: What is it?

Lennon: It's total communication.

Reporter: What is total communication? An invention of John Lennon and Yoko Ono, or is it—

Lennon: No, no, it exists, and we're showing you one example of total communication whereby—

Reporter: Total immersion.

Lennon: Well, that's your version.

Reporter: Are there holes in the bag?

Lennon: There's a hole to get in and out.

Reporter: Have you got a bag with you?

Lennon: [*Laughs.*] It depends what language we're speaking.

Reporter: Cockney in this case.

Lennon: Cockney, I see. I don't think so.

Reporter: Do you get hot in there?

Lennon: It's not too hot yet, thank you.

Reporter: Would you like a drink?

Lennon: No, thank you.

Reporter: If you could change two things with your face, what would it be?

Lennon: I've no idea. Never thought of that.

Reporter: Do you think you're beautiful?

Lennon: I'm quite content.

Reporter: What about your wife?

Lennon: I think she's very beautiful.

Reporter: Thank you.

Yoko Ono: Thank you.

Reporter: Have you conceived a baby?

Lennon: I have no idea. I don't think so.

Reporter: What is the name going to be of your child?

Lennon: I don't want to speculate on the name, really. The Amsterdam thing was a joke, you know. [*A reference to Lennon and Ono's weeklong first "Bed-in for Peace," which began five days after their March 20, 1969, wedding and served as their honeymoon. —Ed.*]

Reporter: Could you change it to Vienna if it [the birth of a child] happens here?

Lennon: Yes, certainly. [*Laughter.*] This is another peace protest, by the way.

Reporter: For peace, or against?

Lennon: For peace.

Reporter: You know, you're in the city of love.

Lennon: Are we? Well, that's beautiful. [*To Yoko.*] We're in the city of love.

Ono: Oh, that's beautiful.

Reporter: This is the room where [*inaudible*].

Lennon: Really? Well, we're highly honored.

Reporter: This is where the Habsburgs used to—

Lennon: Did they? Well, good luck to them.

Reporter: But not in a bag. Somebody said they didn't know whether to pull up the drawbridge or lay on the red carpet.

Lennon: For who? Us or the Habsburgs?

Reporter: The Habsburgs had blue carpets.

Lennon: Ah, did they?

Reporter: What was the special reason for you to come to Vienna?

Lennon: One of the reasons was because we have a film we made [*Rape*] on TV tonight at 10:30, or something. And we thought we'd combine that by plugging the film a bit and also plugging peace a bit from this bag. This is a peace bag. Bag peace.

Ono: This is the first announcement to the world of bagism.

Lennon: Yes.

Ono: We decided to make an announcement of bagism in Vienna.

Reporter: By God, why?

Lennon: Because when we were in Amsterdam doing Bed Peace, halfway through the week we sort of realized a tag to put on what we were doing, which makes it easier for us and you to recognize what we're doing, by calling it bagism. That means that if we have something to say or anybody has something to say, they can communicate from one room to another and not confuse you with what color your skin is, or how long your hair's grown, or how many pimples you've got.

Reporter: How long is your hair?

Lennon: Aha! You have to guess! [*Laughter.*] It's not important. It's only what I say that we're here for.

Ono: We can still communicate.

Reporter: You're not saying very much of interest.

Lennon: Well, you ask the questions and I'll give you an answer, you know. If the questions are going to be banal, you'll get banal answers.

Reporter: Are you gonna come out of the bag once?

Lennon: Not during this press conference, no.

[*Laughter.*]

Reporter: Is there any modern Austrian author you know?

Lennon: No, I—

Reporter: Will you come out of the bag and show us your pimples?

Lennon: I don't have any, actually. But if you're gonna be interested in—

Reporter: Could you prove that to me, please?

Lennon: I don't need to. Take my word for it.

Reporter: Could you give us a reception [*sic*] against pimples?

Lennon: A what?

Reporter: A reception.

Lennon: What's a reception?

Reporter: A recipe.

Lennon: I've no idea. Eat good food.

Reporter: How could you prove that you are John Lennon?

Lennon: I don't have to. I'm here just to talk about peace. It doesn't matter who I am.

Reporter: Are you the ghost of John Lennon?

Lennon: Could be.

[*Laughter.*]

Reporter: Would you come out if we gave you a Sacher-Torte [the hotel's well-known chocolate cake]?

Lennon: We're not coming out for the conference, no. But we'll be out for chocolate cake later.

Reporter: Do you wish to make any statement about the film you are going to show tonight on Austrian television? What it is about, and why did you make it?

Ono: I think the film itself would explain. And I think that it's very important that we are communicating now just by words. We are making a total communication without thinking, as John said, about what sort of face you have or what sort of taste you have in your clothes, et cetera. And those things usually disturb and lock the mind of people, and they can't communicate totally.

Reporter: If you could send anybody to hell out of show business, who would it be?

Lennon: I wouldn't send anybody there willingly.

Reporter: Unwillingly?

Lennon: I don't know, you know. [*Ono giggles.*] I really wouldn't wish it on anybody.

Reporter: Is there any music you especially dislike?

Lennon: I like most music, practically all music. There's some I prefer.

Reporter: Do you hear Viennese music?

Lennon: I've heard the waltzes, you know. I don't think anybody hasn't.

Reporter: I didn't know you went to places where they played waltzes.

Lennon: I don't have to. There's a thing called radio invented a few years back.

Reporter: [*Inaudible.*]

Lennon: That's your own opinion, you know.

Reporter: It brought people like you to the fore.

Lennon: Yes, well, I mean, it brought you into the room.

Reporter: How about this statement Ringo Starr made that you're [the Beatles] never going to appear in public again?

Lennon: Well, all the Beatles made that statement two years ago, but I can say I prefer the Beatles to come out of their bag, as it were, and do another tour. But I'll have to talk to Ringo about that and see how he feels, you know.

Reporter: The opinion is not unique about this problem until now?

Lennon: How do you mean?

Reporter: I mean you've got the same opinion . . .

Lennon: Two years ago we had, and then a few months back . . . I think it was probably when Ringo was making a film that George, Paul, and I were discussing whether to come out on the road again, and we sort of were inclined to come out if we could get some groovy show together. Maybe take Apple on the road or something. And I think perhaps it was a lack of communication between us and Ringo there.

Reporter: Is it only Ringo who has the lack of communication?

Lennon: No, he was making a film, you know. He was in Twickenham [a town in southwest London], and we were just remixing the tracks we'd done. And we were just chatting, like, off-the-cuff. And so when they went to talk to Ringo, he hadn't even been aware of the chat we'd had, you know.

Reporter: Is it true that you said once you would appear free in a concert in Vienna if it would be in the opera house?

Lennon: No, I never said I'd appear free anywhere yet.

Reporter: Is money so important?

Lennon: No, I didn't say that.

Reporter: So what did you say?

Lennon: I said I'd never said I'd appear free anywhere yet.

Reporter: Would you appear for anything free?

Lennon: It depends what it was. The Beatles have done many charity shows. I appeared free in Amsterdam Hotel for peace, for seven days.

Reporter: There only was peace in the room, not outside.

Lennon: The peace was in our minds, really. I mean, we did seven days' press conference for peace in which we donated one week of our two-week holiday for world peace. Now a lot of cynics have said, "Oh, it's easy to sit in bed for seven days." But I'd like some of them to try it, even if they do it for other reasons than world peace, and talk for seven days about peace. All we're saying is give peace a chance.

Reporter: Could you give me an example for anything you've changed with this action?

Lennon: I couldn't give you a concrete example, except for a few good cartoons that came out of it and a few good reactions from readers' letters in England that I especially know about. Some old woman that said she's had the best laugh of her life. Well, if the least we can do is give somebody a laugh, we're willing to be the world's clowns, because we think it's a bit serious at the moment and a bit intellectual.

Reporter: You're not willing to be the world's clowns . . .

Lennon: We *are* willing to be the world's clowns. That's the least we can do, because everybody is talking about peace, but nobody does anything about it in a peaceful way.

Reporter: [*Inaudible.*]

Lennon: If you donate your holiday instead of just sleeping with your wife and giggling, you might do something about it. I'm sure the local press would be just as interested in you relatively as they are in us two.

Reporter: Fortunately, they can see me.

Lennon: We weren't seven days in a bag in Amsterdam. This is a compressed seven days. The Hilton Hotel was a bag in a way.

Reporter: What would you do if you would wake up one morning impotent?

Lennon: Masturbate.

Reporter: If you could send one gift to the pope, what would it be?

Lennon: Peace.

Reporter: What do you think about the Catholic Church?

Lennon: I think it's as far from the truth as any other church. But I think what happened is, the message has been lost.

Reporter: What do you think about the queen?

Lennon: I don't often think about her. I think it's a hard life she has. Her way of communication is shaking hands, as is the presidents' and premiers' way. I don't think it's a very effective way of communicating to the public, because the public know less about the queen and the presidents than they do about us by staying in bed for seven days and what we think about.

Reporter: Do you think the queen should do that, also?

Lennon: If she believes in peace, I think she should do something positive about it.

Reporter: Will you sing us a song? [*Ono begins to sing.*]

LENNON ON . . .

"The Ballad of John and Yoko"

"The follow-up to 'Get Back' is 'Ballad of John and Yoko.' It's something I wrote, and it's like an old-time ballad. It's the story of us going along, getting married, going to Paris, going to Amsterdam, all that. It's 'Johnny B. Paperback Writer.' . . . The story came out that only Paul and I were on the record, but I wouldn't have bothered publicizing that. It doesn't mean anything. It just so happened that there were only two of us there—George was abroad and Ringo was on the film and he couldn't come that night. Because of that, it was a choice of either remixing or doing a new song, and you always go for doing a new one instead of fiddling about with an old one. So we did, and it turned out well."

—from interview with Alan Smith, late April 1969,
published in *New Musical Express* (UK), May 3, 1969

LENNON ON . . .

Working for Peace

"What we're doing is indoctrinating them [people] to think about peace. People's responsibility to change the world for better, although it's gonna change anyway. And we want to indoctrinate them to do it Gandhi's way. That's all. 'Cause everybody's sitting on the sand by the sea talking about 'I'll never learn to swim' or 'Could I ever learn to swim?' or 'The current's too strong' or 'There's sharks in the water' and they spend their whole life wondering, 'Is anything possible? Could we ever get peace?' All we're saying is, 'Dive in,' you know."

—from phone interview with Howard Smith from bed-in, Montreal, May 28, 1969

CONVERSATION

Timothy Leary & Rosemary Leary | May 29, 1969, Queen Elizabeth Hotel, Montreal |
Published June 25, 2012, *Timothy Leary Archives* (blog)

A little more than a month after their Vienna press conference, on May 9, 1969, Lennon and Ono released the second of three avant-garde albums, *Unfinished Music No. 2: Life with the Lions*. The LP sold no better than its predecessor, *Two Virgins*—which is not surprising, because it consisted largely of Ono's screams and the couple singing the text of news reports about their antics.

The pair garnered more attention for their weeklong Bed-In for Peace at Montreal's Queen Elizabeth Hotel, which began May 26, 1969. It was their second such event, following their bed-in in Amsterdam, Holland, in March.

LSD advocate Timothy Leary and his wife, Rosemary, visited Lennon and Ono during the Canadian bed-in, and someone recorded their conversation, which finds Lennon light years from Fab Four territory. Leary intended to use the dialogue in an anthology called *The Beatles as Unconscious Evolutionary Agents (with Conversation with John-Yoko)*. He never published the book, however, and the transcript of the conversation sat in an unmarked envelope for more than four decades, until Leary archivist Michael Horowitz discovered it in 2012.

"The enormous personal and political pressures on the four of them are evident here," Horowitz later wrote. "Despite (or perhaps because of) their global fame, both couples had a difficult time getting through Canadian customs. Both had been busted for marijuana possession the previous year—John and Yoko in London, and Tim and Rosemary in Laguna Beach [California]. A few months after the bed-in, John would leave the Beatles and move with Yoko to the US, where they were closely monitored by the FBI and threatened with deportation. Ten months later, Tim would be in prison; Rosemary would be putting on benefits to raise money for his appeal."

According to the blog *Timothy Leary Archives*, Lennon wrote the earliest version of "Come Together" for Leary's short-lived campaign for governor of California against Ronald Reagan. After the campaign was aborted, Lennon reworked the song for the Beatles' *Abbey Road*. —Ed.

Timothy Leary: Living in a teepee is great. It's pretty basic. It's the first artificial habitat, after all.

Rosemary Leary: It's the sexiest building ever invented.

T. Leary: It's like being in a sailboat, because you have to know exactly where the wind is. You raise the fluttering banners and just look up through the smoke flap and you can see how the wind blows. If you don't have the flaps the right way, the wind will blow the smoke down. We always have to be aware of the wind.

John Lennon: Yeah, Yoko had this plan for us two: to blindfold ourselves for two weeks, y'know, and just work it out. We might do that when we get to the new house and find out about it.

R. Leary: Yes, it'd be a fantastic way to learn about it.

T. Leary: Also, of course, we live with rattlesnakes. That's groovy because it requires absolute consciousness. You just can't go thumping through the brush, thinking of what you're going to do tomorrow. You have to realize that you're intruding on their territory. We don't want to hurt you. We don't want to stumble in and step on you. So your consciousness has got to be focused. And, of course, it's always helpful to have dogs. We learn a great deal from animals.

Lennon: How long have you been there, in the teepee? I mean, before you sussed the wind and everything and, you know, got your senses back?

R. Leary: We had to put the teepee up three times before it was right. It's like you can touch it, and it resounds like a drone, and then it's perfect, the canvas. It's a wind instrument that plays like a drone.

T. Leary: You would really love the teepee, because it's a work of art which involves all the senses. You start with white canvas. Then you get the pine. Each man has to strip the bark so you get the wood smooth. You have to line the poles carefully. There are fifteen of these poles, and if you do it wrong, you end up with too big a hole. It's sculpture. Then once you've got it built, it's a light show, because the moon shines through the smoke hole and you can see the stars.

R. Leary: If you placed it properly to the east, the sun rises right over the opening, so at one point during the day the sun is full blast down into the teepee.

Yoko Ono: Is it very wide?

R. Leary: It's a little narrower than the width of this hotel room.

T. Leary: And at night you have a fire. All right. We're sitting around, with the fire here in the center. That means your shadow is thrown on the screen behind you, big, and I'm gesticulating like this, and you catch my shadow. And the silhouettes flicker. The fire's dancing. So if you are outside, you can tell a mile away what's going on. Then you get the wind coming. It creaks a little. The door, by the way, is shaped like the yoni, and you have to bend your head down as you come in, in honor of it.

R. Leary: The only thing that comes through the yoni is the sun and the stars and the moon; actually, only people go through the lower exit and entrance.

T. Leary: It's a sexy place.

Ono: All those nasty magazines in London, they all call me Yoni.

Lennon: Yeah. Yoni Ono.

Ono: John Lingam and Yoni Ono.

T. Leary: We sent a message to you, through [Barry] Miles [UK countercultural activist who cofounded London's Indica Gallery and helped to launch *International Times*] that said that next time you come to the United States, if you wanted to get away for a few days, there's a place . . .

Lennon: We never got the message from Miles. We miss a lot. Yeah, we've got it now. And if we come . . .

T. Leary: It would have to be done in a way that no one would know you're there. Once you just get into the valley, it's another world. Of course, we've been doing nothing but studying consciousness for the last seven or eight years, and at Millbrook, we had this large estate. You probably heard about it—this big sixty-four-room house. It became like a mecca for scientists and barefoot pilgrims.

Ono: I've heard of Millbrook. I mean, it's famous.

T. Leary: Yes, and police informers and television people. But then we saw how geography was important. The land north of the house was uninhabited. As you got there, you got farther away from the people, and the games, and the television, and the police. What we've been trying to do is create heaven on earth, right? And we did have it going, for a while—in the forest groves where there were just holy people. Just people going around silently eating brown rice or caviar, and when you went there, you would never think of talking terrestrial. You never would say, "Well, the sheriff's at the gate."

Lennon: We were going to have no talking either, for a week.

T. Leary: Well, this was a place where you only would go if you just wanted to. It was set up somewhat like, you know, the [*Hobbit* author J. R. R.] Tolkien thing, with trees and shrines. There was another place where we lived, which we called Level Two, which was in a teepee, and people would come up there, and we would play and laugh. And then you get down to the big house, and that was where you could feel the social pressures starting. And once you left the gate, then you were back in the primitive twentieth century. As soon as you walked out the gate, if you didn't have your identification, then they'd bust you. So it was all neuro-geography. The place you went to determined your level of consciousness. As you went from one zone to another, you knew you were just coming down or going up.

Lennon: That's great.

T. Leary: Now we've got that going again out in the desert.

R. Leary: We're living with a more intelligent group of people this time.

Ono: What did you do with the place, Millbrook? Is it still going?

T. Leary: We were supposed to go there this week. Matter of fact, we may go there tomorrow night. It's still there. But it's the old story. In the past, societies fought over territory. They thought, *We'll hold this space, or we'll force you out.* It's an old mammalian tradition. As you pointed out about Reagan, what we're doing in the United States is transcending this notion of the good-guy cowboy. That's Governor Reagan: he's gonna shoot down hippies, shoot down blacks and college students.

So we gave up Millbrook, because there's no point in fighting over the land and making it a thing of territorial pride. If they want it so much that they're going to keep an armed guard there all the time, they can have it. We'll be back. [*"Two weeks prior to this conversation,"* notes Leary archivist Michael Horowitz, *"California governor Ronald Reagan had ordered the National Guard to shoot at protesting students during the People's Park uprising in Berkeley; it was G. Gordon Liddy, later one of the Watergate burglars, who drove Tim and his extended family from Millbrook."* —Ed.]

Lennon: Yeah, that's where we're shouting at the kids at Berkeley: "Forget the park, move on." They're all saying, "Where?" Y'know, I'm saying, "Canada. Anywhere." There's plenty of space.

T. Leary: There is.

R. Leary: Yes, if you fly over this country in an airplane you'll just be amazed at the amount of space there is.

Lennon: Pioneers. Pioneers are very important today, because people won't go where somebody hasn't already gone. Yeah! That's what we're saying: What did your forefathers do? How did they make it?

Ono: And it's a healthy thing to do, isn't it?

T. Leary: What do the kids say when they talk to you? [*According to Horowitz, "Lennon and Ono had been talking to radio stations all day, and to anyone calling in to these stations to talk to them."* —Ed.]

Lennon: About peace, or about anything in general? On the phone? Well, if they're not saying, "Welcome to Canada," they're saying, "What can we do?" Y'know?

R. Leary: That's good.

Lennon: They're saying, "What can we actually do?" And then we say, "Well, we can't tell you what to do," y'know. We can only sort of say, "There's other things to do."

T. Leary: You're in charge. You don't have to ask.

Lennon: Yeah, think about it. But they're getting it, y'know. I mean, they must be. Our voices must be going out solid about every quarter of an hour. And if it isn't singing, it's talking, and we're just repeating the same bit, y'know, and there's very little "Me eyes are brown and Paul's . . ." Y'know? I mean, I do that for the ones that need it. Most of it's just, "Let's get it together," and it must be going out now like a mantra. We're trying to set up a mantra, a peace mantra, and get it in their heads. It's gonna work.

T. Leary: It's Pierre Trudeau that got us in Canada. Because about a year and a half, two years ago, there was a big university thing in Toronto [Perception '67, a conference/cultural event] and they invited people to speak about drugs. [Writer] Paul Krassner came, [Marshall] McLuhan was there, and I was supposed to come up to give a talk, but the government wouldn't let me in. So I sent a tape, and they confiscated it.

Then I went to the International Bridge in Detroit and handed it across, and the Americans busted me 'cause I wasn't supposed to leave the country. That was two years ago, before Trudeau was premier. This time they checked with higher-ups. They kept us waiting about an hour. They were very polite. They were getting instructions from . . . wherever they get their instructions.

Lennon: They kept us about two hours, searched through everything. Yeah, well, we wanted to get to Trudeau. We're really headed for Nixon.

T. Leary: I am, too.

Lennon: We're just telling them that we want to give them two acorns—a piece of sculpture that we entered in an exhibition. So we wanted to get that to Nixon and tell him, "All we want you to do is make a positive move," y'know. And then they'd either have to accept it or deny it publicly, and then we'd ask, "Why, why, don't you give us that time schedule?"

Leary: How are things in Europe?

Lennon: They're OK there, you know. It's relaxed, and everybody's . . . they're all smoking their cigars and drinking coffee, y'know, and you go to Paris and Amsterdam, and they're all just rolling along.

Ono: And they don't dislike you for smoking.

Lennon: No, it's not the same. They get down about it, but there's none of that . . .

Ono: Not hatred.

R. Leary: I'm always surprised when I read of any of you being busted in England, because . . .

Lennon: Oh, it's again a bit paranoid in England now. It's getting a bit heavy. 'Cause there's a lot of Americans coming in, y'know, sort of refugees, and it's not even that so much. There's just more people around, and they're busting the pop stars. Like they got Mick Jagger and Marianne [Faithfull] yesterday. [*Police arrested Jagger and Faithfull for marijuana possession at their London home the day before this conversation took place. —Ed.*] There's one guy doing it all, one little Sergeant Pilgrim.

R. Leary: Pilgrim?

Lennon: Yes, I think he's on a pilgrimage, collecting scalps.

R. Leary: Your Pilgrim and our Purcell. [*Laguna Beach, California, policeman Neil Purcell arrested Timothy Leary for two marijuana roaches on December 26, 1968; the arrest led to his imprisonment in March 1970. —Ed.*]

Lennon: And he's going around nailing us all; and they're beginning to hound the underground papers now. They never gave 'em any bother before. So it's getting a bit like that. But it's nowhere near stateside size yet, and by the time it gets like that in England, the States will have cooled off.

T. Leary: It's not a yin-yang thing. The energy in the United States is accelerating, and you can go on the negative trip and point to all the bad things happening. But the reason these power trips are happening is because the freedom thing is so strong. I give lectures at colleges, and even down South, and up in Minnesota, in religious, very backwater places where you expected [resistance to change] . . . the kids are just waiting for any voice of honesty and humor.

R. Leary: It's changed. It really has. Even a year ago . . .

Lennon: Yeah, when we were down there, in the States [on the Beatles' last US tour, in August 1966], it was terrifying. That's when they were getting me for saying we're bigger than Christ. Somebody was letting off balloons, and we all looked around to see which of us had got shot.

T. Leary: But the kids there are the same as they are anywhere. Because this thing we're involved in, it does transcend all the old dichotomies of left/right or conservative.

Lennon: They're even playing the "Christ, you know it ain't easy" record ["The Ballad of John and Yoko"] down South on some stations. I didn't think it'd get past the line, y'know, didn't think they'd play it there at all. I asked them [in] Jacksonville, Florida, "Hi! Y'playing the record?" "Yeah, we're playing it. Why did you say that?" "Well," I said. "Uh, heh . . ." [*Laughs.*]

T. Leary: John, about the use of the mass media . . . the kids must be taught how to use the media. People used to say to me . . . I would give a rap and someone would get up and say, "Well, what's this about a religion? Did the Buddha use drugs? Did the Buddha go on television?" I'd say, "Ah . . . he would've. He would've . . ."

Lennon: I was on a TV show with David Frost and Yehudi Menuhin, some cultural violinist, y'know. They were really attacking me. They had a whole audience and everything. It was after we got back from Amsterdam . . . and Yehudi Menuhin came out. He's always doing these Hindu numbers. All that pious bit, and his school for violinists, and all that. And Yehudi Menuhi said, "Well, don't you think it's necessary to kill some people sometimes?" That's what he said on TV; that's the first thing he ever said. And I said, "Did Christ say that? Are you a Christian?"
"Yeah."
I said, "And did Christ say anything about killing people?"
And he said, "Did Christ say anything about television? Or guitars?"

T. Leary: Marijuana . . .

Lennon: Yeah. I couldn't believe it. I really couldn't believe that.

T. Leary: The trick is, though, not to be pulled off into the bullring thing. You've got to keep right on the essence, and if you do that . . .

Lennon: Yeah, I got a bit lost, actually, but I got such a fright. I didn't expect such . . . so much from 'em. It was just a sort of David Frost show with a couple of people on, and we'd just got there, and the hatred was amazing. I was really frightened. But Yoko was cool, so when one of us loses it, the other can cover.

LENNON ON . . .

Emigrating to the United States

"A lot of people don't want me in, you know. They think I'm gonna cause a violent revolution, which I'm not. And the others don't want me in because they don't want me to cause peace, either. Because war is big business, you know, and they like war because it keeps them fat and happy. And I'm antiwar, so they're trying to keep me out. But I'll get in."

—from interview with fourteen-year-old Beatles fan Jerry Levitan, Toronto, 1969

LENNON ON . . .

Unfinished Music No. 2: Life with the Lions

"That's [the album's screeching, nonmusical sound] just saying whatever you want it to say. It's just us expressing ourselves without any words or format, not formalizing the sound we make to make words or to make music or beat. We're just expressing ourselves like the child does . . . and you get it or you don't. . . . What we're saying is, 'Make your own music.' This is unfinished music. We're not giving you finished products wrapped up in a bit of paper and saying, 'Here you are, aren't we clever?' . . . Youngsters don't have any trouble digging it . . . You play it for a twelve-year-old, they just go along with it."

—from interview with David Frost, London, broadcast on ITV (UK), July 10, 1969

LENNON ON . . .

His Campaign for Peace

"Do you want nice middle-class gestures for peace? And intellectual manifestos written by a lot of half-witted intellectuals and nobody reads 'em? That's the trouble with the peace movement. . . . I'm sorry you liked the old mop-tops, dear, and you thought I was very satirical and witty and you liked *Hard Day's Night*, love, but I've grown up, but you obviously haven't. . . . That ['Give Peace a Chance'] was a message from me to America or to anywhere. I used my songwriting ability to write a song that we could all sing together, and I'm proud that they sang it at the moratorium." [*A reference to the November 15, 1969, march on Washington, where Pete Seeger led the crowd in singing Lennon's song. —Ed.*]

—from response to journalist Gloria Emerson, who'd attacked Lennon's antiwar efforts, Apple headquarters, London, December 4, 1969

LENNON ON . . .

His Rift with the Beatles

"Paul and I have differences of opinion on how things should be run. But instead of it being a private argument about how an LP should be done, or a certain track, it's now a larger argument about the organization of Apple itself. Whether we both want the same thing from Apple in the end is a matter of opinion. But how to achieve it—that's where we digress. Mainly we disagree on the Klein bit. [*A reference to whether Allen Klein should manage the Beatles' business affairs. —Ed.*]

—from interview with Alan Smith, early December 1969, published in *New Musical Express* (UK), December 13, 1969

RADIO INTERVIEW

Howard Smith | December 17, 1969, Mississauga, Ontario, Canada | Broadcast December 1969, WABC-FM (New York)

New York radio personality and journalist Howard Smith spoke with Lennon and Ono in mid-December 1969 at the ranch of rockabilly musician Ronnie Hawkins, near Toronto.

It had been quite a fall. In quick succession in September, Lennon and Ono had performed in Toronto with their Plastic Ono Band and Eric Clapton; Lennon had announced at a group meeting that he was leaving the Beatles; and the band's chart-topping and critically acclaimed *Abbey Road* had appeared. October brought the little-noticed release of Lennon and Ono's *Wedding Album*, the couple's third and final avant-garde LP. Then in December, Lennon and Ono released *Live Peace in Toronto 1969*, a recording of the aforementioned September concert. Five days after that came this wide-ranging, previously unpublished discussion with Smith, which covers Woodstock and Altamont, the potential for world peace, marriage and divorce, and the prospects for future Beatles products or tours.

Smith serves as an interesting counterpoint to Lennon and Ono's idealism, calling the youth movement "a marketing concept," questioning what Woodstock ultimately accomplished, and wondering whether most people even understood the meaning of the couple's "war is over if you want it" slogan. Lennon and Ono stand their ground throughout this previously unpublished discussion, but so does Smith. —Ed.

Howard Smith: What did you think of the press conference tonight?

John Lennon: It was very good. They were all tense when we came in. So were we, and it was relaxed by the end of it. It was a very good conference.

Yoko Ono: Good vibration, I thought.

Lennon: I thought the happening of the press conference was great. Just the vibes and what comes out and then we can judge it, really. But the press in Canada are pretty straight with us.

Smith: What—and not elsewhere?

Lennon: Well, see, in London we had the worst time. They're really sort of . . . well, they've always treated Beatles like private property. They think they sort of have—well, they do because we came from there, et cetera—but they have this sort of parent—

Ono: "We made them."

Lennon: —parent/child relationship with us, and the press is generally doing that bit about we're not being preached to by some middle-aged, past-his-best Beatle who's an entertainer—no-entertainer-should-open-his-mouth kind of bit. That's the attitude they usually take in London. So all our best work is done abroad. That's why we did the first bed event in Amsterdam. The only way to get the British interested is to leave and do it somewhere else.

Smith: Is that how they treat other entertainers in England, also?

Lennon: Oh, sure, sure, yeah. They sort of have a little snob thing about America, the way they treat their entertainers: "You ain't in America now, boy." They did that to the Stones when they got back. Stones had a quiet performance—

Ono: In London.

Lennon: In London after America and it was sort of, "Well, you're home now, son—none of that, not Americans screaming," and all that. A bit like that.

Ono: It's a classic case of your hometown treats you differently—and indifferently or whatever.

Lennon: I mean, they had headlines 'cause I shaved. I've been trying to get something in [the papers] on the [James] Hanratty [case] . . . a murder case in England that happened eight years ago, where there's a shadow of a doubt and a big hustling scene going on.

We did a stunt; it sort of happened, but we did it. There was Ringo Starr and Peter Sellers's premiere of [The] Magic Christian, and Yoko and I arrived just at the same time as Princess Margaret, which would have gotten the news, anyway. Also, we were in a white Rolls with [a bumper sticker that read] BRITAIN KILLED, MURDERED HANRATTY on it. All the police were trying to get the crowd to pull it off, and we also came exactly behind her [Princess Margaret's] car—bang, like that.

The press were going mad as if every Beatle was there, like it was Beatlemania. Whoever timed it did it just right. We didn't plan it. Somebody suggested doing it like that, but I said, "I don't want to do it like that." But it happened. We got out of the car with these posters saying, BRITAIN MURDERED HANRATTY. The press were going berserk, TV and everything, and the next day not a peep.

Now if they're going to put in about me shaving . . . Even if they hadn't had the posters, they would have put "Lennon insults Margaret and Tony [Armstrong-Jones, her husband]," but they don't want to know about the hanging case because most of the newspapers are already set on that. All their crime reporters are in with the cops, anyway. If they don't get any stories, they start turning that one around. So that was just killed. They had pictures of [British actress and singer] Britt Ekland or one chick in a see-through thing that nobody saw. Saying this is what happened at the premiere. Or "Is Peter Sellers going back to his wife?" That kind of thing. And what happened that night was us two with them posters. So that's what we're up against there.

Smith: What is the Hanratty case? I'm not familiar with that at all.

Lennon: We've had a test period of five years in Britain where they have not killed anyone, state killing. And at the moment there's a big thing. The Socialists are trying to rush it through, and they just got it through the [House of] Commons to prevent any more killing, to finish it off. The Tories are trying to kill it in the [House of] Lords now. That's what they'll try, and try and make it an election issue because 84 percent of the people want killing, you know, so that's what they're going on.

So while this was going on, this guy's parents, the guy that was killed, came to us and said, "We've been eight years trying to clear our son's name. We have witnesses that say they saw him in another place on the night that weren't called, that only the prosecution looked into." It's like that Kennedy bit, people vanishing.

Ono: It's a real scandal.

Lennon: It's a real scandal. At five years . . . but we're not going down on any side of the guy's innocent or not; we're antikilling. But the thing that hooked us on the case apart from the parents trying and trying, just these two people, eight years going through every channel and being given the runaround and people helping them, sort of, the police saying, "You're interfering with the cause of justice, boy," all that bit. That was while he was still alive.

And the thing that really hooked us was five years after he was dead, the [British government's] Home Office had at least one, I believe two, private inquiries into the case. If the Home Office have an inquiry into a case five years after it, that means there's a shadow of a doubt whether that guy was guilty or innocent. And he was hung. That's only one of a few cases.

But the establishment don't want to know about opening the case again, because it makes them look a fool. But the parents want a public inquiry, so we joined them. And we've been giving them a bit of publicity, and that's what it is, but it's a tough scene.

Smith: Do you think it's going to work? I mean, can you get a—

Lennon: I think it'll work by just building it and building it. Because since we did it, there's a guy that keeps confessing all the time, [Peter] Alphon. He was the first suspect, and then the police dropped him and got somebody else. . . . The Hanratty people have been saying . . . [that Detective Superintendent Robert] Acott or whatever the guy was in charge of the case, the police guy rigged the case. Someone called [*inaudible*] paid the money to have him killed . . .

Since this has happened we've had a lot of calls and things from people, and of course Alphon has confessed again. He's confessed in

Germany, France, everywhere, and one guy that's been with him from before the killing until now has got years of tape of him confessing. That doesn't mean anything, but the guy's still around confessing. Since we did this thing, he's been on the phone again to some guy from *Private Eye* who's writing a book on it, confessing again. He goes between "I'm going to get you" and confessing. This group's been putting pressure on him to break him and the guy behind it. Since then, there's been a lot of people saying, "Yeah, yeah, my friend perjured to get off another case, but we can't give our name," that kind of thing. So I don't know how we'll do it, but we'll do it.

Smith: Do you get approached all the time to get involved in different causes?

Lennon: Oh, sure, everything on earth you can think of, we get approached for. But we're selective because we've only got so much time. But state killing and world killing we'll go for. We've just been approached by [the group seeking to] boycott US grapes.

Ono: Yeah.

Lennon: We know a bit about that, too.

Ono: It's physically impossible to do them all.

Lennon: It's physically impossible to do them all.

Ono: But it's OK.

Smith: But are all the approaches . . . do they reach you?

Lennon: I don't know how much reaches. We go through a lot.

Ono: We do try, don't we?

Lennon: Yeah.

Ono: We don't just—

Lennon: Some people want little . . . like just a little bit of publicity locally. We'll help them. Like Gypsies and things like that have a tough time in Britain. So we do little things for them, which we can do on the phone or just by sending them something [so] that they can say, "Look, they're with us."

Ono: We try to go through all the letters, not just sort of dump it in the wastebasket. [*Laughs.*]

Lennon: Because we don't get Beatle mail, so . . . We get quite a lot of mail between us. So it's still at the stage where we can read it all.

Smith: How much mail, when you say "a lot"?

Lennon: I don't know, maybe we get . . . what's an average day's letters?

Unidentified Man: Twenty or thirty a day.

Lennon: Twenty or thirty a day. We manage usually. We get behind, of course. We can't—

Ono: That's to the office.

Lennon: We don't want any more poetry. Or artists. [*Laughs.*] We have enough trouble getting our own poetry and art out, and that's no kidding.

Ono: And also, if they're really serious about something, they should write two or three times, and then they may get through.

Lennon: Yes, because a lot of stuff gets lost in Apple among the Beatle mail. Telegrams from people we know have sent them, and we don't know where they've gone. Even to the house. We give people our home address. "This will really get through." Telegrams don't come. I don't know what goes on with the British post office, but it seems a lot of important things never get to us.

Ono: Also, if they can write the letter—

Lennon: I'm not saying anyone's fiddling with it. It's just something—

Ono: Also, if they can . . . come to the point in the beginning because I try to read all of it, and I go through it and go through it, and they're just talking about their family or something like that. At the end they come to a point where they say, "Well, actually we want this." So it's better if the first thing they say is what they want and what they think we can do.

Smith: Is almost every single letter you get asking for something?

Lennon: Yeah, yeah.

Ono: [*Laughs.*] Exactly.

Lennon: Everything we do is that. But we don't mind that as long as we've got it, whatever it is they want. But we need to recoup now and then. . . . People sap up energy. But we've been offered things in Canada like help from these people, from the committee. Of course, they'll have their reasons, but the main reason is—

Ono: Peace.

Lennon: —they offer help to do it, and it'll be for peace, and the guy with the station said, "Here, can you use these radio stations?" We said, "Yeah." So that's the first thing. It takes a bit of time. John and Yoko advertise themselves as well as available. Or wanting to help and needing help with the first bed-in in Amsterdam and then the thing in Montreal and then going on and on and on. So eventually we'll get help, and then when we've got enough help together, then we'll start approaching the big-money people and ask[ing] them to match the money we've earned or whatever.

Smith: Do you feel these different things that you've been doing for peace really will have an effect? It seems sometimes that it's just—

Lennon: Well, yeah, I know, I know. But it's like asking Coca-Cola, "Do you think these stupid little ads have effects?" I was in the Himalayas, and they have Coca-Cola; they didn't have anything else.

Smith: But you're dealing with Coca-Cola—it's something that people seem to feel that they need. I mean, I don't see a basic need for peace in people.

Lennon: Who needed soap before they sold it to us? We didn't have soap. We didn't have Coke. Who needs Coca-Cola? We had water. Who needs any soft drink? Who needs most of the stuff we've got in our houses? Who needs it? But once you get 'em hooked on it . . . I think we can get people hooked on peace.

Ono: It's part of culture—soap. Now it's a part of culture.

Smith: There are times that I think that it's just part of our own kind of upbringings that we think there are solutions to a lot of problems, and I'm not so sure myself that there is—

Lennon: Yeah, well, I've gone through that, too.

Smith: —that there's ever going to be peace.

Lennon: Of course, I go through that, but the alternative is to do something or not to do something, and to do something is better than not to do something.

Ono: If we can make it happen, that's the thing.

Lennon: We have that choice, what little choice we have. We have the choice of doing or not doing, and we come for doing. When we've got the energy and we're not too paranoid, we do. And when we're in the other mood, we hide, and then we come out again and do.

Ono: We hide in our bedroom.

Lennon: Yes [*Laughs.*] Watch TV or something insane like that and recoup and think *What the hell?* and all that.

Smith: Why did you decide on the billboards this time?

Lennon: It was a poster event. It was Yoko's idea originally. We tried one poster event in New York. It never worked. Somebody, one person, went around with a poster on his back, and it was to do something for Christmas. We did have some vast plan for Christmas. But we just didn't have the energy or . . . I don't know, we just couldn't have done it.

Ono: No.

Lennon: Maybe we'll do it next time.

Ono: It's very interesting.

Lennon: We wanted to do something at this time of the year, and poster is a good media.

Ono: There are like twenty events we've done, but you see we don't have any control as to whether that would really happen big or not. So this one happened big. I mean, it sort of happened. We wanted it to be big, but every event we do we want to communicate as much as possible . . .

Lennon: Each one is like being colloquial. Like if we had done it in the bed event in Amsterdam, it did get around the world, but the main effect was on the Dutch, on the outlying areas, and the same in Montreal or Canada. It did get around everywhere, and the MBE was British. Of course, it got around everywhere, in those cartoons and whatever. But this [WAR IS OVER billboards campaign] was the only one we've done where we've had sort of a physical manifestation of us in every town. The happening happened everywhere at once, so every town thinks that's the town—we're doing it for them specially. It's not like we love your policemen.

Smith: But putting up a billboard like that with that kind of message . . . I was wondering whether the average person walking by in the street would understand what you meant. It says, THE WAR IS OVER IF YOU WANT IT.

Ono: Yes.

Lennon: Yeah, well, it's as simple as . . . I mean, we can only do what we do, and that's the way we think and that's the simplest thing we've done. Obviously, if we meet people who've got man-in-the-street ideas . . . I mean, like the songs are man-in-the-street ideas, they get through, but we can't just sit on the records all the time. I can't keep writing "Give Peace a Chance" all the time. I'll have to think of another slogan or something. You know what I mean? They only come now and then. So we've got to do everything. Poster isn't our only answer. We're just trying to do TV, film, acorns . . .

Ono: Acorns . . . you know about the acorns.

Lennon: Anything.

Ono: That's John's idea.

Lennon: Whatever idea we have, if we can put it out, we put it out. And whatever . . . if it's the guy in the street or the guy in the office or the president, maybe some of them will get it. And that's all we can do is keep sending out the message in different form, in different languages. It's the same message all the time.

Ono: And also, don't you think that maybe the journalists are sort of thinking that they represent the public and thinking that the public is really dumb? But they're not that dumb. I mean, "war is over" is a very simple message, and I'm sure everybody gets it.

Smith: I had this odd feeling—because the one [billboard] that I saw in New York was right at Forty-Third Street and Broadway—that maybe some people walking past there would think that it's an ad for a movie, because all the other billboards seem to be for movies.

Lennon: Yeah, but with a bit of luck, the press will cover it, and the word will go around. And maybe—it lasts for two weeks—maybe after two weeks they might guess it wasn't a movie. We only could try it. We don't know how people will be affected by it.

Ono: And pessimism is not going to take you anywhere. We have to do something. We're [not] waiting until we die. While you're waiting around, what are you going to do? Just always cry and weep or whatever? Or are you going to make something out of it?

Smith: What are you here in Toronto for now?

Lennon: To set up this July peace festival, folks. [*Chuckles.*] That's the main thing, and to turn these radio stations, we hope, into peace stations. And that's it, really.

Smith: When will it be in July?

Lennon: Let me get my bit of paper. The Peace Bag Festival in Mosport Park [in Bowmanville, Ontario], July third, fourth, and fifth. [*The event, also known as the Toronto Peace Festival, never occurred, because Lennon, Ono, and fellow promoter John Brower failed to obtain the necessary permits. Brower went on to stage the Strawberry Fields Festival, a rock concert, the following month. —Ed.*] I was hoping to set up a peace council, the stage will be the world's largest bed, and we hope to get some—

Ono: Talents. [*Laughs.*]

Lennon: Talents to build that.

Smith: You mean literally it'll look like a bed?

Lennon: Yeah. We'll get a bloody big bed and try and get everybody on there jamming and blowing and then take it to Russia and take it to the Iron Curtain a) 'cause we want to go there and b) 'cause one of the main criticisms is, "Why don't you stop yelling at us and go over there and say something to them damn commies?" So we'll go over and see what the damn commies have to say about it. And if we can get it on tour, that'll be something. I don't know who we can get or how, but I'll ask everybody I know and ask everybody I know to ask everybody they know and hope we get something together.

Ono: Yes.

Smith: What'll it be like? A Woodstock-type event?

Lennon: Well, I don't know how Woodstock was. From where we heard it, Woodstock was just like a great, great thing, and we hope it's as great as that. We've got six months to organize it, and maybe we can sew it up so well that there's nothing they can write about it except that it was a good scene.

Smith: Are you looking for it to be a huge campout-type event? . . . Are you looking for half a million people?

Lennon: The thing that we've not got to do is to frighten whichever area we're going into, into thinking they're going to get a Woodstock. So let's say we're going to have a small peace festival and see what happens. Because if we start saying it's going to be Woodstock . . .

Ono: Then everybody has some prejudice about it.

Lennon: The locals are going to get up petitions, so let's say we're having a nice [event] with a crowd we can control, and in six months' time we'll see what happens.

Smith: Will there be more Beatles records coming out soon?

Lennon: There's a Beatles album coming out in January, which we finished a few months back. That's the next thing, and a Beatle film.

Smith: Which Beatles album? What is this? Original? New?

Lennon: Yeah, *Get Back*. [*Though originally titled* Get Back, *the album was released as* Let It Be *in May 1970. —Ed.*] It was the one that was scheduled from before *Abbey Road*, but now it's after it to tie it up with the film, which is a documentary of us suffering while making the thing. [*Laughs.*]

Smith: Why suffering?

Lennon: Well, we were going through hell. We often do.

Smith: How? I don't understand. To most people it looks like, wow, it's so great. The four of you just get into a studio and you make music.

Lennon: Oh, come on. It's torture, it's torture.

Ono: All artists go through suffering . . .

Lennon: It's torture every time we have to produce anything. Any artist, poet, anything, whatever you call yourselves, listening know what it's like. Well, the Beatles haven't got any magic you haven't got. We suffer like hell every time we make anything.

Ono: I mean, they're flesh and blood.

Lennon: And we've got each other to contend with. Imagine working with the Beatles, man. It's a tough scene.

Smith: Whose songs will be on the album?

Lennon: The *Get Back* one? Well, it's sort of old. I don't know. It's all of us.

Ono: All four.

Lennon: It's a strange album. It's unfinished; we never finished it. We started off with this intention of doing a TV show or something, and it went on and on and on. Paul was hustling for us to do it, and we didn't really want to do it. We never did it, and we never finished the album, never quite finished the songs. We put it out like that, and there's bits of us mumbling and chatting and singing old rockers and all sorts of messing about.

Ono: It [has] a very nice little improvised quality about it.

Lennon: Yeah, it's the Beatles with their suits off.

Smith: How do you decide as to whose songs get on, now that George seems to be writing?

Lennon: We hustle for it, we hustle for it. And in the old days, Paul and I won. That's the problem. I mean, I don't know personally whether there will ever be any more Beatle product with the four of us on again. I mean, that's a decision we make every time, but it gets harder. Because in the old days, Paul and I'd just write most of the songs because George wasn't prolific. We encouraged him to an extent. Subconsciously we would have just made sure we got the LP for ourselves. So now he is prolific. Now there's three of us all trying to squash ourselves onto that fourteen tracks, and then there's the bit about . . . you'd prefer your own songs.

Ono: Every one of them has, say, thirty songs.

Lennon: So do we make a double album every time, which takes six months? That's six months out of your life just to get an album out. So that's why I broke out with the Plastic Ono bit—make my own stuff on the side. I can't wait to get two tunes on an album, and the same goes for the others.

Smith: Why does it take so long to record, though? Isn't there any way to actually speed that up?

Lennon: Well, we used to do 'em quicker, but now we just like [a] certain sound, so it takes a bit of time, that's all. If you want what you want, you have to take time over it.

Smith: Do you know what you want when you go in at all? Or you mean you literally work it all out right in the recording studio?

Lennon: Usually work it out in the studio. We used to have some—

Ono: They have the songs and all that written already.

Lennon: Yeah, we usually have them in quite a finished state, but to get the sound that you've imagined is the hard thing. You know, to put it over. I usually say things like, "Well, 'Heartbreak Hotel' this is, and do it that way." I have some other song in mind to say it's like that, that's what I'm going for. We always used to do that in the old days, trying to tell the EMI engineers in 1960, "We want to sound like [Gene Vincent's] 'Be-Bop-a-Lula,'" and [they'd reply,] "What's that, all that?"

Smith: Do you get into a lot of actual arguments among each other while recording?

Lennon: It's not so much arguments, but there's just tension. It's tense every time the red light goes on for a kickoff. And getting four of you to groove at the same time is difficult with any band; any band goes through that. You get two going, and somebody else drops out halfway through and gets paranoiac and screws it. We're always going for perfection and . . . because you never achieve it, that's why it takes so long.

Smith: When you said you don't know whether there'll ever be any more Beatles product . . .

Lennon: Well, there'll be plenty of Beatle product, but about whether we ever get together and do it again, I don't know. Beatle product we've got. [*Laughs.*]

Smith: But at this point, there's no plans for the four of you to get together and do something?

Lennon: No, well, we've got an album and a film in the can. I'm going to try and maybe hustle Paul or some of them for the peace festival.

Smith: There are always these rumors that go around all the time that you're breaking up.

Lennon: Yeah.

Smith: Is that true at all, or—

Lennon: Well, I mean we've had . . . Ringo's left once; George has left once for a couple of days or something. [*As noted earlier, Lennon at this point had already told his bandmates that he was leaving the Beatles. However, he had agreed to keep the news secret, because Allen Klein was in negotiations to extend the group's record contract with EMI. —Ed.*]

Smith: Is that the longest?

Lennon: Usually, yeah.

Ono: I'm sure every group goes through things like that, but because they're in such a limelight . . . so everything they do . . . Like, he just shaved off his beard or something [*laughs*], and that was big news. [People ask,] "But why?" and "What happened?" and all that.

Smith: You mean the other Beatles wanted to know?

Ono: No, no, no. I mean the press.

Lennon: It gets blown up. George had an argument with Paul, and in the papers it was that me and George had a fistfight. [*Laughs.*] So it gets just blown out to ridiculous things like the Paul [is dead] rumor.

Smith: Have any of you ever had fistfights with each other? Does it ever get—

Lennon: Not ever. I think I once threw a plate of food over George in Hamburg, but that was the only violence we ever had between us.

Ono: That's pretty good.

Smith: The other rumor that keeps going around is that now that [manager] Allen Klein has sort of straightened everything out, you're all going to be leaving him.

Lennon: No.

Ono: [*Laughs.*] No.

Lennon: We made no decision on Klein. What he's straightened out is the past. Now he's got to hustle for the future. It's been tough on him. He wanted the Beatles for seven or eight years, and now they're all sort of going their own way. But he's all right. I believe in everything until it's disproved, and I certainly don't believe all the crap people write about him, because if I believed that, I'd believe all the crap people write about me.

Ono: Yes, well, I know that I'm all right, and I've had many things written about me . . .

Lennon: "Leading John on the wrong road." "He's only gone mental since he met her." But I've been mental the whole time, folks.

Ono: So you see, all that.

Smith: But were things in as much of a mess as had been recorded when Klein took over?

Lennon: Sure, it was complete chaos. We'd been carved up, set up, the whole pop-star story. You've heard all the stories. Well, they're true.

Smith: Were you really going broke?

Lennon: We were spending money at a rate that would have broke us in six months, as I said at the time. When Klein read that, he thought, *Well, now they know. So now they'll be open to somebody to say, "Well, I'll fix it."* Until then there was no hope. It was not till we were aware it was going wrong that nobody [*sic*] could come and say "We're going to help you."

Smith: How did it come together that you got with Klein?

Lennon: He got in touch with me. He'd been trying to get in touch with me for quite a bit through Mick [Jagger] and through [art dealer] Robert Fraser. And I had always put it off. I'd heard so much about him. I didn't want this guy coming—

Ono: You were very scared.

Lennon: Yeah, I was scared to meet him. I'd heard so much about him. Anybody can hustle me—it doesn't have to be a super Klein. I'm gullible to anyone. So I finally said yeah. When he read that [I was willing to meet him] he got in touch. I saw him, and I made a judgment. Whatever happens with Klein or anything, I like him. He's a nice, sentimental guy. . . . We're getting his birthday present together today. I like him, and whatever the Beatles do with him, I'll probably use him.

Smith: Well, what I meant was—

Lennon: Only Klein could take this peace thing around the world. Only he could get it around the world and properly organized.

Smith: But is his contract with you or with the Beatles?

Lennon: It's with the Beatles and Apple, but it's optional every year.

Smith: Every year?

Lennon: Yeah.

Smith: Wow! That must make him very paranoid.

Lennon: No, no, he's not. He's got a lot of money. What's he want? He's in the showbiz, as it were, so he wanted the best, what he considered the best. Now he's got 'em. He's not gonna do any stupid things with the whole world looking at him. He's got all the money he needs. He's just grooving along. He wants a job or something to do that's worth doing. He thinks it's worth doing, that's all. It's as simple as that. What's he in it for—a few more million dollars? He's got it. All he's got to do is cash his investments. What's he in it for? He enjoys the game.

Ono: He'll be bored without this . . .

Lennon: He's got a lot of energy. He wants a lot to do. He's like us. Until we fill up a day, chop a block, and so does he.

Ono: He needs a big game, that's all—Beatles.

Lennon: And it's a big game playing with the Beatles.

Smith: There were these stories that when he went over to London to clear things up, the first thing he did was fire a lot of your old friends.

Lennon: Old friends, Paul's friends.

Ono: OK, that's not true.

Lennon: He found a lot of incompetent people who were living in luxury and flats and airplanes and cars and God knows what and not doing anything. Everybody was saying, "You can't fire them, because the whole thing will collapse." They went, and the thing went on without them and all the people that were fired . . . there was only one guy that had been around for years, and he was always incompetent. And we just could never bring ourselves to face up to it that he was incompetent and screwing it up and a nasty guy, too. I'm not going to name him, but we always knew that guy always gave it to the office girls and was a little Hitler, but we could never do it ourselves. So Klein, in that respect, did fire people.

The other people were just incompetent. They were nice people, but they were just incompetent. They weren't doing anything. They're writing all these articles in *Rolling Stone* and things. Let's see what they're doing in a few years if they're so worth having, and they left.

We gave them an out by saying they weren't fired. We let them have the story that they left because of Klein. They come around writing all these articles, and let's see what they're doing in a few years. That's all. They were incompetent and wasting money, and we have to make the thing run or we'll have to be on the street corner singing. It was just like that.

Just the way we've done things, people like you come up with offers and experience or ideas like that, and that's what we mean by "get it together." John and Yoko are not going to be any leaders of anything. We've all got to do it, and that's how we do it. Once we say, "How about . . ." it's like a great world recording session. I say, "How about doing this song?" And it takes about six months for that to go around the world, and then it comes back and they say, "OK, let's do it in E, and let's put guitars on." It's just going like that. We're just sort of doing the rhythm section now.

Smith: What other peace things are you planning in the next—

Ono: All the things we're planning, they're surprises.

Lennon: All the sort of how-we-get-in-the-press bits, we don't tell because a) I can't think of any at the moment and b) because if you tell them, it's all over.

Ono: Or something will prevent it. It's that, especially in our case.

Lennon: But the main things are this . . . the festival. That, and trying to set up some kind of committee. I'm a bit wary of committees, but I think it'll be good to have some kind of fund that we could use in the way people of our generations think. And use the money the way we think and people, contemporaries of ours, think, rather than the old, established UNICEF charity, all the directors getting a million dollars apiece kick.

Smith: You just did a big UNICEF show, didn't you?

Lennon: Yeah. I don't mind helping them, all the fuddy-duddy charities. But I wouldn't spend a lot of energy with them because I think they waste a lot of money and time. I don't know whether we can do better. We'll find out, though.

Ono: And also, you know, this committee would be like not so much controlling things, but would be like a get-together. Just the fact that, say, somebody in Montreal, some big town, Montreal, and some big town in Russia or something [*laughs*] could come and shake hands or something would be good.

Smith: Yeah, because it's sort of confusing to me what you want to have happen from this peace festival in July here in Toronto.

Lennon: We want to make some bread for a peace fund.

Smith: You're going to charge admission, then?

Lennon: Oh sure, sure. And we're gonna pay the musicians, too, because whatever the politics, they're musicians. My face always dropped a mile when I thought I had to play for nothing, all of us did, and charity shows are always the ones where you were treated like a pig. Like the charity . . . the Beatles did some charity in New York. We were treated like animals. There was no microphones. There was nothing but showbiz celebrities in the audience. They were the worst thing on earth.

I don't want to frighten off the people. I want to do the show by saying, "Come on, man, do it for mankind." The musicians have got to get their bread, the doorman's got to get his bread. But we hope to make the thing so big there's enough bread for everything.

And when I said "the cream" at the press conference, I mean the cream, not the milk. We'll give the milk to the musicians. [*Lennon is referring to a press conference earlier the same day in Toronto at which he said, "People will be paid for their performance and we'll try and cream some off the top to set up a peace fund." —Ed.*] Most of them aren't expensive, not for a thing this big, and to set up a fund that will be run by contemporaries and young people mainly to use in the way we think. And that's what we want to do. That's the aim of it.

Ono: Also the peace vote.

Lennon: Yeah, the vote, but he's talking about . . . and to set up the vote.

Smith: What is the peace vote?

Lennon: We want to set up a thing where . . . to get a vote, a worldwide vote: war or peace, which do you want? And when all these politicians are galloping around with 84 percent want hanging and 200 percent don't like blacks and that bit, well, we'll have thirty-five million say "no war," a no vote. Just a positive move, and somewhere all the youth can send their vibe to.

Ono: Send their votes.

Lennon: And we think Canada's a good place.

Smith: So that's where you want them to send their votes, you mean?

Lennon: I think we'll set it up so they'll send it there, yeah.

Ono: And also you can go to somebody and make them commit themselves, when you say, "Peace or war?" What are they going to say? And then he can vote for war too but then you're sort of . . . you just have to face up to it then.

Smith: What effect, though, will having . . . let's say you end up with seventeen million pieces of paper that say we're for peace?

Lennon: Actually, that's a petition. Let's see what we do with it when we get it. To do the event will be something, to actually have the vote going on and the fact that those people make that move is enough in itself. What we do when we get the seventeen million bits of paper, we'll think of then. It's no good sort of planning what we're going to do when. Let's do it, experience it as it happens, and then work out what to do then.

Smith: You don't want anybody to start sending those yet? Or do you?

Lennon: No, we'll work it out. We've got a few friends who are sort of organizers. We're not, and we'll get them to sort of lay out a feasible, practical way of doing it, and that kind of thing. And then it'll be announced or whatever. [*Laughs.*] People will know when it's time to vote.

Ono: It'll be great then.

Smith: Any other peace events that you're planning in between? The peace vote will take place before the . . . [festival]?

Lennon: I don't know. I'll have to ask our mates there.

Ono: We shouldn't disclose it now, at any rate, because—

Lennon: Yeah, I'm not really sure. We've been here a day, and we just said this is what we're going to do, and in between the press we'll discuss when and wherefore. I didn't even know they had a place where they were gonna do the festival yet.

Smith: What is this fast?

Lennon: Oh, the fast is somebody at Rochester Cathedral—

Ono: Christmas.

Lennon: —asked us to go to a fast over [the] twenty-fourth and twenty-fifth [of December 1969], so that will be the next thing as well.

Smith: Rochester Cathedral where?

Lennon: In England somewhere. [*Laughs.*] Sorry.

Ono: In England.

Lennon: The thing they're doing is against poverty, hunger, and loneliness, and we'll add the word *peace*, and we'll sit with them.

Smith: How long will you fast?

Lennon: I think it's two days, something like that.

Ono: Outdoors.

Lennon: It's healthy.

Smith: Outdoors in the cold? I mean, is it cold there?

Lennon: Yeah.

Ono: Christmas is a time of peace. Not commercial Christmas, that's it.

Lennon: And 'cause it takes things like that to convince some people that we're serious. And a fasting, I think, is good for you.

Ono: Very healthy.

Lennon: Especially after talking to [comedian and political activist] Dick Gregory, who's been [fasting] up to sixty days, and he's topped Jesus—he did forty. You really trip out on those fast kicks.

Ono: We did two days.

Lennon: Yeah, we did two days once and tripped out, and we do the ten-days-rice bit every now and then, get high as kites, and it's good.

Smith: What's the ten-days-rice bit?

Lennon: Well, I thought you New Yorkers knew everything. [*Laughs.*] It's a macrobiotic bit. Every now and then you clean out all the chemicals the government pump into you. And it makes you more aware, folks. It's like a permanent mescaline trip. If you can stay on a pure macrobiotic diet after you've done the ten days rice and cleaned all the poison out of your mind and your body, then you're on a permanent trip, and you can handle things objectively and not paranoically.

Ono: Sound judgment.

Lennon: Your judgment's better, you're more healthy. And we couldn't do what we're doing under the pressure and the speed we do it on any other diet.

Ono: On any other—

Lennon: We slipped off the diet a couple months back, and we really went through hell, so we took two weeks off and cleaned ourselves out again in Greece and India and came back and did the MBE poster event. Met the peace people and a whole lot of things happened just after the ten days.

Smith: And what did you do for the ten days? I don't quite understand.

Lennon: Well, we were in Greece on a boat for a couple of days starving [*laughs*], and then we went to India.

Ono: Just rice.

Lennon: We did rice.

Ono: Brown rice.

Lennon: And then we went to India and did rice. We slipped up into the mountains to see some miracle worker who didn't do any miracles and came back while we were there.

Smith: With being into this sort of food and diet thing, how do you rationalize smoking?

Lennon: Smoking . . .

Ono: Macrobiotic smoking is not that bad.

Lennon: Smoking is not that bad. I'd like to give it up. I've just found it very hard. Smoking doesn't harm you as much as all the chemical crap you eat every morning. Just look at everything you eat. The first thing you don't want to do [*laughs*] is just look at your cornflakes with government-allowed hexamer durafin and coloring. And then look at your tea: they all like dark tea, so that's got a load of chemicals in it, too.

I think in the old days the government used to keep you down by not educating you. Now they keep you down by poisoning you. Every night on TV: "Eat more Hershey smershey, eat more ice cream, eat more, eat more." And I know from not eating and then eating the crap how it affects me. It's just like shooting shit or something like that. We did ten days with rice, and we got back to Bombay and said, "Right, curry!" I had three milkshakes, lime, and all that, and it was like cold turkey I went through.

Ono: We went through torture, didn't we—

Lennon: I went through hell.

Ono: —after that because we just stopped the poison—

Lennon: First time we did ten days of rice, we coasted out slowly and kept pure for months on end and then slipped off. This time, we got right back. I couldn't resist it—milkshakes, the lot. I went through hell for forty-eight hours cleaning out. It was just like I had every drug I'd ever touched in me. And that *really* convinced me. When I'm on it I feel all right, but you forget what it's like before, how you were before. But this time convinced me. It was just hell we went through after eating the shit.

Smith: You recently gave an award back to the British Empire, right?

Lennon: Yeah.

Smith: And Mick Jagger, at his press conference in New York City, when he was asked about what he thought of that, he said he thought it was about time, that you should have done it a long time ago and that they would never give him any at all.

Lennon: They wouldn't . . . he would never get one. But I bet he would have taken it the same a few years back. Until the last two years, he always wanted to be the Beatles. But he will never get one. And he was right. We should have done it years ago. But not right away, really, because I wouldn't have been . . . now was the time to do it.

Ono: It was just right now.

Lennon: When it's useful. It had some use this time.

Smith: Were you dragged that the other three Beatles didn't do it?

Lennon: I didn't ask them. I told them I was gonna give it back over a year or two ago. They were saying, "Oh, just sit on it, forget it, it's not worth it," and all that. I just couldn't live with it. And I was always planning to do it at an event, forgetting—that was before I went on ten days of rice—forgetting that it was an event in itself. Of course, then I got back, and I thought, *Now, do it today.* And I did it the next day. It was the event.

Smith: We don't have any awards like that in the United States for that type of thing, except gold records. That's about all a rock group would get.

Lennon: Come on, you get your local key to the city . . .

Smith: I don't think they ever give that to rock groups, anyway.

Lennon: Oh, we got more . . .

Smith: Is the award you gave back really like an important thing in England? Like it really caused a stir? People just never do that?

Lennon: Well, the only people that had done it before were the people that gave it back when the Beatles received it. A couple of them asked for theirs back now [*laughs*], but one guy, this old ex-policeman . . . he was quite a nice old guy—

Ono: Detective now.

Lennon: Detective now, yeah. He's keeping it in the family. He asked for his back, but they couldn't find it. They keep them in a drawer for you in case you ever change your mind. [*Laughs.*] Yeah, really. So I said he can have mine to save him looking for his. [*Laughs.*] But they're all saying, "We were right. We should never have given them to them creeps."

Smith: Did the policeman take yours, then?

Lennon: No, no, the palace didn't give it to him. They're still looking for his. They do take it very seriously. I mean, you see the fuss going on here in Canada about taking the queen's head off a pound note. Or if you send that award from heaven back, it really means something to the bluebloods and the Tories. Nothing means anything to the queen.

Smith: The award I guess you'd like at this point would be a visa to come into the United States.

Lennon: Yeah, that'd be a nice award, yes. For services rendered. [*Laughs.*]

Smith: Why hasn't that been given to you?

Lennon: Well, I don't know. I can't pinpoint it, but I was waffled a lot. I think they weren't sure what I was going to do.

Ono: They're just plain nervous.

Lennon: I think it's just nerves on their part. I don't even want to talk about it too much because I haven't got it yet. Anything that's like that, that situation, I can't talk about it. Nobody said "Don't talk about it," but I know . . .

Smith: But if you had had a visa, would you have come to the States to do the bed-in and this thing?

Lennon: Yeah, we tried to come in to do it, and we ended up in Montreal, which turned out to be a good thing. That's how the whole Canada thing happened, but we intended doing something. It probably would have been a bed-in. But they were frightened of a bed-in. They're frightened of acorns. It's true.

Smith: Why?

Ono: It was funny.

Lennon: You ask me. [*He's responding to Smith and probably means to say "You tell me." —Ed.*] Why are they killing everyone and all that?

Ono: And the world is—

Lennon: It's fear, and people were frightened of acorns. Really. They're really frightened, and frightened of bed-ins.

Ono: If they accept it . . . say a politician would accept the acorns, he might either—

Lennon: —make a fool of himself or—

Ono: Yes.

Lennon: That's the trouble with a lot of the press, especially in Britain, is that when they're reporting what we do about the MBE or anything like that, in case we're conning them, they go for a story about how upset my auntie is because I took it off her TV set, where she kept it. In case those two con us, we better hadn't commit ourselves either way.

Ono: They just want to laugh it off.

Lennon: Yes, so they go for the satirical side of life, just in case we're conning them.

Smith: Let's say you've got a visa. Would there be any chance that the Beatles will tour ever again?

Lennon: I'd say it's a ninety-to-one chance they won't. It doesn't sound very inviting to me—touring. Touring was a drag.

Smith: Why?

Lennon: It was just a *drag.* I mean, I don't know how the Stones did this tour, whether they took a day off in between. But it was just complete madness from morning till night with not one moment's peace and living with each other in a room for four years on tour. We toured for four years. And of course there were great moments and . . . whenever we talk about it, it's all laughs. But when you get down to the physical reality, it was all pain. Because there was nothing in the music. We weren't getting any feedback. We'd just go on, and we weren't improving; we were just turning out the same old . . . half the time we'd just mime on the mic, because your voice had gone, and the kids would just be howling. You'd get kicked, beaten up, walked into walls, hustled, pushed, and all that.

Smith: But that might not happen now. The Beatlemania seems to have subsided somewhat. I mean, there's still tremendous interest, but—

Lennon: Yeah, I bet you ninety . . . I'll give you ninety dollars against one or whatever the odds are.

Ono: Nine dollars. [*Laughs.*]

Lennon: If we came on the road again, maybe the first time it'd be like that just again, because the myth still exists. I can judge it by the reaction to one lone Beatle and his Japanese bride wandering around. You multiply that four times on the hype and the pressure that'd be out and the publicity that would go with it. You saw what happened to the Stones. They hadn't done it for four years in the States. It was like Stonemania again. So if the Stones can do it, the Beatles certainly would do it, and the way the Beatles did it.

Smith: How long has it been now?

Lennon: Four years or five. I'm not against performing, but performing as a Beatle is like such a myth and an aura about it that they expect Jesus, God, and Buddha—I've said this a lot of times—to come onstage. It's like the Isle of Wight Dylan concert. He was beautiful, the whole atmosphere was beautiful, but the way it was written and said about it, it was a big disappointment because they were expecting God to come on and lay it on them. The press especially. And for the Beatles to come on, we'd have to come on and do a miracle.

Smith: You don't think that it's just a lot of people are out there and they want to see you perform live?

Lennon: Yeah, but it's anticlimax, the buildup of the myth. The myth is bigger than the actual three guitarists and a drummer. The myth is bigger than the reality. So I'm inclined to leave them with the myth. If the

Beatles would split open the group a bit and have Yoko, Billy Preston, Bob Dylan, Eric Clapton, Elvis Presley [*laughs*] in the group, I might be interested. But as the Fab Four, I'm not personally interested in going out like that.

Smith: Are any of the Beatles?

Lennon: Well, a few months back, it was George didn't want to work. I tried; there was a point where I was trying to get them on the road again, and I thought it'd be good. "Come on, let's go," you know. I ended up out here on my own, rocking with Yoko. And now of course George is on tour with Bonnie and Delaney [Bramlett] and Eric Clapton. A great sound going on there, ten guitarists and all that.

So it's that . . . he's out there now playing, and he performed with me the other night for the UNICEF thing. In fact, it was great. We had the whole Bonnie and Delaney band and the whole Plastic Ono Band— seventeen people playing. It was fantastic. We did two numbers, "Cold Turkey" and "Don't Worry, Kyoko," and they lasted one and a half hours. It was like . . . I'd like to come play that in the States, but I don't want to go on as the myth.

Smith: How about Ringo? He seems the one least heard from most—

Lennon: Well, you'll be hearing from him, because his film has just come out—*The Magic Christian*, with [Peter] Sellers. It's not bad.

Ono: Ringo is a natural.

Lennon: And the concept is good, but nobody's got him on film how he should be filmed.

Smith: Is he mainly interested in being an actor now?

Lennon: Yeah. Because he knows the Beatle thing isn't gonna go on. So he's got a job and he's interested in it. He's a natural comedian. Nobody's done it properly yet. I saw him on TV the night before the premiere of the film, and the twenty minutes he was on TV was better than the whole film. But he's got the film, and he'll be filming for a long time. And that'll come out in the States soon, so I suppose that's when you'll hear about it. He was in the States recently, so I don't know why you didn't hear it. He's not as big a hustler as me probably [*laughs*] publicity-wise.

Smith: Often I'd heard that he was the main one that wanted the Beatles to dissolve.

Lennon: No, no.

Ono: No, that's not true.

Lennon: See, there's no main one that wants the Beatles dissolved. There's no decisions like that being made. We're just four guys with different points of view who change every now and then and decide they want to do something, decide they don't want to do something. We're just like any one of you, but we're just in the public eye, so all these myths grow up and all these stories and all that. But we just change our minds every now and then.

Smith: But they're pretty spectacular changes. I mean, going from the whole drug thing to the maharishi thing and now to a peace thing . . .

Lennon: But I mean, lots of people have been through those trips. Everybody went through acid.

Ono: Or something.

Lennon: Everyone who's anyone went through the acid trip; millions of people have been through the yoga meditation trip. I'm now in the macrobiotic trip; everybody's going through it all the time. It just so happens we do it in public. But us two, John and Yoko, have made use of the public, going through our changes in public, and make it into an event.

Like she was saying on TV or something, like [French playwright Jean] Genet and them writing plays about a strange couple and making it into "theater" or "art." Instead of doing that, we're living it; we're doing it right now, not putting it down on paper and getting somebody to perform it later. We are doing it now; this is twentieth-century theater, art, music, whatever you call it. We're living it.

Smith: In spite of your dedication to sort of a pacifist ideal, the world does seem to be going the other direction.

Lennon: I don't believe . . .

Smith: The Arab-Israeli War, the thing in Greece, and Vietnam.

Lennon: Is it any different from what it was twenty years ago or a hundred years ago? It's not going anywhere; it's static, violence-wise.

Smith: Which goes back to my thing of maybe there won't be peace ever.

Lennon: But listen, do you believe this last decade, the '60s, produced negative things? I believe this decade produced positive things—the whole youth movement, the whole whatever it was, the Woodstock, the whole moratorium—

Smith: What has the youth movement produced? I mean, I'm aware of the youth movement more as a marketing concept, it seems. [*Laughs.*]

Lennon: No, what about Woodstock, man?

Smith: What has Woodstock produced *after* Woodstock?

Lennon: Not after Woodstock—Woodstock itself, the thing, the power, and the positive . . . the message that came over to all the kids in Britain, all the kids around the world. The fact that so many people were in one place on earth and weren't there to commit crime and violence, weren't there to kill.

Ono: They weren't soldiers.

Lennon: The fact that that happened is worth everything. That is so positive and fantastic that it—

Smith: It's positive, and I was there the whole time, and I saw it and felt that, but I'm saying, what did that change?

Lennon: It's never happened before. It's never happened before.

Ono: The first time—

Lennon: That's the first one. That's the first time it's ever happened. So if . . . before it, would you have been saying it would never happen and you couldn't have two hundred million [*sic*] people?

Smith: OK, four months later in San Francisco, we have almost the same amount of people and with violence with very bad vibrations at the Stones' San Francisco [concert at Altamont].

Ono: But Isle of Wight was another result of Woodstock. That was another very peaceful event, and we were there, and that was just fantastic. It's like, say, before Woodstock, I'm sure there were instances where many people gathered in one place, but mostly soldiers or something by the order of whoever. They were ordered to gather there to do something. But these people, they just gathered out of their own free will, just to listen to music and all that. And there were very few instances of violence, if I understand. And the thing is, the same thing was in Isle of Wight. Just that report, the myth of it is good enough, just like the Beatles, the myth of it is good enough.

It started to give us hope because John and Yoko even, we were starting to think after the bed event, we think, *Oh, no*. Because everybody was talking negative so much to us. We were saying, "Listen, we didn't do very much. Nothing happened." But then when we started to see the Woodstock scene and the Isle of Wight scene, maybe, not just us, but maybe the whole direction . . . that this is possible. It was a historical thing. Can you name an instance before that that so many people gathered in one place?

Lennon: It gave us hope. It gave a lot of people hope to hear about it.

Smith: But how do you explain the trouble at the San Francisco [concert]?

Lennon: Because there's always—

Ono: There's always something somewhere.

Lennon: There's always that, you know. Like it's the yin-yang bit. It's probably the negative, but the Stones thing wasn't set up in the same spirit or for the same end as the Woodstock thing, and the Stones thing was completely different in the way it was run and everything. It was a completely different scene. The Stones' whole image, the whole idea, the thing they put over, wasn't Woodstock. They have a different way of thinking, a different vibe, and that thing happened because of that.

Ono: But what you're saying is insane. It's like saying, "All right, then, no babies are born in the world because so many people are dying." It's like that. We have to just go on producing positive . . . some heir or whatever. And what you're saying is, "Well, you might be doing that, but look at these people—they're dying." All right, so some people are dying, but then at the same time, you can't deny all the babies born. It's like that.

Smith: The Black Panthers in the United States—is there a similar movement in England?

Lennon: There is. After Malcolm X came over, he got a few things together and produced Michael X in Britain. Not produced him but . . . and there is a movement there, but it's different from the Panthers.

Smith: The Panthers in the States have been through a lot of police trouble. The police on one side say that it's the Panthers that cause it because they arm themselves. The Panthers say that they've just been murdered. I mean, twenty-eight Panther leaders in the last two years are dead.

Ono: Can we say that the '60s was just a start and was the primitive age? We're still in the primitive age.

Smith: What I wanted to ask you was how would pacifism work in the case of the Panthers?

Lennon: I have no idea, because I don't know the ins and outs, but obviously it seems to me they're just being killed, but I don't know how or what. I just know that whatever the monster is, as Dick Gregory puts it to me, "The monster is insane and getting careless, and when it's careless, then that means it's out of control and that's our only hope."

And these people are being sacrificed for the future. And I can't explain it, or say they should have turned the other cheek or all that. I don't know what they were into, what scenes they're into, what magic they're into, what violence they have or had or what, whether they are weapon carriers or what. I have no answer to that. All I've got is hope, and I just hope it's different for the British blacks. We've just talked to Michael X, who is the one there, and there seems hope there, and maybe we can avert it there and God knows what.

I don't know what's going on. I just think the monster is insane, and he's careless and lets people . . . then that's the end of him. I think this is the end of that era. I believe in magic. I believe in evil, but I don't believe in good and evil, but I believe in that kind of thing, and I think that's what it is. And I think we have to fight it on all levels, as well as in the street, and that's what it's about.

Of course, if people have got more questions for me about it, I can't answer. When I believe in magic, what can I say? I'm an idiot. But that's what I believe in: power and vibration, and that's what's going on. And Dick Gregory to me is the representative of the blacks that I know and the blacks in America, and he knows as much about it as anybody, I suppose. I understand him and the way he goes about it. So it's better to ask him about that.

Smith: I did. I did a long interview with him just a few weeks ago, actually.

Ono: That's good.

Lennon: Do you mind if we eat while we do it? If you want more . . . if anybody'd like something? You hungry? You might like this. There's sort of rational food in the kitchen. [*Laughs.*] But this is shrimp—quite nice.

Smith: How do the two of you work things out between you when you decide to do an event?

Lennon: We mumble and talk.

Ono: We see what happens.

Lennon: And react, one against the other. It's like conceptual songwriting.

Ono: And it's very strange because I'll be thinking about something. I don't have to tell John, and then John starts to say something. This is not about ideas necessarily but just anything. It's almost sort of like a telepathy, so I don't even know if I really thought of "war is over," but . . . it's almost a matter of who says it first. It's like that.

So any ideas that we had probably is like a product of both of us; it's just sort of a mutual thing. Because I'd say something and John would immediately say, "Oh, and then this way and that way." And then I'd say this and all that, and it just goes on and on, and then it's made. So it's, like, made in a few seconds in a form of dialogue.

Lennon: That's when we came up with the word *bagism*. We're lying in Amsterdam high as kites—on rice, folks. We weren't trying to think; we were just watching this car. We had this Hilton window, and we just had the city beneath us. We were just lying there after a day's press.

Ono: In bed and all that.

Lennon: And we weren't talking, but we were both thinking, we found out after, how far it could go and where. Just sort of the future . . . those pictures of the future you get, and then we were thinking to describe it.

Ono: I was thinking, and I didn't have to say anything. I just looked at John, and he just went, "Yeah, right! Oh yes, yes," and all that. It just happened, and there's this fantastic string, the *bagism*—

Lennon: Yeah, the word.

Ono: Yeah, the word but—

Lennon: I just said, "*Bagism*, that's what we call it."

Ono: That's what it is, yeah.

Lennon: We had visions of these bags [*laughs*] all over the place.

Ono: The thing that embarrasses us most is all the reporters. They usually first ask how much it costs.

Lennon: And then who thought of it.

Ono: And whose idea was it.

Lennon: But you'd never get away with it, because Paul and I had it for years, and they're still asking who wrote what line.

Ono: Yeah, but especially in our case, it's almost unfair to say whose idea because it's almost like, if we start to really try to copyright whose idea it is or something, then we'll be in trouble because it's like a telepathy thing, really, isn't it?

Lennon: Mmm. If it wasn't, our egos wouldn't manage it.

Smith: In the States—I don't know whether it's true in England, I guess that it probably is—people seem to be having a lot of trouble getting along with each other. I mean, couples. And marriage seems to be virtually on the way out and everything. Both of you seem very, very close. What's your secret?

Lennon: It's called love. [*Ono giggles.*] I mean, we've had previous marriages, and they're the ones you're talking about. Whether you're getting married or not is up to yourself. But love is our secret, and there's nothing to split that up. I mean, you've got to work on it like it is a precious gift and it's a plant, and you've got to look after it and water it. And you can't just sit on your backside and think, *Oh, well . . . we're in love, so that's all right.* But that's the secret. It's all true, folks: all you need is love.

Smith: But what is it that—

Lennon: I don't know how you get it; it just comes. . . . I can't give you the formula for meeting the person you're gonna love, but it's around and it happens. It happened to me at twenty-nine and Yoko at [*mumbles*].

Ono: Whatever. [*Giggles.*]

Lennon: But it's a long wait. I didn't think it was . . . I thought it was an abstract thing. When I was singing about "All You Need Is Love," I was talking about that, something I hadn't experienced. I'd experienced love for people in gusts and love for things and trees and things like that, but I hadn't experienced what I was singing about. It's like anything: you sing about it first or write about it first and find out what you were talking about after. So that's why we say, "Think positive." Even if you kid yourself, con yourself into it, and it happens later. Like all these novel writers in the nineteenth century always wrote their lives out before it happened.

Ono: They do . . . they're very, very frightening.

Lennon: And if you write out a bad scene for yourself, I think you get it. [*Laughs.*] And I'm wondering about them books I wrote in 1964. [*Laughs.*] They were pretty screwed up, and I'll have to wipe them out before that happens. I can see me in a wheelchair.

Ono: So now . . . whenever we do an event or something, we think in terms of "All right, so we're writing our future, too." The strangest thing was that . . . the bed event, we thought of it, and then this whole year after the bed event—

Lennon: We've been in bed.

Ono: —we mostly spent in bed somehow. We didn't plan it, but somehow situations forced us into that, so that's very, very good.

Smith: Why do you think that other couples all over seem to be having such trouble getting along?

Lennon: Well, I don't know. It's just that they're saying it now. In the old days, they pretended that it was all going all right. So now they're just saying, "Christ, man, this is nowhere, drop out, get rid of her," or whatever. [*Laughs.*] That's all I see. It's that. They're just owning up now, that it doesn't work, just choosing the right guy with a nice job, and she has a nice family and all that. They're just owning up now. It's not marriage or love that's not working; it's just that people are owning up.

Ono: Well, I never thought that it would happen in this late stage of my life. [*Laughs.*] I was starting to give up hope, that kind of thing. Becoming very cynical and all that. But it helped me, and it's very, very good. I think most people . . . the whole society is geared toward that thinking that it's sort of almost silly to be in love and stay together and all that. It's not very fashionable, is it? It's that bit, too.

Lennon: Yeah, and as soon as they get together, the whole place is set up so that the guy has to work in Vancouver and his wife lives in Los Angeles, and everybody accepts that right away. Sure, we could never possibly work together because women can't get a job, and men all have to work together. So the whole place is geared to splitting you up as soon as you get together.

Ono: Even us . . . don't you think that almost subconsciously people tried to sort of just split us up in a way? It's very strange the way they . . . very subtle things; they don't even notice it probably.

Smith: I don't know what you mean. How do you mean?

Lennon: You're thinking paranoia.

Ono: OK, all right, we shouldn't go into that maybe.

Lennon: It's all right.

Ono: It's just that, well, we don't drink, so this is not us, but like—

Lennon: —when you give up drink, they'll give you a drink all the time.

Ono: Men go to the pub.

Lennon: But the splitting up he wants to know about.

Ono: Oh yes, yes, yes.

Lennon: All these people are subconsciously trying to split us up.

Ono: So say if somebody quit drinking and all the people who still drink are sort of all nervous. So they say, "Why don't you drink just once? It's OK," and all that, and subconsciously they want this guy to not stop drinking, because everybody else is sort of—

Lennon: Laying around.

Ono: Unhappy or whatever. It's "Oh, come on now, you're not serious," and all that.

Lennon: "Oh, come on, John, you're a musician, you know all about it." But it's just subtle. It's not evil intent.

Ono: No, no.

Lennon: It's just the way people do it with the drinks when you give up smoking: "Come *on*, have a cigarette. Have another bar of chocolate."

Smith: Marriage itself as an official ceremony seems to have somewhat gone out of style. How come you decided to go through with a regular marriage?

Lennon: Because we turned out to be romantic. I mean, we went through the whole intellectual bit about marriage, and it's a bit of paper that some guy gives you, and that's all true. But when he gave it to us, it was very emotional, and it wasn't even . . . we couldn't get a nice vicar or a bishop to do it. [*Laughs.*]

It's completely against what we thought, what I thought intellectually. I thought once, *Never again, if I get out of this one. What a joke, what a joke it all is.* And the next minute I'm standing there and she's crying, and it's like we're soft kids. So we're romantic, and it made a difference. It was like we were living together a year, and she was pregnant and everything before we did it. It was like this difference. Before we got our divorce papers, at first we didn't even think . . . sod divorce, let's just groove around, forget it, we'd forget 'em. We'd leave them, and that's it. It doesn't matter what the papers say, the certificates, but then we went for divorce. Then the difference between knowing the divorce is going through and when the guy comes and gives you the paper, and he says, "You're free," and you are . . .

And you're then aware of what was on your back anyway, that you didn't know about. That you were not free in that way, in that stupid civil way. So that worked—the relief of having the paper that said she was no longer Mrs. Cox and I no longer had a wife was fantastic. So when that worked, getting married was the other way around. It was like another bond. It's a ritual. It's a nice ritual, and we thought of getting married like everywhere we went.

Ono: In every country.

Lennon: And in every religion and get everybody who's got the right to do it to marry us and anybody who hasn't and just keep doing it and tie more and more string around each other, whatever it is. More wedding rings and more ceremonies and more ritual.

Smith: You didn't do that, though.

Lennon: No, but I would if we got a chance.

Ono: No, but we started to think of it like a month ago about that. Our first chance was India, but then it wasn't—

Lennon: We missed it. There was a great Hindu marriage going on, and we thought, *Wow, we'll have one of them!*

Ono: That'd be the first one.

Lennon: [*Laughs.*] We'll make it into an event, probably. That's what we can do.

Ono: Yes, yes, that's right. [*Laughs.*] That's a great thing.

Lennon: So that's what it is. That's my answer. [*Laughs.*]

Smith: Why do you think not that many other rock people are active in peace?

Lennon: I don't know. Because rock people are no different from anybody else, except for they have a different occupation.

Ono: Nobody is really active on peace. Who's really that active?

Lennon: Yeah, just name the people that are active in peace, and we'll get in touch with them, because we're looking for them. I mean, the thing is, I believe in all the songs going on, whether . . . whatever motive they put 'em out for. And at the moment in Britain, there's "The Onion Song" from . . . the American one with Marvin Gaye and somebody else [Tammi Terrell]. There's another one, which is a bit cod, but it's nice about getting blacks and whites, and let's all intermarry and all be coffee. And there's a lot of those songs around. And if a musician uses his talent to sing that, that'll do. It doesn't have to be dedicated like we are—

Ono: There's so many peace and love songs these days.

Lennon: —that kind of fanaticism. It can be on the local housewife level. Just show your colors locally. You don't have to have a whole press ballyhoo to do it. Just do it locally.

Smith: What kind of music do you listen to when both of you are home and you just listen to music?

Ono: Anything.

Lennon: Just anything, anything, that's all. Maybe some record somebody sent us or somebody said, "Do you want to hear Johnny Winter, man?" So whenever somebody says, "Do you want to hear him, man?" I'll listen.

Smith: Any particular favorites right now?

Ono: We're just almost—

Lennon: Not particularly, no. Johnny Winter was the last thing I was listening to. It was a nice track he did with sort of double guitars coming out, and it really blew me. There's a beautiful Lee Dorsey record. [*Deep voice.*] "About everything I do from now on is going to be funky." Like that. [*Laughs.*]

Ono: Well, of course, our *Wedding Album*. [*Laughs.*]

Lennon: Yeah, and our own stuff, of course, folks. Plastic Ono Band, Live [*Peace*] *in Toronto* [*1969*].

Smith: Do you ever listen to your own stuff when you're just around the house?

Lennon: Sure, but normally when we've just done it or then six months after is the time to see what you meant, to get that.

Ono: What was it like?

Lennon: In the old days, the Beatle records, we used to make an album, then listen to it, and then forget about it. Then make another one, and then I'd play them both, one after the other, to see where it was going. But we got so many that [if] I tried sitting there like with *The Beatles* double album and everything right by it, *Please Please Me*, I just couldn't sit through it all. To see what happened, listening to it one after the other. I couldn't make it [*laughs*], not because I wasn't enjoying it, but there's not enough time.

Smith: Something like *Sgt. Pepper* . . . did you listen to it six months later and go, "Oh, why did we do that?"

Lennon: No, I never think that. I used to think that more in the early days, all embarrassed about the early stuff we did, but I got over that. And I don't regret anything we've done. I just have preferences for tracks, things like that, but I don't regret any record we ever made. It was just us then, and it's valid.

Smith: It was you then. In other words, you weren't doing something else; you were doing what you wanted to do right then.

Lennon: Yes, that was where we were then. I think everybody is in that state. Every record or book—anything is a reflection of where the person's at, at the moment he conceives it and puts it into action.

Smith: When you're not actually working on an album with your three partners, how often do you see each other?

Lennon: We usually pass through each other's arms in the office, the Apple office. There's usually one other Beatle up on some other floor arranging his life. I usually see him then. Or if there's a premiere for Ringo I'll go along—things like that. It depends where George gets his new house; if he gets it near, I'll see more of him.

I've got a feeling I'll see more of George because he's mixing around with the musicians, and if I don't know who's a particularly good drummer or anything like that, I always use George [to help me find someone]. Like he originally got me Eric [Clapton] and Klaus [Voormann] and Alan White, that kind of thing. I don't know one from the other most of the time. So I usually see more of him.

Smith: Someone told me that another one of your causes that you've been involved with is cruelty to animals and not killing animals and things like that.

Lennon: We've never done anything specific. I was a vegetarian before I met Yoko, and she was a macro fanatic, and I converted her to vegetarianism, and she converted me to that. And then we just started eating fish. So I am against it—killing animals to wear and everything—but I do happen to have a pair of leather boots now, whereas I never would have it for a bit, for about three or four years.

Smith: What I'm leading up to is somebody told me a funny story [*laughs*] about your coat, your fur coat.

Lennon: Oh, the human-hair coat.

Ono: Oh, that one.

Lennon: Yes, I've got a coat.

Ono: We didn't kill anybody to get that. [*Laughs.*]

Lennon: I've got a coat made out of human hair, which I never wear because it's too heavy and too big. But I saw it in the paper, and I thought, *A human-hair coat, man! I've got to get it.* [*Laughs.*] So I got it, and it's hanging up.

Smith: They told me—I don't know whether this is true; as I said, it's a fourth-received story—and it was that you wanted a human-hair coat because you didn't want to have an animal fur coat because you were against killing an animal. And then they backed it in animal skin?

Lennon: Yes, they did that. They put it on suede [*laughs*], so I sent it back and they put it on something else.

Ono: Jersey.

Lennon: Yeah, because I wanted a fur coat, and I didn't want to get an animal fur coat.

Smith: Isn't that eerie, wearing a human-hair coat?

Lennon: Well, I don't know. It was a bit strange. [*Laughs.*] They were all sort of Asian hair. It looked like I had tons of Yoko's heads on me, just all this sort of black Asian hair. [*Laughs.*] It was funny seeing.

Ono: Both of us are like that, but we have sort of eccentric sides, too. I mean style. [*Laughs.*] We like some weird things once in a while. But I mean, it's sort of overpublicized. It gets to that.

Smith: How about the skinhead movement? I've begun to hear a lot about that.

Lennon: It's not particularly big. The press built it up because it was a new image; they've all got short hair and boots. But they used to be Teddy Boys when I was a kid. It's just that section of society that there is nothing for them to do except for kick each other up in gangs.

Smith: I mean, that's really what they're doing.

Lennon: Yeah, but they haven't done too much. There's been no great skinhead cases of violence.

Smith: That American group that was over there was killed by them.

Lennon: Really? I never heard of that.

Smith: I wish I could remember the name of the group now.

Lennon: You know, they probably will get into that, because they're being billed up as a big, new thing by the press, you see, and they're beginning to react for the press.

Smith: Do you see it taking off, though, really? A lot of people joining there?

Lennon: When Beatlemania was on, we had mods and rockers, and they're not around now. The mentality is always there, and the skinheads are grooving. They've got some good music going, the skinheads. They go for that reggae beat, West Indian thing. It started off as blue beat a few years ago, but it's gotten a bit more subtle now. And it's pretty funky stuff now. I think "Israelites" [by Desmond Dekker and the Aces] is one that made it in the States, and there's some pretty good music coming out in the West Indies.

Smith: "Israelites" is an example of reggae?

Lennon: Yeah, and they're all into that scene, which is pretty good because it sort of . . . it's a new black music, and maybe the skinheads will form some liaison with the British blacks. That's my dream, but I'm a naive peacenik. [*Laughs.*]

Smith: On the peace thing, the thing that keeps bothering me somehow . . . I don't know, maybe I'm more cynical, negative, and all those things, but selling peace as a commodity . . .

Lennon: Well, why not, Howard? Don't you see that they sell war all the time, that Hollywood sold war and still is selling war? That John Wayne has been selling war since I was a kid? That's what selling war is, so all I'm trying to do is get as much space in film and song about peace. That's all, just to give it a chance. [*Laughs.*] That's all it is. They sell war all the time. Every night on telly they sell war, every film, every other film, they sell war and violence and that. All I'm trying to do is equal the balance a bit.

Smith: The Moog on *Abbey Road* . . . how did that come about?

Lennon: George ordered one when he was in the States, and he brought it back, and we used it as best we could. He used it on a few tracks—"Maxwell['s Silver Hammer]," "I Want You." At the end [of that song] we used the [*makes sucking sound*] into infinity thing. I can't remember what else we used it on. We used it on a few tracks. Yeah, I think it's on "Maxwell." [*Makes trumpet sound.*] That thing, it's a fantastic machine. I couldn't face it. George is gonna master it, and it will take him all his life.

Smith: Like he sits and plays it, you mean?

Lennon: Yeah, he did a whole album of it, which is out, folks. [*Laughs.*]

Smith: Do you see using it on other Beatles albums if there are going to be more Beatle albums?

Lennon: If it's around. I personally can't be bothered with all the instruments unless I can play them meself. [*Laughs.*] I just like doing it with guitars. I'd sooner have five hundred guitars.

Smith: Where do you see the Beatles' music going? Let's say you do find yourselves, all four of you, back in a recording studio three months from now. What do you see?

Lennon: I can't imagine, I can't imagine at all. I don't think of it in terms of Beatles music. It's only Beatles music when it comes out under the name *Beatles*. There's no limit to where anybody's music can go, and I think Beatles stood still a bit too long after *Pepper*, and they've got to freak out a bit more. That's where I'd push them. [*Laughs.*]

Smith: Do you think that's the general feeling among your other three partners?

Lennon: You see, because we're all different, we all have different concepts of how far you go. I say, "Go as far as you can." I don't know what the others say. I can't quote for the others, but we don't all think the same. That's why we make individual music. See, like on *The Beatles* double album, "Revolution 9" is the track I'm interested in. I had to impose that on them, really.

Ono: And yet they cut a little, too, because there was some pretty good parts that you cut.

Lennon: I'd like to just be able to go there that way. I still like off-beats.

Smith: Is that what your new company is for, Bag Productions?

Lennon: That really is for our peace efforts, but it handles our music. It's a concept more than anything. It's what we put on when we produce records: Bag produced this. Bagism. It's based on Yoko's old bag scene, which all you New Yorkers will remember.

Ono: I remember that in Amsterdam we suddenly came to something—

Lennon: Oh, bagism, yeah. It's too much to go around that bit.

Ono: Yes, yes, that's right.

Smith: I remember your bag event very well.

Lennon: Yeah.

Smith: I wrote it up in the [*Village*] *Voice* years ago.

Lennon: It's kind of long, though.

Ono: Right, he's the first [*inaudible*] about it.

Lennon: Oh yes, so the bag, the bag carries on. Bagism is what we sort of came to in Amsterdam. It's total communication, et cetera, et cetera, and I can't explain that. But bagism is what we're all doing. We're all in our bags. [*Laughs.*]

Smith: I'm curious about how it actually works with a recording session when you say you sort of had to force "Revolution 9" on the other three. What do you mean? You came in and said, "This is what I want one of the tracks to be"?

Lennon: No.

Ono: More subtle than—

Lennon: More subtle than that. I was just putting it together, and George and Ringo were nipping about, getting tapes and cutting them and all that, and we're just doing it. I just felt as though . . . I felt maybe it was my paranoia. I just felt as though I had imposed it on them, on the Beatle product.

Ono: I remember the last minute you said, "Well, it has to be a bit short because—"

Lennon: Yes, it was just like that. I had to sort of—

Ono: It would occupy too much space and all that, considering the proportion—

Lennon: So I thought, *Sod that. If I want to do that, I'll do it separately, and then there's no messing—*. See, while all the Beatles were on holiday, we'd started doing "Revolution [1]"— the song "Revolution [1]" which is on the album, and I wanted to put that out and "Revolution 9" as the B-side. It was just, literally, the others wouldn't let me.

Smith: But what happens when that happens? Do you all sit down together and have an argument?

Lennon: They all came home, and I said, "Look, I want to put this out as the next Beatles single." They said, "Well, we don't think it's a single." So I said, "Oh, all right," and I redid "Revolution [1]," and by then "Hey Jude" had come along. And I managed to get it on the other side of "Hey Jude," but what I wanted out was the message. Not the song, just the message. And I wanted it out when I wrote it as near to . . . I like to get it out as I think it.

Smith: What was its message?

Lennon: Nonviolence. I mean, it got a lot of people uptight, but that's what I was saying.

Smith: A friend of mine who's very into the Ohsawa macrobiotic diet thought it was the number-nine diet.

Lennon: Oh, well, of course! I never thought of that. It must be that, too.

Ono: Yes, yes, yes. [*Laughs.*] That's beautiful.

Lennon: That was just a tape, some test tape I found. I just chopped up Beethoven, and anybody that was lying around EMI, and stuck them together. Number nine was some test engineer sort of going [*deep voice*], "Number nine." I just cut that bit out and used it, but that's it, isn't it? Number nine regime.

Ono: I'm getting nostalgic about that.

Lennon: Oh, yeah.

Smith: Is that the one that you're on, the number-nine diet?

Lennon: Yeah, yeah, the ten days [of] rice.

Ono: Yes, yes, yes. [*Laughs.*]

Lennon: Would you like a frog? [*Laughs.*]

LENNON ON ...

Cultural Change

"This is only the beginning. This '60s bit was just a sniff. The '60s was just waking up in the morning, and we haven't even got to dinnertime yet. And I can't wait, you know, I just can't wait. I'm so glad to be around. And it's just gonna be great, and there's gonna be more and more of us. [*Humorously, to the camera.*] And whatever you're thinking there, Mrs. Grundy of Birmingham on Toast, you know, [*laughs*] you don't stand a chance! A) you're not gonna be there when we're running it, and b) you're gonna like it when you get less frightened of it. And it's gonna be wonderful, and I believe it. Of course we all get depressed and down about it, but when I'm down, or when John and Yoko is down, somebody else will be up. There's always somebody else carrying the flag or beating the drum, you know. So 'they,' whoever they are, don't stand a chance because they can't beat love."
—from interview with Desmond Morris, December 2, 1969, broadcast on ATV (UK) December 30, 1969

LENNON ON ...

God

"I believe that God is like a powerhouse, like where you keep electricity, like a power station. And that he's a supreme power and that he's neither good nor bad, nor left, right, black, or white. He just is. And that we tap that source of power and make of it what we will. Just as electricity can kill people in a chair, or you can light a room with it, I think God is."
—from Toronto press conference, December 17, 1969

LENNON ON ...

The Plastic Ono Band

"The original idea was *you* are the Plastic Ono Band. I've used two people practically every session, that's [multi-instrumentalist] Klaus [Voormann] and [drummer] Alan [White], but . . . they're not permanent, and the audience is the band, you know. . . . Let's all groove together. . . . When you got the audience as well . . . then we're really groovin'. That's what I want. So it wouldn't matter whether I was on the stage or if I got fed up and went down in the audience for a bit, too. Let's take it in turns to be superstar."

—from interview with Richard Robinson, published in *Hit Parader* (US), August 1970

LENNON ON ...

His Autobiographical Songs

"'Help!,' 'In My Life,' 'Strawberry Fields [Forever],' and a few [other] songs are the same thing. It's about me, you know. I can just probably express myself better and simpler now. . . . It [the Arthur Janov primal-scream experience] was like a mirror. I was given a mirror, and I had to look into my own soul. . . . When you're left with yourself, what do you sing about? I found it easier when I was younger to project stories—'She loves him because he left her'—but I could never really get into it. I always liked first-person novels, and I like first-person songs, too."

—from interview with Howard Smith, Regency Hotel,
New York, December 12, 1970

LENNON ON ...

Being a Genius

"When I was about twelve, I used to think I must be a genius, but nobody's noticed. I used to wonder whether I'm a genius or I'm not—which is it? I used to think, 'Well, I can't be mad, because nobody's put me away. Therefore, I'm a genius.' A genius is a form of madness, and we're all that way, you know, and I used to be a bit coy about it, like my guitar playing . . . I've been like this all me life. Genius is pain, too."

—from interview with Jann Wenner, early December 1970, published in *Rolling Stone* (US), January 21, 1971

LENNON ON . . .

Being an Artist

"If I had the capabilities of being something other than I am, I would. It's no fun being an artist. You know what it's like, writing. It isn't fun; it's torture. I read about Van Gogh, Beethoven, any of them—and I read an article the other day—well, if they'd had psychiatrists we wouldn't have had [Paul] Gauguin's great pictures. And these fuckin' bastards there just sucking us to death. That's about all that we can do, is do it like circus animals. I resent being an artist, in that respect. I resent performing for fucking idiots who don't know anything. They can't feel; I'm the one that's feeling. Because I'm the one expressing. They live vicariously through me and other artists."

—from interview with Jann Wenner, early December 1970, published in *Rolling Stone* (US), February 4, 1971

CONVERSATION

Tariq Ali & Robin Blackburn | January 21, 1971, Tittenhurst Park (Lennon's home), Berkshire, UK | Excerpts published March 8, 1971, the *Red Mole* (UK)

In late September 1970—about four months after the release of *Let It Be*, the chart-topping final Beatles album—Lennon began recording *John Lennon/Plastic Ono Band*, which would become a Top Ten hit. Coproduced by Phil Spector, the record contains highly personal songs about pain, childhood, love, and religion, as well as the political "Working Class Hero." In "God," the often-quoted opening track, he sings, "I was the walrus, but now I'm John / And so, dear friends, you'll just have to carry on / The dream is over." The song also lists all the things Lennon doesn't believe in, ending with "I don't believe in Beatles / I just believe in me, Yoko and me, that's reality."

Lennon finished making the album in late October and, three months later, he and Ono met at their Georgian country home with Tariq Ali and Robin Blackburn, a pair of British writers and political activists. A highly condensed version of their discussion appeared shortly thereafter in the *Red Mole*, a left-wing newspaper edited by Ali. What follows is the much longer original interview, which has not previously appeared in print.

As you'll see, the conversation covers everything from childhood trauma to the Beatles' music and breakup but focuses mostly on politics. Lennon talks much more candidly about revolutionary, socialist, and even communist ideologies than he does in better-known interviews.

The singer found the discussion energizing, wrote Ali in England's *Guardian* newspaper thirty years later. "The day after the interview he rang me," Ali recalled, "and said he had enjoyed it so much that he'd written a song for the movement, which he then proceeded to sing down the line: 'Power to the People.'"

The conversation has already begun when the tape begins rolling. At that point, Lennon is commenting on what he is trying to accomplish with his music. —Ed.

John Lennon: I'm expressing my own feelings, but then the job of that record [*John Lennon/Plastic Ono Band*], really, is to incite in other people's minds: "Is this about me as well? Does this apply to me?" To put that question mark there—that it's not as simple as God or myth will save you. We have to question ourselves about what our position really is, and don't be too comfortable about just being long-haired, you know.

Solutions I don't know. I don't think you give solutions. I think if anybody has solutions to give, it tends to put people in a position of either having to accept it or reject it. And that splits people into Marxists or Trotskyists or Socialists and all that, which is a problem in a way. But of course, according to dialectic materialism and those ideas, that is a natural thing that will always go on.

The thing that all those people and us and the hippies are formally against is status quo conservatism, which is unreal; it cannot be. And so our problem is really to solidify, but how do you solidify under a natural dialectic materialism—splitting and breaking and forming and reforming counterrevolution? I don't know how to come to terms with it. I don't know what the answer to that is. Obviously Mao is aware of that and keeps the ball moving.

Robin Blackburn: You mean in the Cultural Revolution?

Lennon: Yeah. He's obviously going by the letter. Like Russia. You were saying, "What happened to Russia?" It's obvious that it [a bureaucracy] will happen anywhere. Even in Cuba it'll probably happen. Anywhere, once the new power's taken over, they have to try to establish the status quo just to keep the trains running or to keep people running a factory. And then you're in that position.

Blackburn: Ah, but to keep the trains running, do you have to have repressive apparatus like Stalin? Perhaps they'd run just as well with workers' democracy.

Lennon: Yeah, I think that, but I still think that we all have bourgeois in us, and we all get tired now and then, and we all—maybe especially after a revolution—would tend to relax a little. And the amount of fervent revolutionaries after the revolution probably died off a little.

Tariq Ali: In Russia they did, but they died literally.

Lennon: Yeah, but how do you keep people in an activist role once they've achieved what seems to be the aim, which is to take over? How do we or any of us prevent people and ourselves from becoming apathetic again or relaxing without having somebody like Mao, which is something different, which continually doesn't allow that to happen? What happens when Mao goes?

Blackburn: Having Mao is an accidental and partial solution. I mean, it'd be better to have something built in.

Lennon: Yeah, well, I think he's trying to build in Maoism but it's almost the same as building in Confucianism or—

Ali: It's got to come from the masses. That's the crucial thing.

Lennon: Yeah, if Mao personally has to keep doing that, that means when he dies, unless he's really infiltrated all their minds completely, they will go the same way as any other, because people are people. And obviously, as all the Communists always said, you have to keep the revolution going continually or keep purging. That's the difficulty, you know. I mean, if we took over in Britain, then we'd have the job of cleaning up the bourgeois and we'd have the job of keeping people in a revolutionary state of mind.

Ali: Yeah, but one difference between Britain now and revolutionary Russia is that despite the fact that it is bourgeois education, the cultural and educational level of a large majority of the British people today as a whole is much, much higher than it was with the peasants in Russia and China, with the ignorance and backwardness and rural . . .

Lennon: But even though relatively it's the same apart from [the English having] some kind of knowledge of what happened in 1812 or Columbus went to America, relative human feelings are the same. And it's about eating and sleeping and fucking, and "Do I have a roof over my head?" And opportunism . . . well, what would be the solution to that?

Yoko Ono: The young generation take over—

Lennon: Yeah, but they're no different from anybody else—

Blackburn: People are what they are because of the institutions that have formed them. I mean, institutions like the family, informal ones, as much as [political] parties or anything.

Lennon: Yeah.

Blackburn: The basic thing that happened in Russia is the old order collapsed under the strain of the First World War. And the revolutionaries were a tiny group. They were thirty thousand people in a country of maybe two hundred million. You say, "Take over." What would happen in this country is the masses, the great majority of the working people of this country, would have to take over. And if you've got a great mass movement like that—and we'd have to have, because this social [system] is not going to crumble—

Lennon: Not go without a fight, yeah.

Blackburn: That seems to me . . . that it's in the struggle you can develop the institutions which can check arbitrariness, which can check opportunism. And that's why in China, where they had twenty years of struggle, they've been able to check opportunism and arbitrariness much more than in Russia where it was just a few months.

Lennon: But it was instigated by Mao himself, wasn't it? It wasn't like a national feeling of, well, there's too many opportunists and too much apathetic . . .

Ali: No, but—

Lennon: [*Hears someone at door.*] Hello? Who is it?

Voice: Laundry.

Lennon: Laundry, OK. Stick it here.

Ali: The point you raise is not one of Mao on his own. It's basically one of revolutionary leadership, of a revolutionary organization, which has a leadership, which is precisely capable of taking the masses forward when they reach a certain level of consciousness.

Blackburn: But you have to have some followers. He's [Mao's] just one man. If the youth of China hadn't been behind him, the Cultural Revolution would have been impossible. And let's face it, the Cultural Revolution didn't succeed completely.

Lennon: The thing is . . . obviously, they are fairly well behind him 'cause they all got their [Little Red] Book [*Quotations from Chairman Mao Tse-tung*], and they're shouting. . . . If the youth in Britain were suddenly given free rein to destroy the local councils and the local schools, it wouldn't take too much [to get them going]. But I wonder about the charges against Mao. The personality cult doesn't seem to be part of the basic Communist idea.

Ali: It isn't.

Lennon: Khrushchev, in his book, [*Khrushchev*] *Remembers*—I know he's a bit of a lad and all that—but he sort of puts him [Mao] down for that, saying it's like Stalinism. I'd like to know your opinion on that.

Ali: In the first place, I think that a personality cult like the one which has been built up in China is alien to Marxism.

Lennon: Yeah.

Ali: You know, because Marxism is basically about ideas. It is also, of course, about people, but Marx and Lenin and Trotsky and these revolutionaries and even, in the beginning of China, Mao himself, were totally opposed to the personality cult, which is why it's written into the Chinese constitution.

Lennon: So how do they account for it?

Ali: I think it's the fact that one section of the Chinese leadership found in Mao's cult the best guarantee of ousting a right-wing section of the Chinese leadership, a revisionist Chinese leadership, and this has literally got out of control from them, and they find it a bit difficult to withdraw—

Blackburn: It's a weakness of the movement that Mao needed to use this cult.

Lennon: It seems like people need a father figure, someone to lead them.

Blackburn: Even in Russia . . . Lenin hated anyone praising him in public.

Lennon: Well, he didn't like them to say it in public, but he liked them to sort of acknowledge what he did.

Blackburn: Lenin or Stalin?

Lennon: Stalin.

Blackburn: Lenin really was a very modest man. On the other hand, it's true that people seem to need [a father figure], but it's partly when they haven't created an institution of their own, they need a substitute. And partly because the revolutionary institutions were weak in Russia, they needed the little father—Lenin.

Lennon: Yeah, but I think we all do.

Ono: That's the problem.

Blackburn: The day we control our own lives, we don't.

Lennon: Yeah. But to create a more illusionary—that gets like religion—father figure of the state or the image of the workers is superior to individualism, isn't it? I think with Western-style communism in power, it would be possible to create an almost imaginary workers' image of themselves as the father figure.

Blackburn: So long as their life in the factory is being run by somebody else—by capitalists or even a bureaucrat—they'll need a father figure. But if they're running their own life, which is most of the time in the country, I think you're right: they'd still need some ideals. But I don't think it would take the form of a personality.

Lennon: It happened in Russia and China and Cuba. I mean, Fidel and Che and all that. It seems that we all have this basic need for it, you know.

Ono: But people have to have more trust in themselves.

Ali: That's the question. You see, what one's got to very consciously do is instill into the working-class movement a feeling of self-confidence, and you can't only instill that by propaganda.

Lennon: No, no.

Ali: It's when the workers begin to move themselves. They occupy a factory. When the capitalists make them redundant, they say, "OK, you can bugger off, we'll run this factory ourselves." And when they actually *start* running the factory themselves, as happened in France in May of '68, then they begin to feel a sense of their own strength.

Ono: The fact is that you have to give people some responsible position. And all the governments are afraid of that, even Mao. They like to make a revolution, but then after that they get afraid of the people and they try to limit their abilities.

Ali: That's true.

Blackburn: I lived in Cuba for a bit, Yoko, and . . . you see, they've got the Americans just ninety miles away. They're partly wrong and partly right, but they think it's too big a risk [to give the people too much power]. They let the people have a certain amount of responsibility, but until you let them have complete responsibility it's not really a revolution, is it?

Lennon: Yeah.

Ono: You don't trust people.

Ali: That's right. It shows on the part of the leadership a lack of self-confidence that you can't trust the people. And you see, the big difference between Mao and Stalin is this: that Stalin was a counterrevolutionary. He strangled the Russian revolution—literally strangled it, killed all the old Bolsheviks. Mao made a revolution. That's the big difference between them.

And then Mao did what Stalin in his wildest nightmares used to dread. Mao actually mobilized the people themselves. And when he mobilized them, the young Chinese students and workers were out into the streets. Then in many places, like Shanghai and Canton, there were many groups of workers and students who said, "Well, we hate Liu Shaoqi [Chinese revolutionary who was president of the People's Republic of China from 1959 to 1968 under Mao]. But we also think that Mao has made certain mistakes." And it created a fantastic regeneration of things. And this is, in a sense, why some of the people around Mao got scared, because they said if they develop—

Lennon: Loopholes.

Ali: It's a possibility, yeah.

Blackburn: [*Inaudible.*] Everybody wrote their own posters.

Ono: Why do you need Mao's poster all over? They're forcing Mao to take a position of a dictatorship.

Ali: I must confess, I was in Peking [now Beijing] last summer, going on my way to North Korea, and it was a bit religious, this whole bit of seeing small kids passing by and the teacher would instruct them to bow for Mao. I disagree—

Lennon: Because there's bound to be a reaction against that.

Ali: Either that or the kids won't take it seriously. Like learning what they learn in school. It just becomes a part of a sort of convention, which they get over.

Blackburn: But even the counterrevolutionaries or revisionists or whatever you want to call them in China used Mao. Everybody was using Mao.

Can I ask you something which sort of is related to this but concerns your position as a pop music artist? There has been this fantastic colonial revolution where the peasants of the third world have started throwing off the domination of their countries. They haven't created a perfect socialism—and they couldn't because they didn't have any resources—but they've done pretty well to defeat the largest imperialist powers in the world, like in Vietnam. Now when we're talking about relating to that, your music, it's very interesting . . . they thought that was imperialist music.

Lennon: Yeah.

Blackburn: 'Cause it came out of Voice of America.

Lennon: Yeah. Also the Russians had put it out that we were capitalist robots—which we were, I suppose. [*Laughs.*]

Blackburn: But they were pretty stupid, too, not to see that there was something—

Lennon: They're scared of the Western culture. Just recently I read something where some Vietnamese up north had had a secret club where they all dreamt about what they would do if they were capitalists with all the women and they were playing rock 'n' roll. And the actual musicians were playing; they were not playing records. And they were imprisoned for twenty years 'cause of it. I think they're so scared of Coca-Cola and rock 'n' roll—

Ali: You're right, you see, because I'll tell you—

Lennon: But I think that's silly.

Blackburn: But they've got to see the difference, haven't they? In Cuba it was a really big breakthrough in 1967—it was actually when *Sgt. Pepper* came out. They listened to it and said, "This is not bourgeois," and they started playing it on the radio.

Lennon: Amazing.

Blackburn: And of course the Vietnamese also really understand that. But then you get these ridiculous incidents like the one you mentioned, which is very bad.

Lennon: It's the same kind of paranoia that the West has about anything Communist.

Blackburn: But I think that your own development is probably gonna help this, too. Because, as you say, I think they were mainly wrong but they were also partly right to say that the Fab Four were part of the system. As you become less part of the system, then I think they can understand. Of course, the cultural barrier is also very big.

Lennon: But there is the problem, as I've become more radical, with *Two Virgins* or whatever, putting heavy statements out, [that] the influence grows more strong and solid but it diminishes. The Beatles' influence is far superior to any of us individually working. And that is part of my policy, really—to shake off teenyboppers so they won't frighten off the other type of people. We try and get through to them. So the power diminishes then.

Blackburn: But as you say, it's also concentrated more.

Lennon: Yeah, yeah.

Ono: Let's face it: Beatles music was a twentieth century folk song within the frame of capitalism. They couldn't do it otherwise. And to make their names big, they had to play the game, smiling and all that. And if the whole society will change, their song will change, too.

Lennon: Well, we did turn out to be a Trojan horse in a way. We were moved right into the center, and then we said, "Oh, fuck, drugs, and the rest of it." And that's when they started dropping us.

Blackburn: I think you were only a Trojan horse because you were that right from the beginning, actually. There was always that contradiction.

Lennon: Yes, yes.

Ono: He was always like that.

Blackburn: You did come out of Liverpool slums in a way.

Lennon: Well, the first thing we had to do was proclaim our Liverpoolness to the world and say, "It's all right to come from Liverpool and talk like this. Because anybody [from] Liverpool that had made it—like the comedians Ted Ray, Tommy Handley, and Arthur Askey—all had to lose their accents to get on the BBC. I mean, these are only comedians, but that's what came out of Liverpool before us. We stopped the accent game, and all the middle classes were trying to talk Liverpool. That's a fact, you know.

Like [Manfred Mann vocalist] Mike d'Abo was on the other night saying that he always felt embarrassed about his middle-classness and his voice. And for a period he would say [*affects strong Liverpool accent*] "'ow are you?" "all right," and all that. All those people would do that. And the people at Harrow and Eton now are all growing long hair and trying to lose their accents, which is a good change.

Blackburn: Did anybody ever try to get you to stop using Liverpool accents?

Lennon: No, no.

Ali: They wouldn't.

Lennon: We always put it on more.

Ono: So the Trojan horse thing seems to be very successful—

Lennon: But we weren't much aware of it.

Ono: No, but I mean for the future. Like [Yippie leader Jerry] Rubin . . . I like what he did on TV and everything. But he tried to on *David Frost* smoke marijuana or something. That was very good, but it won't work . . . if you just take a marijuana cigarette and you just smoke it . . .

Lennon: Rubin's position is that there's no time for subtlety anymore.

Ali: It's an absurd position, actually, because—

Lennon: I think it helps—

Blackburn: It shakes things up, Tariq. That's the point. People need shaking up.

Lennon: It was the best thing that happened on TV. He took [black-power activist] Michael X on Simon Dee's [show on British television], sneaked him in.

Blackburn: But somehow we're all part of a discussion or being interviewed, and it's not breaking the framework. So even though it could have been better done and all that, at least breaking the framework once was a good thing to do.

Lennon: I thought it was good to sort of incite people to do similar things, you know. Be disobedient in school or whatever it is.

Ono: Stick your tongue out.

Lennon: Stick your tongue out, whatever—just keep insulting 'em.

Blackburn: The schools is where it could start happening, actually, 'cause—

Lennon: Yeah, that's where *Red Mole* should get out—in the schools.

Ali: We are getting a lot there.

Lennon: Especially to the students.

Ali: Yeah, lots of school students now are reading the *Mole*.

Lennon: That's good.

Blackburn: Do you get a different pattern of correspondence these days?

Lennon: [*To Ono.*] It has changed over time, hasn't it?

Ono: Very different now.

Lennon: Seems more intelligent letters than "give my love to Paul," and all that, which used to be.

Ono: Very political these days.

Lennon: Yeah, it's usually, "Will you help this way or write a letter this way?" Et cetera, et cetera. So it's becoming more realistic, the mail.

Ali: John, what were the basic reasons why you split up with the other Beatles?

Lennon: With the others? Well, because, uh, Paul is a conservative . . .

Blackburn: He votes Tory, does he?

Lennon: Well, I don't think any of us have ever voted. But he is a conservative and always was, in a way. He's more interested in putting out pop music than anything that says anything. And it was just that kind of thing. At one period, I just said to them, "Well, I think it's limiting what we're doing together, and I want to work individually and not with the group anymore; the group image inhibits me." And it was just like that, you know? It was just a case of we got to a point where we just couldn't work musically together, because I couldn't be bothered with jog-along happy songs about nothing in particular. I just could no longer feel it.

Blackburn: Funny enough, some of the new record [*John Lennon/Plastic Ono Band*] seems almost to be taking a new look at a lot of things that were there in some of the Beatles stuff, in a different way. I was just thinking, for example, that a lot of the old songs used to be about childhood.

Lennon: Yeah.

Blackburn: Now you're talking about your real childhood.

Lennon: Well, I was always inclined to write about childhood. Most of the childhood stuff would be from me.

Blackburn: Yeah. I mean, it's good stuff, but it had a missing element.

Lennon: Well, the missing element was reality—the fact that I wasn't wanted and that my worst fears had come true in a way. That fear of not being wanted. And when that finally hit home, well, it cleared the air.

Blackburn: Maybe that's why you had to sing about childhood in the previous times.

Lennon: Yeah, because I couldn't face up to what was happening to me now, so I'd sing about childhood. But I just always found that when I was writing, I would always drift back into childhood. It would come out whether I liked it or not. I mean, it's just a fact that that's what makes you what you are, childhood. There's no getting away from it.

Blackburn: Can I ask about a contradiction that comes up out of the new record? The bad things seem to come out of childhood and the family, but the good things also can come out of personal relationships.

Lennon: Well, with Yoko, you mean?

Blackburn: Well, quite. Which is really a new family.

Lennon: Yeah, I'm not against family as such.

Ono: It depends on how aware you are.

Lennon: Yeah, if you're aware of what's happening, well, you can manage. I suppose you could call Communists a family, too. But we just happen to be a family of two. And we found ourselves in the same position with her coming from middle-class Japan and me coming from working-class Liverpool. We found out we have the same experiences really.

Blackburn: That is amazing, isn't it? The cultural and national—

Lennon: Yeah.

Ono: That means that the world is getting smaller and smaller, you know, and we just have to face that. John was saying he thought that he was singing American songs . . . but, I mean, there's Coca-Cola in Britain, too, and we share a strange same culture in a way wherever you go.

Ali: After you and Yoko started living together, did you get a lot of letters from racists and people like that?

Lennon: Oh, yeah, we did. I was going to publish them at one time, but it never happened. I got 'em all together. All things like what the Japs did to us in the war.

Ono: And "She'll slit your throat in the middle of the night."

Lennon: I did this sort of declaration of our living together, the show at Robert Fraser's [art gallery in London], which is *You Are Here*. People walked in, and when they got downstairs, it just said, "You are here."

Ono: That's a reality thing.

Lennon: Flashes of reality were always there. And then I let balloons go, with [a message attached that said,] "Write back to this address." And of course it was all in the press, and a lot of letters came by the press.

And there was a lot of racialism. I was really shocked. Because I hadn't thought about it; it hadn't entered me mind, really. And it was a real shock. All from army people, people in Aldershot [an English town known as Home of the British Army] and these crazy old women and . . . "Jap bastards" and "They'll slit our throats" and "Watch she doesn't murder you at night." I was really, *really* shocked by it. But that brought us closer together, of course.

The subtle difference between racism and antifemale-ism . . . It's just so subtle, you have to really have a light shone on it to realize that—

Ali: You mean there's a lot of male chauvinism?

Lennon: Oh, sure, sure. That's what I was going to ask you: How do you treat your women? Because we can't really have a revolution until we include women.

Ali: Absolutely.

Lennon: They have to be included. And it's so subtle, the way you're taught. It took me quite a time to realize my maleness cutting off certain areas for her. And she's a red-hot liberationist. [*Ono laughs.*] And she was quick to show me where I was going wrong. There was just a built-in sort of reaction. And anybody that claims radicalism, I always just like to see how they treat the women.

Blackburn: Often, pretty badly.

Lennon: Yeah. I mean, it's ridiculous. You can't talk about equal rights and revolution and power to the people . . . the people include both sexes.

Ono: You see, from a woman's point of view, I mean, you can't love somebody unless you're in an equal position at least. You know what I mean? If you're suppressed and all that, everything that you do is out of fear or insecurity, and that's not love. And that's why, basically, I think women hate men.

Lennon: And vice versa.

Ono: So if you have slaves around in your house, how can you make a revolution then?

Ali: Absolutely. Actually, it is a problem which increasingly—I mean, a lot of it exists, but increasingly revolutionary men who are socialists or regard themselves as Marxists are having to come to terms with it because the women they live with, most of them happen to be political.

Blackburn: Not necessarily political but women's liberation—

Lennon: Well, that's political, all right.

Blackburn: My girlfriend's in court today, actually, on the Miss World demonstration. [*Women's liberation activists protested at the 1970 Miss World event, as did people who charged that the contest judging evidenced racism. —Ed.*]

Lennon: Oh, great.

Blackburn: I felt a bit guilty coming here. But when did you come to start thinking like that [about women's rights]?

Lennon: Well, Yoko was into women's liberation before I met her. She had to fight through a man's world. The art crowd is just completely dominated by men. And they're very bitchy, and she fought her way through that, so she was full of revolutionary zeal when we met. There was never any question about it that we had to have a fifty-fifty relationship or there was no relationship, and I was quick to learn. [*Laughs.*] It's as simple as that.

Ono: Amazing, isn't it?

Lennon: She did an article in *Nova* about two years back. She said, "Woman is the nigger of the world." [*Lennon is referring to an interview that Ono gave to the British magazine in 1969. She used the phrase in the Q&A, and the magazine quoted it on its cover. —Ed.*] That was a couple of years back. And she was a friend of [feminist author] Kate Millet's at one time.

Ono: Kate is a very nice girl. But she's suffering, too, from that. Because if we try to be natural, then we naturally become lonely. Because there are so many women who are willing to be a slave, and usually men prefer that so you have to always take a chance of, "Am I going to lose my man?" It's very sad.

Ali: In the last few issues of the *Mole*, we've been doing a lot of interviews with these women night cleaners, who go around cleaning offices—

Lennon: Oh, yeah.

Ali: —and how they're trying to unionize themselves. And it's an amazing story. In the latest issue, we've got a story about one of these bosses in these buildings, the people who pay out the money. He rang up May Hobbs [leader of the London's Night Cleaners Campaign and author of the 1973 book *Born to Struggle*], who's the leader of these women, and said that if she came around to his building and tried to unionize the women working there, he'd come and break her arm.

Lennon: Amazing. Insane.

Ono: So we're very lucky, actually, because we have our own [*inaudible*] together.

Lennon: The more reality you come to face, the more alone you are, because you realize how much unreality is the main program of the day. And the more real we become, the more abuse we take. So it does radicalize us in a way, being put in a corner.

Blackburn: But it's only by linking up with other people against the program of the day that one can really . . . I mean, one just feels better, I find. One can do it by oneself but with another person, that's great, and more people, that's even better.

Lennon: Quite true.

Ono: I really think that books and papers have power. Because there are many people who just read one book and got some kind of enlightened feeling . . . that changed their whole—

Blackburn: You think books and papers rather than—

Ono: Rather than guns. You know, because we always think, *Well, we just have to go to war. We just have to do it that way.*

Blackburn: That's what the Weathermen are doing. Until you've actually built up some group—

Ono: A lot of revolutionaries think that. We're soft to think that there's a peaceful way, but communication's a fantastic power—

Ali: But the crucial thing, surely, Yoko, is suppose you have established roots in the masses, through your propaganda, through your actions. Ultimately, when you challenge a bourgeois system and the capitalists come and try to crush you with force, then there are two options: either you lie down and are crushed or you fight back.

Ono: I know, yes, but before that, and it is before . . .

Blackburn: That's what the Weathermen don't understand. I think they're just beginning to, actually, that one can't get out on the streets—

Ali: —with a gun in hand and think that by even killing two policemen you suddenly radicalize the American working class.

Lennon: It goes the other way.

Ali: Exactly. At the moment it will.

Lennon: What about Ireland, then?

Ali: Ireland is an absolutely fascinating situation, because what has been happening in Ireland is the mistakes or the interests of British imperialism in the '20s and '30s . . . all those chickens are now coming home to roost. They thought they could have a partition, divide a country up on the basis of religion, on the basis of Protestants they had actually planted there a long time ago. And that this situation would continue to exist. And what's happening now is that all these accumulated contradictions are blowing up in their face. No one would have dreamt ten years ago that the British would have to send the army back into Ireland again to keep the population under control. Their women and kids would be put up against the wall and searched. That's what's happening in Belfast and Derry today.

Lennon: It's a good thing [Jerry] Rubin shouted about Ireland.

Ali: Oh, yes. Marx actually once said something very, very crucial in 1870, a hundred years ago now. He said that unless the British working class and the British revolutionary movement understands and supports the struggle of the Irish to free themselves—

Lennon: Yeah.

Ali: —they'll never be able to free themselves. It's absolutely true. They'll never be free.

Lennon: Yeah. Sure. The southern Irish aren't exactly—

Ali: No, the government isn't—

Blackburn: Southern Ireland is as much a creation of that phony setup as the North. And the real revolutionaries in Ireland are just as much against the regime in the South as in the North. But I think the North is gonna be the weak link in the thing. Of course, there are big problems in the North, too. The working class is divided according to religion. The Protestant workers are still—

Lennon: Along with the fact that they don't get a real vote or an equal vote.

Blackburn: They get unemployment, worse housing conditions . . .

Ali: They're the poor whites of Great Britain in that sense. Like the poor whites are always in one sense much fiercer in their antiblack hatred than some of the poor whites in the South. Because the only privilege they had was the color of their skin. Otherwise they were as bad off as the blacks.

Ono: I get very excited when we talk about how there's no choice but to use violence. In American TV I saw this program and a kid who just came back from Vietnam. He's lying down in bed, and the only body he has is from here. [*Apparently indicates no legs.*] He's just like a lump of meat. And he said, "Well, I think it was a good experience."

Lennon: Because he doesn't want to face it. He doesn't want to think, *Well, it was all a waste of time, and I've just got no legs.* That's the problem.

Ono: It's such a painful thing. And when you think of violence, you just think of it conceptually. But what it actually means was maybe your kid or yourself would not have a hand or—

Blackburn: But, Yoko, think of this. Say in Northern Ireland, in those Catholic districts like Bogside, the police were coming in there and just shooting up the place. They killed seven people on one evening in August 1969. What they [the people] were doing was really defending themselves there. They were building the barricades. They weren't symbolic at all. Those barricades were to stop the armored cars coming in. I think when you get defensive popular violence, that is 100 percent justified.

Lennon: Yeah, I do—

Blackburn: But if you go out with a gun and think you can individually pick off . . .

Ono: That's why you do it before that happens—

Lennon: What do we do?

Ono: Well, that's what I'm saying—

Ali: That's the problem, because no social class, no ruling class in the whole of history, has ever given up power voluntarily.

Ono: I know, I know. But you see, I think tradition is created every day. And there was no tradition or precedent of that. But was there any precedent of an age where communication is so rapid and all that? No.

And, for instance, when you publish the *Red Mole*, the leaders tend to be intellectual and they mainly appeal to intellectualism, college students . . . but if you start to have a column for younger kids who are not intellectualized yet, and appeal to their instincts and educate them in a Communist way . . .

Blackburn: [*Inaudible*] in the States is doing some of that.

Ono: And I think in that sense what Beatles do is fantastic. They didn't use guns.

Lennon: Yeah, but as I said, nothing happened.

Ono: Right, right, but I mean there was a definite change. I'm not saying that it was for the better or anything. I'm just saying that sometimes you can make a revolution without using—

Lennon: But you can't take power . . .

Ali: That's the crucial thing.

Lennon: When it comes down to the nitty-gritty, they won't let you have any power. They'll give you all the right to perform and dance . . .

Ono: The thing is, even after revolution, if people don't have any trust in themselves, then they're gonna be slaves for the Communists or government or something. So it's really very important to build people's confidence, that you don't need a father figure.

Blackburn: To do that, you need a focus for people to organize around, and sometimes the trade union does that. Sometimes a factory committee is something they can use.

Lennon: It's a pity that a trade union couldn't open up its own factories . . .

Blackburn: I mean, take Rolls-Royce. They haven't said the workers can take over the factory and run it instead of closing it down, which they could. But in a way, I understand . . . that if you ran it in the capitalist system, you'd have to make a profit.

Lennon: But they could put the profit back into the factory, couldn't they?

Blackburn: Yeah, but part of the way the system rules us is not just the profits . . . You've got to change the system so that men control the economy and not the market. 'Cause at the moment, the market says who is unemployed and who isn't. It's not any individual. Even the capitalists don't decide to let the peasants starve and we live off the fat of the land. . . . It's not Nixon who decides that. It's the market. How are we going to stop exploiting the third world? Only by destroying the international market whereby we get the coffee and all the things that we [*apparently indicates coffee cup*] . . . This probably comes from the Philippines or somewhere.

Ono: Nixon does have a lot of control of the market. The thing is—and I know it sounds sort of very optimistic and all that—but if you make a fashion out of it, some kind of habit or idea spreads rapidly.

Ali: But look, Yoko, at the biggest fashion that has spread—the long hair, hippie fashion, and dropping out. Well, most of the people, in fact, large numbers of them that could afford to drop out, are middle-class kids. And the only reason they could afford to drop out was 'cause they could afford to drop in again.

Lennon: Yeah.

Ali: And they didn't change. Some of the hippies I know who used to come with us on demonstrations to Grosvenor Square [in London] against the Americans in Vietnam and used to be beaten up with us by these thugs . . . I actually saw one of these people the other day in a big, big car going past a demonstration—it was, funny enough, a demonstration on Ireland—honking the horn of his car and churning abuse at the demonstrators as he drove off. And that's just one incident, but it does typify—

Blackburn: How typical is it? I think hippies, some of them have very reactionary ideologies; quite a lot of them become quite radical, really. I don't think they're pure revolutionaries, but who of us is? The general cultural impact increased the size of the movement; it didn't change the structure. This communication you talk about helps you build your movement. But in the end, the aim is not just to have a big movement; it's actually to change society. The form the force will take is difficult to say.

In France in 1968, there were ten million workers on strike. I mean, there really was a big movement there, occupying the factories. It wasn't machine guns in the streets; it was actually barricades and with the police going out with gas and the students fighting back with rocks. And they had these massive demonstrations, half a million workers in the center of Paris, and if they'd occupied the government buildings, which they could have done then, what would they [the government] have done? Sent the army in to shoot down workers? They might have, in which case you'd have to defend yourself. Probably the soldiers wouldn't have fired on workers.

Lennon: The Communists thought that up, didn't they? The Communist Party.

Blackburn: Absolutely. Because they didn't want the revolution; they're scared. They thought they could get it by a deal at the top because they don't like the masses taking the initiative.

Lennon: Madness, isn't it?

Ono: But you know, to talk about an extreme case, Nixon can't be president if 90 percent of the people in United States would have a different idea about it. Then he would start to sing a different tune.

Lennon: But he has the money to communicate. Our position doesn't.

Ono: Yes, but he relies on backers, and if the backers started to change—

Blackburn: But why should the backers change?

Lennon: If he changes, the backers no longer exist.

Ali: Someone else will take their place. That's why you see some comrades say, "Let's go and shoot off a few dozen capitalists." You can do that, but it goes to their wives or their sons. Or otherwise the government buys it and sells it to someone else. It doesn't change anything at all. That's why even our propaganda—

[*The tape is changed, causing a brief break in the conversation. —Ed.*]

Lennon: It's like blaming the failure of Christianity on Christ. It wasn't Christ's fault. It was the others. He was a basic Marxist with a halo on his head.

Ali: When we bring this interview around, there's a very interesting text, which I think you should read, in fact, on the Russian Revolution by Trotsky called *The Revolution Betrayed*, in which he analyzes very concretely what went wrong.

Lennon: I get very muddled up about Trotskyists and this-ists and that-ists, what their position is.

Blackburn: Can I ask you . . . that war-is-over thing . . . did it link up? In Jerry Rubin's book, he talks about a demonstration in New York called "The War Is Over." Was that linked up to that [your campaign with the same name]?

Lennon: Not as far as we know.

Ono: It's the first time I've heard of that.

Lennon: What we did was buy space in all the major cities in the West and just put up billboards saying that.

Blackburn: I think they must have done it at the same time.

Lennon: Maybe they saw the posters.

Blackburn: It's curious because Rubin doesn't say how he arrived at the idea or where they got it from. They had a demonstration in Central Park, and they rushed around, about two thousand of them, ran around Forty-Fourth Street, saying, "The war is over."

Ono: When was that?

Blackburn: About a year ago.

Lennon: The original idea was to try and make fake paper headlines, like *Daily Mirror*, saying THE WAR IS OVER. And then, PRINCE PHILLIP IS GUILTY in small type.

Blackburn: The first thing he [Rubin] said is nobody asked who won. Nobody—even the people who were pro-war—felt they could say they were sorry about the war being over.

Lennon: In New York, the poster was on a giant billboard right next to the induction office for the army.

Ali: What factors would you say had, in fact, radicalized you over the last few years?

Lennon: I'd always been interested, as I said in the *Rolling Stone* article, in China and Russia as a working-class human being and always related to working class, although I was playing a capitalist game. I was not aware of that at the time. I was doing me job. But there was always this . . . I was an atheist as a teenager. And then with the advent of acid and that, there was all this glorious vision and all that shit. [*Laughs.*] And so I tended to go back because we all somehow need a father figure. Even Chairman Mao is that, and the father figures were all laid on the line with the Buddhists and the Christianity. And having been brought up in that, it was an easy switch to, well, you know there must be something to it. This feeling of brotherly love, I translated as a feeling of God.

But having gone through this [primal-scream] therapy and understood the wish for father and mother in life from us all—whether we have them or not, we never got what we wanted from them—and as soon as that was physically felt, there was no question of a God. I had to do it that way, though, to really kill off what the drugs had done. And it was that. And having felt my own pain, literally—I mean, in the therapy, you really feel every painful moment in your life, and it's excruciating. It's like being crucified. And you know that that's your pain and not the result of somebody in the sky; it's a result of your parents and your environment.

Blackburn: Your social context.

Lennon: Yeah. So it just all fell into place. At one time, I used to claim to be a Christian Communist, which is bullshit, really. But that was the position I took because I couldn't disassociate myself with this God shit. But this therapy . . . there was a moment, experiencing some kind of pain and realizing it was to do with nobody else but me and the association with parents. But it was me that was feeling it. Nobody had anything to do with it; it was my own self. And that just finished it; it was the end of it. It wasn't any great revelation. It was just, "Fuck it, what have I been doing?"

And then the thing was what to do about it. Having always, especially since Yoko came, wanted to do something about peace or people. And the point was what to do now. Where do I stand? What education have I got to catch up with? Or should I try and rely on my own common sense, which, now that the myths have gone, leads you to the one conclusion: hell, we're all oppressed, and something has to be done about it.

Blackburn: And you actually were thinking about that even when writing songs like "Revolution [1]" that seem to be knocking politics? In a way, you were thinking about a political problem.

Lennon: Oh, sure. There's two versions of the song "Revolution." Of course, the underground left picked up on the one that says, "Count me out." But the original version, which ended up on the LP, said, "When you talk about destruction, you can count me out in." In and out—I put both in 'cause I wasn't sure.

Blackburn: Yeah.

Lennon: On the one I released as a single, we did it in a more commercial style—the single is much faster than the album version—and I left out "count me in." Because I'm a coward—I don't want to be killed and all the rest of it. I didn't really know that much about the Maoists, but I just knew that they seemed to be so few, and like, painting themselves green and standing in front of the police and getting picked off . . . I just thought it was unsubtle. I don't think the original Communist revolutionaries went around shouting about it. They kept quiet.

Blackburn: They didn't ask to be picked off.

Lennon: Right. They coordinated themselves a bit better. And I was really asking a question.

Blackburn: Also, they got dug in to what the people really wanted. Which is what Mao did. He didn't just wave a red book.

Lennon: So the "Revolution [1]" song was that, really. I was posing a question and saying "in and out." There was three "Revolutions"—two songs and one abstract. I don't know what you'd call it . . . musique concrète, loops and that, which was a picture of the revolution.

Blackburn: That was the last track, wasn't it, on *The Beatles* double LP?

Lennon: Just before Ringo does a Hollywood bit ["Good Night"], yeah. So that was a picture I painted in sound of the revolution, which was complete murder and killing and people screaming and kids crying and all that, which is what I really thought it would be. . . .

Blackburn: Could I just ask you how this ties into analysis? I get the idea that most analysis is working people through their pain into the world. This guy [Lennon and Ono's analyst, Arthur Janov] doesn't seem to be doing that; he's doing the opposite. He's bringing—

Lennon: His thing is to feel our pain, not come to terms with it. We come to terms with it ourselves to survive to the age we are. All the repression pains, which are caused by childhood, aren't literally repressed in you; they come out in arthritis or asthma or whatever. People with asthma and thyroid things are being cured in his place by allowing themselves . . . they're literally trying to kill themselves to get parents' love in a way: "Look, Mommy, now will you love me? I'm a cripple."

And we put it somewhere or other. I put it into my eyes literally: I experienced moments of not wanting to see when I was a child, not wanting to see the ugliness. Not wanting to see not being wanted went into my eyes and into my mind. And he [Janov] doesn't just put you back [in childhood] to talk about it . . . you do most of the work yourself, actually. Once they've started on you, it just happens yourself. Once the machinery for feeling everything that goes on to you is open, you can't stop it. After thirty years of repressing feeling and putting it in my backbone or in my neck—

Blackburn: Well, what's left after his—

Lennon: You're left with yourself and still with the ability to feel daily. Almost daily, we primal, which is cry. Every morning most of us wake up in fear. That's your weakest moment, when you first wake up, and that's usually when your heart's pounding for no reason you can think of. That's just the basic fear inside all of us.

Instead of having your heart going like clappers or some strain in your back and just either taking a pill or saying, "I'll get over it, I'll have a bath," you let your mind go to that pain. And after you've been through the therapy, the pain itself will regurgitate the memory that originally caused you to suppress it into your heart. So you sort of lie there, and your mind goes to this pain, and it goes, "Oh, 1943, this happened." It comes out literally like that, and you cry about it. You feel that feeling.

Blackburn: But even through analysis, you can't cancel out what's happened, can you?

Lennon: No, no, no. It's like all the pain was always channeled into whatever—sex or masturbation or dreaming or God or whatever it is. But once the channels are open for the pain, when you feel pain, the pain actually goes to the right channels, and you express it the right way—which is crying, like children do. But for men, we're told not to cry from an early age. We have to repress ourselves all that time. And there's no harm in crying. You cry, you feel good, like a kid does. It's like after acid. The therapy was literally like a six-month very slow acid trip. The difference between acid and the therapy is acid unleashes all these feelings. There's so many of them, and they're not channeled in the right direction.

Blackburn: Because you don't know what's happening.

Lennon: Well, you do, actually. You get used to it, and you can work it out. But after all those years of channeling it the wrong way, when people have acid they hallucinate, because the pain and the awareness of feeling that you get on those drugs is so much that you cannot take it. It's too much at once and you hallucinate or whatever you do—trip off, away from reality. And the therapy was like a very slow acid trip, which happens naturally within the body.

It's hard to talk about crying and pain and all that. It sounds sort of arbitrary. But the word *pain* to me now has a different meaning, because of having physically felt all these extraordinary repressions I had. And *feeling* is a different word to me, because after therapy and after big primals, it was like taking gloves off. You could feel your own skin for the first time. It was like I'd been wearing gloves all me life, and suddenly there was a literal feeling in my hands.

I don't like talking about it, because it sounds so abstract. You can't really understand if the vocabulary is different between people who've done it and haven't done it. It's a bit of a drag to say that . . . but just the simple pain of living—that's part of a dissolving of the God trip or father-figure trip. Always looking for some kind of heaven. I mean, intellectually I knew that it was yin-yang or black-and-white continually or dialectic materialism—it's the same thing, really. And once God's out of the way, the main asset is to realize there's no good and bad. There's a bit of it in every day, and you just go through it.

Blackburn: You trace that pain first to the family.

Lennon: Oh, yeah. It's directly involved with the family. I mean, the family's what shapes you.

Blackburn: I take it you don't mean your family in particular.

Lennon: No, every family. The extraordinary thing is my father and mother split—I never saw my father till I was like twenty—so I'm an extreme case. But Yoko had her parents there, but she never had 'em. The lyrics of "Mother," which said, "You had me and I never had you," applies to people with parents too . . .

Blackburn: More subtly, perhaps.

Lennon: Yeah, but see, she went through the same pain.

Ono: More pain, really. It's like when you're hungry, instead of getting a cheeseburger, you get a film of a cheeseburger, and it doesn't do you any good.

Lennon: It affects the middle class even more because they're so formalized. There's more middle-class people in this thing [therapy] because they can afford it, and they're the ones that are cracking up. And the middle classes are really repressed; they're the most repressed people. They have all these formalities with their parents, and actually touching is out. It's like intellectual love. Or like she says, films of love. And she was in that school of pain.

Ono: I always wished my mother died so I could at least get decent sympathy, you know. [*Laughs.*] But there she was, a perfectly beautiful mother. Everybody'd say, "How lucky you are to have a mother like that." When it wasn't really true. I wasn't lucky to have a mother with—

Blackburn: In a way, what the parents are doing is transmitting to their children the fact that their lives have been fucked up.

Ono: Exactly!

Lennon: They can't give because they've never been given to. But the problem for most people, and extraordinarily enough for me, who'd had no real impression that my mother actually wanted me—or father—because she wasn't there. But still one of the hardest things is to realize that actually they didn't want you: you're just the result of a fuck. Not many of us are planned. And in fact, their own need is so great that they cannot possibly give to you.

So to allow yourself to feel your own want is a big problem. The thing we all seem to greatly fear is to show the want we have of love from other people, especially parents. To feel it and acknowledge it in your mind: "No, they didn't want me. That is a fact. I was not wanted. No wonder I feel shitty." 'Cause I couldn't explain it as a child. You just know that something is not right, something is not there. And that is the big trauma, to experience that.

And especially the middle-class people who have nice, imagey parents, smiling and all dolled up. They're the ones that have the biggest struggle to say, "Good-bye, Mommy, good-bye, Daddy. I never had you, and I must realize that I never had you and I never will." The middle-class people in the therapy were continually going back to their parents just to see, "Maybe I can tell them about this experience I've had, and I understand them," but the parents could not associate with it.

Blackburn: On the record, I listened several times to that "Mommy's Dead" track [*actually "My Mummy's Dead." —Ed.*], and then I suddenly realized it reminded me of something. Then it seemed like perhaps it was "Three Blind Mice."

Lennon: It was just a feeling. It was almost like a haiku poem. Actually, I got into haiku in Japan just recently. I think it's fantastic. God, it's beautiful. We bought some haiku originals when we were there. But obviously when you get rid of a whole section of illusion in your mind, you're left with a precision. The difference between haiku and Longfellow or something is immense. Longfellow says, "Oh, beautiful yellow flowers standing quietly in the shadowy electric light," when the haiku would just say, "Yellow flowers in a white bowl on a wooden table" and that gives you the whole picture.

Blackburn: It looks much more simple, but like your music is now, it can in fact be listened to many, many times to get into it.

Lennon: Because people's perception of reality . . . they're not used to it, they don't know what it is. So when a simple haiku or a simple statement is made, they're not used to it. They're used to devious intellectual ways of feeling things. I don't know what people who aren't intellectuals do to arrive at the point, but they probably go through some mystic Walt Disney scene . . .

Blackburn: Religion is a very popular need for the reason that you say.

Ono: It's a convention.

Blackburn: But it's more than a convention in that people need religion; it covers up the pain.

Lennon: Religion is a legalized madness—that's what Janov says. You have to allow it. If the government stopped them . . . like all those stories—*1984*, when they replace God with a bomb or a rocket. I mean, they've even discussed it in America: What would we do if we had no war or no rocket to the moon? We've got to give them something to replace the religion thing. I think it was him or George [Orwell] who said opium is the religion of the people now instead of religion is the opium of the people. That's what's happening.

Blackburn: Actually, Marx said that in that essay, that early one. He also said, "Religion is the heart of the heartless world." There's a fantastic passage that's very like the God is—

Lennon: A concept.

Blackburn: But I'm sure you haven't—

Lennon: No, no. [*Rolling Stone* editor Jann] Wenner, when he interviewed me, said, "Do you realize that lots of philosophers or whoever had talked about God being a concept by which we measure our pain?" . . . It wasn't my own revelation. It [my line] was based on something maharishi once said, which was time was a concept by which we measure . . . oh, what was it?

Ono: By which we measure eternity.

Lennon: Eternity. Which is pretty cool. I used that basis to put what I thought about God. But a lot of kids wrote to me via *Rolling Stone*, saying, "Well, what about joy? God is a concept by which we measure our *joy*, John," and all that. So they obviously—

Ono: They were mad.

Lennon: Well, apart from being mad, they were just disappointed that I wasn't saying that. When you've got joy, you don't think about God much. It's only when you're in pain that you start thinking . . .

Blackburn: Look, the people who always have the most intense religious experience are those who are very oppressed and very miserable. Blacks in the States, Indians in Mexico. These are the people who really are obsessed by religion.

Lennon: It's no accident that there's so many fag priests. Like a fag has done—if any of you are fags, excuse me—they've completely reversed their roles to please Mommy and Daddy. They've gone so far that they've reversed themselves [and they say], "Now do you love me? I've not been what I was; I'm now something else for you. Will this suit you?" And Mommy says, "Yes, good boy, come home . . ."

Blackburn: Or it's a revolt perhaps against their parents' classification.

Lennon: I don't think so, because the fags are usually very close with Mother. There's no getting away from it.

Blackburn: That's true, yes.

Lennon: Another interesting thing: somebody recently wrote a book about all the prime ministers here and their life. I didn't read the book, but I read praises of it. That all the main prime ministers we've ever had, including [Sir Edward] Heath—apart from being short people, which that myth seems to be true—they repress themselves so much that they don't grow for Mommy and Daddy's sake. "Look, I'm still a little boy and I'll be good for ya." But most of the prime ministers of Britain have been repressed kids with strange childhoods or loss of parents and things like that.

Blackburn: You can argue that about lots of people. Most very creative artists—

Lennon: Sure, I agree.

Blackburn: It doesn't discredit them.

Lennon: It doesn't discredit them. But art is only a way of expressing pain. I mean, the reason she does such far-out stuff is her pain is expressed in a far-out way. It's a far-out kind of pain. The only reason for sure why I'm a star is because of my repression. Nothing else would have driven me to do all that. I mean, why would I do it if I was normal?

Ono: And happy.

Lennon: And happy. The only reason you go for that goal is because you want to say, "Now will you love me? Look, I'm prime minister," or "I'm head of a department."

Blackburn: That is the driving force, but how people come to terms with it themselves can be in two different ways. I remember once when I met [British prime minister Harold] Wilson, I thought, *What a shriveled up guy he is.* To be successful, he's completely repressed any human emotions he might have shown. And I got the impression in your interview [with *Rolling Stone*'s Jann Wenner] that when you were a successful Beatle, when you were playing the game, you didn't even know you were so successful. I mean, I suppose the most fantastic success of the mid-twentieth century but you still were oppressed by it.

Lennon: Oh, Jesus Christ, it was complete oppression. We had to go through humiliation upon humiliation with the middle classes and show-biz and lord mayors. It was complete humiliation for me, because I could never keep me mouth shut. [*Ono laughs.*] I'd always be drunk or pilled or something to counteract this pressure. And it was hell.

Ono: He was actually deprived more than anything. It's not like he was enjoying the success and being happy.

Lennon: It's a very miserable feeling. Apart from the first blush of making it, your first number-one record—thrilling; first to break into America—thrilling. That was some sort of objective: "Well, I want to be as big as Elvis" or something like that. Moving forward was the great thing. But actually attaining it was a big letdown.

Blackburn: At one point, it seemed like really everybody was using you.

Lennon: Sure.

Blackburn: Wilson wants to get votes by—

Lennon: And the only reason we wouldn't pose with Heath was because he'd insulted me in the House about my book *In His Own Write* by saying, "If this boy had been educated, he would have been a good writer." That's what he said about me, so we wouldn't go anywhere near them. And anyway, we were socialists at heart, and we presumed that Harold would be better than Heath. It was a big letdown for all of us, but it turned out to be better than this. Like [Australian author] Richard Neville said, there's an inch difference between them [Wilson and Heath], and that's an inch in which we live. I think it's true in a way.

Ali: I mean, the Labour government did in fact almost equally nasty things in its time. After all, it kept the blacks out of Kenya nation—

Lennon: Oh sure, sure. That was bad, but it's nothing as bad as now . . . [Black leader] Michael [X] said that as soon as they came in, it was just—

Blackburn: You don't know. Wilson could have changed on that; he changed on a lot of things. This isn't about living in that inch. What Richard said is quite true, but still, we shouldn't be wanting to live in that inch. . . . Heath may be doing us a good turn by forcing us out—

Lennon: I thought of that, too, that he's putting us in a corner so we have to do something . . .

Blackburn: You've got to find out what's oppressing other people, too.

Ono: That's why meeting is so important, meeting with each other.

Lennon: Well, the first thing we did when we got back [to England] was contact you and Richard Neville and Michael [X], because in your individual ways you represent the movement in different spheres, all the different aspects of it. And we got messages abroad that complete repression was going on. You even said it in *Red Mole*, apart from Richard Neville's anarchist tendencies, all power to him because you'll be next, sure as hell you will.

Blackburn: And actually, that's begun to happen now. A lot of the political groups have been raided in the last few weeks, in the wake of that explosion—

Ali: Now in many parts of the country we're receiving information, even in towns which seem politically dead, where *Red Mole* sellers go out onto the streets: the police just refuse to allow the comrades to sell the paper on the streets.

Lennon: Can't you get it out through universities?

Ali: We are. We're doing it a lot through universities. But what worries them now is that more and more *Red Moles* are being sold to young workers who aren't bugged about all the old *Daily Worker* and *Morning Star*—

Lennon: I get it every day to see if there's any hope, but it just seems to be in the nineteenth century.

Ali: It is.

Lennon: So if you can get at the young workers—because obviously when you're eighteen, nineteen, twenty, that's when you're most ripe for . . . that's when you're most idealistic and have less fear. What I was trying to do in the *Rolling Stone* article was influence all the people I can influence who are still under a dream—to just put a big question mark in their mind: "Well, if great guru John says there's no God and it's all pain, maybe the acid dream is over." I'm trying to tell them that is over.

Blackburn: But also there was a very good bit in the interview where he [Jann Wenner] asks you what's really changed. It seems like the great Cultural Revolution wasn't—

Lennon: Oh, yeah. Bullshit, yeah.

Blackburn: You were saying about how the same people were in power—

Lennon: Sure, sure. . . . We cut our hair specifically for that reason, to stop that identification parade going on, that anybody with long hair was a socialist or radical.

Ali: Absolutely.

Lennon: So to confuse those image followers, we keep changing.

Blackburn: Also, I notice you're wearing air force clothes.

Lennon: Well, there's many reasons for that. During the therapy, we weren't supposed to repress anything, and we all became children literally, and we were all eating ice cream in America. All the people on therapy were just eating like children. Because when you're reliving your childhood you become that, and we put on twenty or thirty pounds just during that period. So I couldn't wear any of me clothes. I was not going to buy a new set of clothes for this figure, so I got these. It was as simple as that. And also they're functional. Before I'd wear jeans, but now I can't fit into any of them, so this is the next-best thing. And it's bloody functional. And I don't normally go anywhere where you need a tie, anyway, so . . . I was fed up with being a peacock. I decided I was an artist, not a model. So that was the changing point.

Blackburn: It is true that in the *Red Mole* we can get into contact now with the young workers, but the barriers are still immense. You say that in "Working Class Hero"—the song about the "fucking peasants."

Lennon: Yeah.

Blackburn: Do you think that, as an artist, you can help to destroy [that barrier] . . . because it's really a cultural subordination, isn't it? Thinking that you've always got to be dominated and led.

Lennon: Yeah. Well, it's a cozy feeling for them, like being in prison. You don't have to think. You take your position and stick with it, and it's that, really, which is the problem.

Ono: Plus the desire for a father . . .

Lennon: Yeah, nice big company to look after you and all that.

Ali: The Rolls-Royce crowd seems to have somewhat disproved that.

Lennon: Right, right. Well, the more of that that happens, the better in a way for the workers in the long run.

Blackburn: You know that ten thousand workers held shares in that company under a scheme that was touted as workers and capitalists getting together?

Lennon: Like the Japanese do.

Blackburn: No, they've lost not only their jobs but all their life savings.

Ali: Rolls-Royce is a very paternalist firm. "We really look after our workers. We give them a few shares . . ."

Blackburn: Also, the unions were very tame there—

Lennon: Well, they're more like the Japanese unions, which is just company-run.

Well, I don't know about that problem. Because it seems to me that all the revolutions have either happened with a Fidel or a Marx or a Khrushchev or whatever it was in the early days who were literally intellectuals, whether they were workers or not, and they got a good pocket of people. And I don't know how they got through to the workers except that the workers were in a more repressed state than they seemingly are here. See, the Americans have woken up in a way to the fact that two cars and two tellies does not answer it. But here they haven't had it long and they're still—

Blackburn: But John, it seems to me that in a way this is where the revolutionary artist comes in. Because the workers here are repressed not by guns but by ideas.

Ali: The whole ideas of the ruling class.

Blackburn: It's television and the spectacle. And you're part of that, or you were and then you freaked out of it. But in a sense you're still benefiting.

Lennon: Sure, sure. I'm not sure what to do or where me place is now. I woke up, so I have to sniff around and see what my place is and what I can do, which is why we're all talking.

Blackburn: I think maybe in the [*Rolling Stone*] interview or somewhere else, I read about your influences. Obviously, most of them came from the States, didn't they? There isn't a native tradition here, which is really revolutionary in a cultural sense. Or is there? Perhaps the Newcastle mining towns—

Lennon: The thing was, [when I started,] rock 'n' roll itself was the basic revolution to people of my age and situation then. I think the reason was because we were so unfeeling and repressed, that [we needed] something as basic and as loud as rock 'n' roll . . . to get through [to us].

Blackburn: And also it had to be simple—

Lennon: Yeah . . . and I've forgotten what the question was.

Blackburn: About whether there was something in England that—

Lennon: We all were very conscious of being imitation Americans in the early days. But we delved into the music and found out that it was half white country western and half black rock 'n' roll, African. And most of the country songs basically came from England—all those train songs. Sure they did, Scotland and Ireland. The basic folk song comes from Europe. So it was just a cultural exchange.

I mean, they went to America and Americanized the songs, and they sang about working on the railroads, and the blacks sang about working in the cotton fields. But all the basic songs . . . like lots of Dylan's basic songs are Scottish, Irish, or English folk songs. So that made us feel better. We delved into that side of it. But the more interesting songs to me were the black ones, because they were simpler. And they just sort of said, "Shake your ass and shake your prick about," which was quite an innovation, really.

Blackburn: Look, the good thing about that is that it's getting you to do something, whereas some of the folk-song tradition is about losing.

Lennon: Well, folk songs are completely middle-class, you see. As kids we were opposed to folk songs because it was all middle-class—same as jazz. It was college students with big scarves and a pint of beer and singing folk songs in what we call la-de-da. [*Breaks into song.*] "I worked in the mine in Newcastle" and all that shit. [*Laughter.*] And there was very few real folk singers. . . . I liked [Irish songwriter] Dominic Behan a bit, and there was quite a folk-song tradition in Liverpool, and country and western. But the country and western was complete cowboy gook. But the folk songs, most of them were middle-class kids just singing in very fruity voices.

I heard a few sometimes very old records of real workers singing the songs, and even now you occasionally see on TV some Irish still singing them—the actual people that work every day and go to the pubs singing the songs—and the power of them like that is fantastic, and I began to get a little more interested. But my own class prejudice was that folk songs had always been on the BBC with fruity voices and had nothing to do with folk music. They were just sort of classical reproductions keeping alive some old tradition. It was a bit boring, like ballet or something. . . . Today's folk song was rock 'n' roll even though it happened to emulate from America. That was not really important in the end, because then we wrote our own, and that changed it.

Blackburn: Oddly enough, some of your songs, even when the lyrics were almost nursery lyrics—like "Yellow Submarine," for example . . . Do you know—you probably do—that that was used by workers on strike? And at the LSE [London School of Economics], we had a version of it, which was, "We are all living in a red LSE." And workers had a version of it—

Ali: "We're all living on bread and margarine." They heckled Harold Wilson outside the Labour Party conference, singing, "We're all living on bread and margarine."

Lennon: That's great. I like that. I enjoyed when the football crowds in the early days would sing things like "Yellow Submarine" and "All

Together Now," which is another one that we put out. It just said, "All together now, all together now, all together now" all the time. And I was pleased when "Give Peace a Chance" became a sort of anthem thing. I'd written it with that in mind, really, hoping that instead of singing "We Shall Overcome" from 1800 or whatever it is, that they would sing something [current]. I felt an obligation even then to write something that people would sing actually in the pub or in a demonstration.

Blackburn: That was thinking very politically, actually, wasn't it?

Lennon: Well, I've always been politically minded. I've never not been political. I mean, religion tended to overshadow it during the acid days, which was probably '65–'66, and that was almost a direct result of being in that repressed, superstar position, and then religion was an outlet for that. [I thought,] *There's something else to come; this isn't it, surely? There's more to come.*

But I've always been political. In the two books I wrote, even though they were in sort of [James] Joycean gobbledygook, there's plenty of . . . There's a play about a worker and a capitalist. There's many knocks at religion. I've been satirizing religion from childhood in books . . . I used to always write magazines at school and hand them around and things like that. So I've always been conscious of that, and very conscious of class. They used to say there was a chip on me shoulder. There still is. Because I know what happened to me. I know all the class repression that happened to me; it was a fucking fact. But of course in the hurricane Beatle world, it got a bit left out, you know.

Blackburn: [With the Beatles,] you disproved the class system—

Lennon: Yeah, there was a feeling that the workers had broken through, but I realized in retrospect it was like they allowed blacks to be runners and footballers or boxers; that's the choice. But now you can be a pop star. I mean, that's the outlet they've given you to be something, which is what I really say on my album.

Blackburn: None of the American groups have dared tackle class yet, even when they shout about revolution.

Lennon: Because they're all middle class, and they don't want to show that they're middle class and they're bourgeois.

Blackburn: They're scared of the workers, actually.

Lennon: Sure they are, because the workers are mainly right-wing in America, clinging onto their goods. But as soon as they realize what their class has done, then it's up to them to repatriate the people. But even during the Beatle heyday, I think it was me mainly and George who insisted—we'd been to America a few times—and [manager Brian] Epstein had always tried to waffle us about talking about Vietnam. So there came a time when George and I said, "Listen, when they ask us next time, we're gonna say we don't like it, we think they should get out." And that's what we did—which was pretty radical for the Fab Four at the time.

Ali: Yeah. It had a phenomenal effect also in the States. It brought up all these right-wing radio commentators who'd been drooling about the Beatles: "They showed their true colors."

Lennon: Yeah, it was the first opportunity which I personally took to wave the flag a bit. I'd always held that repression. But it was so involved and the going was so pressurized that there was hardly any means of expressing yourself at that rate. We were just working continually, touring continually, and always kept in this cocoon. And it's pretty hard, when you are Caesar, and everybody's saying how wonderful you are and giving you all the goodies and all the girls, to break out of that. It's hard to say, "Well, I don't want to be king. I want to be real." And the second big sort of political thing was when I said the Beatles are bigger than Jesus. That really broke the scene. I mean, I nearly got shot in America. That was another big trauma for all the kids following us.

Ali: When did you first start thinking about Vietnam, and did it play any part in accelerating your radicalization?

Lennon: I don't really remember. I just remember that we'd had this unspoken policy of not getting involved by answering any questions. I always read most of the newspapers, whether it was shit or not, and read the political bits. And I think the continual awareness of it, as it grew in me, made me feel ashamed that I wasn't saying anything, and that's when it sort of burst out of that period. Because I couldn't play that game anymore. It just was too much for me, the pressure of shutting up. I had to say something. And it was just a buildup, I think. I can't remember first being aware of that war.

Blackburn: Yeah.

Lennon: It was obvious that I would become more aware of it going to America where it was happening and being approached by underground [press] or whatever it was, although mainly it was capitalist press that saw us. There was always somebody there grinding in some way or other. So . . . I can't remember an exact time.

Blackburn: Could I just return to one point from earlier? You were talking about folk and black music. It seems to me that one of the big problems about folk music is it's sort of depressing. It's sort of [about] losing, whereas black music is about fighting. And I think even in Dylan's best songs, you somehow feel they've had it. Maybe it's because it comes out of struggles that were a long time ago.

Lennon: Most urban blues and things like that were mainly about sex and fighting each other on the street over a woman or something. The field songs were mainly just expressing the pain they were in. That's what I like about it, 'cause they couldn't express themselves intellectually so they had to say in very few words what was happening to them. And it was really self-expression. Because there were many different pockets of blues. Originally it was in the fields, and then as they moved to Chicago and places like that, it developed into city blues. It was still an expression of their own individual pain, not the black man in general, but there was never any solution given. It was always, "God will save us." They were laboring under that problem, that God always pervaded their songs. So I don't think there were any answers given. . . .

Blackburn: You've said you don't think answers can be given.

Lennon: I don't think answers can be given. The first thing one can do is to state your own positions, which is what they did with their songs. And then I think the second thing is to find out who else thinks like you, and then there's a group, which is what's evolving there now. And only just recently have they started singing about the war, the blacks, or any kind of revolution. Apart from people like Nina Simone. But most of the blacks, like [comedian and activist] Dick Gregory said, are still doing the boogaloo.

But there is a big change now, with Edwin Starr [who had a July 1970 hit with the song "War"] and all that making more records and stating black positions and black is beautiful and all the rest of it is a big change; it's only happened in the last two years. So they've come to that point now, where they're expressing themselves completely, solidly, and expressing opinions on the position rather than just saying, "I'm in pain, man." They're saying, "We're in pain, and this is why."

LENNON ON . . .

The Beatles' *White Album*

"Paul was always upset about *The White Album* [*The Beatles*]. He never liked it because on that one I did my music, he did his, and George did his. And first, he didn't like George having so many tracks. He wanted it to be more a group thing, which really means more Paul. So he never liked that album, and I always preferred it to all the other albums, including *Pepper*, because I thought the music was better. The *Pepper* myth is bigger, but the music on *The White Album* is far superior, I think. . . . I like all the stuff I did on that, and the other stuff as well. I like the whole album."

—from interview with Peter McCabe and Robert Schonfeld, New York, September 5, 1971, published in *Penthouse* (US), September 1984

TV INTERVIEW

Dick Cavett | September 8, 1971, ABC Studios, New York |
Broadcast September 11, 1971, *The Dick Cavett Show*, ABC (US)

Lennon and his wife held hands during much of this long and revealing conversation, which took place the day before the release of the ex-Beatle's landmark *Imagine* album, his first chart-topping solo release. Besides the classic title cut, itself a top-three hit, the record includes several sociopolitical diatribes ("I Don't Wanna Be a Soldier Mama I Don't Wanna Die" and "Gimme Some Truth") and a few well-crafted love songs to Ono ("Jealous Guy" and "Oh Yoko"). But the album drew just as much attention for "How Do You Sleep?" a biting attack on Paul McCartney in which Lennon proclaims that "the only thing you done was 'Yesterday'" and "the sound you make is Muzak to my ears."

No such vitriol crops up in this interview. Lennon does have harsh words for a few people, most notably Ono's first husband, Tony Cox, and journalist Betty Rollin. But he is charming and funny throughout and appears to be in an upbeat, playful mood.

"Yoko was quite sweet and cordial, and John and I got on instantly," recalled the show's host, Dick Cavett, in a December 2010 *New York Times* piece. "He was too complex a man to be described in a few adjectives, but one of them would have to be 'accessible.' He was easy and comfortable immediately."

The show was "a smash," Cavett wrote, "getting better as it went along. They were nervous at first, evidenced by their killing half a pack of Viceroys between them in the first few segments, settling down gradually into what proved a delightful and increasingly smoke-free ninety minutes."

This interview—Lennon's first on American TV since the Beatles breakup a year earlier—has not previously appeared in print. —Ed.

Dick Cavett: I guess you all know that John Lennon, together with the three other fellows named McCartney and Harrison and Starr, were responsible for becoming I guess the most written about, most listened to, most imitated musical group of the '60s. And for about eight years they were leaders in the musical world, and not only that but probably affected what a decade of young people looked like and thought about and dreamed of. And they achieved the absolute pinnacles of success. They were even honored by the queen, an honor which they eventually returned, I believe. [*Lennon gave back his MBE medal in 1969, but the other three Beatles kept theirs. —Ed.*]

I'm sure it doesn't come as a surprise to anyone that the Beatles are no longer together. In recent months, John Lennon has sort of surfaced in the underground press, where he gave a long interview in *Rolling Stone* magazine in which he talked with some great deal of candor and some bitterness, I suppose, about the old days. And his wife, Yoko Ono, is maybe one of the most controversial ladies since the Duchess of Windsor, Wallis Simpson, kept the duke from becoming the king. Tonight they are, however, quite aboveground, and I am very pleased to welcome them here. Will you welcome, please, John Ono Lennon and Yoko Ono Lennon?

[*Lennon and Ono come onstage to applause following this introduction, which reflects the fact that Lennon formally changed his middle name from Winston to Ono in April 1969. UK law, however, did not permit dropping of a name given at birth, so he officially became John Winston Ono Lennon.*]

Cavett: How are you?

John Lennon: Nervous but OK, thank you.

Cavett: Are you really?

Lennon: Yes, aren't you?

Cavett: A little bit. But it isn't as if we've never met, because we did meet once.

Lennon: We did meet in a dingy hotel room.

Cavett: So you're Jack Lemmon!

Lennon: Yes, and you're Fred Astaire. Or is it Orson Welles?

Cavett: I am not Fred Astaire. Yoko, how are you?

Yoko Ono: Fine, thank you.

Cavett: Good. OK. Is there anything that you want to know about me to start off with? Just to get the—

Lennon: What do you do for a living?

Cavett: Actually, this is my profession.

Lennon: Oh, he lives here.

Cavett: I practically do. I hardly ever get out of here. The chair collapses into a bed . . .

Lennon: It must be hard.

Cavett: Do you have my kind of show—

Ono: In England?

Cavett: —all over the world?

Lennon: They're not quite as good in England at repartee, you know.

Cavett: Why is this?

Lennon: Well, they're more inhibited, that's all. They don't have any way to sort of freak out a little. Unless Jerry Rubin comes on, you know.

Cavett: Oh, yeah. Rubin came over and disrupted a show done by . . . I can never think of the guy's name . . .

Lennon: Favid Drost. [*A play on David Frost. —Ed.*]

Cavett: Favid Drost.

Lennon: Yeah, it was a very exciting show, actually.

Cavett: What actually happened? He came in and broke up the studio—

Lennon: They broke up the studio, and David [Frost] ended up in the audience to show that he wasn't with the young people, which shows where he's at, really. Nothing personal, David, wherever you are, red light . . .

Cavett: You know, I had a terrible feeling that my hair was going to be longer than yours. It was a funny thing, because I met you the other day . . . the recent pictures I'd seen of both of you . . . yours is extremely long, Yoko, and yours, John, was very long. And, of course, people were going around saying, you know, "I can't tell which one is which" and all. That sort of witticism.

Lennon: Last year I cut mine. We both cut it right off down to about quarter of an inch. In '69 or '70—I can't remember—because I had just suddenly realized it wasn't functional. When I had it down here, you just had to keep washing it and combing it. So then I chopped it all off. Then it just grew a bit, and then I just let it grow to this length.

Cavett: What's your favorite length, Yoko? Are you at it right now?

Ono: Well, it depends. We like change. Don't want to stick to one . . .

Lennon: Same old haircut every day, you know? Have a different one every few months, you know.

Cavett: Did you save the hair?

Lennon: Oh, yeah. One time we cut it, we gave it to Michael Malik [a.k.a. Michael X], who was running a sort of black house in London, which wasn't exactly a Black Panther thing, but I think it was something to do with it. And they were just having a community center in London, and we sort of symbolically gave it to them. They were going to auction it off at wherever you auction hair off, you know. That big place in London. I can't remember the name of it.

Cavett: Sotheby's?

Lennon: Yeah, that's it. It never happened, though, but it was a symbolic gesture, really. Solidarity.

Cavett: That hair today, then, is missing.

Lennon: Gone tomorrow. Silly, isn't it?

Cavett: Yoko, do you have fun when you're over here in this country?

Ono: Oh, yes, very much, because, after all, this is my second hometown.

Lennon: She lived here for ten years.

Cavett: People are surprised. They often say, "She speaks very good English." But you've been here a lot.

Ono: Some people ask me, "Can you speak Japanese?" and then I get very offended because I am Japanese.

Lennon: [*Jokingly.*] Now you've offended her, haven't you?

Cavett: Get me out of this, John.

Lennon: Well, a funny thing happened on the way in tonight . . .

Cavett: It never has to me, not once in my life.

Lennon: Nothing happened whatsoever.

Ono: Tell them about that story whenever they talk to us and they're not listening, and then you start about the elephant.

Lennon: Oh, yeah. I suppose you get it, too, when people meet you, like in a restaurant or anywhere, when you're trying to order something. You find that they're so struck by, "Oh, is it really you?" that they don't really hear your order, you know? So when I'm talking to them, I'm saying, "I'd like a steak medium, and two elephants came, and a policeman bit me head and a cup of tea, please." And they're saying, "Yes, thank you." Because they're not listening, you know? Probably half of them aren't listening now, which is a good thing, I suppose.

Cavett: That's a terrible feeling, to think that they're never listening at all.

Lennon: It's surreal. I don't mind that.

Cavett: Have you ever had elephant actually brought to you by someone who was listening?

Lennon: And a bit the policeman's head off. Quite often, yes. It's an old Anglo custom.

Cavett: I'll believe anything. You like being over here, I gather. I've had some English guests on . . . well, do you think of yourself as English, first of all? Let's establish that.

Lennon: Well, sometimes. If you're talking about being over here or being over there, well, I'm from over there, you know. But I suppose I think in terms of cliques and things like that. Like musicians and/or longhairs and/or under thirty, over thirty, et cetera, et cetera. And being married to a Hawaiian, it makes you sort of international. [*Laughter.*]

Cavett: Must be a mistake in my notes!

Lennon: People think of us—especially in England, not so much here, we get a bit more respect in America as artists—but back home, I think it's the case for all artists . . . back home it's a bit like I'm the man that won the pools and the lucky guy who had a spot of luck and married the Hawaiian actress, which isn't true, really. [*To audience.*] Do you get it? [*Laughter.*]

Ono: I'm from Japan and he's from England, so somehow we found out that we're sort of passionately patriotic sometimes, you know. "Well, no, that's Japanese made," or "No, no, English artists were the first ones to do this."

Lennon: I mean, we invented radar and penicillin, you know. But you find you turn into a hard hat when we start discussing . . . Well, we're both islands, and we're both little, and we both did this, and we both did that, and we find ourselves turning quite fascist discussing it. Made in Hong Kong and all that.

Cavett: And you do jokes with each other, and do you kid her about—

Lennon: Always laughing, Dick. [*Laughter.*]

Cavett: I mean, would you stoop to Pearl Harbor jokes and . . . [*Laughter*]

Lennon: Oh, yeah, I do all that. [*With Japanese accent:*] Speak English! English pig!

Ono: Tell the Kabuki thing.

Lennon: There's a Kabuki theater in Japan. And they have a massive stage, and onstage they have the musicians with them, and all the men play the women's parts, you see. [*Pretends to speak Japanese in alternately high and low voices.*] That's Kabuki. I learned it after only one sitting.

Cavett: It's very good.

Ono: Even Japanese start to laugh when he does that, because really he is Japanese when he does that Kabuki.

Lennon: Only our hip nits will notice how funny it is, actually.

Cavett: There are two of them in Utah breaking up right now.

Lennon: I've seen one on TV with yellow glasses, and he calls himself a hip nit. And he pretended to be Italian in the war, I remember.

Cavett: [*To Ono.*] Is Mr. Lennon putting me on?

Ono: I don't know.

Cavett: ジオン に 面会 したいですが。 [Japanese for "I want to meet John."]

Lennon: *Das sind die drei besten Dinge von die ganze Welt.* [German for "These are the three best things in the whole world."]

Cavett: *Yo hablo un poquito de Español.* [Spanish for "I speak a little Spanish."]

Lennon: *Que pasa?* [Spanish for "What's up?"]

Cavett: We have a brief message of interest from people of various creeds and colors, and we will return.

[*Commercial message.*]

Cavett: There we are. Now that we're through making fun of each other's nationalities and other people's, you were saying . . .

Ono: So John was saying that he discovered that I chain-smoke through this article that he was reading about me. Somebody said I chain-smoke. "Ah, is that what it is now?" And since then he never gets off that one. But I just noticed him light me another one.

Lennon: Smoking will kill us, you see.

Cavett: It does. You're setting a bad example for adults all over the world.

Lennon: Didn't work, Arthur. [*A reference to Arthur Janov, the primal-scream therapist, who'd promised to cure the couple of their addiction to cigarettes. —Ed.*]

Cavett: Does that ever happen to you, that you find out something about the other from something you read rather than—

Lennon: Oh, sure, sure. I began to suspect she chain-smoked, because every time I kissed her I burnt my chin. And then I read it in an article, you see.

Cavett: That's a wonderful delivery you've got.

Lennon: Well, you know, back on the boards.

Cavett: What was I going to say just before that? Do you have any idea? We were talking about articles written about you and all that. I know where I was. Earlier I said you seemed to like it here. Because I've had English guests on, British guests, who've said they come here because they're stifled over there, and they can't work, and they like the exhilaration here. And then I've had American writers who have left America because they feel so menaced and threatened that they like the calm of London.

Lennon: Somebody like [actor] Richard Chamberlain went over there and did very well—going from a soap opera to *Hamlet*. And vice versa. I suppose people have come over here and broadened their scope. I think it's just a matter of you have a different kind of feeling when you're abroad; maybe you can loosen up. In Britain we only have two channels of TV, and if you watch the old British movies on TV now here, it's the same old men always on TV in Britain still. They have a sort of school of actors. There's about three new people got into the profession since I was ten. It's a bit limiting, you know.

Cavett: You do see all the same old faces.

Lennon: The best thing about British TV is the live stuff, like plays and things like that. But it just goes off at twelve. So you have a choice in England of either going out to dinner or watching TV. You can't do both. With America, it's great. You just sort of wake up and it's on, and you get back after going out for an evening and it's still on. It's beautiful. I love it.

Cavett: It's nice if you're sick. You know, when you're sick and you're up all night—

Lennon: I'm always sick; that's why I like it so much. [*Laughter.*] According to something I was reading . . .

Ono: But British TV's all right in a way. They have nice—

Lennon: Well, it's not bad, my dear.

Ono: I'm getting used to it more than Japanese TV, of course. I feel British sometimes that way.

Cavett: Did your accent change slightly when you were in England? I feel British sometimes that way.

Ono: I don't know. People tell me that I have a Liverpool accent now.

Lennon: She used to have an American accent, being educated here in those funny schools.

Cavett: Sarah Lawrence [College].

Lennon: Yeah. Ha! It's a funny place, isn't it?

Cavett: Do you still have friends from Sarah Lawrence that you're in touch with?

Ono: No.

Lennon: Ah, well, there was one, turned out to be a snide. Tell him about that.

Cavett: A snide?

Ono: A classmate of mine. About two years ago. That was when we weren't really that famous that we were together.

Lennon: She did an article on us both since we got to America. [*The article, by Betty Rollin, was the cover story in the March 18, 1969, issue of* Look *magazine. In it, Rollin said, among other things, that Ono "is giving me a pain . . . when she's being silly, she doesn't think it's silly. Her boyfriend has infinitely more humor about what he does . . . Yoko is pushy—ambitious is a nicer word." —Ed.*]

Ono: It was very important for me, actually, because I was introduced to America through that article, and she was a classmate of mine. So I thought, *Oh, that's nice.* So she came, and I thought, *Well, since we are friends, I should cook for her and all that,* and I made a nice lunch for her, and then she wrote that . . . what was it that . . .

Lennon: She said Yoko looked fat, like an old witch, cooking—she was nine months pregnant and just had a miscarriage—and that—

Ono: —I resembled—

Lennon: —resembled [actor] Ernest Borgnine. Well, you can see that she doesn't. And that was this old pal that had sneaked in to see us.

Cavett: You do like Ernest Borgnine?

Lennon: I just want to say, "Betty Rollin's legs!"

Cavett: Was it Betty Rollin wrote the article?

Lennon: Yeah. Good old Betty, old pal of Yoko's. Betty Rollin's legs!

Cavett: Oh.

Lennon: Betty Rollin's legs! OK, I think we can leave that one. Silly to be so bitter, isn't it?

Cavett: Oh, yes, but there's something about her legs? I never noticed anything wrong with her legs when I was married to her. [*Laughter.*]

Lennon: You weren't looking, obviously. She kept on long skirts all the time.

Cavett: I was never—

Lennon: Were you really?

Cavett: No, I wasn't, but she wrote an article recently in which she said I was delicious.

Lennon: Well, maybe she's had a pill or something.

Cavett: But you don't go to reunions at Sarah Lawrence? You were only there about a year then, I gather.

Ono: Three years, actually. But I didn't want to graduate. I was one of those early dropouts. I just felt it was so ridiculous to go another year. I just couldn't stand it. In those days people said, "Well, it's so silly to not graduate," you know.

Cavett: "'Cause you'll never get a job."

Ono: Right, right. I was a bit afraid of that, of course.

Lennon: "You'll never make it." That's what they told me, too.

Cavett: If you didn't finish school.

Lennon: One math master told me, "You're on the road to failure if he carries on this way." [*Laughter.*]

Cavett: Do you ever see your old schoolmates?

Lennon: No, I've seen a few old school friends, not teachers, no. Most of them disliked me except for one or two, so I'm always glad to remind them of their incredible awareness they had. [*Laughter.*]

Cavett: Was there ever a teacher who did inspire you?

Lennon: Yes, there was always one teacher in each school. . . . It would usually be an art teacher or an English language or literature kind of thing. If there was anything to do with writing or art, I was OK at it. Anything to do with science or math, I just couldn't get it in, you know. But most subjects were science or math, because supposedly they don't want artists, you know. Even at art school, they tried to turn me into a teacher. They tried to discourage you from painting. Why not be a teacher, because then you can paint on Sunday? I decided against it.

Cavett: You know, your drawings look a little like James Thurber's.

Lennon: Well, I used to love his stuff when I was a kid.

Cavett: Oh, did you?

Ono: He does look a bit like you.

Lennon: Well, he's older than me so he came first, so I look like him. I used to read that stuff. Three people I was very keen on: Lewis Carroll,

Alice in Wonderland; Thurber; and an English drawer, whatever you call him, called Ronald Searle.

Cavett: Ronald Searle. Well, we get him over here.

Lennon: So when I was about eleven, I was turned on to those three. I think I was about fifteen when I started Thurberizing the drawings.

Cavett: Ah, yes!

Lennon: Ah.

Cavett: That was my imitation of Nigel Bruce, one of your actors. "Oh, really, Holmes." Remember he played Watson in the Sherlock Holmes movies? "Oh, really, Holmes." [*Audience doesn't react.*] It's dynamite, usually.

Lennon: Ella Fitzgerald, dear Watson.

Cavett: That was Ella Fitzgerald?

Lennon: No, no, Ella Fitzgerald, dear Watson. That's a pun on *elementary.*

Cavett: Oh, elementary, my dear Watson. That's right. I get it. [*Lennon laughs.*] That's known as wordplay. Oh, I can play that. Sure.

Lennon: Betty Rollin's legs. Our local stations—

Cavett: We will be rolling further after this message from our local stations.

[*Commercial break.*]

Cavett: We're trying to figure what it is I forgot that I wanted to ask you earlier.

Lennon: I just want to thank them [the Cavett show's orchestra] for playing Paul's tunes to me. It was very nice of you. Wonderful, thank you. I sat in a restaurant in Spain, and the violinist insisted on playing "Yesterday" right in my ear. [*Laughter.*] Then he asked me to sign the violin, and I didn't know what to say. I said, "Well, actually, OK," and I signed it and Yoko signed it. One day he's gonna find out that Paul wrote it.

Cavett: That's better than if they'd played "Wedding Bells Are Breaking Up That Old Gang of Mine."

Lennon: I guess so. I guess so. [*Laughter and applause.*]

Cavett: Maybe I should have saved that for later. Well, let's talk about that for a second because, you know, Yoko, you've even been called the dragon lady who—

Ono: Yes.

Cavett: —the lady who brought the Beatles apart, took them all . . . I have trouble with English . . .

Lennon: If she took them apart, could we please give her credit for all the nice music that George made and Ringo made and Paul made and I've made since they broke up? If she did it . . .

[*Applause.*]

Cavett: That's true.

Ono: It turned out all right, didn't it?

Cavett: Yeah. But you're aware of that? I mean, that the press always saw you as the wedge that was driven in—

Ono: The witch.

Cavett: Drive a wedge in three places. I don't know how many spaces there are between four people, but . . . There are millions of girls who would love to have met, let alone married, any one of the four probably, but certainly a lot of them . . .

Ono: Well, I resent to think of him as one of the four, or any one of the four. Because I just met him as another artist, and I didn't particularly realize that part of it, really.

Cavett: You were a Beatles fan before, or would you say you were a Lennon fan before?

Ono: Neither.

Cavett: Neither. You didn't care for either of them?

Lennon: She didn't really know about us. The only name she knew was *Ringo*, because it means "apple" in Japanese. *Ringo* means "apple."

Cavett: *Ringo* means "apple." Did you know that when you named your company Apple?

Lennon: No, no.

Cavett: Just one of those happy accidents.

Lennon: Just one of those happy apples, yes.

Cavett: Happy applesauce. Right number of syllables. *Ringo*, if you spell it sideways, spells *groin*.

Lennon: Yes. *Starr* backwards is *rrats*.

Cavett: I know. Do you do those things, too? I find that I'm always—

Lennon: When we go on the road in the car, I'm always doing the signposts backwards. Anyway, she didn't split the Beatles, because how could one girl split the Beatles, or one woman? The Beatles were drifting apart on their own, you know.

Cavett: Can you remember when you realized that it was inevitable that you would split up?

Lennon: No. It's like saying, "Did you remember falling in love?" Not quite, no. It just sort of happens.

Cavett: How long was it fun?

Lennon: Well, everything's fun off and on, you know. So I suppose it could have gone on being fun off and on, or it could have got worse, I don't know. It's just that when you grow up . . . we don't want to be the Crazy Gang, which they might know over here, which is British. Or the Marx Brothers, which is sort of being dragged onstage playing "She Loves You" when we've got asthma and tuberculosis when we're fifty, you know. "Here they are again! [*Sings, imitating voice of old person.*] 'Yesterday, all my troubles seemed . . .'"

Cavett: Yeah, that—

Lennon: So a long time ago I said that I didn't want to be singing "She Loves You" when I'm thirty. I said that when I was about twenty-five or something. Which in a roundabout way meant that I wouldn't be doing whatever I was doing then at thirty. Well, I was thirty last October, and that's about when my life changed, really.

Ono: Especially for John, I can say that he's at least overgrown, outgrown, whatever they were in, you know. Because I think it's very difficult for four artists who are so brilliant and talented to be together and do everything together. It's just impossible. Whatever they were doing was almost miraculous, you know, that they were together at all.

Cavett: With all the pressures and everything that they had.

Ono: Yes.

Cavett: I guess . . . *A Hard Day's Night*, everybody thought that was what life really was like for you, and that a man with a handheld camera had managed to capture the essence of Beatle life. And that it was always just flitting about in a lovely, carefree, joyful way. Was it ever like that?

Lennon: It wasn't that carefree ever. It was a lot more pressure. That was a sort of comic-strip version of what actually was going on, you know. The pressure was far heavier than that. And that was written after the author spending about three days with us when we played in London and then in Dublin and then back in London again. He wrote the whole of the film based on our characters. You know, club-hopping Ringo, sharp John, whimsical Paul, and stern George. And all the Beatle character myths were formed from three days watching us, you know. Which was a lot of junk, really.

Cavett: [*To Ono, who is lighting a cigarette.*] Would you like me to get that for you?

Ono: No, thank you. I don't believe in that.

Lennon: Female lib.

Cavett: That's why I hesitated, because I've had my fingers snapped off by ladies on the show that I've tried to light—

Lennon: But you do light men's cigarettes as well sometimes, if you feel like it. If you're feeling gay, you know.

Cavett: I do?

Lennon: Well, one does light any sex's cigarettes. Betty Rollin . . .

Cavett: [*To Ono.*] But I interrupted you.

Ono: What I meant was, as a woman it's such a nuisance to have to wait for somebody.

Cavett: And do you make a point of opening the door for yourself?

Ono: No, I don't make a point of it. When I'm tired it's always very nice if somebody opens it. But at the same time I don't make a point about just waiting. That is silly, too, I think.

Cavett: I think so, too. I think I disrupted something there or I interrupted. You were talking about the impression in the Beatles movie that was a comic-strip version of what your lives were like.

Lennon: Well, that was all I had to say, really. It was a comic-strip version, and it sort of stuck with us . . . and now for a small message from we'll be back. Something like that.

Cavett: He's right about that. We have a station break, and we'll be back.

[*Commercial break.*]

Cavett: Oh, we're back again and . . . Yoko, you work in film?

Ono: Yes. We both do, actually.

Cavett: Both of you. But John said somewhere that you were one of the best unknown artists in the world.

Lennon: The most famous unknown artist in the world. She is, yes.

Cavett: Most famous unknown artist in the world.

Lennon: Because she's been in the so-called avant-garde world of New York for almost fifteen years producing—

Cavett: How many?

Lennon: Fifteen years about. Something like that. She was quite an established artist before she met me. And then once she met me, then she became Mrs. Lennon. And that's when they started calling her "Japanese actress," when in fact she never appeared in any movie up till then, really. Mainly, she'd been directing movies and having gallery shows and theater shows and things like that. Then it got swamped with Mrs. Lennon. But now it's just about turning around people to realizing that she's an artist in her own right. But she's still the most famous unknown artist. [*To Ono.*] Do you want to comment on that?

Ono: That was brought up because of the film that we're going to see?

Cavett: Yeah, we have a piece of a film that you did. It's not . . . maybe the most famous film you did was one called *Bottoms*—

Ono: I think so.

Cavett: —which was in fact a film of bottoms.

Ono: It was called *Number Four*, actually.

Lennon: Three hundred sixty-four bottoms . . . five bottoms, that was it.

Cavett: Three hundred sixty-four or 365?

Lennon: Three hundred sixty-five bottoms, one for each day of the year.

Ono: But it actually didn't contain 365 because I thought, *Well, nobody's gonna really* . . . it's a conceptual number. They couldn't possibly count it.

Cavett: You mean, in some cases the bottoms were the same ones posing as other bottoms?

Ono: No, no.

Lennon: It was about a hundred. You see, the interesting thing about the film is all the bottoms were the intellectual and artist people in London, and the soundtrack of the film is all of them trying to explain and be very uncomfortable while they're taking their trousers off. Some guy saying, "Well, I normally do Shakespeare, you know . . ." And then you see his bottom. It's not cut to each bottom, but the whole screen is just two bottoms, each side of the buttocks walking like that. [*Motions with hands.*] All these comments are they're saying, "Well, I normally do Shakespeare" and "What's it all about?" And "The real philosophy about taking your trousers off." And they're all jabbering on like that.

Ono: They're intellectual, so they just have to sort of rationalize it somehow, so they bring up [Soviet leader Nikita] Khrushchev and [philosopher Jean-Paul] Sartre and everybody before they just take off their pants, and it was really funny. But the point was that I was asking to look for intellectual bottoms.

Cavett: Intellectual bottoms?

Ono: Yes. And they would say, "Well, is this intelligent enough?" or whatever. And when you look at it on the screen, it's just all the same, and that was the point.

Cavett: There's a show here called *New Faces*. What would you call . . . well, never mind. Can we take a look at the piece of film you have?

Lennon: [*To Ono.*] Are you gonna explain about it?

Ono: This is a female-lib film in a quiet sort of way. And it's like a diary. It's about a woman who's naked and who's lying down, and a fly's sort of crawling over her body and gradually becomes four and five flies all crawling over her body, and the message is . . . there's lots of things in it and all sorts of levels of understanding, but it has something to do with a life of a woman who is more like taking it rather than doing it positively. The flies crawling over you and just taking it.

Cavett: Passive woman.

Ono: Mmm.

Cavett: Let's take a look at that. Oh, we'll take a look at that in exactly six seconds, because the film has a certain amount of leader on it.

Lennon: [*Singing.*] Take me away . . .

[*Film clip airs, followed by applause.*]

Cavett: There's more to the movie, of course. That was only—

Lennon: It goes from head right through and back again.

Cavett: Never mind!

Lennon: From head to toe. And you notice the women always giggle. It was shown at the Cannes Film Festival and it got an ovation, believe it or not, but the women always giggle like mad, especially as it's getting higher.

Ono: We stopped just before it was getting very interesting.

Lennon: It was just getting interesting, but of course we're on TV.

Cavett: Yes, this is television, after all.

Lennon: This isn't [New York public television station] Channel 13, is it? [*Laughter.*]

Cavett: I didn't even know you could—

Lennon: Betty Rollin! Aye, aye!

Cavett: When the censor found out the movie was called *The Fly* [*Actually, just* Fly. *—Ed.*], you can't imagine what he thought.

Lennon: *Imagine.*

Cavett: Maybe you can.

Lennon: That's a joke on the album title.

Cavett: You must have done an enormous number of retakes to get the fly to do . . .

Lennon: We had an enormous number of flies. In fact, the credits are almost as long as the film because there are so many people catching flies from the back of dirty New York restaurants and things like that. And then we're catching them in the room. The girl was very good.

Cavett: Who was that?

Lennon: Her name was Virginia Lust.

Cavett: Virginia Lust. L-u-s-t?

Lennon: Yeah, L-u-s-t. Get out of that.

Cavett: Did the movie lead to other roles for her or the fly?

Lennon: Well, after two years of making movies—we made about, say, twelve together and apart—we finally got deals here with people called

Genesis in America and somebody else in Britain, and they'll be going around to all the different colleges. So before our films hadn't really been seen, so nobody really knows that we're filmmakers. We've had them in Cannes Festival; they did all right in there. We had them in the Edinburgh [International Film] Festival. There's a chance they're going in the New York festival. They're definitely going in the San Francisco festival. And they should be, later this year, starting . . . about five of them probably will tour America. So then—

Cavett: So you're serious about film.

Lennon: Oh, sure. Film is . . . well, it's like recording, only with your eyes. You just make it visually, and it's just as interesting. And to combine the both is really interesting.

Cavett: How would you feel about me if I were to ask if *Bottoms* was shown at the Cannes Festival?

Lennon: *Bottoms* wasn't, no.

Cavett: That was a bad joke.

Lennon: That was a joke. [*Feigns laughter.*]

Cavett: Well, that answers my question.

Lennon: Yes, we'll be back after this . . .

Cavett: Will you explain the people in the bags before the evening is out? Not now but before the evening is over.

Lennon: [*To Ono.*] Are you going to tell the story of how you started the bag event?

Ono: Yes, well, that was when some composer was going to visit me from Europe and I didn't really want to meet because I'm basically a very shy person. And then I thought—well, people don't believe me when I say I'm very shy, but we're both, actually—and then I thought, *No, I don't want to meet him*, but then there wasn't anything I can do. So finally he was coming, and it was about an hour before he was coming, and I couldn't do anything about it, so I just out of desperation made a bag. And I was in the bag when he came to visit me.

Cavett: An all-over bag or just over your head?

Lennon and Ono: All over.

Cavett: That's a terrific idea.

Ono: [*Inaudible.*] [He said] "Oh, yes, it's you, is it?" And he was pretty calm about it because he'd heard of my work and all that. So he said, "Oh, is this your musical piece or something?" It was very comfortable, because then I didn't have to be seen. I could see him but—

Lennon: And there's no prejudice if people are in bags. You know, if a black man goes for a job in a bag, if everybody had to go in a bag for a job, there'd be no prejudice, you see. You'd have to judge people on their quality within, you know? And we call it total communication.

We were asked to make a film for Austrian TV, which we did, called *Rape*, which wasn't a rape, but it was called *Rape*. It was a rape by camera, in fact. And when we went to Austria to show it, we did a press conference there in a bag, and it was great because all the press came in, and they never saw us; we were just both in a bag. And they interviewed the bag, and they said, "Is it really you?" and "What are you wearing?" and "Will you sing a song?" And they said, "Why us?" And they said, "What is this?" And I said, "It's total communication!" And they said, "Well, why did you pick on us? We've never *seen* a Beatle!" And it was beautiful, and they said, "Do you realize the Habsburgs lived here?" And we said, "Yeah, so?" And it was a great press conference, and they all had a very serious conversation with a bag, and the next day the headlines in Austria were . . . they show a bag and all the important pressmen all just talking to it. So in the audience we have two friends who are in bags . . .

Cavett: We must take a—

Lennon: We must take a break now, yes.

Cavett: That's right, we will take a break, and we will get to them after that. Stay with us.

[*Commercial break.*]

Cavett: All right, would everyone wearing a bag please step up here, so we could see . . . the two people in the second row? [*Two people covered with bags come to the stage.*] I've never had guests . . . Uh, there we are.

Lennon: [*To woman in bag.*] Turn it down, May. [Pang, Lennon's assistant and, later, his lover.] We can see your legs there. What's going on? You see, if they were going to a job, they'd say, "What are your qualifications?"—

Cavett: How do you do?

Lennon: —and "What color are you?" And "Are you Christian or are you Hebrew?" And "Yeah, you've got the job!"

Cavett: Let us know when you're through voting. [*Laughter.*] You know, I have no idea what sex either of you is, and I assume you do.

Lennon: Well, you see you could go in the bag and make love to one of them and find out.

[*Laughter.*]

Cavett: I would, but this is a very short segment.

[*Laughter.*]

Lennon: Oh, I see, OK. [*To people in bags.*] Do you want to go off again? Why don't you dance off?

Cavett: If we had more time . . . Oh, they're leaving. Wait, wait, one thing. One thing, one thing. You will speak to me? It's funny 'cause I don't know where to look. I don't know if your nose or eyes are here. Are you a lady?

Woman in Bag: Yes, I am.

Cavett: Would you hold where you are for just a moment? Just stay where you are. [*Holds out glass.*] I'm offering you a glass of water.

Woman in Bag: I don't drink water.

Cavett: You don't drink water? [*To Lennon.*] Have I made a social faux pas?

Lennon: No, I think it's all right because you don't know whether she's perspiring or thawing in there, do you? So it's all right. See, we did a talk show in England, and every time the man wanted to talk about Beatles, the interviewer, because I'm fed up talking about them, I asked him to go in a bag, and he did it. And the interviewer, the Dick Cavett in England, he was in the bag all the time. So every time the camera panned to him, the audience broke up, so he could never get the questions out. It was a very good show.

Cavett: [*To woman in bag.*] Thank you for being here. Can you find your way down there?

Lennon: You look very nice there.

Cavett: Yes, you're looking a little pale but very nice.

Lennon: They could be changing film, of course.

Cavett: They could be doing anything in there, for all we know.

Lennon: That's what it's about.

Cavett: We'll be right back after this message.

[*Commercial break.*]

Cavett: For similar reasons that I explained either before or after this— I've forgotten—we can't have you [Ono] sing live for us, but your voice is so unique that I wanted to get it into the show. Could you tell us how and what we're about to hear?

Ono: Well, maybe this voice is something else again, but this is going to be a single, my first single independently. I've had singles before with John, but it was always the B-side.

Cavett: You were always the B-side?

Lennon: Now, she's women's lib, she's got her own first single. I think it's a beautiful song, and it's called "Mrs. Lennon." It'll be out now.

Cavett: It's called "Mrs. Lennon"?

Lennon: It's called "Mrs. Lennon," yes. It's a very nice song.

Cavett: Let's give it a whirl, as they used to say.

Lennon: From her new album, *Fly*, out now. Da-ding. [*Laughter.*]

[*Video of song airs, followed by applause.*]

Cavett: How do you know how to make film, John? Have you studied it at all?

Lennon: Well, no. Yoko is quite adept in filmmaking, and she made quite a few films before I met her. I used to make eight-mil films at home and superimpose and do tricks with it and just play arbitrary records with it. But when I met Yoko, she said, "Well, why don't you do it seriously, you know?" So she sort of helped me develop in that area. And I find it's very similar to recording. Just visual, and it's beautiful to work with.

Cavett: You understand the camera and all how it works, and do you use an American camera?

Ono: He's getting so good now. I find it a bit . . . he's too good for my liking these days almost.

Lennon: She taught me filmmaking, I taught her the rock 'n' roll, so I'm getting worried with these singles coming out, and she's getting worried with my films. So it's pretty good.

Cavett: What kind of camera do you use when you—

Lennon: A reflex, 16 mil.

Cavett: Film fans like to know that.

Ono: We use about three cameras at the same time, to get all the angles covered.

Lennon: I mean, we know what a good picture is. So if you know what a nice picture is, then that's the start, you know.

Cavett: Say . . .

Lennon: Say!

Cavett: Is it true, that rumor, when the four of you were together—

Lennon: Who?

Cavett: You and the other fellows.

Lennon: Oh, yeah.

Cavett: That those concerts, many times the din was so uproarious and all—nobody could hear anything, anyway—that they actually played a tape and that you didn't really play? That was a rumor that was going around.

Lennon: We never didn't ever play. There were some times when your voice was so bad, losing your voice, that you virtually wouldn't be singing at all, but nobody would notice because there would be so much noise going on. You could never hear what we were doing. It just would become a sort of happening. Like Shea Stadium was a happening. You couldn't hear any music at all. And that got boring. That's why we stopped, really.

I reckon now if I went out—not as the Beatles but just Yoko and I went out with a group—then people wouldn't be screaming, you know. Because our records are better now, I think, and more mature. I think the audience would be more mature, too. That's what I'm hoping. I don't want any of that jazz, you know.

Cavett: Somewhere you said you'd like to be forgotten, but now you say you'd like to go out and perform again, so you can't really have both—

Lennon: Well, I can still be forgotten when I'm dead. I don't really care what happens when I'm dead, if that's what you mean.

Cavett: No, I thought you meant now. I thought you meant you'd just like it all to go away and all the publicity you've had.

Lennon: Well, you see with people like me and yourself, if you're in a certain mood and reporters are sort of asking questions which are angled to get an answer that they need to sell their paper and you're in a certain mood, you'll say certain things to them. And then people bring it back five years later: "So you said this, did ya?" But you've forgotten all about it. You've changed your mood, it's a different day, it's a different year, you know, and you're feeling entirely different. So you're always held up to what you've said before. And half the time you don't know what you're talking about when you're talking to reporters.

Cavett: I have that same feeling. I always want to say, "Well, either I said it or I didn't say it, or I said it and didn't mean it. Or any of the above."

Lennon: It's like if everybody's words were recorded as they were saying it, there's lots of things you say that either turn out to be silly or you didn't mean it or it's spur-of-the-moment or you meant it or you had foresight or didn't. And it varies, but when people bring it back, you've forgotten all about it. "I don't know what you're talking about."

Cavett: Which are you doing now?

Lennon: How do you mean?

Cavett: I mean, what you're saying now you actually mean?

Lennon: [*To Ono.*] I don't know what he's talking about. What's he talking about? [*To Cavett.*] What do you mean?

Cavett: Which am I doing? We'll be back after this. Stay where you are.

[*Commercial break.*]

Cavett: I've been reading *Grapefruit*, which is a book that Yoko wrote.

Lennon: It comes out in paperback in two weeks' time. Ha ha ha.

Cavett: It may even be out now in certain areas.

Lennon: Oh, yes, it might be out now.

Cavett: If it isn't, you can reserve your copy. But there are things in here that you suggest people do; it's a book you can take part in, such as getting a bag of light and bringing it down and placing it where your lightbulb would be, and so on, which I find difficult to do, but I like it.

Ono: Well, when you do it you'll find that it's easier than—

Cavett: Easier than I think. [*Laughs.*]

Lennon: It's a book of instructions. Yoko says poetry is adjective and prose is . . . what?

Ono: Well, this is just verbs.

Lennon: What's that story you tell about adjective and nouns?

Ono: This is just verbs.

Lennon: You have to *do* the things in the book. It's a book of instructions, and through doing them you have . . . I don't know; you go through a trip, and you go through an awareness; you have an experience.

Cavett: Let's do one fast.

Lennon: OK. What? Which one?

Ono: That one. Listen to your . . .

Lennon: OK, go on. What do you do?

Cavett: Do you want to use me in any way? Tell me what you're going to do. What do you need, John?

Lennon: Well, we listen to each other. [*Grabs stethoscope.*] One of the original instructions in her book was called "Touch Piece," where everybody in the audience had to touch each other, and that was long before Esalen [the alternative-education center in Big Sur, California] or any of those things where people are supposed to touch each other. In 1960 she did that. I'll have a listen. [*Holds stethoscope to Cavett's forehead.*] I can still hear them laughing through your head, you see. Talk.

Cavett: OK. For some reason I feel I should cough or something. [*Laughter.*] Can you hear anything?

Lennon: Well, it sort of echoes like a cave. [*Laughter.*] Try it, try it. Go on. [*Cavett holds stethoscope to Lennon's forehead, and Lennon alternates two funny voices.*] "Hello, Dick, how are ya?" "All right, how are you?" "Fine, thanks. How's Ricky?" "He's in the kitchen with Mom?" "Where's Mom?" "She's in the house watching [*inaudible*]."

Cavett: I didn't hear a thing.

Ono: Listen to me now. Anywhere.

Cavett: Anywhere I want to listen to you? Are you serious, lady?

Ono: I have no [*inaudible*].

Cavett: Well, let me close my eyes and just . . . [*Holds stethoscope to Ono's shoulder.*]

Ono: Anything happening, Dick?

Cavett: It's on her shoulder, for those with bad focus on their television sets. I can hear the audience. It's very strange.

Ono: I think it's a nice way of communication. Total communication equals peace, you know. You can never have peace unless the whole world would have total communication. This is just a process.

Lennon: There's a piece in her book called "Cut Piece," where . . . most artists when they give you something, they make a painting or a record. Are we gonna go away or something?

Cavett: No, we're gonna take a look at your piece of film. We'll talk about "Cut Piece" in a moment. Tell us about your film.

Lennon: This film is called *Erection*, and it's not what you think, ha ha. [*Laughter.*] I was driving through London once, or any city, and you suddenly notice, if you go away, you come back, suddenly there's a big building there. And I suddenly noticed this hotel starting to get built, and I had this idea to show the whole of the film growing, you see. So I got this guy to take still footage in the same position for one and a half years while they built the building. [*Laughter.*] No, he did it once a week, you know, every Friday from the same place. And the film is like a cartoon where these stills over the one and a half years . . . the hotel just grows up in front of you.

Cavett: That's a good idea.

Lennon: And in the left-hand corner, you won't see it [in the clip to be shown now] but you see a bush going through all the seasons, from summer to winter, the leaves come and go, the snow comes and goes, and gradually, at the end of the film, the whole hotel's there. People are in there, and the lights go out. In the very end, the lights go out gradually in all the bedrooms, and then that's the end. It lasts twenty minutes, and it just goes one frame after the other. You can see how it goes now. And the music is from Yoko's new album, out now.

Cavett: Let's take a look. The movie is called *Erection*.

[*Film clip airs.*]

Cavett: That was a short bit out of the middle of the film. I'd love to see the whole thing. That looks terrific. We have a message from our local stations, and we'll be right back.

[*Commercial break.*]

Cavett: Yoko, do you do exhibits of your work now? Can I see it anywhere? A collection of your stuff?

Ono: Yes, of course. If you want to find out about my work, first if you buy this book, which is coming out now in paperback—

Cavett: Oh, *Grapefruit*. Did I mention this earlier?

Ono: But at the same time, in Syracuse there's an Everson Museum, and I'm going to have the first museum show of mine there. That's in New York. Syracuse.

Cavett: Syracuse, New York, yeah.

Ono: Yes, it's a one-woman show with guest artist John Lennon. A retrospective show of all my pieces for fifteen years or so, and new pieces as well. And that's going to be from October ninth. I set it like that because that's John's birthday, and I thought it was a nice birthday gift.

Cavett: Is that your birthday?

Lennon: Yes, it is. Thirty-one.

Cavett: What does that make you?

Lennon: Thirty-one. Again, there's a whole museum, it's a beautiful museum, meant to be one of the best museum buildings in America, and the whole museum is for Yoko's show. She's gonna show ten years' work up to now, with all-new work. Plus films, plus happenings, and whatever. It's gonna be fantastic. Syracuse, October the ninth and onward. Ta-da!

Cavett: I've been listening to *Imagine*—

Lennon: That's nice.

Cavett: —and "Oh Yoko" is going through my head constantly.

Lennon: That's great.

Cavett: The song. There's something about the . . . I don't know what. It goes through your head sort of like—

Lennon: Like "Three Blind Mice."

Cavett: Like a chewing-gum commercial or something. I don't mean that in a—

Lennon: I know. It's a simple love song, you know.

Ono: It's very Zen.

Cavett: Is it Zen?

Lennon: I don't know. It's a simple love song to me.

Ono: Chewing gum is Zen.

Lennon: Bubblegum, you mean?

Cavett: No, just plain gum, like the Wrigley commercial.

Lennon: Well, I'm glad you like it. I thought, of the album, which they're plugging now, out now, we thought "Jealous Guy" and "Gimme Some Truth" was gonna be the ones. But people seem to like "Imagine" and "Oh Yoko" the best. I did not think they'd like "Oh Yoko." They love it.

Cavett: For complicated reasons you can't sing for us here, one of them being that you think you play the guitar badly, which I find amazing.

Lennon: No, I said I'd have to rehearse a group first. And because we're doing something else, I can't rehearse the group before I come on. I can't just play one off like that without rehearsing. [*Applause.*] However . . .

Cavett: However, through the magic of ingenuity, we will in any case see you do "Imagine."

Lennon: This is a clip from a film we're making showing my new songs from the album and some of Yoko's new songs from her album. And this first clip is the beginning of the film. It'll be slightly changed in the end, but this is roughly how the film starts. Called *Imagine.* On TV, probably this September.

Cavett: And here it is . . .

[*Film clip airs, followed by enthusiastic applause.*]

Cavett: We have a message from our local stations, and we'll be right back.

[*Commercial break.*]

Cavett: Oh, we don't have much time left. Does anyone have any idea how much time we do have? Let me confirm quickly a couple of rumors with you.

Lennon: Yes.

Cavett: One of them . . . Has it ever been settled whether "Lucy in the Sky with Diamonds" was a code for anything?

Lennon: It never was, and nobody believes me. I even saw some famous star—I've forgotten who it was—introducing a Lennon-McCartney show. Ah, it was Mel Tormé, saying about how "Lucy in the Sky with Diamonds" is about LSD. This is the truth: my son came home with a drawing and showed me this strange-looking woman flying around. I said, "What is it?" He said, "It's Lucy in the sky with diamonds." And I thought, *That's beautiful.* I immediately wrote a song about it. The song had gone out, the whole album had been published, and somebody noticed that the letters spelt out *LSD*. And I had no idea about it. And of course after that I was checking all the songs to see what the letters spelt out. They didn't spell out anything, none of the others. And it wasn't about that at all.

Cavett: They could do that. "Eleanor Rigby" stood for *erotic*—

Lennon: There was Henry the horse in a song I wrote called "[Being for the Benefit of] Mr. Kite!" The lyrics, which I got most of off an old poster for an old-fashioned circus from the 1800s, were all about Pablo Fanque's Fair, and the horse was there, and they said Henry the horse was horse [heroin], which I didn't know anything about then.

Ono: And "Happiness Is a Warm Gun."

Lennon: And "Happiness Is a Warm Gun" was another one. Which was banned on the radio. They said it was about shooting up drugs, and there was the front of a gun magazine, which said, HAPPINESS IS A WARM GUN. You know, they're advertising guns. I thought it was so crazy that I made a song out of it.

Cavett: I don't know if you knew Janis Joplin well or Jimi Hendrix or—

Lennon: We didn't meet, but she sent me a birthday tape on my birthday, last birthday. Yoko asked all different people to make a tape for me, and she was one of them, and we got it after she died; it arrived in the post. She was singing "Happy Birthday" to me in the studio.

Cavett: What do you think could be done about drug overdosing in or out of the profession of music?

Lennon: I think the basic thing nobody asked is, "Why do people take drugs of any sort from alcohol to Aspro [aspirin] to hard drugs?" And that question has to be resolved first, before you think, *Well, what can we do for the poor drug addict?* Why do we and you and anybody have to have these accessories to normal living to live? I mean, is there something wrong with society that's making us so pressurized that we cannot live in it without guarding ourselves against it? So it's that basic, the problem.

Ono: Total communication.

Lennon: I think if people were allowed to be a bit more free and express themselves, they wouldn't have to inhibit themselves by taking drugs to not be hurt. People take drugs and drink so they don't feel what's going on around them.

Ono: Total freedom for everybody is our goal, you know. That way, you know, it would be a utopia.

Lennon: People are frightened of freedom. They think, *Freedom, oh, there'll be excesses.* Of course, there would be excess to an extent, and then it would settle down. The way the porno films don't pull so many people in now. It'll level out. And all forms of freedom will be the same as that. If people are allowed to be completely free it will level out, and people will be less inhibited and not be frightened of each other and wouldn't have to take drugs to prevent being hurt by each other.

Cavett: We're almost out of time. Was that your house, by the way, in the film?

Lennon: That's our house, yeah. I just wish to mention that my son visits me every weekend at that house, which is a beautiful home in Ascot [in England] with eighty acres of ground. Yoko's daughter is not allowed to visit us because her ex-husband won't let her see her own daughter. All Yoko wishes is that now and again Kyoko could be brought to that house to spend some time with her mother and with my son, Julian, because it's a beautiful home, and we have eight or ten children living there that belong to the staff.

Cavett: That's wonderful.

Lennon: And we're not allowed to see our daughter, and Yoko's going mad as any mother would, because her daughter's being withheld from her. That's all we have to say about that. But that's the house waiting for her, if you're watching, Kyoko.

Cavett: We must take a message from our locals, and we'll be right back.

[*Commercial break.*]

Cavett: We've come to the end, and there are a lot more things we could talk about. Maybe you can drop back sometime when you're stateside.

Lennon: We'd love to. Maybe next time we'll really perform live for you. I'd like to do it. [*Applause.*]

Cavett: Oh, that would be wonderful. Thank you, John.

Lennon: I'd just like to say we're going on the road next year, John and Yoko and the band that I'm putting together, and we'd like to come and do a live performance wherever we can.

Cavett: We'll have the carpet out. And we're going away right now. Thank you, John. Thank you, Yoko.

TV INTERVIEW

**Dick Cavett | September 8, 1971, ABC Studios, New York |
Broadcast September 24, 1971, *The Dick Cavett Show*, ABC (US)**

Dick Cavett's September 8 interview with Lennon and Ono, which aired September 11, went so well that the show's crew kept the cameras rolling after the host and his guests ran out of time and said good night. Two weeks later, Cavett broadcast more of the original footage, which included the couple's responses to questions from the audience. Like the September 11 broadcast, this material has not previously appeared in print. —Ed.

Dick Cavett [*in intro taped after September 8*]: The other night, I did a show with John Lennon and Yoko Ono. And there's an enormous amount of curiosity about them and anyone who's had that much celebrity and that much press and all of those . . . the various lives that John Lennon has gone through in the last few years. And a lot of people were very curious about Yoko, and we taped the show with them, and it was going so well. And the audience had a lot of questions they wanted to ask them, that I . . . we went on, and there are some other segments, too.

This is one that was not in the show. It's just a segment; it's not the questions I don't believe. But later, John answers some questions about his songwriting and the rumor that Paul was dead and an interview in the *Village Voice* that made him angry. But as we came out of the segment that you won't see into the one that you will now see, I had just been talking to Yoko about the people in black bags. This was an idea that she had. They once gave an interview in black bags and freaked out the press.

"Freaked out" is an expression John doesn't use. I thought that was one of the refreshing things about him. He doesn't use all of those tired old vocabulary words like that. But anyway, here again are John Lennon and Yoko Ono. Or Yoko Ono and John Lennon. Six seconds? Or John Yoko and Ono Lennon. Here they are.

Cavett: Yoko, is there anything that I didn't grasp about the bags?

Yoko Ono: No, no. I was just saying that I stood in Trafalgar Square in London—

Cavett: Mmm-hmm.

Ono: —wearing that bag before I met John, and I was thinking that if everybody wore this bag then it wouldn't be any racial war, things like that. I get obsessive about things like that and think, *Oh, well, I should go in front of [the] White House or something and wear a bag, and if I get shot or something, maybe the whole world will become peaceful.*

John Lennon: Another hair-raising idea is if all the world leaders just before they met took their trousers down for the peace meeting, they might have a peace meeting. Or if all the soldiers before they charge had to take their trousers down, you see, nobody could fight in that situation. [*Laughter.*]

Cavett: You know, I had seriously thought of—before my face was known to a lot of people like it is now—I used to think . . . you know the days you want to go out of the apartment or the house but you don't want to run into anybody or talk to anybody, and I thought of wearing a sack over my head. Just put eyes in it. I don't know why people don't do that. But you can't—I found out it's illegal.

Lennon: To wear a bag?

Ono: Amazing. Why?

Cavett: It's illegal to wear a mask in public, I was told.

Lennon: We've got some great footage in the film—

Ono: I have a mask now.

Cavett: You have a mask now?

Ono: In my mind. [*Smiles.*]

Lennon: We have great footage in our film we're just making with a man in a bag wandering all over London. And most people don't take any notice of him. He's just walking around. That's fantastic, yeah. There's another old bag walking. Some people have made a profession of it. I've seen two sacks doing a comedy show on TV in America. And she [Ono] was doing this in '61. The first bag event was done in '61, and since I've seen people—like, there's a comedy team in America that wears sacks.

Cavett: Appearing in sacks. Yeah. There's times I've been asked to. What was it the man yelled out in the audience in *The Eamonn Andrews Show* in England? I read several clippings in your album called *Wedding* [*Album*]. There were letters to the *London Times* and other papers saying, "Thank God someone in the audience finally yelled out to John Lennon what we've all been wanting to say to him." And then with excellent British reporting, they didn't tell what it was.

Lennon: Oh, I don't know what it was. We went on this show—it was a terrible show. Eamonn Andrews was very nice. . . . We went on, and then suddenly we were doing a peace campaign. And suddenly the audience started shouting all sorts of abuse at us. And we were thinking, *What the . . . what's going on?* You know, it's like now, we're just talking, and suddenly the audience starts shouting, "Get your hair cut!" and "You longhairs, go back to where you came from!" All that kind of jazz.

You know, and they were shouting and [classical violinist and conductor] Yehudi Menuhin was on there. And we're discussing peace, and Yehudi Menuhin goes, "Sometimes it is necessary to kill." It was a really freaky show, and we were horrified, and the audience was sort of calling names. I've forgotten what they were saying. . . . I was speechless. We were terrified. And I thought they were going to come and attack us. "People like you! We fought the war for you!" and all that old jazz. Al Capp crap, you know. [*In an encounter caught by cameras at Lennon and Ono's 1969 bed-in in Montreal, conservative American humorist Al Capp argued intensely with the couple about their political activities. —Ed.*]

Cavett: Was this before or after you had spent your week in bed with all that publicity?

Ono: After.

Lennon: After probably.

Cavett: Because that set a lot of people on edge. I don't know what they thought—

Lennon: The same guy, Eamonn Andrews, after we had done one of the bed events in Amsterdam or Toronto, had us on his show, and he did the show from a bed. So he was nice, you know . . . he thought we were genuine in our demonstration for peace. But a lot of people say, "Well, we don't want you to demonstrate for peace that way. We want you to do it our way." And that's what usually upsets people. But we're individuals, and we like to do things that are more conceptual than anything else. Where the idea is more important than whatever you're doing, or the painting. And that's how we like to do things. So we don't fit into most people's bags.

Cavett: So to speak.

Ono: But no one should fit into anybody else's bag. We should all have our own bags.

Cavett: You know that when you did that week in bed, I don't know if everyone still knows exactly what happened. I'm sure people think that tremendously lurid things took place, and the press was, I think, expecting—

Lennon: Well, the first time we did it, we did it in Amsterdam. You see, we were getting married. We knew we were going to get married. And we knew we were going to get chased by the press. And Yoko had always been doing things for peace. All her work—like she said, she'd been standing in Trafalgar Square—and she had done lots of different things for peace as an individual. And when she married me, I said, "Look, I'm not going to stand in Trafalgar Square, I'll get slaughtered." So she wanted to work for peace. . . . We had to sit around and think of something we could both do together. We were going to get married, and we knew we had just seen Jackie Onassis and, uh . . . whatever . . . Aristotle and that. And all that chasing that they had . . . we're not as big as them, but all that chasing that they had, and they couldn't get away. Even with all those millions, he couldn't get away. So we thought, a) we are going to be chased, so let's invite them around.

Ono: Use this!

Lennon: Let's use this occasion. Instead of just saying, "Oh, whoopee, John and Yoko got married," the front page. What? There's no news in that. Let's use this. We're going to be in the papers, let's use this space, and just say *peace* instead. So what we did was we invited them to our so-called honeymoon. And they all thought we were going to make love in bed.

Ono: Why did they think that, though?

Lennon: And all the press from all around the world came. And they opened the door, and they're fighting to get in, you know, like this with their cameras [*mimes fighting to get in holding cameras*], and then their faces drop when we're sitting like angels, saying, "Hello. Peace, brother." And all their faces dropped, and we were just in bed. And we thought it was a great practical joke that most of the world's headline newspapers, especially the European and British, was, MARRIED COUPLE ARE IN BED. Whoopee. It makes a change.

Cavett: It's a novelty.

Lennon: Yeah.

Ono: But, you know, I really wonder about that. Because we are, actually, a pretty sort of square, nice, old couple. I mean, sort of quiet and all that. How did they ever think of *that*? You know, I mean that we would . . .

Lennon: Because we'd done *Two Virgins*.

Cavett: I can't imagine. I think of you as [dance instructors] Arthur and Kathryn Murray. [*Laughter.*]

Lennon: That's very nice. I think of you and Ozzie and Harriet Clark. [*He clearly meant Ozzie and Harriet Nelson, of the American radio and TV show* The Adventures of Ozzie and Harriet. *—Ed.*]

Cavett: Didn't they get a vice squad out after you? One city, Amsterdam or somewhere, announced that the vice squad was going to close your bed or something.

Lennon: Not for the bed, no. Well, when they heard we were going to do it, they thought it was going to be all that. Because people have such devious minds, they mostly sort of have these strange ideas about our life, which is fairly normal, actually, in an abnormal situation. And so there was talk about that, but of course all we did was talk from bed. All we did was allow the press in, because they're always asking to interview us, and they said they're giving us three minutes. And we just said, "You can have as long as you want. Ask anything you want."

You know, "You always think there's something to hide; well, ask anything." And we said, "We'll give you as much time as you want for seven days," from the time we started it to the time we ended it. And they asked us everything, and we talked to people from Czechoslovakia, reporters from Hungary, and all around the world. And we did a lot of communication with the young people in the East part of the world. People from Russia and everywhere. And we thought that was good to communicate with them, and allow them to ask, even if it's "What did you have for breakfast?" over and over again. We answered everything they wanted to know.

Cavett: Weren't you exhausted at the end?

Lennon: Yeah.

Ono: And we didn't do it for money.

Cavett: Didn't do it for money?

Ono: No. Because Al Capp said we did it for money.

Lennon: No, we didn't make any money on it. We made a documentary of that, which we might get some bread on now because it might go out, but up till now—people said we made money out of our peace events— we're probably quite a few dollars in the red from the peace events, but we don't care 'cause that's what we think we ought to do.

Cavett: Is it possible that you or any of the other three fellows could have financial problems the rest of your life?

Lennon: Well, you can always get unlucky and turn into [actor] Mickey Rooney and have to work for your tax, you know, or [boxer] Joe Louis. There's always that danger. But if your manager's all right, well, you're all right then. Hi, Al. [*A reference to Allen Klein.*] [*Ono waves.*]

Cavett: Do you ever wish it hadn't all happened, John?

Lennon: Well, I don't regret anything in my life, really, because I've met Yoko and I'm very happy with her, and I feel as though if I didn't go through all that I went through, I wouldn't be with Yoko now. So I don't regret the past. I'm always just trying to live for this moment.

You know, I once said I wish I was a fisherman, meaning I wish I didn't have the kind of mind that makes me want to perform in public, whatever, make records, make films, always be working. I wish I was satisfied to just be peaceful. I thought [the life of a] fisherman was so easy. You know, you just get your breakfast out of the water, you eat it, and you go to bed. A simple life. I have a sort of longing for that. I think everybody does. I dream of us being an old couple on the south coast of Ireland or something. "Hey, remember when we were on *Dick Cavett*?" And being a nice old couple like that.

Ono: It's really a miracle that we met, because I come from Tokyo, and he comes from Liverpool and, you know, as he says—

Lennon: Mark Twain was wrong, though. The twain shall meet.

Cavett: The twain met. Now, excuse us.

Lennon: Oh, we will.

[*Commercial break.*]

Cavett [*in intro taped after September 8*]: We then let the audience who was sort of anxious to ask some questions of their own ask John and Yoko some questions, and here is that. Are you ready? Eight seconds? That's a lifetime. First question is, why can't we get into it sooner? Here it is.

Cavett: John and Yoko, Mr. and Mrs. Lennon, I have an idea for a happening. Let's let the audience ask us anything that happens to be on its mind.

Lennon: Well, that's real crazy, Dick. Far out, man!

Cavett: Where's your nerve, baby? Oh, there's already a man in the aisle. How convenient. Yes?

Man in Audience: I'd like to know how you write your songs and how you think your songs have progressed since you first started.

Cavett: The man would like to know how I write my songs . . . [*laughter*] how you write your songs and how the songs have progressed since you first started.

Lennon: In many ways. All the combinations you can think of. Either sitting at the piano and having a word that you write a song around. Or having a word and playing the guitar. Or you have a guitar chord change. Any combination of that. The best ones are usually inspirational, which just sort of come when you're not expecting it, and you just go and write it out almost in full.

The earlier songs . . . in the early days, Paul and I, we wanted to be the [Gerry] Goffin and [Carole] King of England, you know. Goffin and King were very big in those days, and we used to want to be Buddy Holly and Goffin/King, et cetera. And so we wrote pop songs with the kind of mind that that's a pop song, like bubblegum, and that's real life. And I used to write *In His Own Write* and the books I wrote then like [*A*] *Spaniard in the Works* with one half of my brain, and [with] the other half I sort of would churn out pop songs.

And then with the advent of Dylan and a few other interesting people I'd meet or hear about, I suddenly realized I was being silly. I should put all my energy into writing the song, into the lyric. So then I transferred any writing ability I had completely to the songs. And the song lyric got better and the structure of the words got better, and they became as important as the tune then.

And I think the songs are better. . . . I have a lot more experience than I had when I was twenty. I'm older, and it's true you get more experience 'cause there's just more time span, that's all. And so your songs get more experienced. And there is a tendency for them to get a bit . . . you know, like you can rip 'em off easy. But I try not to write songs anymore unless I really want to. You know, I no longer have to . . . "Oh, the Beatles need an album, you and Paul better go and write twenty songs tomorrow" kind of thing. I just write when I feel like, you know.

Cavett: That must be nice.

Lennon: Oh, it's wonderful.

Cavett: This gentleman right here. [*Points.*]

Man in Audience: How have drugs affected your music writing?

Lennon: Drugs have not affected my music writing any more than cornflakes, living in America, not living in America, going on tour, living with four men, living with one woman. The drugs were no more a help or a hindrance to creating—I don't believe in creation but to writing songs—than any other experience I've had in life. None was more important—i.e., drugs are not more important than the environment. I think my environment is more important than any drugs or outside influence that came when I was a teenager. Most of the things I write about are basic things that come from me that I've had all my life.

Cavett: Man on the aisle there.

Man in Audience: Do you listen to much music now? And if you do, what do you listen to?

Cavett: Do you listen to much music now and, if so, what?

Lennon: Well, I think, like most artists, they get less time for listening to other people's music. You can either be an artist or the audience. Audiences are always listening to other people's music. Artists are always creating their own music. I spend more time creating than listening to my own, because that's what I'm involved in. I like people like Yoko, of course. I like [Frank] Zappa and a few people. Dr. John. And I like some of the pop music. I can't think of it offhand. There just are records that come out I like. I'm still a rock 'n' roll fan of early Presley, early Jerry Lee Lewis, and all those people. That's the music I really love is rock 'n' roll. It's great.

Cavett: Does anyone have a question for Yoko or a question you can ask Yoko through John? There's a lady there, or vice versa. Oh, I'm sorry. Yell it out, and I'll repeat it.

Woman in Audience: I want to know how you as a woman feel about overpopulation in the world and its relation to polluting the environment.

Cavett: How does Yoko feel about overpopulation as a woman?

Ono: Well, I think the problem is not overpopulation as people believe it to be, but it's more of the balance of things. You know, like food. Some part of the world is wasted food and some parts, nobody has food. That kind of balance . . . if that is solved, I don't think we'd be worried so much about overpopulation.

Lennon: I think it's a bit of a joke the way people have made this over-population thing into a kind of myth. I don't really believe it, you know. I think whatever happens will balance itself out and work itself out. It's all right for us all living, saying, "Oh, well, there's enough of us, so we won't have any more; don't let anybody else live." I don't believe in that. I think we've got enough food and money to feed everybody, and I think the natural balance, even though old people will last longer, we have enough room for us. And some of them can go to the moon, anyway.

Cavett: You mean, you think there's enough if it were just distributed?

Lennon: Yeah, I don't believe overpopulation. I think that's just a kind of myth that the government has thrown out to keep your mind off Vietnam and Ireland and all the important subjects.

Cavett: Oh, I think you're wrong about that.

Lennon: [*Jokingly.*] Oh, I don't care. [*Laughter.*]

Cavett: [*Pointing.*] Yes, the gentleman there. [*Pretending to be tearful about Lennon's comment.*] He doesn't care!

Man in Audience: It seems that a while back, as people followed you, you were really into peace, not at any cost but just very peaceful—peaceful means of revolution—and I read an article in *Ramparts*, and you're into violent revolution, and now—

Lennon: I'm not.

Man in Audience: Well, that's what it stated.

Lennon: No, the article in *Ramparts* was basically about socialism, right? And I don't believe in violent revolution. Yoko stated it very well, which is violent revolutionaries are playing the same establishment game. I believe in some of the things Jerry Rubin and Abbie Hoffman have done, like the theater-in-court kind of revolution. I believe in the revolution of happening and artists.

Yoko says artists don't create, any woman can create, a man can destroy with a Coke bottle. And an artist revalues. If I'm a revolutionary or we're revolutionaries, we're revolutionary artists, not gunmen. I believe in the Black Panther original statement, the ten-point program, which is not violent, which says to defend yourself against attack. I might consider that. But anything else I don't consider. So I'm still for peace, peaceful revolutionary. But I'm an artist first and a politician second.

Man in Audience: I don't know if the article was wrong or not, but it said you were saying in your song "Revolution" that you wanted to change a few of the words from "count me in" to "count me out" or "count me out" to "count me in."

Lennon: No, I have both versions. "Revolution," there's three versions, number one, number two, and number nine. Number nine's an abstract picture of revolution. Number two is the single because the other boys didn't like number one. They said it wasn't fast enough, so I made it fast, and sometimes I said, "count me in, count me out." The thing I regret was making a reference to Chairman Mao, which might spoil any chances I have of going to visit China, like those Ping-Pong people. I'd love to go and see what's happening there. But I wrote the Chairman Mao line in the studio 'cause I didn't have any words.

What I was trying to say to the Maoists, or anybody that wanted to change the world [was,] "Why go stand in front of a policeman with a red Communist flag in your hand and a big suit and then get hit?" I thought it was unsubtle. So in the song, I wasn't putting down revolution. I was saying, "Isn't that a bit unsubtle?" But if you want to really change the thing, do it subtly in a way that the establishment can't attack—i.e., theater in court and/or bed events, *Two Virgins*, things like that, things that the establishment don't understand. Therefore, they can't kill it.

Man in Audience: Yeah, well, the last part of my question is—

Cavett: Gentleman down here now. Sorry.

Man in Audience: You wrote a letter to the [*Village*] *Voice* in defense of Yoko as an artist—

Lennon: And myself. [*Published August 26, 1971, the letter was a response to a rant by writer Harold Carlton that had appeared in the* Voice *a week earlier under the headline* YOKO NO NO. *—Ed.*]

Man in Audience: Yes. It was a rather strong letter, and I wondered if you've regretted it since, especially in the light of the strong reaction that it has provoked.

Lennon: I don't mind if a few fat liberals got excited about my letter. One of the replies to the letter I wrote was, "It's nice to see how well John and Yoko take to criticism." The letter [that Lennon was responding to] wasn't criticism. It said, a) our films wouldn't be shown unless we were John and Yoko. I said that's a lie. I think our filmmaking stands on its own. That'll be proved by them standing on their own. They've been accepted in many festivals; I don't see why Mr. Carlton can't accept them. He said Yoko was a has-been artist that was no good, anyway. He's never seen her work, read her books, or seen any of our films. And instead of going into an intellectual/liberal load of guff, I just told him to sod off.

Cavett: And did he?

Lennon: Yeah. I hope he did. I don't feel like spending . . . I'm not an intellectual. I'm not articulate. I'm working class, and I use few words. I use the words that the people around me used when I was a child. I talk like that. So if somebody's going to say a lot of [*word deleted by network censor*], I'll say a lot of [*word deleted*]. It's as simple as that.

[*Applause.*]

Cavett: Don't say too much [*words deleted*].

Lennon: Hey, how about if I go [*words deleted*] to insert it? This is to insert [*words deleted*].

[*Laughter.*]

Cavett: I was trying to find someone where we have a microphone. [*Points.*] Yes?

Man in Audience: I was wondering . . . last year we had a big thing about Paul McCartney being dead.

Lennon: Yeah.

Man in Audience: And I was wondering how much of it was planned and how much was planned by you.

Lennon: It had nothing to do with me. [*Laughter.*] There is a rumor that he is dead, actually, but the first I heard about it was in the press, you know, or from . . . I don't know how it happened. It's a mystery to Paul, and it was a mystery to me. None of us knew what it was about or whatever. But of course they credit it to me or Paul, saying it was publicity-seeking and we did it. It was too far out for us to have thought of it, you know, and it wasn't a very . . . I don't know, it was a peculiar thing. I don't know what it was about.

Cavett: Do you and Paul speak?

Lennon: We have spoken. I spoke to him about an hour or so on the phone about three weeks ago. That was the last time we spoke. But I hugged George two days ago, and I sent a postcard to Ringo last week. All right? [*Laughter.*]

Cavett: We have a message . . .

[*Commercial break.*]

Cavett: We're back. You wanted to say something about—

Ono: I just wanted to reply quickly to what John said about artists and all that. You know, artists can offer some sense of humor to life, to relax people, and it would make people less violent and all that. This

Village Voice thing that he wrote, I thought it was beautiful because it was almost like literature. The usage of words and all that was sort of fantastic vocabulary that I could never dream of having, and it's just so beautiful. And if you take it with a sense of humor, it was beautiful. And what American culture offered to the world in the last fifty years or something, I believe, personally, is a sense of humor. People like Andy Warhol, who's a fantastic original, beautiful artist that you have, added something very important to the art world, which is sense of humor.

Cavett: That's right, he did. And a lot of people still don't get the joke. What do you want to know about me? I know that I'm an international enigma and that there are things that—

Lennon: Well, I've heard the first thing babies say now is "Dick Cavett!" when they smack them.

Cavett: That's right.

Lennon: I'd like to know some things about you. Things like . . . when we first met, you brought me that album of Sioux Indian music.

Cavett: Oh, I did, yeah.

Lennon: I'd like to know how interested you are in Indians, and are you interested in the "red revolution"? And power for the red Indian, that kind of thing. Are you interested in what the American people are doing for Indians? That's a big question over in Europe.

Cavett: Yeah, I'm getting more and more interested in that. At first, I was just interested in Indians like a kid at the cowboy movies. That's how it started. And I come from the Midwest, where there are—

Lennon: Real ones.

Cavett: —Indians everywhere. But I used to see some as a kid. And then, I don't know, I guess you just develop a feeling. That's so tragic . . . that whole period of My Lai–like incidents—the Sand Creek Massacre, Custer's wiping out of the Indians at Washita—

Lennon: I just saw something very interesting on . . . what are those Indians down . . . the Incas and those other ones that could write?

Cavett: Aztecs and . . .

Lennon: The Mayans. Somebody on TV was talking about how when the Spanish came, these priests burned for thirty days all the Mayan books, so there was none left. And his reason was, it's either the word of God and we've already got that, so we'll destroy it, and if it isn't, it's the work of the devil. So they destroyed the whole Mayan culture of literature, which was very good and very aware. And there was about three books left, which sort of say, you know, "Got up and went to work," and there's not enough words left for them to work out what the language was.

Cavett: That's right. One man destroyed a whole written culture. Also, the man who led the cavalry against the Indians at the Sand Creek Massacre was a man of the cloth.

Lennon: Oh, yeah.

Cavett: Not that all men of the cloth are—

Lennon: You had an interesting Indian on this show you were telling me about, too.

Cavett: I had a man who was also a great authority on Indians.

Lennon: He was at Custer's Last Stand with him.

Cavett: No, he was a friend of Curley, who was Custer's scout, John Neihardt.

Lennon: [*To audience.*] You didn't know he was an Indian freak, did ya? So what about the red revolution, then? What's gonna happen—

Cavett: You get so frustrated at what was done to the Indians in the past that you feel like you should do something for their descendants now, who are still getting it six ways.

Ono: Terrible.

Lennon: I know, illiterate and not educated and not looked after. I don't know if they're having it worse than black people here, but it's pretty rough for them, isn't it?

Cavett: Yeah, it's very bad, and I think it's good that people have a sense of conscience about it and are doing something about it.

Lennon: Well, they've made so much money out of the Indians. First they took the land and then they made movies about them taking the land, you know. [*Laughter.*] It's a bit mean, you know. But we always used to stick up for the Indians in Britain in the movies.

Cavett: One movie they were making in which they did the Custer battle, which has never been done well on the screen, but anyway, they used the Crows as the ones who attacked Custer. Whereas, actually, the Crows were the scouts for Custer.

Lennon: Oh, I see.

Cavett: And the Sioux who were working on the picture were furious and said, "If it hadn't been for us, there wouldn't have been any Custer battle. You should use the Sioux."

Lennon: It's like Nixon having a Japanese watch, isn't it?

Cavett: Having a what?

Lennon: Japanese watch.

Cavett: Does he have a Japanese watch?

Lennon: He does, yeah. A Spiro Agnew watch.

Cavett: I didn't realize that.

Lennon: But what's happening with the Indians? What are they doing for them?

Cavett: Not enough.

Lennon: Don't they legally really own the land?

Cavett: Interestingly enough, some conservative politicians seem to be more concerned for the Indians than some liberal politicians.

Lennon: Maybe they've realized how many there are in the whole American continent, including the South. People think there's only a few Indians left. There's millions of them in the whole continent of America, which includes South America, and one day they're going to be asking for their rights. I wouldn't be surprised if they were standing next to the black people, too. So it's either give now or die later, I reckon.

Cavett: What else do you want to know about me?

Lennon: I'd like to know where you got your shirt.

Cavett: Where I got my shirt?

Lennon: It's very nice.

Cavett: It is rather nice, isn't it? I was going to ask you the same question.

Lennon: It's very funny. I was in the German airport, and I had an American army mac on, and a guy came up and said, "I've just got out of the army in Vietnam, and if you'd like these clothes, I'd love to give you them." I said, "All right." And he sent me all these army clothes through the post. A few years ago that was.

Ono: May I ask a question? What do you want to be remembered for?

Cavett: What do I want to be remembered for? I don't know. I don't feel that I've done anything yet to be remembered for—with the exception of tonight's program, of course.

Lennon: I've asked this of a lot of people, Dick. What's your definition of love? Ho ho ho. [*Laughter.*]

Cavett: My definition of love is never having to read *Love Story.*

Lennon: Do you know what mine is? You can ask me mine. I'll tell you what mine is: love is having to say you're sorry every five minutes. That guy [*Love Story* author Erich Segal] doesn't know anything about love. He's obviously never been in love, whatever his name is. Fred Segal or something.

LENNON ON...

Being with Yoko Ono

"If you love somebody, you can't be with 'em enough. . . . We don't want to be apart. . . . We can live apart. Part of [primal-scream therapist Arthur] Janov's thing was to separate us for a night or a day or a few hours or whatever it was at various times. . . . It was torture, but we can live without each other, if people want to know that. But we don't want to. It's just too good . . ."

—from interview with Howard Smith, St. Regis Hotel, New York City, September 9, 1971

LENNON ON...

Whether Anyone Could Do What He and Ono Do

"If Fred and Elsie Smith [i.e., an unknown couple] had done the bed-in in Yorkshire, the *Yorkshire Post* would've done it [reported it], and it might've been picked up by the *Daily Mail* or *Mirror*. I'm tellin' you, anybody could've done that bed event. If somebody suddenly appeared who had got married in a bag in the local church, it'd be everywhere! You see things like that. . . . The English are famous eccentrics. I'm just another one from a long line of eccentrics."

—from interview with Michael Watts, published in *Melody Maker*, October 2, 1971

LENNON ON...

Imprisonment

"They've been putting people in prison for a thousand years. It hasn't improved anything. . . . I understand that society hasn't worked out what to do with people who kill and violent people, but there's a lot of people in jail who aren't violent and don't kill, and they're in there for no reason at all. And then they go mad in jail, man. Do you think everybody in jail is really a criminal? They [judges and juries] never make any mistakes?"

—from conversation on *The David Frost Show*, December 16, 1971, syndicated by Group W network (US), aired January 13, 1972

RADIO INTERVIEW

Howard Smith | January 23, 1972, 105 Bank Street (Lennon's home), New York | Broadcast January 23, 1972, WPLJ-FM (New York)

Like the tapes of the 1969 Howard Smith interview that appears earlier in this book, the ones for the conversation that follows sat in a box for four decades. The interview, which has never previously appeared in print, took place on Lennon and Ono's bed in their two-bedroom apartment in Greenwich Village.

As they talk, the couple and their guest munch on snacks and listen to—and comment on—the songs in a Beatlefest radio broadcast on WPLJ-FM, the station that aired Smith's radio show. The conversation also includes much candid talk about the Beatles' early years, primal-scream therapist Arthur Janov, and other topics.

At the time of this discussion, *Imagine* and its title cut had given Lennon major hits, and he and Ono were working on the follow-up, a double album of live and studio recordings that would be called *Some Time in New York City.* —Ed.

John Lennon: Well, look who popped in. [*Laughs.*]

Howard Smith: I just happened to be walking past, right here where you live at [*deliberately mumbles unintelligibly*] Street, and I heard Beatle music coming out of the window.

Yoko Ono: You just caught us!

Lennon: Here we were . . . we were just sitting at home listening to PLJ Beatle '72, and Howard Smith walks in with a tape recorder! So we thought, *Well—*

Ono: I know. Such a miracle!

Lennon: Miracle of modern science. So we said, "Welcome, Howard, and let's get it on a little."

[*Laughter.*]

Smith: What do you think, listening to all of this stuff [on the Beatles special on the radio]?

Lennon: I think it's fantastic. I hear things I hadn't heard for a long time. I get off on a little guitar solo or a lick I've done in the past. "Oh, wow, I didn't know I could play that." Or there's some stuff Yoko hasn't heard which is especially good. I say, "Listen, listen, you've not heard this," because she couldn't possibly have heard all that music. I mean, the Americans got thirty albums out of it; we only made about ten, I think, but somehow there's thirty. And it's fantastic.

Ono: I get very emotional about it, too, because there's some parts that you can see obviously that they're going very well, just beautiful. In other words, it was like under the name Beatles, somehow they all threw in their talents together, you know? And in some cases, it's just blossoming, you know. And for anybody, it's very sad that that's gone. I get emotional about that, too.

Lennon: But they play the new stuff too, so . . .

Ono: Yeah, the new stuff is beautiful, too.

Smith: Were you guys aware back then of the impact each album had on people? Other than commercial success. I don't mean just that, "Wow, a million people bought it" or something. I mean—

Lennon: I don't know . . . no, I don't know whether we were aware of what impact . . . only the fact that so many people would buy it. At that stage, 1963, that would signify to us how much we were liked by how much we sold, you know.

Smith: Yeah, but what I meant was things like—

Lennon: [*Listening to radio.*] That's not Beatle music. What are they playing?

Smith: That's a commercial.

Lennon: Oh, I see. [*Laughs.*]

Ono: Can we hear that commercial?

Lennon: Yeah. There's a level where you can hear it.

Smith: What I meant was . . . I don't know whether you *are* aware of it then, but each time a new album would come out—especially I remember it with the *Sgt. Pepper* album—

Lennon: Oh, by then they began to have some kind of double life or something. People were reading all sorts [of things] into them.

Smith: No, I didn't even mean that. . . . People would sit around, and it would be the latest Beatle album, and there would be a whole room full of people, usually stoned out of their minds and going, "Wow! They did it again! Another fantastic album."

Lennon: People still do that, not only about our music. I mean, I've had friends of mine [who] have done it with the new albums I've made. Friends of ours have done mescaline trips on *Fly* and things like that, you know.

Ono: Yeah.

Lennon: And they get off on the Stones and all the artists that way; they all get together. I think it's still there. It's just, there's so much good stuff out, you'd have to spend all your life locked up in a room listening.

Smith: You told me one time—two years ago when I talked with both of you in Toronto—that you used to sit and stack up all the records, the Beatle records—

Lennon: Oh, yeah. Well, in the early days—

Smith: —in chronological order just to see whether there's been progress made. But I guess you just don't do that anymore.

Lennon: It's just got too many. I know there isn't thirty. I mean, there is thirty if they've got thirty, but I think there are some repeats in there somewhere. But I used to play them, the first four albums, one after the other, just to see the progression musically, and it was interesting. I got up to about *Revolver* and then it got too many probably; or it'd be too much listening time. But you could hear the progression as we learned about recording, as the techniques got refined and everything like that, you could hear it . . . [*Stops talking, listens to "Eleanor Rigby" playing on radio, and starts singing along.*] "The lonely people . . ."

OK, where are we?

Ono: And then I was surprised you just told me that mostly you had about fourteen tracks on a side or something. Does it mean that—

Lennon: Each album in England used to have fourteen tracks a side. [*The UK releases often had fourteen tracks per LP, but Lennon persists in insisting there were fourteen per side. —Ed.*]

Ono: If it's real hot rock or something, you can't put fourteen tracks on a side.

Lennon: You can, because some of the tracks would only be two minutes long, you see. We still would not have more than—

Smith: Fourteen on each *side*?

Lennon: Fourteen tracks. See, when we were kids, we'd end up buying Elvis records ten times in England, and all of them would have the same tracks on them. I know it happened with Beatles in the end as things got out of our control. But in the early days, we were really set on giving people their money's worth off the record, 'cause we'd been up in the sticks there in Liverpool paying overhead prices where we'd get the same "Heartbreak Hotel" and the same album ten times and all that jazz.

And that was our policy at first, just to put fourteen tracks a side that were brand-new and never put singles on the albums, which everybody did, was have a hit single and make an album of it. And that continued for a bit, but then they had to do it different over here because they would only allow us ten tracks a side in America for some reason or other. [*He's misspeaking again; in the United States, Beatles albums typically had ten to twelve tracks total, not ten per side. —Ed.*] That's why each album wasn't the same in America.

Only I prefer the English albums, you know, because that's how we produced them, and we put them in that order specifically and released them in that way. So if you're really going to get into it, it's best to get them English albums. That's the progression, because as they were recorded, naturally they're in that order. [*It is the English versions that ultimately appeared in the United States when Capitol reissued the material on CD. —Ed.*] But over here they got jumbled, and you get one year's work mixed up with the year before. So if you're really getting into that, what is it, chronology, you couldn't do it because it was so messed up here.

Smith: I know that you're into a whole other life and everything like that, as all the Beatles are at this time, but do you miss any of it at all? You know, listening to this music or anything, or any other time—

Lennon: The thing I miss most is just sitting down with the group and playing. And as you know, we've been playing with these Elephants lately, Elephant's Memory, and when we were gigging with them, just rehearsing and playing around, it reminded me of the early days in the Cavern [Club in Liverpool], you know. It was really nice to have a solid group, you know. The fact that they [Elephant's Memory] are a group themselves was nice, and it was really good working with them.

And that's the thing I miss—just working with a group, you know. But with the Beatles it got less group-like when we stopped touring, and then we'd only get together for recordings. So therefore, the recording session was the thing we almost rehearsed in as well. So all the playing was in the recording session. And sometimes it'd be a drag. You know, it's like an athlete—you really have to keep playing all the time to keep your hand in. And we'd be off a month and then we'd suddenly come to the studio, be expected to be spot-on again. It would take a few days getting loosened up and playing together. And so, therefore, the Beatles musically weren't as together in the last years, although we'd learned a lot of technique. We could produce good records, but musically we weren't as together as some of the earlier years. And that's what we all miss.

If you sit down with any of us . . . Yoko's seen us sitting together—George, Ringo, Paul was here last week—anytime we talk about the past at all, it's always pre-making it.

Ono: Right.

Lennon: We always talk about the Cavern and the dance halls in Liverpool, 'cause that's when we were really hot musically. And Hamburg. And we never talk about after that because the music to us stopped existing, live music stopped existing, once we left the dance halls and moved into theaters where you had to do a show that only lasted twenty minutes where up till then we'd been doing an hour or two.

You know, suddenly everything had to be done in twenty minutes. Then in twenty minutes you had to do all your hits. And then you'd do two shows a night, because the theater only held three thousand people. And that started killing the live music. The times we talk about are the times, as I was saying, before we made it, 'cause that's when we were making good live music, you know.

Ono: And whenever they just talk about, "Oh, that's like Cavern" or something, their face really lights up. Even with John, whenever he says, "Oh, this is really like in those days," they never mention about when they were making it.

Lennon: That's like that bootleg you found, the one with the Decca audition and "[I'm Gonna] Sit Right Down and Cry (Over You)." We were still together musically there. You can hear it's primitive, and it isn't recorded that well, but the power's there, and the musicians were together musically on those tracks. And that was more like the stuff we used to do onstage in the dance halls in Hamburg.

Ono: And "Love Me Do"—

Lennon: "Love Me Do" is one of the first ones we wrote ourselves, you know. Paul started writing that when he must have been about fifteen. We finished it up over the years and recorded it. It was the first one we'd sort of dared do of our own. Because we were doing such great numbers of other people.

Smith: Was it a big event? Like you talked about it a lot?

Lennon: To do one of our own numbers? Yeah, yeah. That started later in our life, around Liverpool and Hamburg, when we started introducing our own numbers. It was quite a traumatic thing because we were doing such great numbers, you know, of other people. Ray Charles and [Little] Richard and all them. It was kind of a hard thing to come in and suddenly start singing "Love Me Do." We all thought our numbers were a bit wet, you know. But we gradually broke that down and decided to try 'em.

Smith: This tape, the Decca tape, that you were talking about . . . that was for a Decca audition on January 1, 1962.

Lennon: That they turned us down on. I listened to it. I wouldn't have turned them down on that, not in those days. I think it sounds OK, especially the last part of it. The period it was . . . there wasn't any people playing music like that then.

Smith: Were you guys very disappointed? Do you remember it?

Lennon: Oh, it was terrible, yeah. See, Brian Epstein had come down to London, and then he'd come back and say, "I've got you an audition." We'd all be excited, it was Decca and all that. We met this Mike Smith guy [an A&R assistant for the label], and we're gonna go down. So we went down, we did all those numbers, terrified nervous. You can hear it on that album. It starts off terrified and gradually settles down, and then we went back and waited and waited, and then we just found out they hadn't accepted it. We really felt that was it then.

Smith: What? That that was all—

Lennon: That was the end, yeah.

Ono: You think the sound was too far out for them or something?

Lennon: They always said it's too bluesy or too much like rock 'n' roll, and "That's all over now," they used to be telling us.

Smith: What?

Lennon: The first day I got interested in rock, the first six months, when Presley's "Heartbreak Hotel" came out in England, they were saying rock was gonna die already. "Is calypso gonna take over?" That was what they were talking about then. Even in Hamburg when we auditioned for those German companies, they would tell us to stop playing the rock and the blues and concentrate on the other stuff, you know. 'Cause they all thought rock was dead, but they were wrong. They're still saying rock is dead.

Smith: Did you ever meet the guy who turned you down in later years?

Lennon: I think George and Paul met Dick Rowe, the famous head of Decca [*Actually, an A&R man and producer at the label. —Ed.*] who turned us down.

[*Listening to radio.*] Oh, here's a nice one—"Rain." It's the first time we used backward voice on this track, "Rain." This is a song I wrote about people moaning about the weather all the time. Whatever it is, is OK; it's meant to be. I went home with it about three o'clock in the morning. In those days, we used to take a seven-and-a-half-inch cut of it, take it home, and by the next night arrange what we're gonna put on top of it. Whoever's song it was, was [their] responsibility.

I went home; I was out of my mind stoned. We'd been working till five in the morning. I got home, six in the morning. I stuck the tape on, stuck it on backwards, and I played "Rain," and it came out backwards on the tape, and I had the earphones. I was thinking, *Wow, it's fantastic!* So the next day I went in and said, "Look, let's at the end of the song have the whole song again backwards." We didn't do that, but we just laid my voice track and guitar track over the last half minute backwards. You can hear it at the end. It sounds like I'm singing Indian or something.

Ono: Who thought of that?

Lennon: Well, me. It was an accident because I was out of me skull and I put the tape on backwards.

Ono: That's beautiful.

Smith: How did it go with Paul? You said that you saw him. That must have been the first time in a long time.

Lennon: Was it the first time in a long time? Yeah, I've been talking to him on the phone a lot, so I guess I forget that I don't see him. It was fine, you know. We just talked mainly about business, 'cause we both want to get it all over, you know.

Ono: They were very close to each other. You know that thing they always say, something about snide remarks about Paul and Linda. Paul and Linda seem to be very close to each other, and it seems like it's going fine. They're really sort of family people, you know?

Lennon: They just basically want what we want, you know. How to do it was always the problem. Well, I really don't want to go on about it because we decided not to go on about it in public anymore, the two of us, because it was giving the media too much fun. The media makes the most out of an argument and then starts attacking you for arguing in public.

Smith: *I* wouldn't do that . . .

Lennon: No, I know *you* wouldn't. You're not the *media*, Howard . . .

Smith: But about the thing you said to Paul when I tapped your phone when he was here . . .

Lennon: Anyway, so Paul and I decided and Linda and Yoko decided to call it a day on that jazz.

Ono: But there was never an argument between Linda and I. Many people wanted to make it that Linda and I were really scratching each other. But you know it's not that at all, because I felt such a rapport with Linda in a sense that it's very tough to be a wife of a Beatle. It is. I have that sympathy for all the Beatle wives. So there was never an argument between us. In fact, when there were sessions and all that, we were two girls who were sort of waiting around and talking quite a lot and friendly. It's just that when Allen Klein came in, that's the only time that she expressed her dissatisfaction, that she wasn't very happy about that. And she told me that. But that's the only time when we got a bit like that, you know, because of that.

Smith: But it was never a great big battle, you mean?

Ono: No, never.

Lennon: There was never actually many big battles. There was arguments, but they were mainly the lawyer kind of battles or things in the press . . . statements made. The lawyers all try and get the best out of you to make an attack in court. Most of the real heavy stuff came out in the court cases, you know. It's like a divorce. You might make a decision to divorce your wife amicably between the two of you, but once you both get your own lawyer and they say, "Well, don't talk to anybody unless . . . don't talk to him or her unless I'm here," and then you get into that position of you can't talk unless the lawyer's there, and then you get into that position of making your statements. And then you read their statements through their lawyers. "He couldn't say this" . . . "What the hell?" . . . "Who said that?" . . . "That's not true!" And you start saying your side of it, and it builds and builds and builds. Enough of that, folks, as I chew my sour ball.

Ono: I mean, especially between John and Paul, because they're so close to each other, I'm sure in the past ten years they'd be sort of nagging at each other, whatever, you know, every day. And also cheering together, that kind of thing. Any couple would go through swearing at each other to kissing and hugging.

Smith: Love/hate.

Lennon: It is a strange thing, though, for four men to stay together, because the world would like four men to stay together—

Ono: [*Laughs.*] I know!

Lennon: —in blissful youthfulness, always shaking their heads and being the Fab Four. And never having any women in the scene. Very strange: the world wants four fags to go on together forever.

Ono: Very male chauvinist—

Smith: Well, that's what the suggestion would be by now if that's actually what had happened. You'd be attacked for other things.

Lennon: Believe me, people'd have been a lot happier if the Beatles had just gone on disintegrating like the Marx Brothers for a hundred years. No offense to the Marx Brothers, but people would really like us to give that happy Fab Four image. I've said it many times: anybody who wants that can make Beatle tapes out of the individual albums. It's a cinch.

Ono: And even with Paul, the fact that he's now with Linda, and they're sort of doing things together and all that, shows a tremendous growth, you know, and advancement from the time that they were just sort of four brothers, you know. Because as people, the fact that he's starting to care about a woman is very beautiful. And I'm sure the female-liberation movement and all that would be glad of it. But as a whole, the society still likes the idea of four men in the front, and let the wives just suffer in the background, and forget about them, and they just sort of have a nasty he-he-he nice feeling about the fact that the women aren't there. That bit. And that's so silly.

Smith: You took a lot of the resentment for a long time. I don't think that's over yet completely. You know—that you were the one that broke up the Beatles. I still hear that from people all the time.

Ono: When you're accused so much, you start to believe. "Is that true?" Though it's not really true at all. I mean, you couldn't move four men, so determined four young men, into something so—

Lennon: A musical breakup had already started long before the women came into it, you know, and it was inevitable. Let's get on to something—

Smith: But I'm just curious . . . it's all over? I mean, there's no doubt? You know, everybody after listening to Beatles music all day . . . there's still going to be that question: "Oh, if they ever would play again . . ."

Lennon: But it probably wouldn't work. I mean, you have to go through a lot of changes to fit into a foursome, you know, to be a quartet.

Smith: You mean there've been no discussions about that? Even to get together for one last record?

Lennon: What would be the point? There's no reason to. There's just no reason on earth for us to do it.

Ono: And people don't be happy about the fact that there's a human development, you know, that's involved in this process of change. I mean, they don't see that side at all.

Smith: No, they want it frozen back there.

Ono: Right, right.

Smith: I feel a lot of times that way, also. It's like, well, why can't you all just go back for a while . . .

Lennon: People want us to live their dream for them. I mean, it's odd enough that people are living vicariously through stars as it is, but never mind wanting them to remain in limbo in effervescent youth forever, bubbling and singing.

Smith: A recording studio filled with formaldehyde.

Lennon: Yeah, occasionally letting the cameras in to see that we're all right, you know. [*Starts singing along with Paul McCartney song on radio.*] Maybe I'm amazed, da-do, dao-do.

Ono: And also—

Lennon: Can we drop it?

Ono: No, we're not going into that.

Lennon: Oh, I see.

Ono: I think the message that was the strongest was the feeling of it's OK. There's something about old Beatles songs that would say to you, "It's OK, let's be as we are and we're OK."

Lennon: Everything's gon' be all right.

Ono: Yeah, everything's gonna be all right, and that was the strong message. And I think that should still go on because, yes, it's gonna be all right. But at the same time, I think all of the Beatles on their own, they're starting to see the side that's not OK, and they're starting to bring that out.

Lennon: They were playing "All You Need Is Love" earlier on. I was saying to Yoko, I still believe all you need is love. But I don't believe that just saying it is gonna do it. I still believe in the fact that love is what we all need, that makes us all so desperate, frenetic, or neurotic, et cetera, et cetera. But I still believe there's many ways of getting to that situation. There's a lot of changes in society to come before we can ever get to a state of even realizing that love is what we need, you know? But I still believe in it. And I've read cracks about, "Oh, the Beatles sang 'All you need is love,' but it didn't work for them," you know. But nothing will ever break the love we have for each other, and I still believe all you need is love.

Smith: It worked for a long time—

Lennon: I don't have to live with three guys to prove that love is the basic necessity of all of us.

Ono: And George is bringing out this Bangladesh thing—

Lennon: We wouldn't have had Bangladesh, which is the most fantastic thing, [if the Beatles had stayed together]. And they're blowing that movie up to 70 mil., apparently. And it's gonna earn millions and millions for those people. It's fantastic. And George is virtually an ambassador in the world now. And I think it's fantastic. And he's gonna go to India and Bangladesh and see where the money goes. He's following it through. He's taken on a great responsibility, and he's doing it because he's on his own and he's found what he wants to do. And I think it's fantastic.

Smith: He especially couldn't have grown like he did, right, because he was definitely below you and Paul—

Lennon: I think there would have come a point where he . . . I mean, his songs were getting so much better. And he was demanding his rights. I mean, the reason why the Beatles made a double *White Album* [*The Beatles*], not *Pepper* again, is because George had so much material, John had so much material, Paul did, and even Ringo had material. And we made a double album 'cause it was gonna be a double album forever. *Abbey Road* was like a freak, you know; it was an effort at trying to produce something that we used to produce. The fact is it was already disintegrating on *The White Album*, because there was so much material.

And either we would have had to make double albums every time or Paul and I would have had to say, "Well, OK, we're only gonna have two songs an album each," and that wouldn't have been fun for Paul and I, so it had to break, it had to go somewhere else.

Ono: Well, George one day, remember, said that he wanted to call it quits long before—

Lennon: Who was the first one? George was the first one to quit, or was it Ringo that time?

Ono: No, no, Ringo was the second. George was the first.

Lennon: Anyway, George and Ringo quit a long time before I did.

Smith: That's interesting. Most people assume—

Ono: George said, "Well, look, I want to quit because I have friends outside of the Beatles," you know. Musical friends.

Lennon: And Ringo came a few months later and said, "I want to quit because I feel as though I'm no longer necessary in this group. And nobody knows what they're doing." [*Hears song on radio.*] Oh, this song, I've forgotten what it's called. I wrote it. "Not a Second Time" was one of those ones that was written [about] by [critic] Thomas [*actually William —Ed.*] Mann in the [*New York*] *Times* with the Aeolian cadences—I still don't know what it means—at the end. The chords at the end are like Mahler's *Fifth Symphony*. All that jazz. To me, I was writing a Smokey Robinson or something at the time. But it had Aeolian cadences, and all that jazz started after that.

Ono: Amazing. Individually now, the Beatles, instead of just saying "It's OK," are starting to point out the troubles in the world. Like George sings "Bangladesh" and Paul is doing something about . . . not the weather but what is it? The pollution, you know. Everybody's starting to bring out the problems, and that's beautiful, I think. It's healthy.

Lennon: When you're on your own, you have to face up to the reality of the world on your own or within your family group, and it looks a lot different when you're on your own.

Smith: This thing with Elephant's Memory—

Lennon: Oh, yeah.

Smith: What have you been doing? Rehearsing with them and playing with them in a recording studio?

Lennon: No, we haven't been in a studio yet. We've just been playing with them, and we did a few Mike Douglas shows with them, believe it or not. And that's how we started.

Smith: *The Lawrence Welk Show* is next.

Lennon: Well, we're gonna build up slowly to Lawrence Welk, finally ending up in the sermonette at about five o'clock in the morning if we really make it big. But we've been playing with them, and they're very compatible and very aware, and they play nice rock, you know, and it's just very nice to perform with them.

It was so hard when I was sort of thinking in terms of Klaus [Voormann], who lives in England, and Nicky Hopkins, like he's living half in L.A. and half in the South of France. It was so hard every time we wanted to do a quick gig somewhere to get these big artists to come across. I had to exactly know when we were gonna play and all that. It was getting to be sort of a problem. And then, say, Klaus, if I want to record, well, maybe George is recording at the same time; he'll have a split loyalty there. And Nicky had the same problem with the Stones, 'cause he's committed a lot to them. It was just getting such a hassle for me and for both of us to say . . .

You know, somebody invited us to do a charity gig fifty miles outside of New York. I have to contact half the world to do it, or stand up and do it acoustic, which I was doing. And it was a great trauma for me to do that. I haven't done it since I was fifteen, but it's a funny feeling when there ain't no bass and drums coming and backing you, and you're out there on your own.

So then we bumped into Elephant's Memory. We're having a trial marriage, as it were. We're gonna see how we get on together and how it fits. We don't want to envelop them so they become invisible, you know. You might have read somewhere I said, well, maybe we could have a relationship like Dylan and the Band, except it'd be John and Yoko and the band. [*Turns up radio.*] Oh, this is a great one! They never play this. "Happiness Is a Warm Gun."

Ono: Oh, I love it. I love it. I remember the day that he was making it. This was when we were in Kenwood. You were making this song in Kenwood.

Lennon: Oh, yeah. [*Listening.*] This is the bit I like.

Ono: Yeah.

Lennon: They said this is about drugs, and it wasn't. [*Sings.*] "Shoot, shoot!"

Smith: I was positive it was about drugs. This was the one that I was convinced was about drugs.

Lennon: Nobody believes me about that.

Ono: I didn't even notice it, and then later—

Smith: That was the one that everybody said it was most clear. There was just no doubt it was a drug song.

Lennon: It's just camp, you know. I thought this song covered the whole gamut of rock 'n' roll in a way, the different phases.

Ono: Collage—it was a collage.

Lennon: Anyway, "Happiness Is a Warm Gun," as I've said many, many times, was from the cover of a gun magazine, which [producer] George Martin had in the studio when we were making the double album. And it had HAPPINESS IS A WARM GUN on the cover, and on the cover it had a picture of a gun that had just been shot. It was smoking, you know. And I thought, *How incredible that happiness is a warm gun that has just shot something or somebody.* And that's why I wrote the song.

The first half, which goes [*sings*] "she's not a girl who misses much" was something I was writing vaguely connected with Yoko just when I was first meeting her, and these were all just segments of songs and I wove them all together, different songs, stuck them all in one piece and made like a little miniature—

Ono: Collage it was.

Lennon: Collage. Instead of an album collage like *Pepper*, this was all done in the one song. And it went through the different styles of rock, and it also was about a gun, not about heroin or anything. In those days, I had no idea about heroin. I'd never seen it, knew anybody that ever touched it or taken it.

Smith: Well, we're out of tape on this reel. This is Howard Smith. We'll be back with John and Yoko just in a few seconds.

Lennon: Well, here we are in the Marinal hotel in Upper Berkeley Barkside in East Lower Hampshire Fifty-eight Thirty-nine.

Ono: You were saying Mother Superior—

Lennon: Mother Superior was you. She was rabbiting on in the car one day, as is her wont, and I was saying, "Oh, Mother Superior jumped the gun again." She's always one jump ahead. So that was about Yoko, really, that little segment. And they're all separate songs. I was telling you that.

Ono: I really liked it because I didn't realize that they can do things like that. They do that in classic songs, you know. Instead of thinking of A-B-A, music form, sometimes they do collage things, you know. Not in Beethoven period, but later, much later, they started the collage things. And I didn't see that in pop, and then he started this Mother Superior thing with "Happiness Is a Warm Gun." It's a whole collage. That was very beautiful.

Lennon: I don't think it's the first time we'd done it. But it was definitely a collage. And it was camp—that bit at the end: "Shoot, shoot, bang, bang!" Like the guy was saying, instead of "shoop shoop, doo wah doo wah," the fact that it was about a gun . . . we said "shoot, shoot" and "bang, bang" instead. And we were cracking up when I was doing all that. [*Sings.*] "When I hold you in my arms . . ." All that bit. Very funny. So you're gonna ask me that one, right?

Smith: Did you get annoyed when people were reading things in—

Lennon: I didn't mind people reading things in, and we would stick little bits and pieces in. "That'll get 'em. Let them work that one out."

Smith: Oh, you *did* do that!

Lennon: Yeah, bits in between tracks. . . . I mean, we never thought it would evolve into sort of the Mansons. [*A reference to cult leader Charles Manson, who claimed to be influenced by "Happiness Is a Warm Gun" and other songs on* The White Album. *—Ed.*] We had no idea it would go that far.

Smith: But you didn't start it. You mean the people started reading it in, and then you started putting things in?

Lennon: Well, you see, in the early days we used to hear like in the end of Elvis's "[Baby] Let's Play House," Elvis is laughing. He cracks up a little: "Whew, ba-by, ba-by," and he just laughs a little. Obviously having a good session. He was cracking up at his own style. And you'd hear little things in "Hound Dog" at the very end: "You ain't nothing but a hound dog," he said over the riff. Things that you weren't sure were on at one period. So it was going on long before Beatles. So then we liked to put in little things that would faze people as well, the way we'd been fazed by a lot of early rock records, partly because we didn't know what they were talking about or partly because tape echo was making these crazy noises, you know.

[*Hears song on radio.*] "Strawberry Fields [Forever]." That was the first one Yoko ever heard of the Beatles.

Ono: And it was so funny. I was in sort of a cocktail party that was given by an art critic, you know, and then he said, "Listen to this," and he just put that on. And I said, "Can you imagine pop songs coming to this? What do you think . . . the world's come to this, pop singers start doing this?" I thought, *Wow!* And that's why even now, I get emotional when I hear this one. That's the first Beatles song that I've heard.

Lennon: Have you ever noticed on this track, "Strawberry Fields," that the voice changes completely in tone about the second verse? 'Cause it's two separate takes stuck together. Sometimes when I had a song I really loved like "Strawberry Fields," we'd try so hard with it that we'd ruin it. We did many versions—it was a real hard one to record—and the first half is one take and the second half is another take, but they were both in different keys, different rhythm; we tuned different. [*The Beatles recorded twenty-six takes of the song. —Ed.*] So we had to slow the second-half track to match the first half. So I start off singing in me own voice, whatever the first words are—la-la-la-la—and then suddenly the second verse. [*Sings in slowed voice.*] The voice is slowed down a bit: "but it's all right." It's not my voice.

Ono: It sounds sensational, because in the end you have this weird thing that goes on like funny music coming back and all that . . . it sounds like an electronic thing.

Lennon: It wasn't electronic. It was a mellotron. It was a machine that some guy in Britain invented. They have them over here now under different trade name. And he had tape loops of jazz bands and trumpets and flutes and rhythm sections on it, and I used that a lot on this track. [*Listens.*] That's George's Indian instrument.

Ono: That's another thing John and I this morning were sort of talking about before you came. It's almost like this big karma. You know, like George's relationship with India and all that. And then John mentioned it's so funny that the film that they made first has an Indian joke in it.

Lennon: The first time we were aware of anything Indian in a way was . . . we were making the *Help!* film. Remember there was a card thing about an Indian, like an Eastern sect that had the ring and the sacrifice and all that? And on the set in one place, in a restaurant, they had these sitars and things, meant to be the Indian band playing in the background. And George was looking at them. We recorded that bit in London, in a restaurant.

And then we're in the Bahamas, filming that section of it, and this little yoga [yogi] runs over to us. We didn't know what they were in those days. This little Indian guy comes legging over and gives us a book he'd signed to us on yoga. And we didn't look at it. We just stuck it along with all the other things people had given us. And then about two years later, George had started getting into that yoga. And from looking at the instruments on the set, and they were all sort of out of tune and everything, that's how he got involved in Indian music. All from that crazy movie.

Ono: Isn't that interesting?

Lennon: And then years later, he met the guy that gave us that book, this [yogi] guy. I've forgotten what his name was, because they all have Baram Baram Badulla Bram, all that jazz. But whoever he was, we met him years later, or George met him, and all that Indian involvement came out of that film *Help!* And here he is taking fifteen million dollars to Bangladesh shortly, I guess.

Smith: Yeah, as you said, that's karma of some kind. [*Laughs.*]

Lennon: That's a real trip.

Ono: It's a weird thing. And then they went into that maharishi thing and all. And at that time, I don't know if this has anything to do with karma, but I went to this Indian guy in London who does a palm reading and all that, and he was saying, "Oh, it's all very well that the maharishi got the Beatles." They were just sort of talking about another Indian behind the back, you know. And then he read my palm and said, "Oh, you've just met somebody that is going to change your life, and you're sort of like a wind that's going on and—"

Lennon: Who is this?

Ono: You know, the palm reader.

Lennon: Oh, that one in London. I know that story.

Ono: "Just sort of change your life, you know, and it's gonna . . . the life that you're gonna go into in this next four years is gonna be something that you never dreamt of. It's a complete different kind of life. And very few people have lived that kind of life" and all that. So I was scared, you know. So he said, "No, it's gonna be good, so don't worry." And then he said that "you've just met somebody who's like a big mountain, and you're like a wind, which is going around the world very fast, you know. But now, because you've met this person who's like a mountain, he's going to not stop you but make a connection with you and the world. Not the wind that's going faster and faster but—"

Smith: Had you met John already?

Ono: Yes, I did, but I didn't know that [person the palm reader meant] was John, because I didn't think that meeting was anything connected there.

Lennon: That was the first meeting in the gallery, after that.

Ono: And then he said, "Also, this mountain is going to make you become physical so that you would be visible to the world, because you're like a wind that's going fast and you're invisible almost."

Lennon: Well, if I didn't believe in magic, I'd say there was something funny going on.

Ono: Right!

Lennon: But I don't believe in that jazz no more.

Ono: No. But we did talk about isn't it strange about the karma and all that in the morning in the bed. It's a weird thing, and that's all.

Lennon: That's all, folks.

Smith: I remember that press conference that you and Paul— [*Voice on TV says, "I'm gonna find out who did it."*]

Lennon: Oh, good. He's gonna find out who did it.

Smith: The TV set. I should describe what we're doing. [*Laughs.*] I'm sitting and talking with John and Yoko on their bed.

Lennon: This bed that we inherited from the previous owner and used to be a . . . made out of church pews.

Smith: Oh, I see.

Lennon: Isn't that fascinating? So we're in a very holy bed here. And the three of us are on the bed. All dressed, of course. *The Saint*'s on, on Channel 5. The green staircase, as described in the *New Yorker,* has now been painted white.

Ono: We were gonna paint all white, anyway.

Lennon: Everywhere we have in England and here is white, but we hadn't painted it by then. It still needs a coat of paint. They have to do it in between us getting off this bed and running off—

Ono: And we have three skylights.

Smith: Three skylights. And this is a very nice block here on [*slurs word*] Street.

Lennon: Wonderful, yes.

Ono: It's like a quiet village, really quiet. Like in a quaint village or something. And the three skylights give us enough light so that during the day it has a feeling of under the water, you know, that lighting, talking under the water.

Smith: You've been spending a lot of time in New York.

Lennon: Yes, we have, Howard.

Smith: This is your eighth year here now.

Lennon: Yeah, something like that, yeah, yeah. We're just passing through, you know. [*Laughs.*]

Smith: Are you gonna eventually make America your home?

Lennon: I don't know, you know.

Ono: We'd like to stay here. We like living here.

Lennon: We'd really like to be able to come and go without any problems, and we do love America. And there's been many reasons why we've had to stay here. . . . Yoko and her child was one of the main reasons we had to be here, all these court cases. And also because we love the place, you know. And we can't really say anything about it, because we don't know what's going on. We don't know where Kyoko [Ono's daughter] is. [Ono's ex-husband] Tony [Cox] and Kyoko ran off somewhere.

Smith: Again?

Lennon: Again, from Texas. But still we have to go back—

Smith: That means he'll have to go to jail unless—

Lennon: I think they put him in for two days, and he was released on bail, and then he didn't come back. Anyway, he ran off, and we still have to go down to Texas and finish off the court case and all. Things like that. So we really don't know what we're doing, actually.

Ono: It's sad.

Lennon: So we really do like being here, and we wish we were here under happier circumstances. Meanwhile, we're grooving on being here, of course, 'cause it's a great place to be.

Smith: Is the main difference between living in England and here one of energy levels? Is it like you're more charged here?

Lennon: Oh, yes, definitely. Because we were brought up on the same Americana you lot were. We were brought up on Coca-Cola and Doris Day too, in Liverpool. And we were like the fifty-ninth [sic] state. I mean, America runs our economy, and our prime ministers used to hustle over here to see if they were allowed to do anything, you know. And all that jazz, and that still goes on. Now they've joined Europe, and good luck to 'em. So I've forgotten what I was saying, anyway. [Referring to TV:] There's The Saint again.

Smith: About the difference . . .

Lennon: Yeah, the difference is that it's like going back in the past, going to England. It's much slower. It's going back to Europe. England is in Europe. And if you want to rest and that, it isn't swinging. It's very quiet, you know. And there's not much happening there, and it is all happening in America. It's a different energy level. It's like going back a few decades, going back there. And that's no detriment to it. It just happens to be a few decades behind, you know. And therefore, it's more interesting to be here, where things are . . . you know, this is what's happening now.

Ono: Also, going back, it just came to my mind, so I don't see how we could go back there, I think. It's about John Lennon/Plastic Ono Band and Imagine, you know. That difference . . . it's so difficult how people receive things. The thing is, John Lennon/Plastic Ono Band—that is really a masterpiece, a real masterpiece.

Lennon: The "Working Class Hero" album.

Ono: Right, right, the "Working Class Hero." And then the other one, which is *Imagine*. Obviously *Imagine* was more popular, because it has a little sort of sugarcoat on it, as John puts it. You see, the Beatles' popularity was . . . the main thing was they were just saying, "OK, OK," to people. "It's gonna be OK." And then suddenly John comes out with this *Plastic Ono* album, "Working Class Hero" and whatnot, "God" and all that, saying, "It's *not* OK—there are these problems."

Obviously, that makes him less popular because people don't want to know about that. People want somebody to always tell them it's OK. And so maybe George Harrison, John, all of them, now pointing out these problems, it's gonna be a little bit less popular or whatever, I don't know. But it shouldn't be if the world gets more mature. They should understand that that's more important somehow.

Smith: That album [*John Lennon/Plastic Ono Band*] was written right in the middle of the whole Janov thing, right?

Lennon: A lot of it was. A couple of tracks, which one would suppose were written under therapy, like "Look at Me," were written about a year before therapy and things like that.

Smith: You were getting ready to go into therapy.

Lennon: Yeah, it sounds like it. But the theme was the same, you know: "Look at me," "Who am I?" all that jazz. So that's why I stuck it on that album, but actually it had come from beforehand.

Smith: How do you both feel about Janov at this point? Do you see him at all?

Lennon: No, we don't see him. We can manage on our own now. We learnt whatever we had to learn from them, and we're doing OK.

Ono: It was very educational. The first time when I saw the book, when I said, "Oh, wow, it's so interesting, let's read it." It said *Primal Scream*. Because the scream thing was my thing, you know; I was screaming before that. And so I read it, and it was very interesting. We both got very excited over it. I think the book is very beautiful. I think the practice of it is a bit difficult. The book itself is much more enlightening. And now people tell me that I'm screaming because of the primal scream.

Lennon: That's a bit of a drag. Every time she does her usual performance, they say Yoko is doing a primal scream. But that's life, I guess. I think Little Richard was doing his primal scream as well in 1950.

Smith: Do you both feel that in your own personal growth that's been going on—obviously, I'm pretty sure both of you feel that you're constantly changing—

Lennon: Well, if we aren't—all of us—we'd better give up.

Smith: All right, but do you feel you're going to need some other form of outside help to continue the growth at all, or just the two of you bouncing off each other will—

Lennon: We're always going to need other people, whether—

Smith: I don't just mean "other people." I mean, like a Janov, like the maharishi was at one point.

Lennon: I think we're past those kind of trips. I would never know what we're gonna do. I mean, when we do go into something, we really go into it.

Ono: We both do.

Lennon: I think the main thing with Janov . . . see, Janov was a lot of Freud, too. Janov, I saw him on TV saying that if people had understood Freud, his primal therapy would have been developed a long time ago. And there's a lot of truth in that. See, some of the claims they were making I just can't agree with, because I was in there and it didn't happen to me, you know. I don't want to go into specifics. Other things . . . it was worth it for me, because it did help me a lot to go through my past childhood, you know, and delve into it and find out what made me tick. And what the hell? [*Apparently looks at TV.*] *The Saint's* still on, "Day in the Life"'s playing and all that.

Ono: [Wilhelm] Reich has done a lot of things that . . . I've seen this film recently with John . . .

Smith: *W.R.: Mysteries of the Organism.*

Lennon: Oh, yeah, that. That looked a lot similar, actually, but you couldn't really tell, because they were writhing about on the floor, screaming and all that.

Smith: It's such a pastiche. I hear the movie, it hasn't done that well in this country . . . it's one of the *huge* successes in England right now.

Ono: Oh, really?

Smith: Lines around the blocks. It's one of *the* successes right now.

Lennon: They probably all want to cry and have a scream, really. When you're attracted to that stuff, they want to get in on it.

Ono: That's true, yeah.

Smith: England isn't very psychoanalytically oriented, I understand. People just don't go into analysis.

Lennon: Very suspicious of psychiatrists. Janov . . . if it hadn't been for his book, I would never have touched a psychiatrist. The fact was that in his book it came across that his psychiatry wasn't like anybody else's, because I always thought most psychiatrists need a psychiatrist. I don't believe anybody else can tell you how you are.

Ono: Mmm.

Lennon: And one thing about their therapy is they never told you how you were. You had to tell them. That was the difference. Whereas most psychiatrists, you lie there telling them how you are. I mean, what's the point of that? It's all . . . what's that word? Semantics?

Ono: Symptomatic.

Lennon: Symptomatic. People talk about their symptoms in most psychiatry, and I think the English are right to be suspicious of that. It's all right to talk if you're lonely, but you pay a lot of money to talk to a psychiatrist over twenty years. I think Janov used to be one of those psychiatrists at one time, so he knew about it. People'd come in and talk and talk and talk for twenty years, you know. And never make any impression on the inside of them.

Ono: Well, you see, *symptomatic* means the doctor will tell you, "Well, you are this way and that way." But you *know* that. You want to know how you can cure it.

Smith: I personally feel, from having had lots of friends in analysis and everything like that, one of the big failures of analysis is getting it off of the theory part, off of the talking part. It's much harder to make a change in yourself, much easier to understand it, to just go on forever understanding all the nooks and crannies.

Lennon: There's a point in yourself beyond talking, and that's where Janov's thing was more advanced than the others. That's why I still would say—

Smith: It is Reichian. That's what he was about. He believed that you had to get with it.

Lennon: I don't think any old psychiatrist can help you, and I don't think . . . you know, I think it's up to the individual, et cetera. But with the Janov thing, you have to do it yourself. It was really a self-done thing. He showed you how to get in there because there were some leads from Freud and things like that.

Ono: But many people who are disappointed that they can't be actually treated by Janov, because there are too many people wanting to be treated by Janov, and they get a no answer from Janov . . . they should know that if they read the book thoroughly, that's about it in a way. They can probably do it themselves.

Lennon: Some of them can do it themselves. But it's not that easy.

Ono: Because when they get together, there is that side of telling each other, "Oh, you are crazy." "No, I am not." "Well, you're crazier." They go into all that. And that side of it was not particularly helpful. Then again they became symptomatic, telling each other that.

Smith: How about in Japan? Is there a lot of analysis over there?

Ono: No, no, Japan is like England. There's not very much of that. And I think it was a natural growth on John's part.

Lennon: It had to happen in America.

Ono: John was the first one, practically the first one, who was really interested in psychoanalysis in England.

Lennon: [*Inaudible.*]

Ono: That's what I was saying.

Smith: But it isn't common like in this country; especially in New York, almost everybody you meet is either in it, is about to start analysis, or has gone through one.

Lennon: Well, I think America's more neurotic than anywhere else. Just a little more. Most places are very neurotic.

Ono: I wouldn't say that, but I would say that they're more *aware* of being neurotic.

Lennon: Yeah. Whatever it is, it's more here, good or bad.

Ono: That's another thing that's very good because it's almost like living in a symbolic city here. You get everything—

Smith: More than Tokyo? Because I've never been in Tokyo.

Ono: Exactly, exactly. More than Tokyo.

Smith: More even than Tokyo? From a distance that to me looks like it would even be more than New York.

Ono: Not really, no. I think this place is more concentrated. And it's very interesting. We both have that side of . . . we are sort of an exaggerated something, and we fit into this exaggerated city. That's why we're very comfortable here. Especially like having TV twenty-four hours a day.

Lennon: Suits me fine. Suits me fine.

Smith: What are your favorite programs?

Lennon: The psychiatrist on about three o'clock in the afternoon, that's a wonderful one. No, what do I like? I like the movies. I still like the talk shows, although I'm beginning to spot that everybody's the same on each show. I have a horror that one day I'm gonna have seen every movie in America, and I'll have to go to some other country. [*Laughs.*]

I just like TV, you know. To me it replaced the fireplace when I was a child. They took the fire away, and they put a TV in instead, and I got hooked on it. Yoko was an intellectual, and she thought TV was something you didn't bother with.

Ono: [*Laughs.*] Right.

Lennon: I've met a lot of people like that. But TV is what everybody in the world watches, and TV is what everyone talks about [the] next day at work. And if you want to know what everybody, twenty million Americans, are talking about or twenty million Britons are talking about on Saturday night, it's what they saw on Friday night on TV.

Smith: I'm not sure I want to know. [*Laughs.*]

Lennon: Well, it's nice to know what other people are thinking. And also TV is a window on the world. Whatever it is, that's that image of ourselves that we're portraying.

Ono: And if you're thinking that don't exactly explain to you . . . instead of looking at TV as events, even if you look at it as abstract pictures—

Lennon: It's surreal pictures without sound on.

Ono: The complexity of it is incredible. So you can observe TV on many levels actually, many different levels.

Lennon: I was a great one as a kid for standing and just looking out of windows for hours and hours and hours. The TV does that for me, except the view changes immensely. One minute it's *The Saint*, the next minute it's a rocket in Vietnam, and it's very surreal. I leave it on whether I have the sound on or not.

Ono: And the next minute you're in India. We don't have to go to India anymore. You don't have to go anywhere.

Lennon: It's like [author and counterculture figure] Paul Krassner said: "All I ask in life is a waterbed, a TV, and a typewriter." Well, I'll just have an ordinary bed, a TV, and a guitar. Apart from Yoko.

Smith: He used to watch more TV than anybody I knew, Paul. He used to sit in his contoured chair in front of it.

Lennon: Well, Paul and Jerry and John are in the runnings for the square eyes.

Ono: Paul Krassner and Jerry Rubin, right.

Lennon: Thank you for translating. Keep America warm.

Ono: And also these days, because this is John's influence definitely, and I do start to see that side, so I'm ordering all Japanese weekly magazines, which is supposed to be nonintellectual, and intellectual Japanese would not even dream of reading them. It's just sort of about what's happening among the people in Japan, nothing intellectual. And I order all of them and read all of them, which is fine. It's like looking at Japanese TV at the same time, you know.

Smith: How about the different shows that both of you have been on? Do you have any more that you're gonna do? I mean, are you really gonna be on *The Lawrence Welk Show*?

Lennon: Well, we believe in communication. I don't know about Lawrence Welk, but when you understand that *Mike Douglas Show* has the biggest audience on TV—

Ono: Supposedly, yeah.

Lennon: —I want to know what's going on there, and I want to investigate it and see it and try and communicate with some of those people that are watching, you know. And that's why we did it, and you'll see the shows, and some of them are political and rather heavy for a *Mike Douglas Show* and some of them aren't. And we're just trying something, you know. And whether it comes off or not, we'll see.

Ono: See, we still believe in love and peace definitely. And I know that it sounds very corny and simple—a sweeping statement—but still it's true: we have to have love and peace. [*Listening to radio.*] What is that one?

Lennon: [*Sings.*] "The same old song." Another Christmas record.

Ono: And I have to always fight with the movement people, the avant-garde. The avant-garde, what they were mainly up to was to alienate people with their art. And I was in the avant-garde. I was always trying to communicate rather than to alienate, and that's why I was an outcast there. They didn't like the way I was doing things 'cause it was too communicative or whatever. And now we meet these movement people in the political field. They have the same snobbery as the avant-garde artists. They want to alienate people, you know, and they believe in that.

Smith: You mean elitism?

Ono: Yeah, elitism. Also, when they go on TV, instead of trying to communicate with the housewives—because they basically despise the housewives—they try to alienate housewives, you know, by making them angry. Like saying, "Well, look, you better know what's happening," and all that. But we don't believe in that. We believe in really reaching a hand and not saying, "Well, it's only the very young who's all right and the rest of them are no good." But to say, "No, no, even if you're forty, fifty, and you're not with it, it's fine. Let's try to communicate and understand each other."

Smith: I see. Before you go on these TV shows, are you put through any changes just before you go on? Do they ever take you on the side and say, "Don't talk about drugs" or "Don't do this," or do they pretty much leave you alone?

Lennon: Let's say there's been a lot of things happening, and let's finish all the shows first before we talk about 'em.

Ono: It's been very exciting.

Lennon: It's been a very thrilling time doing these shows, and we have learned a lot.

Smith: Maybe someday you'll have your own *Sonny and Cher* [*Comedy*] *Hour.*

Lennon: It'd be nice if John and Yoko became the Sonny and Cher of the left. And if anybody wants to offer us a show, we're certainly willing to run it, you know.

Ono: Yes, yes, because we have to communicate, too.

Smith: Instead of *Laugh-In*, you could call it *Bed-In*.

Ono: Right. [*Laughter.*] Exactly. And the movement people, they could never really communicate, because as long as they have that attitude about, oh, the whole world is wrong and they're the only ones who are right . . . in a way, they're right, but we have to somehow try to change the situation by understanding the other side too, you know.

Smith: We're going to take another break while we change the tape right at this point. We'll be back with more John and Yoko in a moment.

Lennon: They talk about over here—I even heard George puttin' down American TV— they talk about how British TV is great. Well, let me tell ya. It's only great inasmuch as we do get some good plays on it, because it's still primitive, and we still have live shows. But this *Great American Dream Machine* that they have on [New York–area public television station] Channel 13 is as good as, if not better than, anything that's on British TV, including *Monty Python's Flying Circus*, which is not as heavy as the *Dream Machine*. And the way this Channel 13 is developing . . . I know there's a lot of fors and against it, but I'd rather have it than not have it. It's really good, and it has a freedom that the BBC doesn't have.

Smith: There's a lot of trouble with the BBC now. Have you heard?

Lennon: I don't know, but that's where they have it over BBC here. There's so much going on in Britain of censoring the news of what's going on in Ireland. It's incredible.

Smith: Exactly. That's what the trouble is there now. There's a whole inside guerrilla group at the BBC now trying to outfox the hierarchy.

Lennon: I know. I mean, they're so determined to whitewash the British people about what's going on in Ireland that it's disgusting.

Ono: Jumping subject again—

Lennon: As usual.

Ono: That Janov thing . . . one thing I want to say is the whole thing is they want to act out madness in order to become sane, in order to become not mad. And that's what I was doing and I was saying in exactly those words, you know, explaining about my *Grapefruit* before I met Janov. All the instructions in *Grapefruit* was about that—it was acting out madness in order to stop becoming insane, you know. So in the art world—

Lennon: The only trouble with Janov is he's a chauvinist—

Ono: And he just couldn't take it.

Smith: A male chauvinist?

Lennon: Right.

Ono: He didn't want to admit it. And when he found out that I was doing that, and he didn't want to even listen to it—

Lennon: He'd deny it to us. He'd say we were sick to say it, but he is. And the straightest person in the Janov camp actually is his wife.

Ono: Right.

Smith: Is she a therapist?

Lennon: Yeah, yeah.

Ono: Yes, she's a therapist. And she's a beautiful woman. She's just marvelous, but she's in the shadow of Janov now.

Lennon: She's in the shadow, but she's a very important part of that therapy, and she's the most . . . I mean, he knows he's balmy, but she's the most sane there in the camp.

Ono: He says, "I know I'm crazier than Vivian" and all that, but it's true. So that's what sort of freaked me out, the fact that he couldn't take me straight, you know, and admit about those things as well. So you see it's very important, actually, to act out madness in order to stop becoming insane.

Lennon: I think people do it unconsciously, anyway. I think anybody that's onstage in a way is acting out madness in front of the whole public. If you think of the public as one big sort of parent that you want to make love you. And you go up onstage or you're on the radio here and you're really . . . what you're really doing is saying, "Please love me, please love me, please love me." And all the people out there say, "Yes we will, yes we will, yes we will."

Smith: Well, I'm constantly amazed that experienced performers still go through that. Because I was with you up in the light booth at the Fillmore the night that you played, and you went through all kinds of changes. "I don't know . . . you go, Yoko." "I don't know . . . you go."

Lennon: Listen, Howard, it's all right for you bandless wonders with your microphone—

Smith: I was very surprised. I would have just—

Lennon: —sittin' in little black boxes up talking in the dark . . . radio's the easiest one, you know. You can do it in your undies in bed, right?

Smith: That's the way I always do it.

Lennon: But I had the choice of going up there with a band I'd never played with before to do a number I'd never sung since the Cavern.

Smith: All I'm saying is this was an eye-opener. I'm not saying, "Oh, I would have just walked through it."

Lennon: It's terrifying. That's why I've decided to get a band, so I don't have to go through that torture every time.

Smith: And Leon Russell, who looks like he could do it in a snap, right? He looks like he never shows anything—

Lennon: Don't believe it, don't believe it.

Smith: I asked him, what does he go through just before he goes on?

Lennon: Hell.

Smith: And he said his insides bleed. And I said, "Does anybody know that?" And he said, "I wish they did, because then they'd leave me alone just before I go on."

Lennon: If people knew what it was like to go onstage . . . it makes you wonder why we do it. One period, 'cause I was really going into it in therapy, [I thought,] *Why am I up there?* You know, *What am I doing up there performing like an animal?*

Ono: It's therapeutic to go up there, though.

Lennon: You put yourself in front of the public, and it's like the Roman theater. You put your hands in their lives [*sic*], whether you live or die, you know. It's a very sort of masochistic scene to stand up there day after day, offering yourself as a target for their love or their hate, depending on how good you are or how they feel that night. And it's very peculiar. At one point, I was thinking I would never do it again. I really thought, when I began to see what it meant that I would be up there like a performing flea, *Why should I be up there like a performing flea? Get somebody else to do it.* But now I'm doing it 'cause I want to do it.

Ono: And you're actually acting out madness. In the therapy, there was one guy who stood up and started to bang his head on the wall. I was watching that, and I said, "Oh, that is my piece." In *Grapefruit*, it says, "Bang your head against the wall."

Lennon: She says, "This is my piece!" I said, "This is my therapy; I'm going through changes." She said, "No, on page twenty-eight in *Grapefruit*, I said . . ." [I said,] "Listen, get out o' here." [*Laughs.*]

Ono: But really, it's a fantastic, strange way of exposing yourself. You go on a stage and you act out madness in front of two thousand witnesses. That's what it is. It's just therapeutic; it's to become sane. That's what they're all doing.

Smith: There was an analyst—I can't remember his name. He had a thing where if he had a patient that was very paranoid and would say, "I know there are people looking in my window at night," this therapist would hire people to look in the guy's window.

Lennon: Oh, that's balmy. [*Laughter.*] Maybe good, I don't know.

Smith: He felt that you should go all the way, completely, with every fantasy.

Lennon: Well, that's nice. I don't know.

Ono: All the therapists are like that; I mean, that's what it's about, probably, to expose yourself.

Smith: Yeah, to see how bad it can really be and that it isn't so terrible and you'll come back. That's kind of what it is.

Lennon: The Janov therapy's like that, but you go into your own head with your own . . . you do it in your head rather than . . .

Ono: Yeah, but you do it in front of the group therapy.

Lennon: Oh, yeah, I guess so.

Ono: I mean, it is a big group therapy when you are right on the stage and there's two thousand people watching you.

Lennon: [*Hears the Beatles' "I'll Cry Instead" on radio and turns it up.*] They left this out of *Hard Day's Night*. [Director] Dick Lester didn't like it. [*Talks over parts of song.*] I'll cry instead . . . couldn't get laid . . . gettin' me own back on me mother.

Can we go away from therapy, too? Isn't there something nice we can talk about?

Ono: We can go away from everything.

Smith: How about your new albums? You have new albums you're working on?

Lennon: No, not really. It's so complicated. We've got all this live material from the Lyceum Ballroom [in London], from Frank Zappa's ballroom, and now from Ann Arbor [Michigan], and maybe I'll release all that. We had remixed it and got it all ready to release, and then we did the Ann Arbor and then we did the Apollo [Theater in New York], and we've got all this live bits and pieces. I don't know what to do with it. But we want to go in the studio shortly, if we can, and sweat a few tracks out with Elephant's [Memory].

Ono: There are a few political songs that we made recently, several, so maybe we can make an album out of—

Smith: "John Sinclair"—

Lennon: Maybe we'll do "Attica State" electric and make an electric version of it. I don't know, it's just a matter of going into the studio. We have a few songs to do, that's for sure.

Smith: How about movies? Any new movies coming up? Events? Anything?

Lennon: Well, we're still stuck with *Imagine*, which we've been showing to a few, what is it called, film version of *Imagine* that we made. But they don't seem to understand it, the TV people. "It's nice, but . . ." So it looks like we'll have to send it out just on the road in theaters. [*Listening to radio.*] What?

Smith: That's a commercial.

Lennon: Is it?

Ono: I see. Even the commercials are trying to imitate—

Lennon: People are talking about Beatles music. The commercial music on TV they use for the back of ads is as good as *Revolver*, it sounds like to me. When you make a decision about the kind of music you're gonna make and you listen to what they're making on adverts, which is pretty competent, technical, produced pop mulch bubblegum, you have to decide you're gonna sing about something real when you hear that. Because they're doing it as well as anybody, you know. Selling soft soap and Tricky Dicky [Nixon] and the rest of it.

Smith: Did people attempt to get you guys to do commercials?

Lennon: There were offers many times for different things, like maybe Coke and things like that, but Beatles . . . we never wanted to associate ourselves with one product. We all thought it was a bit demeaning, you know.

Smith: I've been disappointed seeing Johnny Cash lately. Have you seen him doing all those commercials?

Lennon: I'm never surprised at any of it. There's so many people . . . suddenly somebody's in because they did this and that. Now they're out because they did that. I'm trying to keep out of that, for or against it.

Ono: We do commercials for certain organizations, like the fact that we go to some rally or Apple—

Smith: Peace is a commodity, I remember you telling me that.

Ono: Right, peace is a commodity.

Lennon: They took it off our hands and bombed the TV with peace and love ads. You know by the time it's on TV it's really been the rounds.

Smith: But do you still see peace as a commodity?

Lennon: I don't know, I don't—

Smith: I know, early in the interview now you said that you know it's a little more complicated—

Lennon: I think you can sell an idea still to people.

Smith: Like they're saying the war is over—

Lennon: They're selling the idea that the war in Vietnam is over when it's bigger than ever now. And so they're not dying, so many Americans. But millions of Laotians and Cambodians and Vietcong are dying. And the air war is bigger than ever. But they're selling us through the media the fact that the war is over. And it ain't over. It's bigger than it ever was. And that's a commercial we have to keep pushing. The fact that Nixon has not ended the war, and it's bigger than ever, and we have to tell people that. Because people really begin to think it is over. And it ain't.

Ono: We're promoting peace from a different angle by putting a spotlight on all the things that have been done that's not peaceful. And also, I really think that a politician is an entertainer—an entertainer in the sense that he does communicate all the things that's happening.

Smith: We have too many entertainer politicians.

Ono: When they say TV is entertainment or TV is communication . . . but if a politician goes on a TV and says something, is that communicating or not? It should [communicate], just on a level of entertainment.

Lennon: I heard there's a clique of superstars took over New York. There's word going around—

Ono: Right.

Lennon: Have you heard that one? About a clique of superstars. There's a clique of superstars sittin' on this bed.

Smith: Jerry Rubin is—

Lennon: And New York is divided into pro–John and Yoko camp and anti–John and Yoko camp. All the rumors we heard—

Ono: Have you heard that one?

Smith: Oh, yeah. There's a lot of people who go around very mad that you've had an impact on New York. Things like that.

Lennon: What do they want us to do?

Ono: We're not trying—

Smith: I believe that when you get to a certain point of fame like you both are and have been for some time, that you're damned if you do and you're damned if you don't. If you didn't do anything, then people would be saying, "Oh, they just sit around," you know. And then if you do too much, you're trying to take over.

Lennon: When the Beatles didn't communicate with anybody for about a year, people were complaining that we were elitists and we wouldn't speak to anybody. And then I sort of changed. We're literally doing in New York and America what we do in England, you know. We get involved in certain things, and we do a couple of shows, or something will happen like that. It's all just happening naturally. And people will come up to me and say, "Why don't you be cool, like Dylan, and don't say anything and hide away?" Now what happened to Dylan? They start attacking him for hiding away, and they attack him if he says anything, and with us it's the same. If we do something, they attack us, and if we don't do something, they attack us. And it's just a joke, really.

Smith: I think it's one of the prices you pay for your fame, that's all. It's part of the—

Lennon: Yeah, I guess so. I'm sure it happens to everybody to a degree. It makes us laugh, this clique business.

Ono: At least we're using our name not to plug Coca-Cola, but we're trying to plug something that's useful to people, you know.

Smith: But you've become very tight with Jerry Rubin, and from what I can figure out, he believes much more in the demonstration, you know, the action . . .

Ono: He's changing, too. I think even on a strategy level, he thinks, tactically at this point, it's not wise to use violence. I don't think he's for violence in that sense. I think he thinks that we have to somehow change the world at this point with peaceful methods.

Lennon: We can't speak for Jerry, really.

Ono: Yeah, but that's what he was saying—

Lennon: Because we know of him as an individual. I mean, we know of him about different things but just as a guy to hang about with. He's good fun, you know. And we'll probably be friends with him for a long, long time regardless of whatever political differences or togethernesses we have about what to do about certain things.

Ono: Exactly.

Lennon: But just as a friend, you know. It's like the difference between somebody onstage doing their performances and somebody off. Even if you try and be real onstage, you are onstage and you do give a performance. And Jerry offstage is completely different from Jerry media, and that's the one we really know.

Ono: He's a very nice guy.

Lennon: He's just good fun. And he lives nearby, and we hang about with him.

Ono: Also, people like Bobby Seale—he's gonna be on [*The*] *Mike Douglas Show.* But you do connect Black Panther immediately with violence, and the past few years has been mainly showing their anger and resentment for not being treated right, and they were justified for that. In this *Mike Douglas Show*, you will see that Bobby Seale is showing you a side of the Black Panther Party plans. Instead of just being angry, what they're doing is just trying to get together the whole community—

Lennon: See, we met Jerry first. I'm sorry to interrupt. I was gonna say about how we felt. This is the same with Frank Zappa, Jerry, Abbie [Hoffman], Bobby Seale, and a lot of people we've met. You have this image of them that the media have given you. And we were really nervous about meeting Jerry and about meeting Bobby Seale.

Smith: I was gonna say you met Jerry and Abbie in the park, and both of you were *very* uptight.

Lennon: Right, because we didn't know who they were. We'd only read. . . . And you'd think people like us would know better than to believe media images. Because if our image is anything like us, well, we don't exist. We aren't really anything like our image, and neither were they. And there were so many positive things that they were saying and doing that bore no resemblance to what we'd heard about them. And then later on we met Bobby Seale, and he told us so many fantastic things they were doing like these free-food programs and plumbing and factories they have that give away shoes, food, you know, free hospital . . . they're just really trying to help people in the community way. And we were so nervous about to meet them, thinking that they were gonna be real bomb-throwing, freak kind of people. And they had so many positive things that they were doing that were nothing to do with what we'd heard about.

Ono: They're much together.

Lennon: And we thought we'd try and give them a chance to say that on TV. I think Bobby Seale and his people really put it over well. You'll see on *The Mike Douglas* [*Show*] what incredible, positive things they're doing that have nothing to do with guns and violence. And we wanted to give them that chance to show that side of them.

Ono: And they don't use the words *love* and *peace*, but what they are in fact doing is to show their plans, the program that is based on love and peace more than violence or anger or resentment. And it's beautiful. And Jerry, too, when he communicates with us, it's on a level of just really nice friendship. And peace not as a moral issue, but just from a strategic point of view it's now working.

Lennon: We have many heavy talks about it.

Ono: We don't say morally we should promote peace. We're saying even from a strategic point of view, peace does communicate, whereas violence doesn't, you know.

Lennon: We're in a position in America and in England . . . but if we do anything else other than in a peaceful way, they're just gonna shoot us, that's for sure. And that's another tactical reason for having a non-violent approach to things, because things are so bad that they're not messing about anymore.

Smith: I think the San Diego [Republican National] Convention is gonna be another one of those turning points.

Lennon: I think if they're gonna do something in San Diego, if the youth and the movement are gonna do something, it should be explicitly nonviolent. And it should be seen to be that before it happens, and that should be the main idea in people's heads. Because they have the weapons and we don't, and it's silly—we don't stand a chance. Not at the moment.

Ono: And you know, many of those very radical leaders are starting to get aware of that. That's the point that they're trying to push on *The Mike Douglas Show*, for instance. I don't know if it's successful or not; I don't know if it came across. But you'll see.

Lennon: [*Sings.*] Yo ho ho and a bottom of rum . . .

Smith: I don't know, is there anything else?

Lennon: I don't know.

Smith: I'm trying to think what else.

Lennon: Let me think . . .

Smith: I keep getting some of these letters. I forward them to you sometimes. Sometimes I give them to Peter. [*Possibly a reference to Lennon's friend Peter Shotton or to former Beatles assistant Peter Brown, who became president and CEO of RSO Records. —Ed.*] But is the mail still enormously heavy? I mean, like you get bushels of it every day?

Lennon: It's usually about ten a day regular, I think.

Smith: That's not too bad.

Lennon: It's got a lot more sensible than it used to be. It's not just . . .

Smith: Not just asking for money.

Lennon: Well, they're normally asking for money, help, or autographs. Or to be pen pals. There's less of that kind of jazz these days and more sort of just intelligent letters coming in that we can respond to.

Ono: We really enjoy them, and we make sure that we read most of it, really.

Lennon: Yoko gets withdrawal symptoms if there isn't mail there, so keep writing.

Smith: And the address here to send the mail is [*mumbles words*] Street.

Lennon: Box fifty-nine, Great Arkansas, Alaska, Naybub 1053. And I'll repeat that. Fanning DI93, Field Course Typist 159.

Smith: [Beatles fan and collector] Dave Morrell, the guy that gave you that Decca audition tape thing—

Lennon: Oh, yeah. Did he find the tapes?

Smith: Gee, I forgot. I'll ask him. He's gonna be on tonight, on this show live.

Lennon: Oh, I see. Otherwise, we'll put it out as it is.

Smith: You're gonna put it out?

Lennon: I think it'd be—

Smith: Oh, it'd be great! It'd be great!

Lennon: I was talking to George about it. I really think it's worth putting it out because I enjoyed it, and I'm sure anybody that has a sort of soft spot for Beatles would like to hear the audition that was turned down. [*The fifteen songs on the audition tape have since been made available on several legitimate and bootleg albums. —Ed.*]

Smith: That'd be the absolutely first Beatles album.

Lennon: Yeah, the real first one.

Smith: He [Morrell] wanted to know . . . he said that he'd heard that all the early concerts, like the Shea [Stadium concert in New York on August 15, 1965] and all of that stuff, that you really had hated it, that you'd said that in many interviews. And he was there, he felt the place shaking, he couldn't believe that you had taken in $305,000.

Lennon: Three hundred five thousand dollars?

Smith: Three hundred five thousand dollars was how much you got for the Shea concert.

Lennon: Is that what we were paid?

Smith: That's what you were paid.

Lennon: I thought we were supposed to get a million dollars every time we did it, or is that a dream?

Smith: No, it was $305,000.

Lennon: I see.

Smith: And he said, "Is it true that you really didn't like doing that?"

Lennon: Doing which?

Smith: That concert, you know, in front of that many people.

Lennon: One was enough. I think we did two, right?

Smith: Right.

Lennon: It was a great experience. I mean, it was just incredible, the first one, all that happening going on, everybody yelling and shouting, but we were just disappointed musically. It just got a joke. And you can see in the film of us, George and I aren't even bothering playing half the chords, we're just messing them up. There wasn't enough in it for us musically, and we're basically musicians. And it was beginning to get worse and worse musically. And that's why we lost interest in it. As an event and a happening it was fantastic, and we enjoyed it. But as far as music was concerned, it was nowhere, you know.

Smith: Because the year before that you had appeared at Carnegie Hall.

Lennon: Oh, that was terrible, because the acoustics were terrible, and they had people sitting onstage with us. It was like all [then New York governor Nelson] Rockefeller's children backstage and all that kind of jazz. And it got out of hand. It wasn't a rock show. It was just a sort of a circus where we were in cages being pawed and talked at and met and touched backstage and onstage. We were just like animals, you know.

Smith: It shows how fast the thing went. You got paid $6,000 for two shows at Carnegie Hall.

Lennon: Is that all?

Smith: That's all. Six for both shows.

Lennon: Terrible, isn't it? I'd like to know how much the promoters made.

Smith: Well, [promoter] Sid Bernstein says that he made more money from Carnegie Hall than he did from Shea. Shea Stadium he ended up with something like . . . I think he said two or three thousand dollars net profit because there were so many security problems—helicopters and armored cars—that by the time the gross was divided up and everything, he was left with nothing.

Lennon: Believe me, the Beatles got least of it all. Whatever it was, they got more than we ever did. We apparently still haven't been paid for it yet. I wouldn't be surprised. Most of it never got to us. It was all ripped off. We ain't got any millions in the bank, I'll tell ya that.

Smith: Even at this point?

Lennon: I mean, even my album *Imagine* and the other album is owned not by me. I don't own the songs or nothing. They just go straight into Northern Songs and [British media executive] Lew Grade's fat pocket. [*Grade's company owned a majority stake of Northern Songs, publisher of the Beatles' music.* —*Ed.*] And between Capitol, EMI, Lew Grade, and all those people, we get sod all out of it, even now. Anyway, enough of that. Everybody knows the story. We're just like any other artist, musicians—we were ripped off from start to finish.

Smith: Another Dave Morrell question. Clapton plays guitar on "[While] My Guitar Gently Weeps." He [Morrell] wonders why he wasn't given credit on the album for it.

Lennon: Probably a contractual thing. They probably weren't allowed to say who it was. It was the early days of people sitting in on each other's sessions.

Smith: Oh, I see. Whereas now it's "courtesy of . . ."

Lennon: Nowadays, the record companies are understanding that they have to let musicians play together whether they're contracted or not. It's a problem for 'em. And in those days they'd put "Eric Wonderdog" or something, and you'd have to guess who it was.

Smith: How about Nicky Hopkins on "Imagine"?

Lennon: He's not on "Imagine." He's on the album, not on the song "Imagine." He's credited on that.

Smith: On the jacket? I didn't think he was.

Lennon: Yes, yes. I think he was left off something by an accident, but he's credited. I've got the inside sleeve here. Yeah, everybody's credited on that circle that goes on the middle. There was something about Nicky that somebody said left off something. But he was on finally, I think. That was an accident of printing if he was missed off one batch of records.

Ono: In fact, we're proud that he was on.

Smith: When the Beatles were coming up in that early stage where you were getting more and more and more popular, what groups scared you? Like were there groups where . . . could you guys get together and go, "Wow, we'll never be more popular than . . . whoever"?

Lennon: Well, it was just usually Elvis or something like that. Or Bing Crosby.

Smith: Well, you beat him this year with [his] "White Christmas." [*A reference to Lennon and Ono's "Happy Xmas (War Is Over)." —Ed.*]

Lennon: Well, I don't know about that. Capitol's screwed it up so bad it didn't have enough chance to get in there, you know.

Smith: No, my Singing Dogs beat you out this year. [*A reference to a 1950s novelty recording of "Jingle Bells" that found a new audience after Smith played it on the air. —Ed.*]

Lennon: Well, they should have released it a bit earlier than two weeks before Christmas. You need at least four weeks in America. [*In fact, "Happy Xmas" had nearly that much time in the United States, where it came out on December 1, 1971; in the United Kingdom, it was released even earlier, on November 24. —Ed.*] They held it up, trying to make out that Yoko didn't write it and it's a Beatle record really and all that jazz.

They suddenly decided that Plastic Ono Band are the Beatles. In the early days, when we were making *Two Virgins* and even "Give Peace a Chance," they said, "Well, it's one of John's crazy things, sod him—they can have a different relationship, a different deal," and they let us have a different deal. Suddenly when we got a hit with "Instant Karma!" suddenly the Plastic Ono Band is really the Beatles, so we don't want to pay Yoko, and we don't want her to do this, and this has got to be like that, and this is a Beatle record, and we'll pay your Beatle royalty, after they'd already given us a Plastic Ono Band royalty . . .

[*Listens to radio.*] Why do they keep playing "She Loves You" every ten minutes? That's what I'd like to know. [*Voice on radio says, "If you take people off the assembly line you must slow it down or you're gonna get the results like you have."*] That's what I've been trying to say for a long time. [*Laughter.*]

Smith: OK, thank you both again.

Lennon: It's our pleasure, Howard. Are we going now? So we're going to listen to it? What time is it on?

Smith: It'll be on at ten o'clock.

Ono: We'll listen to it, and our lawyers are listening to it, too.

Lennon: The whole damn world will be listening to it.

Smith: Let's start the motor on this bed so we can get uptown right away. [*Lennon makes sound of revving engine.*]

PRESS CONFERENCE

February 1972, Philadelphia

Shortly after talking with Howard Smith, Lennon and Ono gave a press conference in Philadelphia along with their friend Jerry Rubin, the Yippie leader and antiwar activist. The primary subject: the couple's recent taping of a full week of *The Mike Douglas Show*, a popular daytime TV talk program, where Lennon and Ono had appeared as cohosts.

Douglas's show wasn't exactly a product of the counterculture; its namesake looked and dressed a bit like an insurance salesman, and his guests typically appealed to a conservative audience. Not surprisingly, then, the week with Lennon and Ono had its bizarre moments. One minute, Douglas would be singing a Las Vegas–style version of the Beatles' "Michelle," the next Lennon and Ono's friends would be onstage talking about revolutionary change. But in the end, the couple had no regrets about the experience. —Ed.

Reporter: Now that it's over, how do you feel about the Douglas show?

Yoko Ono: It was beautiful.

John Lennon: It seemed like three months, at one point. We think it's worth it. And I think when we see the shows, we'll really know. But I wouldn't have missed it.

Reporter: Jerry Rubin was talking last night before the show that there were a lot of political-type negotiations as far as [choosing] of guests . . .

Lennon: [*To Ono.*] What do you say, fifty-fifty?

Ono: Yes. We wanted to do the shows to show that we are working for peace and love, and also to change the world, not with violence but with love. And everybody that we selected is participating in efforts to change the world.

We were trying to show that not just slogans and demonstrations are gonna change the world, but we have to change the whole lifestyle. So that's why we brought in [the] macrobiotic [cook] and this blood-pressure [biofeedback] thing, et cetera, to show that we're not just freaks just sort of shouting and screaming about it, but that we think in terms of a balanced life, of changing it gradually through our daily lifestyle.

There were about twenty people that we wanted to bring in, but we felt it would be unwise to bring that many in. Usually they have about five people [each] show. Instead, John and I felt like concentrating on about two or three people, so that we can do it in-depth, instead of just saying, "Hi!"—you know, that showbiz thing. So we limited the number of people.

Lennon: There were no particular people that [the Douglas bookers] were more upset about. Course they were upset originally about the idea of Jerry [Rubin] and [Black Panther leader] Bobby Seale being on, but we explained that they were the first [guests] we'd like to bring on if we do the show. And they got over that; it was just nervousness. But there was a point when they said, "Well, haven't you got any friends that aren't political? Have you got any other interests?" So we said, "OK, OK, we do have other interests," and so that's when we went into the [biofeedback] thing, and things which you'll see are other interests of ours.

Reporter: Did you get anybody to talk about the ecology?

Ono: No, but food is definitely connected with ecology. That's also why I wanted to go into macrobiotic cooking. And ecology has a lot to do with our minds. You see, usually people think in terms of just changing the chemical or physical situation. But our minds really control our bodies, and therefore, with a problem of ecology, too, we can develop a beautiful scene if we have a real awareness in our minds. That's why we brought [in] the blood pressure [biofeedback expert], showing that it's not just special people who can lower their blood pressure. We have this idea about Indian gurus and all that, but it's not that. It's no mystery that every one of us has the power to control our body with our mind.

Reporter: Do you think you were successful in reaching the Mike Douglas audience?

Lennon: Well, we won't know till it's all over, but let's say that some of the people around the back of the show who were nervous about certain aspects of what we were doing were happy about it at the end. They felt it was worth it themselves, although they went through a lot of changes while they were doing it. We won't know till the five shows go on one after another, 'cause it was somehow spread over three weeks or so, and it didn't have that feeling of being five shows, but it is five shows, and I guess when we see them we'll know.

Reporter: John, did you make it easier for the next person coming on that show to get these kinds of guests on? Do you think you kind of pioneered a little bit?

Lennon: Well, we hope so. We hoped what it did was to make them less frightened of the fact that a Black Panther would like to say something, which doesn't mean he's gonna come and shoot you to put his point of view across. Maybe we've opened their eyes a little to that.

Ono: The initial fright that we had when we were going to meet Jerry, for instance . . .

Lennon: We had the same prejudices almost . . .

Ono: The same fright they share with us. So we wanted the [Douglas audience] to go through the same process that we went through, to discover that they're just beautiful.

Reporter: How did Chuck Berry become a guest?

Lennon: When [the Douglas bookers] first said, "Will you do the show?" we said, "Yeah, can we bring Jerry and Bobby?" And we mentioned a few other names—Chuck Berry, Bo Diddley, Little Richard. And the only ones they could get, or find, were Chuck Berry and Little Richard, but Little Richard was ill that day or something, so he couldn't come. I wanted Bo Diddley and Jerry Lee [Lewis], too, and just every day have something like that, you know. None of us got exactly what we wanted, but it was worth it just to be with Chuck Berry, man. It was just worth it!

Reporter: Yoko, have you made plans to further your relationship with Ralph Nader?

Ono: Yes, we have plans to get in touch with him again. We have the same kind of interests, and probably our work and his will be a parallel kind of thing. But I don't believe in centralization, and probably rather than coming together, I think it's nice that he's there working independently and we're working here, and we should all start working . . .

Lennon: Our own area, wherever that is.

Reporter: You've seen *The Mike Douglas Show* and how he gets to the Middle American people. Did you have specific things [to do] in mind, or were you just trying to get some people out there to start thinking . . .

Lennon: Well, that partly, and the fact that [Douglas] offered [the chance to reach his audience]. They'd sort of offer things, and then we'd go, "Oh, OK, OK." And also, they know they've got Middle America, but they're also slightly interested in youth, believe it or not. And the idea was that maybe we could bridge that gap for them. They'll have to change their policy after these shows if they want to get youth, obviously. But that was their idea, and ours was that, what you said.

Ono: Jerry, you were with us for five days at the show, and you were watching it . . . I'd like to know what you think about it.

Jerry Rubin: I thought that on the whole it was really good. I think John and Yoko have a great ability to speak to all kinds of people, to straight America. If they represent young people . . . you saw how the [studio] audience changed. The first two days, the audiences were—

Lennon: Purple-haired!

Kal Rudman [publisher of music-industry trade publication *Friday Morning Quarterback*]: Jerry, what specific points did they communicate? What did you get across?

Rubin: I'll tell you a specific thing that did happen. I saw the first show and got angry; I didn't like it. I thought that John and Yoko had been co-opted by the format. I don't like the format of these talk shows. They're totally rehearsed, totally planned. Nothing spontaneous can happen. People watching it don't get challenged in any way. And I thought that on the first show John and Yoko had become part of that format.

And so I told them that, and they said, "But look at how many people we're reaching, and maybe we should, like, lower people's fears until everyone listens, and then bring [the controversial guests] in, because you're gonna be on, and Bobby Seale is gonna be on, and Chuck Berry, et cetera."

And so I began to think that maybe I was just acting out of reflexes—you know, if you can't do what you want to do, you shouldn't do it. But maybe the existence of John and Yoko offers a new possibility to reach millions of people.

Lennon: But what happened then, the next week [when the second show was taped]?

Rubin: I was on the second show . . .

Ono: Yeah, you were great.

Rubin: Yeah, and I thought that was OK [*laughter*] . . . but then John was saying that he was getting fed up . . .

Lennon: I was getting fed up. I was taking the position [Jerry] took the [show] before. Because with the first show, they asked us on the first show to cool it, you know, and then gradually get a bit heavier. So I finished the first show, but after the second show I was gettin' annoyed.

Rubin: Each time [John] was positive, but it was not as good as if John and Yoko had their own television show and for an hour could do whatever they wanted to do. Then they could really blow our minds. It wasn't as good as that, because it was this format, within that format. Bobby Seale usually isn't on with, you know, what's happening musically.

And then the two nonpolitical shows were really very political. Talking about the food people eat, and talking about what people do to their bodies, that's very political. So you take the five shows as a whole, and it was a total cultural offering to the American people, that they'd never get [otherwise], and I don't think *The Mike Douglas Show* will ever be the same. So I think, on the whole, it was really positive.

Lennon: The idea was what I liked, you know, the mixture [of guests]. Except it should be somehow compressed and packaged a bit better, so's people would take it.

Rubin: More special.

Lennon: Yeah, yeah.

Reporter: There was an incident with the surgeon general [Dr. Jesse Steinfeld, a guest on day two]?

Rubin: Well, by accident we just found ourselves in the same place at the same time. No one planned it. He was a Nixon administration official . . .

Lennon: They always insisted on having one of that ilk on each show . . .

Rubin: He came on first and said his piece, and then I came on, and then I was just talking about the war [in Vietnam], the repression of the government. And he made a point that he came from Europe and he made it. Then I said, "What about the Indians and the blacks and the Vietnamese?" And then, when the show was over, he was really petrified of losing his job, because he sat with me [on camera] for fifteen minutes and didn't really respond. It wasn't pretty. I don't know what happened; he went back to Washington . . . [*Laughter.*] You have to realize that people like us never get on television.

Lennon: That's what really surprised me about [American] TV . . .

Rubin: The only chance we have to get on television is on the Walter Cronkite show when we make news. For us just to be on, just to express our . . .

Lennon: Five minutes of a freak, and they shout, "Equal time! Equal time!" And they've got it all, man, they already got 99 percent of it . . .

Rubin: I mean, Nixon's on TV every night making some new announcement . . .

Ono: There are two things that we tried to accomplish with [Mike Douglas's shows]. One is that we wanted to bring some people in, like Jerry, who really can't go on TV otherwise. And the other is the fact that there's such a gap between the young generation and the old generation now, and because this is a show that really communicates more with the older generation, we wanted to reach our hands out to them and say, "Don't be afraid of us. And we shouldn't be too hostile to you, either. Let's work it together, because we have to work it together."

Lennon: We are supposed to be the young, hip generation that knows what's going on, and they're the ones that don't. So we can't expect them to try and communicate with us. I don't know what chance we have to communicate with them, but it's up to us to try, rather than the other way around.

Rubin: Unfortunately, they have all the power, don't they?

Lennon: Yeah, but not them housewives out there. I'm talking about them, about the middle, you know, the ordinary people.

Ono: We have to keep trying to reach. At first they may be afraid, but the next day, they'll change. People are changeable, and it's great.

Reporter: What have you learned from Jerry Rubin, in terms of media tactics?

Ono: Well, he's an artist, you know. When I came back to New York, I met many artists who looked so commercial, like Madison Avenue–type people. And then I met [Jerry], and he looked like an artist. And then he said that we were the politicians . . .

Rubin: Yeah, they said that Abbie [Hoffman] and I are the artists, and we said that they're the political revolutionaries.

[*Laughter.*]

Ono: And our awareness level is the same, and we just feel very close to them.

Rubin: Now, from my point of view, the honesty that John and Yoko express in music and in art, and just in this interview, is exactly what I've been trying to do politically. So it's like art, music, and politics come together. And I've seen the Yippies as doing politically what John and Yoko are doing musically and artistically.

Lennon: Yeah, he said it well. That's what I feel, too.

Reporter: John, can we assume more events are coming up?

Lennon: Yeah, we'd like to, [but] we're not allowed to say we're gonna do this event, or work, because we ain't got our permission to work. We'd like to do things like that, sure.

Reporter: Can we expect a Lennon album soon?

Lennon: Well, it's a long story . . .

Ono: It's a political one that might come out very soon.

Lennon: Yeah. And there's a few bits of pieces of live recordings that we want to put out.

Ono: And I hope you all realize the marvelous performances that Elephant's Memory gave in these past five days as well.

Reporter: What are you and Elephant's Memory planning, if anything?

Lennon: I've said this before, but Elephant's and Yoko and I are having a trial marriage. I don't want to make them become an invisible band, you know. I think they should retain their own identity, still make their own albums and do their own gigs. I think we can have a relationship like that. I call it like Dylan had with the Band. I don't actually know what their human relationship was, but the way it appeared, the Band kept their own identity, and so did Dylan, but they worked together, and neither lost anything, but they gained a lot.

Ono: [Elephant's Memory] is a very strong band.

Lennon: I hope we can work that way with them, because they're a really good band.

Reporter: When can we expect some concerts?

Lennon: In the second half of February, we hope to be able to do that. And I want to stress a point to anybody that's gonna talk to the kids about it: I'm gonna be performing with Yoko, and she's gonna be performing too, and anybody that doesn't want to see us both perform, please don't come.

Ono: They say, "Well, why don't you go back and let John come out?"

Lennon: I don't feel like doing it if I can't do it with her. We enjoy working together, and we don't intend to stop. I don't care if the crowd goes to fifty a concert, I'll still groove.

Reporter: At the moment, are your hands kind of tied from doing a tour of some sort 'cause of [work visa] problems?

Lennon: Yeah, that could be sorted out within a couple of weeks, actually. . . . Oh, I can't wait, you know, I can't wait!

Reporter: Do you have any plans in the near future to return to England?

Lennon: I'd like to stay here for a while, so's we . . . I'd like to be able to just go and come as I like.

TV INTERVIEW

**Dick Cavett | Early May 1972, ABC Studios, New York |
Broadcast May 11, 1972, *The Dick Cavett Show*, ABC (US)**

Less than a year after their first interview for *The Dick Cavett Show*, Lennon and Ono returned, ready to deliver on the first show's promise of a live performance. But there was a hitch.

As Cavett explains in an introduction to a DVD of this appearance, somebody at the network objected to the inclusion in the show of the couple's performance of their song "Woman Is the Nigger of the World" (from the about-to-be-released *Some Time in New York City*). "I heard, 'That song must be cut,'" Cavett recalls. "I said, 'You don't get the Lennons on your show and probably outrate the other shows that night and then cut their damn song.'"

Cavett refused to go along. "There was more compromising and chicken-dribble behavior," he says, "and finally some genius came up with, 'How about an insert?'—sort of apologizing ahead of time for the song. . . . So they wrote this insert and it was the predictable, usual thing: 'You may be offended by this, but we want to treat you as a mature audience' . . . and all that kind of junk. And then they would play the song and then they [the censors] were only half terrified of what would happen as America rose up against the network. Well, I did it that way, and actually a lot of complaints did come in. But all of them were about the mealymouthed message you [the network] made Cavett say before the song and *none* about the song itself."

Here's a transcript of the conversation, which has not previously appeared in print. —Ed.

Dick Cavett: My next guests taped a ninety-minute show with me a little less than a year ago. Can't be that long! No, quite a lot less than a year ago. Like a week ago. No, sometime, anyway. They said at that time that they might come back and sing sometime. There was so much to talk about that the taping actually ran on beyond the ninety minutes, and we ran some of it on a later show. Anyway, they have kept their promise, and I'm grateful because not only is it interesting to see them perform, but they are involved in a crucial court case here in New York which will determine whether or not they can remain in the country or whether they face deportation back to England. Will you welcome, please, John and Yoko Lennon?

[*Lennon and Ono appear and share handshakes and embraces with Cavett and actress and fellow guest Shirley MacLaine. Lennon whispers to Cavett.*]

John Lennon: I couldn't resist it.

Cavett: I'll bet you don't have the nerve to say that out [loud], what you said to me.

Lennon: I do. Tieless in Gaza. [*A pun on the title of the book* Eyeless in Gaza *and a reference to the fact that earlier in the show, Cavett had removed his tie and auctioned it off to an audience member.* —Ed.] They've got to know that book, otherwise it's no good.

Cavett: Is that a favorite book of yours?

Lennon: It was a good book, yeah. Aldous Huxley wrote it.

Cavett: What a terrible pun.

Lennon: I thought it was a nice pun.

Cavett: Nice to see you. Nice to see both of you.

Lennon: Same to you.

Cavett: I didn't see you backstage at all. I wasn't avoiding you—

Lennon: We were rehearsing, and you were putting your tie on—

Cavett: I was doing whatever it is that I do.

Yoko Ono: I was watching you [Shirley MacLaine]. It's beautiful, what you believe in and all that.

Shirley MacLaine: You say it, John. You're leaving, anyway.

[*Laughter.*]

Lennon: I thought it said McCARTNEY. [*Referring to MacLaine's McGov-ERN FOR PRESIDENT button.*] Forget it, forget it.

Cavett: So you're not fat. I couldn't help noticing that you're—

Lennon: [*Stands up.*] Malted milks! I eat malted milks; I drink malted.

Cavett: There's a rumor going around that you had gone practically overboard, as we say in America, on malted milk.

Lennon: I know. You see, we don't have things like that in England. Most kids like it here—not adults, right? But I'm crazy for it. You often see me down at Nathan's [Famous, the fast-food chain], sucking on a malted.

[*Laughter.*]

Cavett: What do they have in your poor, underdeveloped country?

Lennon: Well, they have not as many ice creams and lousy milkshakes.

Cavett: Curds and whey.

Lennon: Really sort of plastic stuff. And I really dig it. . . . I was on cheeseburgers, but I got over them. [*Laughter.*] A round of applause for cheeseburgers. Breadfruit! . . . Somebody clapped for cheeseburgers; I thought we'd get a round for breadfruit.

Cavett: You have to be careful of your adolescent complexion, don't we?

Lennon: Well, I do, and at thirty-one . . .

Cavett: Say . . . happy birthday, in the past.

Lennon: Thank you. You haven't seen me since then.

Cavett: Way over thirty.

Lennon: Thirty-one and rising. I wouldn't go back, though.

Ono: Why don't you tell them how you like TV? You always say the thing is, even after . . .

Lennon: Another thing about America is that. . . . Like in Europe or especially where I come from, London, you have to choose if you want to go out for the evening or go to a theater or go to a movie or watch TV.

But here you can do it all, at any time of night. It's fantastic. You don't realize how great it is. They send you to bed at twelve in London or ten. And twelve is the latest it goes on at the weekend. If we're really lucky, we get a late-night movie up till twelve or twelve-thirty. And it's just boring. Because a lot of people in our business never get a chance to see anything.

Cavett: Aren't you late sleepers, anyway? What's the opposite of rise? Late fallers?

Ono: In a way.

Lennon: Late swingers. Yeah, that's it.

Ono: We just watch TV, and it's great, you know.

Cavett: I've seen very good reviews on your art exhibit—

Lennon: Syracuse. That's what we were doing our plug for that time. We got accused of plugging too much last time.

Cavett: I wonder: Did you see [George] Harrison when he was on here?

Lennon: Yeah, what was he saying? "Capitol! Capitol!" [*In his own appearance on Cavett's show, Harrison had mentioned Lennon and Ono's Capitol Records–distributed "Happy Xmas (War Is Over)." Poking fun at what he suggested were the couple's excessive promotional mentions, Harrison had noted the release of this single, which he'd said was "the one thing they forgot to plug." —Ed.*] He started a riot with that thing.

Cavett: Yes, he did a joke about you. Well, I should explain that.

Lennon: Oh, yeah. I saw it.

Cavett: Harrison came on, and he said "I want to plug . . ." I forget what it was of yours, because he said there's something you forgot to plug.

Lennon: That was nice of him, too. It was the album probably or whatever. I can't remember.

Cavett: But I should have explained that on that show it did look like there were sort of three plugs in a row, but it was because we taped and then we had so much that we put it together out of sequence—

Lennon: Thank you, thank you.

Cavett: And it looked like you—

Lennon: I'm not ashamed of plugging because, you know, people come on to plug something, right? Everybody's selling something.

Ono: And we believe in what we do.

MacLaine: Plug everything but presidents, right?

Lennon: Yeah, sure. I think we did it all right. [*Reads cue card.*] "Lead in through clever—"

Cavett: Oh, no, you don't have to read that. I do want to know about something that's in the papers. [*Laughter.*] There's more than one show going on here.

Lennon: Are they seeing a different show?

Cavett: It's a two-ring circus. Someone may have tuned one of the monitors to another program.

Lennon: It's not as surreal as last time. Last time was a bit fast, wasn't it? We didn't know what was going on in between the commercials. None of us knew what we were talking about. It was going so fast because we were nervous, and he must have picked it up and it was just [*makes sound*] through the whole show.

Cavett: We were hyperactive.

Ono: Well, it's not exactly slow now, but . . .

Lennon: Tell him about the case and everything.

Ono: See, we're really frightened now, because some people feel that we have to maybe leave this country. And that puts us in a position, especially for me, that I have to choose between my husband and my child.

Cavett: Explain that—why you got in that situation.

Ono: First of all, because, well, I have a child who's eight years old and she's an American citizen, and we're looking for her. We can't find her.

Lennon: Shall I explain about Texas and everything quickly?

Ono: Right.

Lennon: See, her former husband is American and so therefore her daughter is. And Yoko never took out American citizenship, 'cause she never needed it. She was here half her life, she was educated here, and then she married an American. And it never came up to change citizenship. It was just always easy to come and go. She never thought of it. So when the divorce came and there was no arrangement made for the child, because at that time we were more amicable, the two ex parties . . . but you know how things get, and they got worse and worse and worse until it came that we couldn't see Kyoko anymore. The child's called Kyoko.

And we've been chasing her in Europe, in Denmark, in Spain, in Hawaii, in America, back to Europe, back to . . . this has been going on for two or three years. And finally we thought, *Oh, let's go to court in the place where the divorce was.* That was in the US Virgin Islands. So we went there, and we only just got in. At the last minute, immigration still hadn't given us a form to get in, and they told us, "You can have just enough time to go for the court case." And that was gonna be one day. And we said, "That's fine."

But even as we got to the border, still the thing hadn't come through, so we said to the man, "Look, they're expecting us. Call Washington to let us in. We have a court case today." And I was still stuck in the British Virgin Islands 'cause I couldn't get in. They let us in. We won the court case. And on the way in, they said, "How long do you want?" after they told me we could only have three days. I said, "Well, what have you got?" They said, "Three months." So I said, "OK, I'll have three months."

But as it happens, we finished the court case quickly, we got custody, we went up to New York for a little sort of social business because our firm is up there, Apple, and then we went back to England. Next time we applied, somebody said—and these are all things you can't prove 'cause it's all . . . "Well, you didn't use your three months, you didn't use your three months." I said, "You didn't want me to use . . ." "You weren't grateful to use your three months."

So I said, "Well, I'm sorry about it, but we have to come back to the court case." So the court case was going on. There's a few different episodes in it. Finally we got custody, but during that, her ex-husband, Tony Cox, opened a court case in Texas, where his parents-in-law are, and he set up an establishment there for the first time in two years, set up a residence, and was carrying on all the family life down there. And he chose Texas as then a forum to fight our case in the Virgin Islands.

So then we had another case going that was in Texas, so obviously we had to keep coming and going. And immigration was getting upset with us and saying, "Well, tell us when it's gonna be." We said, "We can't tell you; it's up to the judge when it happens. We have no control." So finally, as we start winning the case in Texas, Mr. Cox runs away with Kyoko again.

Ono: As usual.

Lennon: So it's easy for somebody to go in court and accuse people like us in public of terrible things. And by the time we've waded through it all and said, "No, we haven't done a damn thing, actually . . . all we're trying to do is talk to her." She [*points to Ono*] hasn't spoken to her for a year. By the time the judge has seen through all the games, the man's run away again. They give us custody again, and this is temporary custody, only if we bring the child up in America.

Ono: 'Cause she's an American citizen.

Lennon: 'Cause she's an American citizen, and the judge felt she should be brought up here. And we don't mind. We'd like to be here and bring her up. So a) we have the two papers with custody, but we don't know where she is still. We haven't a clue where she is; she's in America somewhere. So we've no idea. We can't tell immigration or anybody when it'll be all over or when we'll know what's gonna happen.

And they began to intimate to us that we were using that as an excuse to go on [*The*] *Mike Douglas* [*Show*], [*The*] *Dick Cavett* [*Show*], and things like that. But all it is, we're not just gonna sit in a box while we're in between court cases. We have to live our life, and to work is the only way we can keep our minds off it. 'Cause it's killing her. It's two years since she's seen her and one year since she's spoken to her on the phone, and immigration's policy has always been not to split a family.

So they're saying that seeing as Mr. Lennon is not eligible because I was busted in England in 1968—planted by the way, but bust. I pleaded guilty on lawyer's advice. She was three months pregnant and all that. It was a real drag, but I did it, and I paid my hundred-dollar fine or whatever it was. And then they say because I'm not eligible, "Rather than split a family, although there's nothing against Yoko Ono, you'd both better get out." And I'm saying, "Well, if you don't want to split a family, let us stay here, because our daughter's here." She has to choose between me and the daughter. And a) she doesn't know where the daughter is—we don't have a clue. We just know she's in America somewhere.

Ono: See, even if she's not in America—I really don't know where she is—but the thing is, from a mutual friend we've heard that my ex-husband is saying that all they have to do is hide and wait until we're kicked out. And of course that's the cleverest way. And then this will be a haven for them, because they don't have to worry about us coming in.

Lennon: Yoko always said in all the transcripts of the court cases, too, we don't want to take the child away from Tony.

Ono: No, I'm not—

Lennon: He's paranoid about it. He thinks we're big, powerful people that are going to do something to him, and we're not. We're saying, now if you're watching, there's nothing John and Yoko could do to Kyoko. We couldn't hide her anywhere like you because we're too famous; there's nowhere we can go. And Yoko always said in court and out of court, she thinks the child should have both parents, be able to see both parents. And we don't care what kind of arrangement he wants to make, just so the child does have the benefit of both parents.

Cavett: [*To Ono.*] But at the moment you're split between either, well, as you said, choosing between your husband and your child.

Lennon: They're saying, "No matter what, you're a criminal, and you've gotta go."

Cavett: Well, let's talk some more about that. Excuse me, Yoko, because we have to take this pause now. Then we'll be back. Sorry.

[*Commercial break.*]

Cavett: This picture of your little girl, Kyoko—

Ono: Kyoko, and she's eight years old and, you see, in Texas court a teacher testified that she's three years behind the studies because she's been running around the world so much. And that's one of the reasons I'm very worried about her.

Cavett: I think it'd be on your mind all the time.

Lennon: It is. There's no way out.

Ono: Well, John has to switch the TV to another channel whenever I see a child because I just can't stand seeing a child, you know.

Lennon: And it comes out every night in nightmares, it really does. If we work all day to not think about it, it has to come out somewhere, and it comes out every night about five o'clock.

Ono: And you know, John said, this drug case, which is possession of marijuana case in 1968 . . . it's four years ago, and it was planted, and the sergeant who actually came to arrest us is now suspended from his previous job.

Lennon: He also did the same to George Harrison.

Ono: You know, there's some question about his method of arrest. And they're all saying, the immigration office is saying, "Well, this is only because of the drug case, you know, and nothing else." But the strange thing is, people like Donovan, Keith Richard[s]—

Lennon and Ono: —Mick Jagger, George Harrison—

Lennon: —all have exactly the same case as me.

Ono: Exactly the same record, around the same time, and they can come and go.

Lennon: And the same policeman, I think. [*Laughter.*] It was. He was a headhunter.

Cavett: So what is it they're after you for?

Lennon: They're after us because we talk about peace, you know. I mean, because we want peace. We've said the same thing for two years one way or another, and we believe in it.

Ono: The only thing we promoted was peace and love, and there've been some rumors, like we might go to San Diego to disrupt the Republican convention, things like that.

Lennon: We're getting blamed for the Chicago convention now. [*Laughter.*] It's no kidding. When we approach people for help, somebody somewhere rings them up and says, "These people are criminals." We were given a job on the drug-abuse council to help people try and explain drugs in a realistic way to kids, because nobody else is doing it. Then immediately [after] we got the offer, somebody rings up the people that offered us [the position] and says, "What are you letting those criminals on for? Don't you know they're this, that, and the other? Don't you know . . ." And somebody else rings up and starts talking about, "Don't you know they had something to do with [disruptions at the 1968 Democratic convention in] Chicago?" And the first time we ever heard of Chicago was we saw a play of it done on British TV. They think we're going to San Diego or Miami or wherever it is. We've never said we're going. We ain't going. There'll be no big jam with us and Dylan, because there's too much going on. We never said we were going. That's it.

Cavett: There was an editorial in the [*New York*] *Times* the other day, and I know there have been in other papers—

Lennon: That was great, yeah.

Cavett: —which I completely agree with, and I think it's shocking if you're being deported. And it's ironic that it would happen in the same year that [Charlie] Chaplin was given an award after twenty years after a similar kind of nonsense.

MacLaine: You're more responsible for the expression of love and peace in the arts than anyone practically in the twentieth century.

[*Applause.*]

Lennon: That's very nice. Thank you.

This is a bit hard for me to explain, but our lawyer's name is Leon Wildes. And he's not a radical lawyer, he's not a William Kunstler, nothing like that. We went to an immigration lawyer who knew about immigration. And he has really been surprised, because he worked in immigration fifteen years. He's really been surprised by some of the things that have gone on.

[*Reading.*] "It's very ironic that the government approved our application as outstanding artists whose presence is beneficial to US cultural interests and the public welfare." The federal judge had approved that and the government has, but we had to fight for it. And it's the only time that he's ever had to go to court to force the government to consider an application like that obtained by an injunction. Meaning that one way for us to come in is as outstanding artists or scientists—there's a special clause.

Now we put that in our case, and nobody looked at it. And it's the law that they have to look at the application. They didn't look at it. And our lawyer went down, said, "You haven't looked at it." So he took them to court. And the judge and the federal judge said they have to look at it, and they have to take this into consideration. "Yes, they are outstanding artists and would be of benefit to this country." And it's the only time he's had to go in and fight for it.

Ono: Also, you know, if there's anybody who's interested in helping us, petition does help, too, and we have about ten thousand people roughly—

Cavett: There's a telegram from a union leader—

Lennon: Oh, yeah, you want to mention that? It's great, you know.

Cavett: We've run into another station problem here. We have to take a break for a message, and we'll be back.

[*Commercial break.*]

Cavett: [*Separately recorded message.*] At this point in the show, which was taped a week ago, John and Yoko got into something which ABC feels may develop into, in their words, "a highly controversial issue." It revolves around the song, "Woman Is the Nigger of the World" and the obvious fact that some members of our black audience will or may be offended by the use of that word. In the next segment, John Lennon gives his reasons for writing the song and for using the word. I permitted this insertion into the show that I'm doing now as the only alternative to a full deletion by ABC of the segment. Watch it, and let us know what you think.

[*The show resumes.*]

Cavett: Just quickly, it's interesting that the support for this is growing and does not just represent what you might call one kind of person. This is a telegram that should interest you. Immigration and Naturalization Services it's addressed to:

"It would be an outrage and a tragedy for this country if John Lennon and Yoko Ono are deported. Their strong antidrug stand and their clear, eloquent commitment to nonviolence and their participation and action for constructive social change are messages badly needed in America today, particularly for our youth."

He goes on to say about the personal tragedy that Mrs. Lennon is forced into by choosing between her husband and her child. "I join thousands of other concerned Americans in asking you to take favorable action enabling John Lennon and Yoko Ono to remain in this country. Signed, Leonard Woodcock, president, United Auto Workers."

Lennon: Right on, Leonard. [*Applause.*] Just one other reason we want to be here is because we really dig it. We dig America, we always have. She loves it, and she's converted me to be one of those New York fanatics. OK, you want to talk about the—

Cavett: Do the song. Tell me about it.

Lennon: Yeah, I hate it when I leave New York now.

Cavett: Anyway, yes, you have a record here that bears some explanation because there's a bit of hassling going on as to whether it can be sung or not.

Lennon: Yeah, there's always . . . every other record I seem to have a hassle with. Well, this is a song about the women's problem. It was written by Yoko and I, and the song is called "Woman Is the Nigger of the

World." And obviously there was a few people that reacted strangely to it. But usually they were white and male.

I'll tell you a story of how it came about. In 1969 I put it on the cover of the single so's it helps you explain it a bit. Yoko did an interview with a woman about the women's problem, and I didn't have anything to do with it. And then I noticed the cover [of the publication where the interview appeared]. It was called *Nova*. It's an English women's magazine like *McCall's* or something like that. And the first time I heard about it was I saw it on the cover of *McCall's* [*sic*] like that, and it said, WOMAN IS THE NIGGER OF THE WORLD.

Well, at the time I was more of a chauvinist than I am now, and I must say, I was saying, "Well, come on, what about this and what about that?" and I argued a lot. And then, like everybody else, we talked more and more about it in the last two years. It became more of a thing, and I had to find out about myself and my attitude to women, and this phrase of hers kept coming through my head: "Woman is the nigger of the world, woman is the nigger . . ." So I said, "Come on, Yoko, this is it. You've said it here. I agree with you now—I think she is the slave of the slaves." That's what [Socialist leader James] Connolly said; he's an Irishman. And so we sat down together, and we tried to write together the whole story as best we could in a three- or four-minute song. And it's called "Woman Is the Nigger of the World."

And then luckily for me—because a lot of stations were saying, "Well, we're not gonna play this because it says *nigger* and a white man shouldn't say it"—all my black friends feel I have quite a right to say it 'cause they understand it. And then strangely enough, the chairman of the black caucus, that great guy Congressman Ron Dellums—Democrat, California, it says here—he came out with this, which is fantastic: [*Reads.*] "If you define *nigger* as someone whose lifestyle is defined by others, whose opportunities are defined by others, whose role in society is defined by others, then good news: you don't have to be black to be a nigger in this society. Most of the people in America are niggers." [*Applause.*]

I didn't say that. Oh, my goodness. We'll never get permission to stay in [America] now. I think the word *nigger* has changed. It does not have the same meaning as it used to, and I think he put it very succinctly there. And I really believe women have the worst . . . whatever it is, however badly or poor people are, it's the woman that takes it when they get home from work. [*Applause.*]

Cavett: Would you two menaces to society do your number?

Lennon: Thank you, yes. We'd love to.

[*Lennon, Ono, and their band, Elephant's Memory, perform "Woman Is the Nigger of the World," which is followed by applause and a commercial break.*]

Cavett: Oh, we're back. We were speaking about your far-out attitude. It's not fashionable to like New York these days, and sometime you must come tell us why an Englishman who has a country home and can live in the rolling green hills of England was so anxious to settle here. It's refreshing and nice.

Lennon: I was brought up on America . . .

Ono: And it's not just a single reason that we want to stay here. It's a lot of things we're planning. This was sort of regardless of the immigration attitude. We were . . . since a year ago we were thinking of making a music library in New York, opening a music library in New York that is free, and it's for the poor and for the young. Things like that. And also the [*inaudible*] organization in New York is inviting us as artists in residence to help the summer program, to cool the summer in New York. So we'd really like to stay here and do a lot of things.

MacLaine: They should erect a monument.

Ono: That's beautiful. Now may I quickly . . . because this is so important that—

Lennon: She's been organizing this; it's like a political campaign.

Ono: [It's about] Children's Medical Relief International and this hospital in Saigon called Center for Plastic and Reconstructive Surgery. And this is the only modern facility in Vietnam that's designed to treat the thousands of children injured directly and indirectly from the war. And actually it's very sad, because now the government is cutting funds, and because of lack of funds, maybe they have to close down. And they really desperately need money immediately, and anyone who's interested in helping them or doing something about it, the address is CMRI . . . [*Gives address.*]

Cavett: CMRI is what? Children's Medical Relief International.

Ono: Yes. And it's so sad because even if they go on treating the children, it takes thirty years to treat all of them to get well. It's that bad. What happened is, you know, if you think that if your own child is injured. . . . What happened was, backstage I had these photographs of them and Kyoko's photo together, and I was just gonna take Kyoko's photo out, and I took it out— she's my daughter—and I got a shock because I thought she was injured.

Cavett: Shows how it's on your mind.

Lennon: [*Holds up photo.*] This boy was hit by a phosphorous grenade in the crotch, whatever it is. I don't know what it is, but it sounds awful. Phosphorous grenade in the crotch.

Ono: It's really terrible.

Cavett: We have to take a message. We'll be right back.

[*Commercial break.*]

Cavett: Here again are the Lennons, John and Yoko, and the number, as soon as we get the buzz out of the speaker. . . . It will be "The Flight of the Bumblebee" if we're not careful.

Ono: This is called "We're All Water," and it's a song from our latest album, called *Some Time in New York City.*

[*Lennon and Ono perform the song with the band, then return to their seats with Cavett and MacLaine.*]

Lennon: The band there, that's a New York group, Elephant's Memory.

Ono: We're going to be performing in Washington Square [in New York's Greenwich Village] this Saturday.

Lennon: Washington Square this Saturday, Methodist Church, for a benefit.

Cavett: Are you sure it's this Saturday?

Lennon: Yeah, it's this Saturday.

Cavett: OK, I see. How dare you foreigners walk in here and induce hysteria in our studios? It's frightening.

Say, have I met the best two of the former Beatles, would you say? I know you and Harrison. I know that puts you on the spot.

Lennon: No, I wouldn't say that. I think you should meet Paul, and you should meet Ringo. I think Ringo you'd have a good time with.

Cavett: What does Ringo do with his time? What does he read, for example?

Lennon: Read? He loves science fiction. In fact, he loves it so much, he's handling Apple Films a lot these days, and he was in some mad spaghetti western. We won't mention that. But he was all right in that. Weird film.

Cavett: I didn't see that.

Lennon: But he's making a movie out of [rock star] T. Rex [*Born to Boogie*, a 1972 concert film directed by Starr and released by Apple Films], which is a new phenomenon. The kids are all crazy on him in England. And he's [Starr] making movies and acting in them. So he's happy there.

Cavett: When you two were performing just now, it must get you up in a way that it doesn't to just sit and talk.

Lennon: Yeah.

Cavett: Can you stand a person who doesn't like music? You know, there are people like that.

Lennon: I've never met one, you see.

Ono: There isn't anybody.

Lennon: Oh, there was one man when we were playing our acetates, you know, when you get test pressings of a new album. We were playing them in our loft, and he came banging on the window, saying, "Turn it down! It ain't that good!" [*Laughter.*] That's the only guy.

Cavett: [Vladimir] Nabokov, who wrote *Lolita*, has said that he finds music boring and uninspiring.

Lennon: Well, he's an intellectual, you see, and they can't hear or feel anything.

Ono: And many people hate my screaming so, in the beginning, all the engineers, when I started screaming, they used to just go out of the engineering room.

Lennon: You have to feel music. You don't intellectualize it or watch for it or study it—you feel it. You either play it or you feel it.

Cavett: You and George Wallace, always denouncing intellectuals. We'll be back after this message. Stay where you are.

[*Commercial break.*]

Cavett: We only have thirty seconds left. John Lennon, Yoko Ono, Shirley MacLaine. Or Lemmon, if you prefer. I notice the lady who bought my tie [at the beginning of the show] has left with it. That's interesting; her seat is empty. Monday night, Bette Davis and Peggy Wood, and Tuesday night, ninety minutes with Jack Paar, believe it or not. And we'll see you all then. Good night. [*Lennon and Ono flash peace signs.*]

LENNON ON . . .

His Favorite Beatles Songs

"Of mine I like 'Strawberry Fields [Forever]' and '[I Am the] Walrus.' Of Paul's I like 'Here, There and Everywhere.' Of Ringo's I like 'Honey Don't.' And of George's I like 'Within You Without You.' Of course, I still like 'Eleanor Rigby,' and another I liked was 'For No One.'"

—from interview with Chris Charlesworth, October 1973, published in *Melody Maker*, late 1973

RADIO INTERVIEW

Dennis Elsas | September 28, 1974, WNEW-FM studios, New York |
Broadcast live, WNEW-FM (New York)

Lennon followed 1972's *Some Time in New York City* with the more successful *Mind Games* in November 1973. Then, on September 26, 1974, came *Walls and Bridges*, which would become his first number-one album since *Imagine* and would spawn two hit singles: the chart-topping, sax-spiced "Whatever Gets You Thru the Night," which features a vocal assist from Elton John, and the ethereal "#9 Dream," which, coincidentally, made it to number nine.

On a rainy Saturday, two days after the album's release, Lennon paid an on-air visit to New York disc jockey Dennis Elsas. This was one of several radio appearances over the years in which the ex-Beatle didn't simply answer questions; he read commercials, announced the weather, introduced songs, and spoke directly to the audience. As he told Elsas, disc jockeying is "my second-favorite occupation."

Indeed. People often asked Lennon what he might have wound up doing if he hadn't made it as a musician, and he gave a variety of answers—everything from actor to fisherman to Beat poet—but on the evidence of transcripts like the one that follows, I think it's at least as likely that he might have become a disc jockey.

Elsas had first met Lennon about a month before the singer visited him at the station. The DJ, who was then music director at WNEW-FM, had been invited to the Record Plant recording studios to watch Lennon put finishing touches on *Walls and Bridges*. The singer, who had separated from Yoko Ono the previous year, was there with May Pang, his girlfriend at the time. And Elsas suggested to Pang that Lennon visit the station.

"As a major Beatle fan, I was well aware that none of the Fab Four had ever been to WNEW-FM, but I figured I had nothing to lose by asking," Elsas told me. "A few weeks later, I was surprised to receive a phone call from May, who told me that John would like to come."

They set a date, and Lennon showed up at the appointed time, along with Pang and a friend named Richard. "As the interview began," Elsas recalled, "I was still in a bit of shock that I was actually talking with John Lennon and doing it live on the radio. I was focused on making sure to introduce his new album to our audience, since I was well aware that this must have been the primary reason he'd come to the station.

"What I really wanted to do was ask a thousand and one Beatle-related questions," Elsas continued, "but that didn't seem appropriate. However, I did ask whether '#9' in the new album's '#9 Dream' title might refer back to the Beatles' 'Revolution 9,' and that did open the door to some Fab Four discussion.

"While tracks from *Walls and Bridges* were playing," Elsas told me, "John and I talked off the air about what songs to schedule next. Remember, this was live radio; nothing was scripted, and there was no producer. John and I were sitting across from each other, divided by two turntables. Joe, the engineer, was in the other room making sure the tapes were running to record the show. I was in charge of controlling all the mics and music.

"We played 'Watch Your Step' by Bobby Parker, one of the songs that Lennon said had influenced him," Elsas continued, "and he suggested we segue from that to the Beatles' 'Day Tripper,' which is on *Yesterday and Today*. The album is well known among fans for its notorious hidden 'butcher' cover, and—after I pulled that LP from the huge wall of records behind us—I was surprised to see how eager John was to share the story behind the controversy. Suddenly, I realized that he was still a Beatles fan himself. I relaxed, and the rest of the afternoon was magic."

A full audio recording of Lennon's appearance on Elsas's show has never been released in any authorized format, though brief excerpts have been available on the DJ's website and a couple of other places. Here's a transcript, which has not previously been published. —Ed.

Dennis Elsas: Now, I've been talking about this . . . I don't like to do this—I'd like to have told you all afternoon what was going to happen, but now that it's gonna happen, why don't you just say hello?

John Lennon: Surprise, surprise. It's Dr. Winston O'Boogie at your service. [*Lennon, whose middle name was Winston, used this pseudonym in the credits for some of his work, such as his vocal and guitar backup on Elton John's version of the Beatles' "Lucy in the Sky with Diamonds."* —Ed.] I am Dennis's surprise, actually.

Elsas: And he didn't come out of a cake or anything like that. John Lennon is with us and will spend some time this afternoon to talk about the new album and a whole bunch of things . . . and maybe even do some disc jockeying?

Lennon: Yeah, yeah, it's my second-favorite occupation.

Elsas: We'll get into some good music.

[*Lennon's "Whatever Gets You Thru the Night" plays.*]

Lennon: Ah, hello, folks. That was them singing together. And, uh, are we going to the news, or are we going to drop the news?

Elsas: No, I think we'll listen to news later on today.

Lennon: OK, we know what happened, don't we?

Elsas: That's the single ["Whatever Gets You Thru the Night"]?

Lennon: Yeah, and it's wild and rough. I call it "Crippled Inside," y' know? It's like releasing "Crippled Inside" from the *Imagine* album instead of "Imagine." But I took a consensus of opinion because after I'd done it, I just couldn't make head or tail which one could be commercial, y'know, so they told me that one. So here we go, and it seems to be doing all right.

Elsas: Was that done . . . was the whole album done in New York?

Lennon: Yeah, Record Plant. In fact, I've recorded everything since I've left England in Record Plant. Anybody listening from Record Plant? They're a good gang there. And Al . . . what is it?

May Pang: Carmine.

Lennon: Carmine—I keep calling Al "Carmine"—is just mixing it down to quad 'cause I couldn't face it again. I just arrived in L.A., and I got a note saying, "We want it quad."

Elsas: Aha.

Lennon: I said, "Are you kidding? I just mixed the whole thing—you should have told me that first." But he's doing a good job . . . for the twenty people who buy quad.

Elsas: Well, you never . . . the cover is . . . for those of you who haven't had the chance to see it yet in your favorite record store—

Lennon: 'Cause it ain't out yet! It's this week, actually.

Elsas: It's not in the stores yet?

Lennon: I don't know if . . . well . . .

Pang: It is.

Lennon: Richard, a friend of mine here, went down to get it the other day and they hadn't got it yet. I guess it will be early next week. It'll be in the shops.

Elsas: All right. Now, there's a drawing on the front . . .

Lennon: You could call it that, yeah. It's . . .

Elsas: Uh . . .

Lennon: Well, it's hard to explain, isn't it? 'Cause it's all flapped over. A guy at Capitol designed it. It's a nice design.

Elsas: The album comes in two parts.

Lennon: Yeah.

Elsas: Is this a drawing? It says, JOHN LENNON JUNE [19]52, AGE 11.

Lennon: Yeah, that's true. There's an exam they have in England that they hang over your head, y'know. There's a couple of them. But one of them is called Eleven-Plus. And they hang it over you from age five, y'know. If you don't pass the Eleven-Plus, which you take at eleven, obviously, then you're finished in life. So that was the only exam I ever passed, because I was terrified.

And after that exam's over, the teacher said you can do whatever you want, so I just painted. And of all the childhood sort of drawings and paintings I did, these were the only ones that ever got saved. And I was originally going to use them for the oldies-but-goldies album with [producer Phil] Spector, but that sort of fell apart in the middle because of his [nearly fatal 1974 auto] accident. And that and the guy'd already started the design, so I said, "Oh, they'll fit the new album anyway, so use them." And there're three or four pictures that I did at that age.

Elsas: And *Walls and Bridges* . . . what is that? Is that a prophetic title?

Lennon: I don't really know. I mean, I get these things that sound nice, y'know. I had the song "#9 Dream," [which] was [originally] called "Walls and Bridges," and I just had the title "Walls and Bridges," and I tried to fit it in anywhere like a jigsaw. So it didn't seem to fit any of the songs, and I hadn't written anything, so I just shoved it on as the album title. It seemed to be sort of wide enough to cover everything. It's like communication, y'know, walls . . .

Elsas: Right.

Lennon: Four walls, bridges you go over. I think I heard it on a public-service announcement. On TV—one of those late-night things where they make you feel awful. In between the movies, you know.

Elsas: [The song] "#9 Dream" was [originally called] "Walls and Bridges"?

Lennon: Was called "Walls and Bridges." I mean, some of them have had twenty titles. I change them all the time up to the last minute.

Elsas: All right. Well, let's take a listen.

Lennon: OK.

Elsas: "Number nine" [in the song title "#9 Dream"] has no reference back to the old "Number nine, number nine" [in the Beatles' "Revolution 9"]?

Lennon: Well, yeah, if you look at the cover, and those of you who don't have it will get it. In June 1952 I've drawn four guys playing football, and number nine is the number on the guy's back, and now that was pure coincidence. And I was born on the ninth of October and that "Number nine, number nine" Beatle thing was an engineer's voice, y'know. And, it just sorta seems to be my number, so I stick with it.

Elsas: All right. It's just about four o'clock, and so I need an official station break.

Lennon: OK. This is John Lennon with Dennis on WNEW-FM, and we're mucking about on a Saturday rainy afternoon 'cause we've got you all trapped in your rooms, you see, because it's too wet to go anywhere.

Elsas: We even have the four o'clock temperature readings.

Lennon: We do? Oh, let's see how hot it is. Temperature is 68—no wonder I'm sweating. Humidity 93 p-c-t, whatever that is.

Elsas: Percent.

Lennon: Oh. Why don't they do those little round things? Barometer 30.3 and falling. Oh, disgusting. Winds southeast at 8 miles an hour. Cloudy. And, somebody said the air was unacceptable today, but I accept it. Sounded all right to me.

Elsas: That's the official forecast.

Lennon: Here's the official WNEW weather forecast: mostly cloudy with periods of rain this afternoon, tonight, and tomorrow. High times . . . oh, no! Ha ha, wish it was! High this afternoon and tomorrow in the seventies. Low tonight in the mid-sixties. Watch out for it. That's about my period. Monday's outlook: fair and cool, man.

Elsas: OK, Metromedia stereo at WNEW-FM in New York. John Lennon.

[*Lennon's "#9 Dream" plays.*]

Lennon: Ah, so there we are. That was some, uh, Gaelic words. *Böwakawa poussè.*

Elsas: I'm trying to follow the lyrics in here. There's a lyric sheet, thank goodness, for the album.

Lennon: Well, I print them even if I'm not pleased with them, you know, 'cause I always tend to, on a few tracks, bury the voice.

Elsas: There are drawings within the lyric book, too. Are those also from . . .

Lennon: Yes, same period. There's about one that isn't. There's a picture of a horse, I think, I did about a year or something later, which is at the end. What they did was sort of jumble them up on the cover and then repeat some of them back inside.

Elsas: It's not . . . I mean the package is really nice.

Lennon: Well, it's the first time since I was a Beatle, as it were, that I let the package out of my hands. I used to even make the cover on like

Mind Games. I handmade it, you know. I cut out little pictures. I enjoyed it. But I didn't really have time, you know.

Elsas: Yeah, and . . .

Lennon: So . . . and I'm glad because I let it go, and the guy came up with something creative, and it's a surprise for me now. I can look at it and enjoy it without sort of discussing, thinking, *Oh, I should have done this, I should have done that.*

Elsas: You have all kinds of friends [on the album]—Jim Keltner, Jesse Ed Davis . . .

Lennon: Yeah, Klaus Voormann, bass; Nicky Hopkins, piano; Ken Ascher, keyboards; Arthur Jenkins, percussion; Bobby Keys; Howard Johnson; Eddie Mottau on rhythm guitar; Bobby Keys and Howard Johnson on horns; Steve Madaio; and somebody called Frank [Vicari]; and somebody else . . . I'm not quite . . . May?

Pang: Ron [Aprea].

Lennon: Ron. I had a five-piece horn section, which was weird. It was just the amount of people that turned up, you know.

Elsas: All right, well, we'll be spending the rest of the afternoon with John Lennon in Metromedia stereo. Some commercials and more talk and music. Dennis Elsas here at WNEW-FM. Here we go.

[*Commercial airs for Mahavishnu Orchestra and its* Apocalypse *album.*]

Lennon: Don't miss the Mahavishnu Orchestra at Avery Fisher Hall, Wednesday, October the second. The newest album is available at all Alexander record departments at $4.19. Not a bad price at all.

Elsas: Did you hear—

Lennon: It's nice to hear [Beatles producer] George Martin's cooking, right? [*Martin produced Mahavishu Orchestra's* Apocalypse. —*Ed.*]

Elsas: When was the last time you did work with him?

Lennon: Uh, *Abbey Road.*

Elsas: Have you seen him? Do you—

Lennon: I saw him in California, in the Beverly Hills Hotel . . .

Elsas: Ah . . .

Lennon: In the bar. I went to see him, you know, and we got a little tiddly and had a little, you know—

Elsas: He's working now.

Lennon: —an old-time discussion.

Elsas: With the America album, the new one. [*Martin, who had produced America's recently issued* Holiday, *was now working on its* Hearts *album, which would be released in 1975. —Ed.*]

Lennon: He's working on that, too?

Elsas: Yeah.

Lennon: I don't know what he's working on. The last thing he was doing, he was talking of selling or had sold AIR [Studios in] London, which is his recording setup in England, and buying a boat and putting it all on it. And having a—

Elsas: A recording—

Lennon: Yacht, yeah. I said, "Can't wait," you know, "Call me when you've got it," you know! If they can balance the tapes and not make it all fall in the water, it would be great.

Elsas: John has brought along a couple of records that he thought all of us might be interested to hear. You know, more often than not we do things on the air where we show you that one riff may have been borrowed from another record, an older record. Maybe you could explain this one a bit.

Lennon: Well, yeah, I brought four singles. This is one of them oldies but goldies, as it were. This is an early '60s record by Bobby Parker called "Watch Your Step," which I call "Son of 'What'd I Say.'" I mean, there was the great record "What'd I Say" by Ray Charles, which is the first electric piano I ever heard on tape because nobody could work out what it was on record. And then, shortly after, maybe it could have been a year, because it all blends in, but this was the next move after "What'd I

Say," which is "Watch Your Step." The lick you'll recognize, 'cause I've used it, all the Beatles have used it, sort of in various forms. Recently, I heard it this last year. The Allman Brothers used the licks straight as it was for some song, which is cool, you know. And here it is. It's one of my favorite records.

[Bobby Parker's "Watch Your Step" plays, followed by the Beatles' "Day Tripper."]

Lennon: Number one, never was . . . Ha, ha, we're on, are we?

Elsas: [*Laughs.*] Yeah, you know, I was mentioning to you off the air that the *Yesterday and Today* album, I always take the cover and I try and peel back . . .

Lennon: Peel it to look for the dead babies bit, yeah.

Elsas: How did that happen that that album cover never saw the light of day or, if it did, got pulled off fairly quickly?

Lennon: It went out . . . we took the pictures in London at one of those photo sessions. By then we were really sort of beginning to hate it. A photo session was a big ordeal, and you had to at the time look normal, and you didn't feel it. And the photographer was a bit of a surrealist, you know? And he brought along all these babies and pieces of meat and doctors' coats, so we really got into it, and that's how we felt, yeah! So we sort of—I especially—pushed for it to be an album cover, just to break the image, you know?

Elsas: Um-hmm.

Lennon: And it got out in America, and they printed . . . about sixty thousand got out, and then there was some kind of fuss, as usual, and they were all sent back in, or withdrawn. And they stuck that awful-looking picture which you have in front of you, of us sitting, looking just as deadbeat, but supposed-to-be-happy-go-lucky foursome.

Elsas: You look very unhappy!

Lennon: Yeah! Right, right! So we tried to, you know, do something different.

Elsas: Album covers were much simpler then, right? Just the cover?

Lennon: Yeah, you just walk in, take your photo, and walk out, you know? Especially in America, we made only, say, ten albums actually in America. There seem to be thirty of them. And so we would design a cover or have control of it, more of our own covers in England; but America always had more albums, so they always needed another picture, another cover.

Elsas: We used to be very upset because England would have fourteen tracks per album . . .

Lennon: Yeah.

Elsas: And then we'd only get twelve.

Lennon: Well, we used to say why can't they put fourteen out in America, you know, and stop them, because we would sequence the album how we thought they should sound, and we put a lot of work into the sequencing, too. And we almost got to not care what happened in America, because it was always different. They wouldn't let us put fourteen out. They said that there was some rule or something that would—

Elsas: Greed. *Greed*, I think, is the word.

Lennon: Well, whatever it was, you know . . . and so we almost didn't care what happened to the albums in America until we started coming over more and noticing like on the eight tracks they have outtakes and mumbling on the beginning, which is interesting now, but it used to drive us crackers because we'd make an album, and then they'd keep two from every album.

Elsas: There was also an album out on the Vee-Jay label. Whoever was dealing the contracts at that time before Capitol had *Meet the Beatles*.

Lennon: Yeah.

Elsas: And then at the same time *Introducing the Beatles* came out in America on something that's called the Vee-Jay label, which doesn't exist anymore, though the album's still—

Lennon: They had "Love Me Do." I don't remember what else they had.

Elsas: Well, it was rereleased later. Capitol got the rights and then called it *The Early Beatles.*

Lennon: I only remember "Love Me Do." I think that was a Vee-Jay record.

Elsas: We have also in front of us here *The Beatles' Second Album.*

Lennon: That's what it's called, yeah; I don't know what it is.

Elsas: "Electrifying, big-beat performances [*Lennon laughs*] by England's Paul McCartney, John Lennon, and George Harrison and Ringo Starr, featuring 'She Loves You' and 'Roll Over Beethoven.'"

Lennon: And "Roll Over Beethoven."

Elsas: You know, many of these things have been remixed to stereo.

Lennon: Oh, it was awful.

Elsas: I think the original mono recordings are—

Lennon: I didn't realize it happened, when they put out that package last year.

Elsas: The Blue and Red? [*A reference to the 1973 anthologies titled 1962–1966 and 1967–1970. —Ed.*]

Lennon: The two albums, and I just thought, I presumed, that they would just copy 'em from the masters and put them out. I didn't even listen to it until after it was out, and I took it back, and I played it, and it was embarrassing, you know. I mean, some of the tracks survived, but it was really embarrassing. Some fool had tried to make it stereo, and it didn't work.

Elsas: Yeah, people should stay with the mono and not be so concerned . . .

Lennon: Yeah, because, you know, there's a difference between stereo and mono, obviously. And if you mix something in mono and then try and fake it . . .

Elsas: Yeah.

Lennon: It just . . . you lose the guts of it, you know. And a lot of them lost, lost the . . . the fast version of "Revolution [1]" was destroyed, you know. I mean, it was a heavy record, and then they made it into a piece of ice cream. [*Elsas laughs.*] But never mind. It's all the past, isn't it?

Elsas: Well-chosen words. We're at WNEW-FM, Dennis Elsas with John Lennon, our guest this afternoon, and from *The Beatles' Second Album*, you said that there would be something to listen to carefully in the middle of this song.

Lennon: Oh, when you presented the album to me, I noticed "I Call Your Name," which was a song I wrote when I was about sixteen except for the middle eight, which we did ska. Now it's called reggae, or it was blue beat. It was a bit like rock 'n' roll there. Reggae went through different periods; it was blue beat, then it was ska, then it became reggae. And this is our first attempt at sort of Jamaican, and it's in the middle eight.

[*The Beatles' "I Call Your Name" plays.*]

Elsas: The Beatles and "I Call Your Name" at WNEW-FM.

[*Commercial for Joffrey Ballet airs.*]

Lennon: Ah, yeah, the Joffrey will be at City Center from October the ninth—happy birthday, John—through November the third. The box office on Fifty-Fifth Street, between Sixth and Seventh Avenue, opens every day at 10 AM. Reserve tickets on a major credit card by calling 489-6810. Don't miss it.

Elsas: Hmm . . .

Lennon: Yeah, my auntie used to like ballet, but she didn't like the men's crotch. She said, "It's all right except for those terrible crotches!" [*Elsas laughs.*]

We're going to play Electric Light Orchestra, from last year. "Show-down," which I thought was a great record, and I was expecting it to be number one, but I don't think UA [United Artists] got their fingers out and pushed it. And it's a nice group. I call them Son of Beatles, although they're doing things that we never did, obviously. But I remember the statement they made when they first formed was to carry on from where the Beatles left off with "[I Am the] Walrus," and they certainly did.

Now, for those people who would like to know where licks and things come from, like I do, because I'm always nicking little things myself, this is a beautiful combination of "I Heard It Through the Grapevine" by Marvin Gaye and "[Lightnin'] Strikes" . . . Lou Christie, and it's a beautiful job with a little "Walrus" underneath.

[*"Showdown" by Electric Light Orchestra plays, then "I Heard It Through the Grapevine" by Marvin Gaye.*]

Lennon: Ah, we're having a break here. It's John Lennon and Dennis Schulnetz [*sic*] on WNEW Metromedia stereo, if you've got the equipment. Otherwise, it's on your cable TV. [*Elsas laughs.*] Which is just as good, I always find myself. We're just looking through to see what else to play. Oh, we've got something lined up here, right.

Elsas: Yeah. First we've got to do some commercials.

Lennon: Oh, we've got to do some . . . oh, I love commercials.

Elsas: Now, the official . . . you know, you have to tell us what we . . .

Lennon: Oh, the official . . . oh, that was "Showdown," Electric Light Orchestra. That was the one before that one. And "Grapevine" was one of the parts of inspiration for it by Marvin Gaye. ELO was on UA and Marvin Gaye was on his own.

Elsas: You've been producing.

Lennon: Oh, yes, I've been producing all sorts.

Elsas: I mean, there's your own album, the new one, *Walls and Bridges.* And then there's this one, this odd album. [*A reference to Harry Nilsson's* Pussy Cats *album, which Lennon produced. —Ed.*]

Lennon: This odd album by John Lennon and Harry Nilsson having a fit in L.A., yes. Well, I was in the middle of the [Phil] Spector album, which is . . . some of you will know what it is. I was making an oldies-but-goldies album with Spector, and he had a few car accidents and was . . . that was the end of that for a bit.

Elsas: Will it happen? That record?

Lennon: I have nine tracks which Phil sent me three days before I went into the studio to make *Walls and Bridges*—out soon!—and so I couldn't do . . . I was waiting and waiting for months, and I was just sort of hanging around with Harry Nilsson and people in L.A. and getting into trouble and, whenever we got into trouble, it was *my* name in the paper, so I thought, *Forget this.*

You know, every time we go out for the night, I end up in the paper. [*Elsas laughs.*]

So, you know, I said to Harry one hangover morning, "What are we doing, man? We're wasting our time here. We might as well put all this energy into work." And I knew he was going to make an album. I didn't feel like starting a new one because I had one half finished, so I said, "Look, I'll produce ya," which means I'll sit behind the desk and make sure they get the drums on, you know, and things like that. And keep 'em together as they take off.

And we had a good time making it. We had a lot of friends in there playing. I won't go through the list again; half of them are on my album, half of 'em are on Ringo's. You know, the usual crew with a few added extras, like Keith Moon. Some tracks are beautiful, some tracks are a bit weird, but, uh, Harry Nilsson and John Lennon together is a pretty weird combination.

Elsas: Why the goldies?

Lennon: 'Cause Harry . . . I don't know. He wanted to do certain tracks, you know, like he wanted to do "Loop de Loop." He wanted to do "Rock Around the Clock" because he thought it would be good fun, and he said nobody's ever covered "Rock Around the Clock." We open *Billboard* and there it is, 108, by Bill Haley, you know, while we're doing it. [*Elsas laughs.*] [*Haley's 1955 hit reentered the charts in 1974, reaching number thirty-nine in May, thanks to its use as the original theme song of the TV show* Happy Days. —*Ed.*] We're doing "Save the Last Dance for Me," which he played me a tape of some of his songs he'd written, which wasn't many, and also just a sort of demo tape of him singing "Save the Last Dance for Me." And it was really beautiful, and it was like we did it on the album, only because we orchestrated it and put a lot of other stuff on it. And it was just very nice the way he did it, and we were very excited doing it. And we liked the record, and then we looked in the charts and there was, uh, DeFranco—

Elsas: DeFranco Family. [*That group had a Top Twenty hit with "Save the Last Dance for Me" in May 1974. —Ed.*]

Lennon: —Family, but it was not quite the same style. But, so everything, as we were cutting it . . . we look and someone would come in and say, "But someone's just done that." So we thought, *Hell, we're doing them anyway.* We enjoyed it, and some he picked and some I picked. But mainly they were his choice, and this is "Save the Last Dance," which we both rather like. I hope you like it, too.

[*"Save the Last Dance for Me" by Nilsson plays.*]

Lennon: Harry! Great chamber echo they have down in . . . what was that studio in . . . Burbank Studios, Los Angeles, giant place. I'd better take this cookie out of me mouth.

Elsas: [*Laughs.*] All right.

Lennon: The weather is still weather.

Elsas: Yeah, oh, here's the new weather, John.

Lennon: Oh, boy! More weather!

Elsas: But there's no temperature reading, so we'll fake it.

Lennon: Occasional periods of, oh, this is the weather, folks. Occasional periods of rain tonight and tomorrow, ending tomorrow night. Low tonight in the sixties, high tomorrow in the seventies, cooler tomorrow night with a low in the fifties. Oh, talking of the '50s, we've just been there. Monday's outlook: sunny, windy, and cool. Oh, remember that old joke? Tomorrow will be sunny followed by munny, tunny, wenny, thunny, and Friday? Tomorrow will be muggy followed by tuggy, weggy, thurggy. Tomorrow will be just the same as today, only different.

Elsas: I've got here . . . a new album from George—

Lennon: Splinter. [*Splinter was a two-man vocal group recorded by George Harrison. —Ed.*]

Elsas: The new label, George's Dark Horse.

Lennon: Dark Horse, yeah! It's a nice-looking label, right?

Elsas: What . . . do you see them? Do you see the three of them?

Lennon: I've seen Paul and George, Paul and Ringo, a lot this year because they've been over here. Paul was here about a month ago, and I spent a couple of Beaujolais evenings with him reminiscing about when we were only thirty-eight. And Ringo I've seen a lot of, 'cause he's been over here recording. I was just down . . . in the middle of my album, I just took a break and went down and did a track I'd written for Ringo on his new album. And then I went to Caribou and sang "Lucy in the Sky" with Elton John and then came back and finished my album off. So . . . and Paul and Ringo, yeah. George I haven't seen, but he's coming over in October to rehearse. So I'll go and see him then.

Elsas: Relationships are cordial?

Lennon: Oh, very warm, warm! Very warm, my dear!

Elsas: All right.

Lennon: "Are they getting together?"

Elsas: Yes! Are they getting together?

Lennon: Well, we'd have to be on Dark Horse label the way things are going! We never talk about it because the four of us have never gotten into a room together, because of green cards and immigration and all that jazz. George and Paul have a little trouble getting in and out of this country, too. And so the four of us have never sat in a room together for three years, although we've managed to get three together in one room. That was Paul, Ringo, and me. That was sometime in the summer, in the middle of Harry's album, actually.

And so there's always, I . . . if you say no, it's a negative—they all hate each other. If you say yes, it's "*Rollin'* [Stone] *Crawdaddy Creem* says they're getting together," you know, or "Harry's bringing them together" or something. There's always a chance we'd work together because, you know, if we see each other, we tend to fall into that kind of mood. But I can't see us touring or anything like that. We've never discussed it. I can see us making records. You know, why not? But that touring bit, I don't quite fancy that meself.

Elsas: There's no definitive plans for an album, though.

Lennon: No, no, no, no. We're more liable to be inclined to work together in '76 when the contract comes up. I mean, to be very commercial about it . . . we'd be stupid to give away anything new at the rate we get paid now.

We're going to play ya some Splinter, which is a group George has just produced. I haven't heard the album; I've just heard a bit on your radio station the other day on cable TV, actually, and the singer, Bill Elliott, I used on a sort of . . . not a charity record but a record that I made for an underground paper in England called *Oz*, and they were having a lot of hassles in court, and Bill Elliott was one of the singers. He sang something, whatever . . . "God Save Oz." And here's the first track from side one on the Splinter album, and we'll see. It sounded like George on the radio last night.

[*"Gravy Train" by Splinter plays, then "I'm the Greatest" by Ringo Starr, then "What You Got" by John Lennon.*]

Lennon: Well, it was hours ago when we played these records, but we'll tell you what was happening hours ago, 'cause if you're like me, you wait and wait to hear what it was, you know. Why don't they tell you what it is? A few hours ago . . . oh, it's not this list up there; oh, it's not that bad. "Gravy Train" was that . . . the writing is amazing, Dennis. [*Elsas laughs.*] "Gravy Train" by Splinter on Dark Horse, brackets A&M, which was George Harrison's production of Splinter. Sounds pretty good, too.

"I'm the Greatest" we heard; you probably recognized that. Ringo, on Apple, [doing] the song I wrote for him and sang along with him. Should've been a single, I always said. They wouldn't even give me the B-side. Next time I'll get it! And then we went to *Walls and Bridges*, which happens to be my new album, and I'm Dr. Winston O'Boogie, otherwise known as John Lennon. And that was "What You Got." The guitar lick was inspired, should we say, by "Money, Money, Money" [*The song is actually called "For the Love of Money." —Ed.*] by the O'Jays, was it? Yeah. 'Cause you'd never recognize it now, and that's on Apple or Capitol, and it's available at all those record stores that I keep mentioning.

Elsas: We need . . . it's just a minute past five o'clock, so we need an official . . . and you have to give the FM after the WNEW and you have to give the city.

Lennon: The city?

Elsas: Right.

Lennon: But we know what city we're in.

Elsas: No, but in case someone from—

Lennon: OK, and you do Metromedia before or after—

Elsas: Well, that's not legal. You can just throw that in.

Lennon: OK. This is, ah . . . I keep getting your last name lost in…Schulitz?

Elsas: It's— [*Laughs.*]

Lennon: Dennis will do. OK, this is John Lennon with Dennis Schulitz on Metromedia radio on WNEW-FM, New York City. It also comes through on Sterling Cable Manhattan TV, on Channel N and Channel 3, and it's very good, you know? They don't even know it themselves. I've been told the people here, they don't know it. Well, are we going to play this record now?

Elsas: No, we have to do commercials.

Lennon: Oh, well, here's a nice little commercial, and I'll have a Whopper, if it's a Whopper.

[*Commercial airs for conductor Pierre Boulez's recording of Igor Stravinsky's The Rite of Spring.*]

Lennon: Pierre Boulez, folks, listen to this. Play cart, C1. Pierre Boulez's album, *The Rights of Spring*, spelled r-i-g-h-t-s—ha ha, very subtle—is available at a special low price. No wonder, I tell meself. At all Korvettes stores for only $3.87. Or you can get my album instead, but that's a matter of choice. [*Elsas laughs.*]

Tonight, the Joint in the Woods—guess who's there? It's ladies' night. They won't like that. Women's night. Featuring the exciting eight-piece, all-female group Isis or Is Is, depending where you come from. All females admitted at half price. Oh, good, well, Bowie can get in. [*Elsas laughs.*] Also, dancing party with Lock, Stock & Barrel. That probably is a group because it's in inverted commas, coming next Wednesday, October the second, to the Joint in the Woods. Nothing like a joint in the woods, he says, losing his green-card possibilities in one blow. [*Elsas laughs.*] T. Rex on Friday. Now, that's a good band, now he's getting—buy a couple of his records—he's getting fat with worry. On Friday, October the fourth, Martha Reeves. She's great. And Saturday, October the fifth, Buzzy Linhart. She's great, too. [*Elsas continues laughing.*] For more information, call . . . get your little pencils ready! 201-335-98 naught, naught. Ninety-eight hundred. Joint in the Woods . . . Parsippany.

Elsas: Yes! Well done!

Lennon: Got it this time. Sounds like a group. New Joisey. Where the stars shine! All right. We're not gonna bother with the weather, just look out of the window. You want the weather?

Elsas: It's up to you.

Lennon: The degrees have changed. Oh, this is a nice degree. The temperature's 69. [*Breathes heavily.*] Get it? [*Elsas laughs.*] Yeah? The humidity is 90 percent. Number nine, that's all right. The barometer thirty point naught one three—that's another nine—inches and falling. Inches and falling? That sounds like a song. Wind southeast at 6. See, it's all six and nines—very deep, man, very deep. The weather in Central Park is still there. And it's cloudy. OK? That was UPI. We're only giving you one version of the weather so that you don't get confused.

Elsas: Ah, yes.

Lennon: Are we going back to the . . .

Elsas: Yeah.

Lennon: My favorite goldies and oldies?

Elsas: We are, so everyone can tune in properly, at 102.7.

Lennon: One-oh-two-seven, in case you're not quite on the dial there. Otherwise you get that terrible hissy-treble jazz, you know?

Elsas: And John Lennon is our guest.

Lennon: Yes, he is.

Elsas: Or maybe it's the other way around.

Lennon: Well, depends which . . . no, I think I'm the guest because I'm sitting behind the thing, aren't I?

Elsas: Yeah.

Lennon: Although I do have the sweeties and the . . .

Elsas: But you brought the records along.

Lennon: I brought four only, you know. I didn't know how you'd take it. I nearly brought a hundred, but you know . . . I forget to play me own album, I'm so busy playing these others. This is . . .

Elsas: What is . . .

Lennon: Another American record, that nobody I know over here seems to have ever heard of. And it's called "Some Other Guy," by Richie Barrett. There is a strange bootleg of the Beatles singing it rather crappily from the Cavern somewhere way back in '61. This is another what I call "Son of 'What'd I Say,'" "Son of 'Watch Your Step,'" "Son of 'Lick'" records, and this is a guy called Richie Barrett, who's also a songwriter. I think he's still around, but I don't know what he's doing. This is "Some Other Guy." You'll notice the intro is slightly like "Instant Karma."

[*Some Other Guy" by Richie Barrett plays, followed by a live version of "What'd I Say" by Ray Charles.*]

Lennon: Every band in the world—are we on?—yes, every band in the world used to do that song. That was an album version. [It] wasn't the original single, which as far as I know is the first electric piano on record that I ever heard. And "What'd I Say" seemed to be the start of all the guitar-lick records, because none of us had electric pianos, so we all did it on guitar, to try and get that low sound. And before that, everything was mainly licks like you get on the Little Richard rock 'n' roll records, like "Lucille" licks where the sax section and the guitar played it. And "What'd I Say" started a whole ball game, which is still going now. And that's all I've got to say about that! Dennis Elsas, you see I got his last name from Roberta. Are you listening, Roberta? She's making chocolate pudding, and I'm starving! [*Elsas laughs.*] All right!

Elsas: We are Metromedia stereo, WNEW-FM, and with John Lennon. In 1963 and '4 and '5, when the Stones were the group that was coming up hard and strong behind the Beatles, were you all friends?

Lennon: Yeah, we went to see them at . . . I believe the place was called Crawdaddy, in Richmond. And also, I think another place in London. And they were run by a different guy then, [music manager, songwriter, and producer] Giorgio Gomelsky, who also discovered, brackets, you know, quotes, the . . . what's that group everybody goes for that Jeff Beck was in? Oh, what . . . I can't remember the name. One of those mid-'60s English groups, anyway, which I never thought were much except for Jeff Beck. Every one of those, everybody went through the . . .

Elsas: Yardbirds.

Lennon: Yardbirds. That was it. Son of Stones. But they never really had a singer, you know, or a performer. And immediately we started hanging around London. The Stones were just up-and-coming in the clubs then, and we knew Giorgio through [Brian] Epstein, and we went down and saw them and became good friends. And the story on how . . . this song we're gonna play, "I Wanna Be Your Man," which we virtually finished off in front of them because they needed a record . . . they'd put out "Come On" by Chuck Berry, and they needed a quick follow-up.

And . . . we met Andrew Oldham, who used to work for us or used to work for Epstein, and he'd then gone with the Stones and probably got them off Giorgio Gomelsky, and he came to us and said, "Have you got a song for 'em?" We said sure, you know, we thought, 'cause we didn't really want it ourselves, which is one way of putting it. We went in, and I remember teaching it to them, you know. And the whole story of it, which helped my memory of it, 'cause it all fades away, is in that book on Mick, which Mick's not keen on. I understand that—

Elsas: That's the Tony Scaduto book [*Mick Jagger: Everybody's Lucifer,* published August 1974]?

Lennon: Yeah, yeah, but it's all right for people who they're not writing about, those books. You know, if it was about me, I wouldn't like it probably, either. But I must say, I raced through it for all the juicy bits, like everybody else, right? [*Elsas laughs.*] And it's very interesting. I don't think it really harms him, you know? It shows that he knows what he's doing, which is cool. I don't think he did anything to Brian Jones, either. So here's "I Wanna Be Your Man" by the Stones themselves.

[*"I Wanna Be Your Man" by the Rolling Stones plays, followed by the Beatles' version of the same song.*]

Elsas: That's the only one that the two groups [both] ever did.

Lennon: Yeah. The only records we covered, I mean that we both did the same, yeah. They did it first; we did it with Ringo after. And that was it. That was the Stones' second single. I don't know what happened over here, but in England it was—

Elsas: You're still in touch with them, and you speak with them?

Lennon: Yeah, I see . . . I know Mick's around now, haven't seen him this trip, but last time I saw him was L.A. In fact, we were jamming together down in Record Plant West, and we made quite a good track. [*"Too Many Cooks,"* which has appeared on bootlegs. —Ed.] I was so-called producing it, meaning sitting behind the desk. And—

Elsas: Was there ever talk then, or is there talk now, of the groups getting together and doing something?

Lennon: We never talked about it, because in the early days we just had our own careers to look after, and we used to . . . we hung around in two separate periods. One was when they were initially still playing in the clubs. I remember the first thing one of them ever . . . Brian Jones came over and said, "Are you playing a harmonica or a harp on 'Love Me Do'?" 'Cause he didn't know how I got . . . he knew I got this bottom note and he suspected . . . I said a harmonica, you know, with a button, which wasn't real funky blues, you know, if you're supposed to be . . . you couldn't get "Hey! Baby" licks on a blues harp, when we were also doing "Hey! Baby" by Bruce Channel at that time. [*Elsas laughs.*]

And then the later period was when we both were sort of riding high, and there was a discotheque scene in London, and the main club we all went to was the Ad Lib. There was a couple more, but they were never as big: Bag O'Nails, but we used to just go in there and dance and talk music, and generally get drunk and stoned and high. And one of the records we always played was in the Ad Lib itself, folks, with all of us sitting there, listening and dancing, looking super stoned, and the record was called "Daddy Rollin' Stone" by Derek Martin, which the Who later did a sort of version of, like the English usually do of these great records, not too good, that's including us.

Elsas: This was an American record?

Lennon: Oh, yeah. Another great American record. That's all we ever played, American records. There's no such thing as English records, those days. So, here's "Daddy Rollin' Stone," Derek Martin, on Sue Records. About '63 probably.

[*"Daddy Rollin' Stone" by Derek Martin plays.*]

Lennon: I want a Whopper.

Elsas: Oh, yeah?

Lennon: Ha ha, don't you? I love them things.

Elsas: Derek—

Lennon: I'm five pounds overweight, and I want a Whopper. Isn't that—

Elsas: Derek Martin . . .

Lennon: Yeah, Derek with a D-e-r-e-k. "Daddy Rollin' Stone." Now you heard the real one for all you Who freaks.

Elsas: Station break and commercials is what's next.

Lennon: OK, this is WNEW-FM, New York City, New York [at] 105, 102.5, no, 10 . . . which is it? But if you're listening, you're tuned in. That's the main thing.

Elsas: One-oh-two-point-seven.

Lennon: One-oh-two-point-seven. I just turn it around until I hear what they say. And here's a nice Whopper commercial. [*Laughs.*]

[*Commercial airs.*]

Lennon: Ah, time; we're on the air and it's, oh, it's a minute past half past five, which, I guess is thirty-one minutes to six. You have a funny way of saying things, before . . .

Elsas: Twenty-nine minutes before the hour . . .

Lennon: The hour!

Elsas: And thirty-one minutes past.

Lennon: "What hour?" I ask myself, every time they say it. Which hour are they talking about?

Elsas: Is it, um . . . we've got just twenty-nine minutes left . . . [*Lennon gasps*] and about eight thousand questions. It went . . . our two hours or so have gone quickly.

Lennon: About eight thousand records to play, too.

Elsas: Hmm. Is it easier to be John Lennon, celebrity, in New York? Are people less apt to hassle you and bother you with things? Can you go about your life? Can you have dinner in a restaurant?

Lennon: Oh, yeah, yeah. Well, there's no . . . that goes for L.A., Frisco, anywhere. I think people are a bit cooler in New York, hmm, hmm, hmm. And I've been here three years, and people sort of will wave or something. Or a taxi driver will say, oh, you know, "Are you still here?" Or whatever, "Good luck" and all that jazz about immigration, hmm, hmm, hmm.

Elsas: Can we, uh . . .

Lennon: Yes, we can. [*Laughs.*]

Elsas: Yeah, what about all that?

Lennon: And so anyway, I do get . . . one of me biggest kicks is just going out to eat or going to the movies, you know, and doing things I couldn't do when I was in the middle of the Beatles stuff. And I really get off on that. And people occasionally ask for autographs or just want to shake hands . . . which is cool with me, and I'm just known enough to keep me ego floating but unknown enough to get around, which is nice.

Elsas: You like New York?

Lennon: I love it, you know, and that's why I'm fighting so much to stay here. So's I can be in New York, you know, maybe they could just ban me from Ohio or something, you know? [*Elsas laughs.*] Nothing against Ohio!

Elsas: What's the status? I mean, we saw photographs of you walking in and out of court buildings . . .

Lennon: With my suit on.

Elsas: Yes. You looked very nice.

Lennon: Oh, well, thank you! Yeah, well, every now and then, this is the way, as it appears to me, which is virtually like it appears to the public, 'cause I don't follow it in detail unless the lawyer calls me—Leon Wildes, nice guy. Every now and then, I suddenly hear that I've got thirty days to get out of the country. Last time, I was on the way to Record Plant, I was in a taxi, and the radio was on, and I just heard it announced over the radio. So, being jocular, I said, "Drive me to the airport, Sam." [*Elsas and Lennon laugh.*]

And we were laughing about that, and apparently me lawyers hadn't told me, because they didn't want to depress me in the middle of the album, but I got it over the airways instead. And they say you've got thirty days to get out, and then my lawyer appeals it, and that gives me another six months or something like that, and it goes round and round in circles.

The last time I was in court was . . . I think the government had taken me to court for something or other, and our plea was, could we interview the prosecution counsel that had originally been the government's prosecution counsel and the head of immigration? Could we have them on the stand, you know, to examine them or whatever? But we were not granted that, you know, so we're not allowed to talk to their ex-lawyer, who's a nice guy and a straight guy, and he'd probably tell us the truth, you know, so somebody doesn't want us to interview them.

But I seem to be still here, and I don't have any intentions of going. And I'd like to thank all the people that write to me. And 'cause I don't usually answer, because I have no answer, you know, about how they can help. But one thing that does help, I think: the fact that you write to me is helpful, because it cheers me up when I think about it. And the other thing is, if you just write to your local senator or congressman, that keeps the thing in their minds, and it isn't like, "Oh, he's already gone, what happened?" Because those senators and congressmen are a bit like advertisers: if they get a letter from one person, they reckon it represents fifty or a hundred, and it just reminds them when they're sitting over their cigars somewhere and the case occasionally comes up. They might think, *Oh, well, yeah, you know, my constituents wrote me a letter about that.* So that's about the only way you could help.

Elsas: Yeah, it was, you know, it was sad when Charlie Chaplin—

Lennon: I know.

Elsas: —finally came back to America—

Lennon: That's what I don't want to happen to me.

Elsas: After all those years, gosh.

Lennon: I'd hate that, you know. They'd wheel me on at sixty and give me a plaque for "Yesterday" . . . [*Elsas laughs.*] And Paul wrote it, you know? I mean, I can just see it, you know? I don't want that. I'd like to live here, you know. I don't harm anybody. I've got a bit of a loud mouth—that's about all. And I make a lot of music, and that's mainly what I do. I'm making music, watching TV, or listening to the radio. And occasionally I get into a little spot of trouble, but nothing that's going to bring the country to pieces.

Elsas: No, certainly not.

Lennon: And I think there's certainly room for an odd Lennon or two here.

Elsas: I agree, and I know everyone out there does, too. We're sitting with the new album in Metromedia stereo at WNEW-FM. John Lennon's here, and this is a track called . . .

Lennon: Oh, this is a track called "Scared," which means at the moment I was writing it that's how I felt, but now I'm quite happy, thank you.

[*Lennon's "Scared" plays.*]

Lennon: Oh, that was "Scared"!

Elsas: "Scared."

Lennon: "Scared," yeah.

Elsas: From *Walls and Bridges*.

Lennon: Out soon or out now at all those record stores mentioned. Come on, [record retailer Sam] Goody, put it in the window now. [*Elsas laughs.*] And let's not forgot Harry Nilsson's *Pussy Cats*, hmm, hmm, hmm.

Elsas: Let's hope so. Um, some commercials?

Lennon: Yeah, why, you're gonna put your own commercial on, aren't you?

Elsas: I think so.

Lennon: It must be funny putting on your . . . well, it's like me here plugging me own record, right?

Elsas: [*Laughs.*] Well done.

[*Station commercial airs.*]

Lennon: Ah, are we on?

Elsas: Yes.

Lennon: OK, all twenty-nine White Castles in the New York, New Joisey area are open twenty-four hours a day. Locations at Roosevelt Avenue and Sixty-Ninth Street, in Woodside Rockaway Boulevard and

Ninety-Seventh Street, in Ozone Park, and at Northern Boulevard and Eighty-Eighth Street in Jackson Heights. And if you can't make it today, you go to my friend Richard's restaurant called Home on . . . uh, I've forgotten the name of the avenue, Richard. [*Elsas laughs.*] Ninety-First and Second, and they rock like hell in there, so they're going to kill me, but what the hell.

Elsas: That's a nice place.

Lennon: It is a nice place, yeah, and they play good music.

Elsas: This is—

Lennon: And thank you, [record retailer] King Karol, for putting Harry in the window! [*Elsas laughs.*] I'm getting them all in. Hello, Mother! Father! Auntie Joyce! [*Elsas and Lennon laugh.*]

Elsas: Um . . . it's very odd for me to be sitting here, in a way. I guess it's odd for you to be sitting here, too. I don't know, because, you know, ten years ago, I was just a Beatle freak sitting there taping you off *The Ed Sullivan Show* . . .

Lennon: Just a Beatle freak, oh!

Elsas: And buying the records and so on and so forth . . .

Lennon: Now you get them for free.

Elsas: That's true. [*Lennon laughs.*] And sitting here, and . . . does it make sense to you, to have been so important, and to be so important to so many people, and to have been a member of a group that changed hairstyles and clothing? And does all of that make any sense at all? Can you deal with that enormous—

Lennon: Well, I have to deal with it 'cause I was in it, you know. When I look back on it, it's sort of vaguely astounding, you know, the fact that I was in there. But when you're in it—we always call it the eye of the hurricane, you know—it was calmer right in the middle than it was on the peripherals. And, uh, what was the rest of it you said, because you got me on to that Chuck Berry thing, right?

Elsas: Yeah, I was—

Lennon: That's what we were talking about before.

Elsas: Yeah, I wondered, you know, because I sit here now as a disc jockey playing the record and interviewing John Lennon as a guest on the program, but ten years ago—five years ago, three, four years ago—this would have been the most unlikely thing in the world to me, and I find it wonderful and ironic and very weird at the same time that it would happen this way.

Lennon: Well, I guess I understand your point, because I was doing a radio thing on the phone with a radio station somewhere—I don't know where, I can't remember where it was—and the guy was talking the same way, you know. [He] said it was strange, 'cause he'd been sixteen in the middle of all of Beatlemania.

Elsas: Mmm-hmm.

Lennon: And there I was on the phone, mumbling, you know. And he put it well: he said it was like when he saw me on *Mike Douglas Show*, the way I was acting towards Chuck Berry. Because although I was there with Chuck Berry, and I'd been sitting backstage with him, I met him a few times over the years, I still have that feeling, that when I was sixteen, those were the records I listened to [in] what we called "milk bars" in England, with a jukebox. And I could never quite see him as a human 'cause there was one of my idols, actually talking to me.

And I understood when I used to order, you know, a steak and something and the waiter just didn't hear me because he was too busy looking at me saying, "It talks!" you know, "It talks!" So I understand it in a way, 'cause if I see any of those people from that period of my life when I was sixteen, I really don't know quite if I'm all there when I'm talking to them, you know. It's sort of an effort to see, "Oh, yeah, it's a human, but it is Chuck Berry, isn't it?"

Elsas: It's very nice to know that it's a human being. I mean it's delightful to feel as comfortable as you've made me the last hour and a half.

Lennon: Well, vice versa because this is your territory, not mine, you know?

Elsas: I'm glad you came up, too, because you know you've been in New York three, four years, and, uh, we've played the records, and it's a delight to finally have you come down and say hi. And I do hope that you'll come back again, too.

Lennon: Well, you know, you can see I'm enjoying it. I wish I had brought more of me oldies, but I thought I wouldn't want to flood all these young glitter kids with oldie records from the '60s. But I really do enjoy it, and I always felt a bit more strange about doing radio in New York, because I began to feel as though it was my hometown. And it's like almost putting on an act to go on the radio. I did a lot of TV in the early days I was here, but that was different. TV's big, and it goes everywhere, and it really is a show in a way.

But I tend to feel as though I could do radio easier in, say, L.A. or Frisco, where it was like being in a foreign country almost. But here it feels, well, the people know me. They see me on the street; I've been in almost every cab in New York.

It's strange to be sort of talking through a microphone to people. But I do enjoy it. And, as you know, I've told you that I listen to your station because they've always been good to me and my friends and the music and, as I've said before, it comes through the cable TV, and I'm a TV freak! So there you are, playing the stuff, and I thought, *I always meant to come down.*

But I always think, *Well, what do you do? I'm John Lennon and I'm coming down to play records.* You know, you feel such a fool. But here I am, and I talked to Elton John, who's a good friend, and he does it, and I thought, *He is the big one now, you know. There's not many bigger than him at the moment. And he feels comfortable; he enjoys himself.* He told me he had a good time, and he sort of almost turned me on to doing this kind of thing again. In the Beatle days, when you were a kid—

Elsas: Ahem . . .

Lennon: Well, we used to, we were so overawed by American radio, they had . . . Epstein, our manager, had to stop us. We phoned every radio station in town just saying, "Will you play the Ronettes doing this?" I mean, we wanted to hear the music, we didn't ask for our own records, we asked for the people—

Elsas: I know there was an historic afternoon which you spent in a hotel room with Scott Muni—

Lennon: Yeah, yeah. Hello, Scott, if you're listening.

Elsas: One of the few people to make that transition from being then one of the king of the Top Forty people and, uh, now runs this station. He's the boss, and he's on in the afternoon. And he, of course, was at that old station [WABC-AM in New York], the old call letters, but they took the B and made it [WA] "Beatle" C. [*Elsas is referring to the fact that during the 1960s, the DJs at WABC announced the station's name as "WABeatleC." —Ed.*]

Lennon: Aha. Yeah, I remember those days. It was good, and I didn't see Scott today because he wasn't here, but maybe next time I come, I can sit around with Scott for a bit, you know. He's a good lad. [*Elsas laughs.*] It's nice to meet the ones that've been around, you know, 'cause it's like we all went through it together. You asked me before about how did I assimilate it, and you know that bit about we changed everybody's hairstyles? But something influenced us . . . whatever's in the air to do it, you know, and pinpointing who did what first, you know, doesn't really work.

We were part of whatever the '60s was, and we were like the ones that were chosen to represent whatever was going on on the street. It was happening itself, you know. It could've been somebody else, but it wasn't. It was us and the Stones and people like that. And here we all are, you know? And we all went through it together. And now we're gonna play a track from *Magical Mystery Tour*, which is one of my favorite albums because it was so weird, and it's "I Am the Walrus." It's also one of my favorite tracks because I did it, of course! But also because it's one of those that has enough little bitties going to keep you interested even a hundred years later. And this is for the ELO freaks.

[*The Beatles' "I Am the Walrus" plays.*]

Lennon: Know what they're saying at the end there?

Elsas: No.

Lennon: "Everybody's got one! Everybody's got one!"

Elsas: What's *King Lear*? There's a bit of *King Lear* at the end of that, too.

Lennon: Yeah, that was live radio coming from the BBC, though they never knew it. When I was mixing the record, I just heard a radio in the room that was tuned to some BBC channel all the time, and we did about, I don't know, half a dozen mixes, and I just used whatever was coming through at the time. I never knew it was *King Lear* till years later somebody told me, because I could hardly make out what he was saying. But I just sort of . . . it was interesting to mix the whole thing with a live radio coming through it. So that's the secret of that one.

Elsas: That's really interesting. I mean, I had no idea that that's how it was done. Um, you're talking about secrets. How much of "Revolution 9," John, from *The White Album* [*The Beatles*] . . .how much of that was accidental, if any?

Lennon: Uh, well, it's like an action painting. You don't . . . "Revolution 9" is the weird one, right?

Elsas: Mmm-hmm.

Lennon: I had a lot of loops, tape loops, which is just a circle of tape . . . if people who don't understand it . . . it repeats itself over and over. And about ten of them on different mono machines all spinning at once with pencils and things holding them. I had a basic track, which was the end of the "Revolution" song where we'd gone on and on and on and on. And I just played it sort of live into another tape and just brought them in on faders like you do as a DJ and brought them in like that, and it was accidental in that way. I think I did it twice, maybe, and the second one was the take. And the "Number nine, number nine, number nine" was an engineer's voice, you know. They have test tapes to see that the tapes are all right.

Elsas: Mmm-hmm.

Lennon: And the voice was saying, "This is, uh, number nine mega-cycles," so he was talking like that, and I just liked the way he said "number nine," so I just made a loop of him saying "number nine" and brought that in whenever I felt like it, and ninth of October, I'll be 105, and nine seems to be my number, and it's the highest number in the universe. After that, you go back to one.

Elsas: Yeah, we just were playing underneath, sneaking it up here, a little bit of "Beef Jerky."

Lennon: "Beef Joiky"! Yes, I like this one because I don't sing, and I can stand listening to it without hearing me voice all the time.

Elsas: This is from the new album.

Lennon: From the new album, *Walls and Bridges*, available somewhere and, uh, you can find it if you want it.

Elsas: All right. I just need an introduction to the six o'clock news, which is thirty seconds away.

Lennon: Ah! In thirty seconds, you will hear the doomsday voice of the six o'clock news telling you what happened twenty-four hours ago because we never know exactly what's going on at this minute.

Elsas: And I hope you'll come back soon.

Lennon: I'll be back someday. Who knows when—only the Shadow knows!

Elsas: This is Dennis Elsas thanking John Lennon at WNEW-FM in New York.

Lennon: Thank you, Dennis.

LENNON ON . . .

His Obsessiveness

"I've had to adjust to being like that 'cause that's part of me personality, and it's a bit to do with the artist side, like you said, you know. If something's going on and it's around me, I['m] sort of like a chameleon, you know, and I just really get into it. If it's cornflakes or . . . even with my food, if I get into a food, I eat only that food for weeks until I'm sick to death of it. . . . That's the only way I know. It's like at school they always used to say, 'He's intelligent, but he only does what he wants to do,' which is supposed to be a bad point. Or, 'He's only interested in things he's interested in.' That was the kind of dialogue they give you. If I'm interested in something, I like to really get inside it. I don't care if it turns out to be not the answer to the universe when I've been through it. Because there's that side of you which is always like a journalist—that sort of objective self that's watching all the time . . ."

—from interview with John Houghton, WZMF-FM, Milwaukee, Wisconsin, circa late September 1974

LENNON ON . . .

His Drug Arrest

"One morning we're just lying there asleep. Suddenly there's a banging on the front door and Yoko goes to the door and presses the button, says, 'Who is it?' And they say, 'It's a message from Apple.' Our office. Eight o'clock in the morning, a message from Apple? It was a woman's voice. She [Ono] opened the door, and there was a woman and about five guys there. And then they started to push the door. They didn't say 'We're the police' or anything. She [Ono] shut the door and ran in and sort of collapsed on the floor and said, 'There's a whole pile of people at the door.' Meanwhile, there's another one at the bedroom window by then. They'd come over a roof. I mean, this is very well organized. And they were banging and banging. We were terrified—and naked. . . . I said 'I want to just put my trousers on.' But they said, 'No, if you don't open it [the door], we're gonna bust the window and the door down.' I was really terrified."

—from interview with Jim Hartz, broadcast live on *Today*, NBC, December 17, 1974

LONG NIGHT'S JOURNEY INTO DAY: A CONVERSATION WITH JOHN LENNON

Pete Hamill | Early February 1975, the Dakota (Lennon's home), New York | Published June 5, 1975, *Rolling Stone* (US)

Though he faced deportation proceedings with the US government and financial negotiations with ex-manager Allen Klein, John Lennon seemed relatively content by the beginning of February 1975. He had put an end to a year and a half of drinking, partying, and carrying on in L.A. with friends like the singer Harry Nilsson and assistant-turned-lover May Pang. And he had reconciled with Yoko Ono in New York.

Musically, things were looking up as well. As noted earlier, Lennon had topped US charts in the fall of 1974 with *Walls and Bridges*, which yielded two hit singles. Now, he was anticipating the February 17 release of *Rock 'n' Roll*, a collection of covers of early hits by such personal favorites as Fats Domino, Gene Vincent, Buddy Holly, and Chuck Berry. (Work on the album, which would reach number six on the charts, had dragged on for a year, apparently due to delays by Phil Spector, who'd produced some of the tracks.)

Shortly before the record went on sale, Lennon met with veteran New York journalist Pete Hamill to talk about the LP, his current life, and his relationship with Ono, whom he'd moved back in with only three days earlier. —Ed.

"The time has come," / The Walrus said, / "To talk of many things . . ."
—Lewis Carroll

Here is John Lennon: thin bare arms, a rumpled T-shirt, bare feet, delicate fingers curled around a brown-papered cigarette, reaching for a cup of steaming coffee. A pale winter sun streams into the seventh-floor apartment in the Dakota, an expensive apartment house that stands like a pile of 19th century memories on the corner of 72nd Street and Central Park West. Earlier, the Irish doorman had expressed surprise when I asked for John, because this is where Yoko Ono had lived alone for a year. The building, with its gargoyles and vaulted stone turrets, has seen a lot, and has housed everyone from Lauren Bacall and Rex Reed to Rosemary's baby. There is certainly room for Dr. Winston O'Boogie.

And now John Lennon is talking in a soft, becalmed voice, the old jagged angers gone for now, while the drilling jangle of the New York streets drifts into the room. He has been back with Yoko for three days, after a wild, painful year away, and there is a gray morning feel of hangover in the clean bright room. Against a wall, a white piano stands like an invitation to begin again; a tree is framed by one window, a plant by another, both in an attitude of Zen-like simplicity, full of spaces. I think of Harold Pinter's words: "When true silence falls we are still left with echo but are nearer nakedness." There is, of course, always echo when you are with John Lennon, an echo of the loudest, grandest, gaudiest noise made in our time. But John Lennon is more than simply a Beatle, retired or in exile, more than just an echo. At 34, he is moving into full maturity as a man and an artist and seems less afraid than ever before of nakedness.

On that first morning, and later, we talked only briefly about the Beatles. For the moment at least, talk of a reunion is only a perhaps. "What we did was what we did," he said in 1970, "but what we are is something different."

The 20 Beatles albums are there; the voices are forever young. John Lennon, the young man with the guitar who went to Hamburg and played the eight-hour gigs with the others, popping pills to stay up, drawing on some tough maniac energy. "You see," he explained later, "we wanted to be bigger than Elvis. . . ."

Bigger than Elvis. Bigger than Sinatra. Bigger than God. John told everybody how the Beatles were more popular than Jesus Christ and for a couple of weeks that summer most of the Western world seemed to go into an uproar. Was the world really that innocent so short a time ago? No. It was just that John Lennon was explaining that the world had changed and the newspapers had to catch up; we were not going to have any more aw-shucks heroes. So we could all run in the endless emptiness of the rugby field in "A Hard Day's Night," rising and falling, in slow motion or fast, but sooner or later we would have to grow up. The Beatles were custodians of childhood. They could not last.

And yet . . . and yet, it seemed when it was finally over, when they had all gone their separate ways, when Brian Epstein lay dead and Apple was some terrible mess and the lawyers and the agents and the money men had come in to paw the remains, it often seemed that John was the only one whose heart was truly broken. Cynthia Lennon said it best, when all of them were still together: "They seem to need you less than you need them." From some corner of his broken heart, John gave the most bitter interviews, full of hurt and resentment, covered over with the language of violence. In some way, he had been the engine of the group, the artistic armature driving the machine beyond its own limits, restless, easily bored, in love with speed the way Picasso was in love with speed, and possessed of a hoodlum's fanatic heart. Part of him was Pinkie from [the film] "Brighton Rock"; another was Christopher Marlowe dying in a barroom brawl at 29. John provided the Teddy Boy darkness behind the smiling face of the early Beatles; it is why they were not the Beach Boys. I remember going up to the Ad Lib in London with [writer] Al Aronowitz in '64, and the Beatles were there drinking hard with the Rolling Stones, the music deafening, the floor sagging under the weight of what seemed like half a thousand dancers. Paul McCartney was talking easily; Ringo was kidding and nice; George, as the stereotype told us, was quiet. But John Lennon was a son of a bitch. I felt an anger in him that was even fiercer than my own. We came close to violence, the words reduced to Irish immigrant code as anger bumped against anger, and Aronowitz had to move in and smother the anger with his easy kindness. Later I was ashamed of myself, and the memory of that night has stayed with me through all the years since as I watched John from a distance, engaged in his reckless dance with tragedy.

"One comes back again and again to the criminal," wrote Joyce Carol Oates, "who is the most important person because he alone of all people

acts; he alone, by causing others to suffer and by passing through suffering himself, makes happiness possible."

She wrote about Dostoevsky, but the words have always reminded me of John Lennon. We only know a small part of what really has happened to him in the years since he met Yoko Ono in 1966 at the Indica Gallery in London. The details belong to John Lennon alone. But we know how the other Beatles stood in judgment ("like a jury") on Yoko. We know how viciously the press in England sneered at them and attacked them. Yoko saw the artist in him: "John is like a frail wind . . ." But reviewers were already saying that Yoko had ruined his art.

> *Christ! You know it ain't easy*
> *You know how hard it can be*
> *The way things are going,*
> *They're going to crucify me.*

There was no literal crucifixion, but John moved through everything else: Bed-Ins, peace posters, a phony drug arrest, the acorns planted in the plastic pots in the Coventry Cathedral. He followed Yoko into the rare air of the avant-garde, banging up against Cage and Bartok, undergoing a re-barbarization of his music as if running to some older, purer vision he had of himself, created in the loneliness of the Liverpool art school when he was convinced he was a genius. Bagism, Shagism, Rubin and Hoffman, acid and anger; the marriage in Gibraltar, 17 stitches in a car crash in Scotland, the MBE handed back to the Queen, the Plastic Ono Band, his hair long, his hair short, the neat, precise features wearing a series of masks, his life with Yoko a series of public events. Working Class Hero. Some Time in New York City. Power to the People. And ever deeper into America: into its crazed, filthy Nixonian heart and the immigration case, and that form of the Higher Paranoia that comes because you are a victim in a time when all the other victims have proof and you have none.

"All we are saying . . ."

It was a long way from Chuck Berry.

Until finally people started to write him off. His records were selling but it wasn't like the Beatles, it wasn't even like the other ex-Beatles. John was the one Who Had Gone Too Far.

A year ago, he and Yoko split up and some people cheered. We live in strange times.

And then, as if from nowhere, came "Walls and Bridges." John had a big hit single with "Whatever Gets You thru the Night." And the music was wonderful: full of invention, tenderness, remorse, more personal than anything he had written before; the music clearly showing the effects of his time with Yoko. More than anything else, though, the songs were essays in autobiography, the words and music of a man trying to understand a huge part of his life. "I've been across to the other side / I've shown you everything, I've got nothing to hide. . . ."

What follows is the result of two long talks with John Lennon at the end of a difficult year. As an interview, it is far from definitive, but nothing will ever be definitive in John Lennon's life: He is the sort of artist, like the aforementioned Picasso, who is always in the process of becoming. I think of this as a kind of interim report from one of the bravest human beings I know. Oh yes: He looked happy.

What's your life like right now?
Well . . . Life: It's '75 now, isn't it? Well, I've just settled the Beatles settlement. It must've happened in the last month, took three years. (*pause*) And on this day that you've come here, I seem to have moved back in here. In the last three days. By the time this goes out, I don't know. . . . That's a big change. Maybe that's why I'm sleeping funny. As a friend says, I went out for coffee and some papers and I didn't come back. (*chuckles*) Or vice versa: It's always written *that* way, y'know. All of us. You know, the *guy* walked. It's never that simple.

What did happen with you and Yoko? Who broke it up and how did you end up back together again?
Well, it's not a matter of *who* broke it up. *It* broke up. And why did we end up back together? (*pompous voice*) We ended up together again because it was diplomatically viable . . . come on. We got back together because we *love* each other.

I loved your line: "The separation didn't work out."

That's it. It *didn't* work out. And the reaction to the breakup was all that madness. I was like a chicken without a head.

What was the final Beatles settlement?
In a nutshell, what was arranged was that everybody get their own individual monies. Even up till this year—till the settlement was signed—all the monies were going into one pot. All individual records, mine, Ringo's, Paul's—all into one big pot. It had to go through this big machinery and then come out to us, eventually. So now, even on the old Beatle royalties, everything goes into four separate accounts instead of one big pot all the time. That's that. The rest of it was ground rules. Everybody said the Beatles've signed this paper, that means they're no longer tied in any way. That's bullshit. We still own this thing called Apple. Which, you can explain, is a *bank*. A bank the money goes into. But there's still the entity itself known as Beatles. The product, the name, the likeness, the Apple thing itself, which still exists, and we still have to communicate on it and make decisions on it and decide who's to run Apple and who's to do what. It's not as cut and dried as the papers said.

Do the old Beatles records still go in a pot?
No one of us can say to EMI, "Here's a new package of Beatle material." We still have to okay everything together, you know, 'cause that's the way we want it anyway.

There's still a good feeling among the guys?
Yeah, yeah. I talked to Ringo and George yesterday. I didn't talk to Paul 'cause he was asleep. George and Paul are talkin' to each other in L.A. now. There's nothin' going down between us. It's all in people's heads.

You went to one of George's concerts; what are your thoughts on his tour?
It wasn't the greatest thing in history. The guy went through some kind of mill. It was probably his turn to get smacked. When we were all together there was periods when the Beatles were in, the Beatles were out, no matter what we were doing. Now it's always the Beatles were great or the Beatles weren't great, whatever opinion people hold.

There's a sort of illusion about it. But the actual fact was the Beatles were in for eight months, the Beatles were out for eight months. The public, including the media, are sometimes a bit sheeplike and if the ball starts rolling, well, it's just that somebody's in, somebody's out. George is out for the moment. And I think it didn't matter what he did on tour.

George told ROLLING STONE *that if you wanted the Beatles, go listen to Wings. It seemed a bit of a putdown.*
I didn't see what George said, so I really don't have any comment. (*pause*) *Band on the Run* is a great album. Wings is almost as conceptual a group as Plastic Ono Band. Plastic Ono was a conceptual group, meaning whoever was playing was the band. And Wings keeps changing all the time. It's conceptual. I mean, they're backup men for Paul. It doesn't matter who's playing, you can call them Wings, but it's Paul McCartney music. And it's good stuff. It's good Paul music and I don't really see the connection.

What do you think of Richard Perry's work with Ringo?
I think it's great. Perry's great, Ringo's great, I think the combination was great and look how well they did together. There's no complaints if you're number one.

George said at his press conference that he could play with you again but not with Paul. How do you feel?
I could play with all of them. George is entitled to say that, and he'll probably change his mind by Friday. You know, we're all human, we can all change our minds. So I don't take any of my statements or any of their statements as the last word on whether we will. And if we do, the newspapers will learn about it after the fact. If we're gonna play, we're just gonna *play*.

In retrospect, what do you think of the whole "Lennon Remembers" episode? [A reference to Lennon's long and candid 1970 conversation with Rolling Stone *editor Jann Wenner. —Ed.]*
Well, the other guys, their reaction was public. Ringo made some sort of comment that was funny which I can't remember, something like,

"You've gone too far this time, Johnnie." Paul said (*stuffy voice*), "Well, that's *his* problem." I can't remember what George said. I mean, they don't care, they've been with me for 15 or 20 years, they know damn well what I'm like. It just so happens it was in the press. I mean, they know what I'm like. I'm not ashamed of it at all. I don't really like hurting people, but Jann Wenner questioned me when I was almost still in therapy and you can't play games. You're opened up. It was like he got me on an acid trip. Things come out. I got both reactions from that article. A lot of people thought it was right on. My only upset was Jann insisted on making a book out of it.

"Walls and Bridges" has an undertone of regret to it. Did you sit down consciously to make an album like that?
No, well. . . . Let's say this last year has been an extraordinary year for me personally. And I'm almost amazed that I could get *anything* out. But I enjoyed doing *Walls and Bridges* and it wasn't hard when I had the whole thing to go into the studio and do it. I'm surprised it wasn't just all *bluuuuuuugggggghhhhh*. (*pause*) I had the most peculiar year. And . . . I'm just glad that *something* came out. It's describing the year, in a way, but it's not as sort of schizophrenic as the year really was. I think I got such a shock during that year that the impact hasn't come through. It isn't all on *Walls and Bridges* though. There's a hint of it there. It has to do with age and God knows what else. But only the surface has been touched on *Walls and Bridges*, you know?

What was it about the year? Do you want to try talking about it?
Well, you can't put your finger on it. It started, somehow, at the end of '73, goin' to do this *Rock 'n' Roll* album [with Phil Spector]. It had quite a lot to do with Yoko and I, whether I knew it or not, and then suddenly I was out on me own. Next thing I'd be waking up drunk in strange places, or reading about meself in the paper, doin' extraordinary things, half of which I'd done and half of which I hadn't done. But you know the game anyway. And find meself sort of in a mad *dream* for a year. I'd been in many mad dreams, but this. . . . It was pretty wild. And then I tried to recover from that. And (*long pause*) meanwhile life was going on, the Beatles settlement was going on, other things, life was still

going on and it wouldn't let you sit with your hangover, in whatever form that took. It was like something—probably meself—kept hitting me while I was trying to do something. I was still trying to carry on a normal life and the whip never let up—for eight months. So . . . that's what was going on. Incidents: You can put it down to which night with which bottle or which night in which town. It was just sort of a mad year like that. . . . And it was just probably fear, and being out on me own, and gettin' old, and are ye gonna make it in the charts? Are ye not gonna make it? All that crap, y'know. All the garbage that y'really know is not the be-all and end-all of your life, but if other things are goin' funny, *that's* gonna hit you. If you're gonna feel sorry for yourself, you're gonna feel sorry for everything. What it's really to do with is probably the same thing that it's always been to do with all your life: whatever your own personal problems really are, you know? So it was a year that manifested itself (*switches to deep actor's voice*) *in most peculiar fashion.* But I'm *through* it and it's '75 now and I feel *better* and I'm sittin' *here* and not lyin' in some weird place with a hangover.

Why do you feel better?
Because I feel like I've been on Sinbad's voyage, you know, and I've battled all those monsters and I've got back. (*long pause*) Weird.

Tell me about the "Rock 'n' Roll" album.
It started in '73 with Phil and fell apart. I ended up as part of mad drunk scenes in Los Angeles and I finally finished it off on me own. And there was still problems with it up to the minute it came out. I can't begin to say, it's just *barmy,* there's a jinx on that album. And I've just started writing a new one. Got maybe half of it written . . .

What about the stories that Spector's working habits are a little odd? For example, that he either showed off or shot off guns in the studios?
I don't like to tell tales out of school, y'know. But I do know there was an awful loud noise in the toilet of the Record Plant West.

What actually did happen those nights at the Troubadour when you heckled the Smothers Brothers and went walking around with a Kotex on your head asking the waitress, "Do you know who I am?"

Ah, y'want the juice. . . . If I'd said, "Do you know who I am?" I'd have said it in a joke. Because I know who I am, and I know *she* knew, because I musta been wearing a Kotex on me head, right? I picked up a Kotex in a restaurant, in the toilet, and it was clean and just for a gag I came back to the table with it on me head. And 'cause it stuck there with sweat, just *stayed* there, I didn't have to keep it on. It just stayed there till it fell off. And the waitress said, "Yeah, you're an asshole with a Kotex on," and I think it's a good remark and so what? Tommy Smothers was a completely different night and has been covered a million times. It was my first night on Brandy Alexanders and my last. (*laughs*) And I was with Harry Nilsson who was no help at all. (*laughs*)

What's your relationship with Nilsson? Some critics say that he's been heavily influenced, maybe even badly screwed up by you.
Oh, that's bullshit.

. . . and that you've also been influenced by him.
That's bullshit too. I haven't been influenced by Harry, only that I had a lot of hangovers whenever I was with him. (*laughs*) I love him, he's a great guy and I count him as one of me friends. He hasn't influenced me musically. And there's an illusion going around about my production of Harry's album. That he was trying to imitate me on his album.

You mean that he'd gone into his primal period . . .
That's it. They're so sheeplike—put this in—and childlike about trying to put a tag on what's going on. They use these expressions like "primal" for anything that's a scream. Brackets: Yoko was screaming before Janov was ever even heard of; that was her stint, usin' her voice like an instrument. She was screaming when Janov was still jackin' off to Freud. But nowadays, everything that's got a scream in it is called *primal.* I know what they're talkin' about: the very powerful emotional pitch that Harry reaches at the end of "Many Rivers to Cross" on the album I produced for him [*Pussy Cats*]. It's there, simply enough, because when you get to a certain point with your vocals, there ain't nowhere else to go. Was Little Richard primaling before each sax solo? That's what I want to know. Was my imitation Little Richard screams I used to put on all the Beatles records before the solo—we all used to

do it, we'd go aaaaaarrrrrrrggggghhhh! Was that primaling? Right? And the other thing is about Harry becoming *me* on his album. That's the other illusion that all the little rock writers wrote about. It's bullshit. I go in to produce the guy, expecting to hear Harry Nilsson singing and the guy has no voice. We'd committed studio time and we did one track, virtually, and that's the end of his voice. So then I'm stuck with one of the best white singers in America—with no voice at all. Harry didn't tell me till nearly the end of the album that he was coughin' up *blood*.

Jesus.
I didn't know 'cause he *always* looked so wiped out. I didn't know what it was. I was always treatin' him like a doctor, gettin' him to bed at night and tellin' him, you know, don't drink, don't smoke, etcetera, etcetera. Don't do any stuff, man. Not only have you got no voice but they're gonna blame me. Which they did. I think it was psychosomatic. I think he was nervous 'cause *I* was producing him. You know, he was an old Beatle fan when he was in the *bank* or something. [*Nilsson worked in a bank before pursuing a musical career. —Ed.*] But I was committed to the thing, the band was there and the guy had no voice, so we made the best of it. So they say, oh, he's tryin' to sound like you. The poor guy couldn't get a note out and we were lucky to get anything out of it.

Richard Perry has described you as a superb producer but maybe in too much of a hurry.
That's true. (*laughs*)

But supposedly, when making the Beatles records, you were painstaking and slow.
No, I was never painstaking and slow. I produced "I Am the Walrus" at the same speed I produced "Whatever Gets You thru the Night." I would be painstaking on some things, as I am now. If there's a quality that occasionally gets in the way of my talent, it's that I get bored quick unless it's done quick. But "I Am the Walrus" sounds like a wonderful production. "Strawberry Fields" sounds like a big production. But I do them as quick as I possibly can, without losing (a) the feel and (b) where I'm going. The longest track I personally spent time on was "Revolution

Number Nine," which was an abstract track where I used a lot of tape loops and things like that. I still did it in one session. But I accept that criticism and I have it of myself. But I don't want to make myself so painstaking that it's boring. But I should (*pause*) maybe t'ink a little more. Maybe. But on the other hand I think my criticism of somebody like Richard Perry would be that he's great but he's *too* painstaking. It gets too slick and somewhere in between that is where I'd like to go. I've only produced two albums of me own, actually, completely on me own. And I find something out each time. I'm a learner of production, although I've been at this business so long and I used to produce my own tracks with the help of George Martin and Paul McCartney and George Harrison and everybody else. I would be in charge of me own tracks. But really to produce a thing all on me own—I've done very little. I keep finding out all the time—what I'm missing that I want to get out of it.

Is there anybody that you'd like to produce? For example, Dylan?
Dylan would be interesting because I think he made a great album in *Blood on the Tracks* but I'm still not keen on the backings. I think I could produce him great. And Presley. I'd like to resurrect Elvis. But I'd be so scared of him I don't know whether I could *do* it. But I'd *like* to do it. Dylan I could do, but Presley would make me nervous. But Dylan or Presley, somebody up *there* . . . I know what I'd do with Presley. Make a *rock & roll* album. Dylan doesn't need material. I'd just make him some good backings. So if you're reading this, Bob, you know . . .

Elton John has revived "Lucy in the Sky with Diamonds" and David Bowie has recorded "Across the Universe." How do you feel about both artists?
I like and respect them both. I'm closer to Elton because I've known him longer and I've spent more time with him. Elton sort of popped in on the session for *Walls and Bridges* and sort of zapped in and played the piano and ended up singing "Whatever Gets You thru the Night" with me. Which was a great shot in the arm. I'd done three-quarters of it, and it was, "Now what do we do?" Should we put a camel on it or

a xylophone? That sort of thing. And he came in and said, "Hey, ah'll play some piano!" Then I heard he was doing "Lucy" and I heard from a friend—'cause he was shy—would I be there when he cut "Lucy"? Maybe play on it but just be there? So I went along. And I sang in the chorus and contributed the reggae in the middle. And then, again through a mutual friend, he asked if it got to be Number One, would I appear onstage with him, and I said sure, not thinkin' in a million years it was gonna get to Number One. Al Coury or no Al Coury, the promotion man at Capitol. And there I was. Onstage.

I read somewhere that you were very moved by the whole thing.
I was moved by it, but everybody else was in *tears.* I felt guilty 'cause I wasn't in tears. I just went up and did a few numbers. But the emotional thing was me and Elton together. Elton had been working in Dick James's office when we used to send our demos in and there's a long sort of relationship musically with Elton that people don't really know about. He has this sort of Beatle thing from way back. He'd take the demos home and play them and . . . well, it meant a lot to me and it meant a hell of a lot to Elton, and he was in tears. It was a great high night, a really high night and . . . Yoko and I met backstage. And somebody said, "Well, there's two people in love." That was before we got back together. But that's probably when we felt something. It was very weird. She came backstage and I didn't know she was there, 'cause if I'd known she was there I'd've been too nervous to go on, you know, I would have been terrified. She was backstage afterward, and there was just that moment when we saw each other and like, it's like in the movies, you know, when time stands still? And there was silence, everything went silent, y'know, and we were just sort of lookin' at each other and . . . oh, hello. I knew she'd sent Elton and I a flower each, and we were wearin' them onstage, but I didn't know she was there and then everybody was around us and flash flash flash. But there was that moment of silence. And somebody observed it and told me later on, after we were back together again, and said, "A friend of mine saw you backstage and thought if ever there was two in love, it's those two." And I thought, well, it's weird somebody noticed it. . . . So it was a

great night. . . . And David [Bowie] just seems to be livin' in New York now, and I've got to know him a bit and we've had some good nights and he just said, "I'm gonna cut 'Across the Universe'—will you come down?" And I said okay, and went down and played the guitar. That was it. No big deal.

There seems to be a lot of generosity among the artists now.
It was around before. It's harder when you're on the make, to be generous, 'cause you're all competing. But once you're sort of up there, wherever it is. . . . The rock papers love to write about the jetsetting rock stars and they dig it and we dig it in a way. The fact is that yeah, I see Mick, I see Paul, I see Elton, they're all my contemporaries and I've known the other Beatles, of course, for years, and Mick for ten years, and we've been hangin' around since *Rock Dreams*. [*A reference to the bestselling 1973 book by illustrator Guy Peellaert and writer Nik Cohn. —Ed.*] And suddenly it's written up as they're-here-they're-there-they're-everywhere bit, and it looks like we're trying to form a club. But we always *were* a club. We always knew each other. It just so happens that it looks more dramatic in the paper.

How do you relate to what we might call the rock stars of the Seventies? Do you think of yourself as an uncle figure, a father figure, an old gunfighter?
It depends who they are. If it's Mick or the Old Guard as I call them, yeah, they're the Old Guard. Elton, David are the newies. I don't feel like an old uncle, dear, 'cause I'm not that much older than half of 'em, hehe. But . . . yeah, I'm interested in the new people. I'm interested in new people in America but I get a kick out of the new Britons. I remember hearing Elton John's "Your Song," heard it in America—it was one of Elton's first big hits—and remember thinking, "Great, that's the first new thing that's happened since we happened." It was a step forward. There was something about his vocals that was an improvement on all of the English vocals until then. I was pleased with it. And I was pleased with Bowie's thing and I hadn't even *heard* him. I just got this feeling from the image and the projections that were coming out of England of him, well, you could feel it.

Do you think of New York as home now?

Oh, yeah. I've been here, well, this is almost the fourth year. Yeah, this is the longest I've ever been away from England. I've almost lived here as long as I've lived in London. I was in London from, let's see, '64, '65, '66, '67, actually *in* London 'cause then it was your Beatlemania bit and we all ended up like a lot of rock & rollers end up, living an hour away from London in the country, the drivin'-in-from-the-big-estate bit. 'Cause you couldn't live *in* London, 'cause people just bugged the ass off you. So I've lived in New York *longer* than I actually lived in London.

In view of the immigration case, is one reason you've stayed here so long because if you left, they'd pull a Charlie Chaplin on you and not let you back in?

You bet. There's no way, they wouldn't let me back. Not after I've dug in so much as it is. There's no way. And . . . it's worth it to me. I can last out, without leaving here, another ten years, if that's the way they want to play it. I'll earn enough to keep paying them. I'm really getting blackmailed. I'm *paying* to stay. Paying takes, on one hand, about a half-million dollars, and I've hardly worked very hard for that. I mean that's with sittin' on me arse and I've paid a half-million in *taxes*. So I'm paying *them* to attack me and keep me busy and harass me, on one hand, while on the other hand I've got to pay me own lawyers. Some people think I'm here just to make the American dollars. But I don't have to *be* here to make the dollars, I could earn American dollars just sittin' in a recording studio in Hong Kong. Wherever I am, the money follows *me*. It's gonna come out of America whether they like it or not. This is where the money *comes* from, in *this* world. It's not that the government allows people to earn money from America, the government *wants* people to earn money, otherwise they wouldn't've set up this damn system, right? I also give a lot of *jobs* to a lot of Americans.

Right. And the government doesn't choose that John Lennon makes money. The people who buy your music do that.

The implication is that John Lennon wants to come to the land of milk and honey 'cause it's easier to pick up the money, so I can pick it up directly instead of waiting for it to arrive in England. Or Brazil. Or wherever I decide to do it. I resent that implication, especially as I'm payin' through the nose. I don't mind paying taxes, either, which is strange. I never did. I don't like 'em using it for bombs and that. But I don't think I could do a Joan Baez. I don't have that kind of gut. I did never complain in England either, because, well, it's buying people teeth . . . I'm sick of gettin' sick about taxes. Taxes is what seems to be it and there's nothin' to be done about it, unless you choose to make a crusade about it. And I'm sick of being in crusades because I always get nailed up before I'm even in the crusade. They get me in the queue while I'm readin' the pages about it: "Oh there's a crusade on, I wonder should I . . ." I mean, I get caught before I've ever even done anything about it.

You went through a period of really heavy involvement in radical causes. Lately you seem to have gone back to your art in a more direct way. What happened?

I'll tell you what happened *literally*. I got off the boat, only it was an aeroplane, and landed in New York, and the first people who got in touch with me was Jerry Rubin and Abbie Hoffman. It's as simple as that. It's those two famous guys from America who's callin': "Hey, yeah, what's happenin', what's goin' on? . . ." And the next thing you know, I'm doin' John Sinclair benefits and one thing and another. I'm pretty *movable*, as an artist, you know. They almost greeted me off the plane and the next minute I'm *involved*, you know.

How did all of this affect your work?

It almost *ruined* it, in a way. It became journalism and not poetry. And I basically feel that I'm a poet. Even if it does go ba-deedle, eedle, eedle, it, da-deeedle, deedle, it. I'm not a formalized poet, I have no education, so I have to write in the simplest forms usually. And I realized that over a period of time—and not just 'cause I met Jerry Rubin off the plane—but that was like a culmination. I realized that we were poets but we were really folk poets, and rock & roll was folk poetry—I've always felt that. Rock & roll *was* folk music. Then I began to take it seriously on another level, saying, "Well, I am reflecting what is going *on*, right?" And then

I was making an *effort* to reflect what was going on. Well, it doesn't work like that. It doesn't work as pop music or what I want to do. It just doesn't make sense. You get into that bit where you can't talk about trees, 'cause, y'know, y'gotta talk about corruption on 54th Street! It's nothing to do with *that*. It's a bit *larger* than that. It's the usual lesson that I've learned in me little 34 years: As soon as you've clutched onto something, you think—you're always clutchin' at straws—*this is what life is all about.* I think artists are lucky because the straws are always blowin' out of their hands. But the unfortunate thing is that most people find the straw hat and hang on to it, like your best friend that got the job at the bank when he was 15 and looked 28 before he was 20. "Oh, *this* is it! *Now* I know what I'm doing! Right? Down this road for the next hundred years" . . . and it ain't never *that.* Whether it's a religious hat or a political hat or a no-political hat: whatever hat it was, always looking for these straw hats. I think I found out it's a waste of time. There is no hat to wear. Just keep moving around and changing clothes is the best. That's all that goes on: *change.*

At one time I thought, well, I'm avoidin' that thing called the Age Thing, whether it hits you at 21 when you take your first job—I always keep referrin' to that because it has nothing to do, virtually, with your physical age. I mean, we all know the guys who took the jobs when we left school, the straight jobs, they all look like old guys within six weeks. You'd meet them and they'd be lookin' like Well, I've Settled Down Now. So I never want to settle down, in that respect. I always want to be immature in that respect. But then I felt that if I keep bangin' my head on the wall it'll stop me from gettin' that kind of age in the head. By keeping creating, consciously or unconsciously, extraordinary situations which in the end you'd write about. But maybe it has nothin' to do with it. I'm still mullin' that over. Still mullin' over last year now. Maybe that was it. I was still trying to avoid somethin' but doin' it the wrong way 'round. Whether it's called age or whatever.

Is it called growing up?
I don't want to grow up but I'm sick of not growing up—that way. I'll find a different way of not growing up. There's a better way of doing it

than torturing your body. And then your mind. The guilt! It's just so *dumb*. And it makes me *furious* to be dumb because I don't like dumb people. And there I am, doing the dumbest things. . . . I seem to do the things that I despise the most, almost. All of that to—what?—avoid being normal.

I have this great fear of this *normal* thing. You know, the ones that passed their exams, the ones that went to their jobs, the ones that didn't become rock & rollers, the ones that settled for it, settled for it, settled for the *deal!* That's what I'm trying to avoid. But I'm sick of avoiding it with violence, you know? I've gotta do it some other way. I think I will. I think just the fact that I've realized it is a good step forward. Alive in '75 is my new motto. I've just made it up. That's the one. I've decided I want to live. I'd decided I wanted to live *before*, but I didn't know what it meant, really. It's taken however many years and I want to have a *go* at it.

Do you think much of yourself as an artist at 50 or 60?
I never see meself as not an artist. I never let meself believe that an artist can "run dry."

I've always had this vision of bein' 60 and writing children's books. I don't know why. It'd be a strange thing for a person who doesn't really have much to do with children. I've always had that feeling of *giving* what *Wind in the Willows* and *Alice in Wonderland* and *Treasure Island* gave to me at age seven and eight. The books that really opened my whole being.

Is there anything left to say about the immigration case?
I don't know what to say anymore. It stands no different from the time ROLLING STONE did it last. It's going from court to court and I'm getting no relief, as the legal term puts it. They're still playing that attitude that, you know, we're treating you like this because of this law. Sure, the law exists. And so do all the Nazis here and the drug dealers that are not American born and all the killers that are allowed in here. They're still pretending that they're doing it on the strict letter of the law.

You know, I can resurrect it and do more press, and keep appealing to the American people. But they're *human*. People get *bored* with hearin' about Lennon's immigration case. *I'm* bored with hearin' about it. The only interesting thing is when I read these articles people write that were not instigated by me. I learn things I didn't know anything *about*. I didn't know about *Strom Thurmond*. I had no idea—I mean I knew *something* was going on, but I didn't have any names. I'm just left in the position of just what am I supposed to do? There doesn't seem to be anything I can do about it. It's just . . . bloody *crazy*. Terry Southern put it in a nice sort of way. He said, "Well, look, y'keep 'em all happy, ya see? The conservatives are happy 'cause they're doin' somethin' about ya and the liberals are happy 'cause they haven't thrown you out. So everybody's happy! (*pause*) Except you!" (*laughter*) I'm happy I'm still here. I must say that. And I ain't going. There's no *way* they're gonna get me out. No way. They're not gonna drag me in *chains*, right? So I'm just gonna have to keep *paying*. It's bloody ridiculous. It's just . . . beyond belief.

So nothing has changed with the departure of Nixon.
I'm even nervous about commenting on politics, they've got me that jumpy these days. But it's a bit of an illusion to think 'cause Old Nick went that it's all changed. If it's changed, prove it, show me the change. In all honesty, it's a political decision. No matter how many letters the immigration people write to newspapers saying it isn't, it's a political decision. Somebody's gotta make up their mind either to let this go on or to leave me alone. It could be that it's an embarrassing situation for the government, because they started the thing. It might just be embarrassing to them if someone just made a call to someone to pull the dogs off. What's Lennon gonna *do* then? Is he gonna say, ha ha, I tole yiz? What does it entail if they give in? If they relax about it? How much constituency does Lennon have? And his friends? What does it mean to the public in general? But they also know that the public forgets.

When you heard that Thurmond and these other creeps were making a guinea pig out of you in the immigration case, what was your gut reaction?
My gut reaction was ha ha ha, I *told* you so. And I'd like to thank ROLLING STONE for their pieces on immigration. They helped bring it all out again. They were great.

Does the case get in the way of your work?
It did. It did. There's no denying it. In '72, it was really gettin' to me. Not only was I physically having to appear in court cases, it just seemed like a toothache that wouldn't go away. Now I just accept it. I just have a permanent toothache. But there was a period where I *just couldn't function*, you know? I was so paranoid from them tappin' the phone and followin' me. . . . How could I prove that they were tappin' me phone? There was no way. And when they were followin' me, I went on *Dick Cavett* and said they were followin' me and they stopped followin' me. But when they *were* followin' me, they wanted me to *see* they were following me. I was so damned paranoid. . . . And what with the Rubins, and the people I met through *that* school of music, and as I traveled around the country, I got more information about every one of those politicos, so that I couldn't trust *anybody*. This was pre-Watergate. Even when I said it to reporters, or on the *Cavett* show, that people were following me, they'd look and say, "Don't be an egomaniac, we know you've got a problem, but who's gonna chase *you*? You're not that *important*." And I wish I wasn't. I wish they didn't find it such an important thing.

Give me an example of how the case has affected the work.
Well, there was a period when I was hangin' out with a group called Elephant's Memory. And I was ready to go on the road for pure *fun*. I didn't want to go on the road for money. That was the time when I was standing up in the Apollo with a guitar at the Attica relatives' benefit or ending up on the stage at the John Sinclair rally. I felt like going on the road and playing *music*. And whatever excuse—charity or whatever—would have done me. But they kept pullin' me back into court! I had the group hangin' 'round, but finally I had to say, "Hey, you better get on with your lives." Now, the last thing on earth I want to do is perform. That's a direct result of the immigration thing. In '71, '72, I wanted to go out and rock me balls off onstage and I just stopped.

Have you made any kind of flat decision not to ever go on the road again?
No. I've stopped making flat decisions. I change me mind a lot. My idea of heaven is *not* going on the road. And this was *before* George's tour.

What groups do you listen to these days?

I'm still a [singles] record man. There's nobody—including meself—on earth that I can sit down and listen to a whole album. *Nobody.* The same voice going on. . . . Nobody can sustain it. Even as a rock 'n' roll fan of 15, there were very few albums I could sit through. Even Elvis, and I adored him, or Carl Perkins or Little Richard. There were always a couple of tracks to miss and go on to the next ones. So I don't sit 'round and listen to artists' albums. Unless they're friends of mine. I like records. I like "Shame, Shame, Shame." Shirley and the gang. Some of this disco stuff. Great. I like just individual records. One of me favorites last year was "I Can Help." Billy Swan. A real old Elvis imitation kind of record. I like singles. I like jukebox music. That was the thing that turned me on. That's the thing I like.

What was the Grammy show like?

It was great fun. It was chaos backstage. But I enjoyed it. I was hoping Elton would win. Nothing against Olivia. I hope it didn't show on me face when they announced it. I opened the thing and somehow I was expecting to see Elton John, y'know, and I went . . . uh . . . and here is Olivia . . . Newton . . . John. And I thought, oh, me face has dropped, hehe.

Will you ever be free of the fact that you were once a Beatle?

I've got used to the fact—just about—that whatever I do is going to be compared to the other Beatles. If I took up ballet dancing, my ballet dancing would be compared with Paul's bowling. So that I'll have to live with. But I've come to learn something big this past year. I cannot let the Top Ten dominate my art. If my worth is only to be judged by whether I'm in the Top Ten or not, then I'd better give up. Because if I let the Top Ten dominate my art, then the art will die. And then whether I'm in the Top Ten is a moot point. I do think now in terms of long term. I'm an artist. I have to express myself. I can't be dominated by gold records. As I said, I'm 34 going on 60. The art is more important than the thing and sometimes I have to remind meself of it. Because there's a danger there, for all of us, for everyone who's involved in whatever art they're in, of *needing that love so badly* that. . . . In my business, that's manifested in the Top Ten.

So this last year, in some ways, was a year of deciding whether you wanted to be an artist or a pop star?
Yeah. What is it I'm doing? What am I *doing*? Meanwhile, I was still putting out the work. But in the back of me head it was that: What do you want to be? What are you lookin' for? And that's about it. I'm a freakin' artist, man, not a fucking race horse.

LENNON ON . . .

Reuniting with Yoko Ono

"I would like really to dedicate this whole album [*Rock 'n' Roll*] to my very special friend and wife, Yoko, who you might not have heard that I'm living with. And as I put it, our separation was a failure. . . . Those two inimitable loonies are back together again, and we're very happy. . . . [We got back together] about a week ago, something like that, and it's not really been out. I think a little news came out in England. I can't really remember how it got there, but I'll say it again: our separation was a failure. John and Yoko have got back together in their bag, as it were, together. And rock on!"

—from interview with Scott Muni, February 13, 1975, broadcast live on WNEW-FM (New York)

HE SAID, SHE SAID

Frances Schoenberger | March 1975, New York | Published October 1988, *Spin* (US)

In this conversation with Hollywood journalist Frances Schoenberger, Lennon touches on a few of the same subjects that he covered with Pete Hamill about a month earlier, but he also addresses a variety of other topics—everything from meeting Elvis Presley to taking his son Julian to Disneyland and Disney World. Schoenberger doesn't hesitate to ask personal questions about subjects like the artist's finances and sex life, and Lennon's answers are as direct as the queries.

By now, the singer was settling back into life with Yoko Ono and most likely knew of her pregnancy. (The couple's son, Sean, would be born on October 9.) He appears to already be contemplating his upcoming five-year withdrawal from the public eye when he answers a question about what makes him most comfortable now with "peace and quiet, and a piano."

Schoenberger recalls today that Lennon showed up alone at New York's Park Lane Hotel, where she was staying. "He was in an amazingly good mood," she told me, and he was singing Ringo Starr's "No No Song," which had just been released in late February. Joined by photographer Bob Gruen, Schoenberger and Lennon drove to a park in Yonkers, conducting the interview along the way.

As I noted in the preface, this piece and the ones immediately preceding and following it originally appeared in print are therefore being reproduced exactly as they were first published. One exception: in this article, I've corrected the name of primal-scream therapist Arthur Janov, which was misstated in *Spin* because of a transcription error. —Ed.

Frances Schoenberger: Why do you think the immigration people are making it so difficult for you to stay here?

John Lennon: I am trying to think of his name, so I can give him credit for his quotes. [*As Lennon said when he cited the same lines to Pete*

Hamill, the quote is from writer Terry Southern. —Ed.]. . . He put it this way: "It keeps all the conservatives happy that they are doing something about me and what I represent. And it keeps the liberals happy that I am not thrown out." So, everybody is happy but me. I am still being harassed. Liberals don't feel too bad because I am still here.

Schoenberger: It seems to me that they really use you?

Lennon: Yeah. It keeps all the other pop stars in line. In case they get any ideas about reality. Keep them in their place. They also hassle Paul, George, Mick Jagger . . . obviously Keith Richard[s].

Schoenberger: What does Elton John do—he is here most of the time? David Bowie?

Lennon: Elton John has a clean image. David's image . . . they probably haven't realized what it is yet; it takes them a bit of time. Bowie, they probably just think he's something from the circus. He's never been busted and he didn't get mashed up with lunatics like Jerry Rubin. And Abby [Abbie] my boy Hoffman.

Schoenberger: Are you still friends with them?

Lennon: I never see them. They vanished in the woodwork . . . Jerry has been nothing but trouble and a pain in the neck since I met him. I decided, as he didn't lead the revolution, I decided to quit answering the phone.

Schoenberger: Why do you want to live in New York now? Why in the U.S.?

Lennon: Because it's more fun here. Some of the nasties think I'm here for tax reasons. But it's hardly worth explaining to people. I only decided to live here after I'd moved here. I didn't leave England with the intention . . . I left everything in England. I didn't even bring any clothes. I just came for a visit and stayed. If I had wanted to do it for tax [reasons] I should have informed the British Government; I would have gotten an amazing tax-refund for one year. But I forgot to—so I just ended up paying taxes anyway, here and there. If I'd only thought of it, I would have made a million pounds or something. In America, they should stop saying I do it for the tax. I like it here! Is anywhere better?

Schoenberger: Do the English get upset when you say that?

Lennon: The English tend to get a little ". . . you've left us!" They never say it, but you can tell it by the way they write about you. But, it's too bad. The Liverpool people were the same when I left Liverpool. Or when the Beatles left Liverpool. It was all "You've let us down!" You know, "You should stay here forever and rot . . ." I'm not really interested. I like people to like me. But I am not going to ruin my life to please anybody.

Schoenberger: What kind of life do you live in New York? It doesn't seem like the kind you'd expect a star to live.

Lennon: Pretty normal. I don't know what a star lives like.

Schoenberger: Some live it up. It seems you don't.

Lennon: I don't live it down. I've lived it down, played it both ways. Especially when you first get money—you live it up. I had all the biggest cars in the world . . . and I don't even like cars. I bought everything that I could buy. The only thing that I never got into is yachts. So, I went through that period. There is nothing else to do once you do it. I just live however makes me most comfortable.

Schoenberger: What makes you most comfortable right now?

Lennon: Peace and quiet, and a piano. It's all basically that. And occasionally spurting out to some event. Just to prove I'm still alive.

Schoenberger: You said once on radio that your separation from Yoko was just a failure. What did you mean?

Lennon: Well, it's a joke. They always say, "Their marriage was a failure," at every divorce. Ours was the other way around; our separation was a failure. We knew we would get together one day, but it could have been 10 years. Like Natalie Wood and Robert Wagner—we could have gone that long. It was fate, or our decision, or whatever. I don't know how it worked. We knew we'd get back together one way or another, but had no idea when. We probably would never bother getting a divorce. I mean, if you're living apart you are as divorced as can be.

Schoenberger: What if you wanted to marry again?

Lennon: I don't think I'd ever bother. If this one didn't work out, then it ain't worth bothering about.

Schoenberger: How is your relationship with [ex-lover] May Pang now? I'm surprised she is still working for you.

Lennon: I just didn't wanna "OK—quit!"

Schoenberger: How does she handle it now?

Lennon: She's handling it alright. It's hard to know, because I'm hardly spending any time with her. Any time at all, actually. I don't know. . . . But what can I do about it? She knew what the scene was from the start. There was no question . . . neither Yoko nor I left each other for another person. We just sort of blew up. Blew apart. And then sort of filled in . . . so as not to be alone at night. I don't wanna put May down. She is a nice girl. But she knew what the scene was. I was always talking to Yoko on the phone. I never went anywhere without telling her. "I'm going to L.A." And she said "Good luck to you."

So, we were still good friends. We just blew apart. We didn't even plan to get back together. I was just going to visit her. And I visited her many times before. And I just walked in and thought "I live here; this is my home. Here is Yoko, and here is me . . ." The other time I visited we've been a little . . . we've spent hours together, but I haven't been relaxed. The last time I went I just never left. It was the same . . . I physically left Yoko in the apartment, but I didn't leave her. And she didn't leave me.

Schoenberger: Would you mind telling me how you live? How big . . .?

Lennon: It is a big apartment, and it's beautiful, but it doesn't have grounds . . . you know, it's secure. And people can't get in and say, "I'm Jesus from Toronto," and all that. That still happens. Which was happening in the other apartment. You just couldn't go out the front door, because there would be something weird at the door.

Schoenberger: Why did you live in L.A. for a little while?

Lennon: The separation was physical as well as mental. Our only communication was really on the phone. I just went there to get out of New

York for a bit. Trying to do something down there. But I spent most of the time drunk on the floor . . . with Harry Nilsson and Ringo and people like that. And ending up in the papers . . . that went on for about nine months. It was just one big hangover. It was hell. But that's why I was there.

Schoenberger: *Rolling Stone* mentioned John Lennon "playing second fiddle . . ."

Lennon: That's garbage. What second fiddle? I'm not playing second fiddle to Ringo when I play rhythm guitar. It's all right for me to play rhythm guitar in back of Ringo's record, but if I play rhythm guitar in back of Elton's record, or in back of David Bowie's somehow I'm lowering myself. . . . I think they are good artists. And they are friends of mine, and they asked me to go and play. It's like in the old days. Like Brian Jones is on a track of the Beatles years ago. And he played saxophone. In those days you weren't allowed to say, the record companies wouldn't allow it. So it was never mentioned. Everybody used to play on each other's sessions, but nobody ever said anything.

Nowadays it's always said. And Elton asked me to play on "Lucy." He said, "I'm gonna do this song. I'd love it if you came and played." He was too shy to ask me. He got a friend that we both have to ask me. . . . And I said, "Sure, I'll come." So I went to play and sang chorus or some garbage. Why is it not belittling for Mick Jagger to sing in back of Carly Simon? Why am I some kind of God that isn't allowed to do anything?? It's bullshit.

Schoenberger: How do you feel about people doing covers of all those old Beatle songs?

Lennon: I love it. I was thrilled he [Elton] was doing it. People are afraid of Beatle music. They are still afraid of my songs. Because they got that big image thing: You can't do a Beatle number. . . . You can't touch a Lennon song; only Lennon can do it. . . . It's garbage! Anybody can do anything. A few people in the past have done Beatle songs. But in general they feel you can't touch them. And there are so many good singles that the Beatles wrote that were never released. Why don't people do them?

It's good for me; it's good for Paul. It's good for all of us. And Elton would have had a No. 1 record without me; he didn't need me. And anyway, I was only Dr. Winston O. Boogie on it . . . 'cause they weren't sure; and we didn't have time to get real permission . . .

Schoenberger: What about going on tour?

Lennon: I think it would be a drag. I am sure I enjoyed parts of it, but not much of it. My decision was already made on touring, long time ago. I always changed my mind about things; and then everybody got angry, and said, ". . . but he said . . . " I don't know if I'll ever tour again; I can't say. But just the idea of it . . . it's just . . . you gotta pull a group together, invent a group. And then you gotta whip them into life, make them a real group, and not a bunch of guys. Then you gotta go around all those snotty little dressing rooms—and all you get is money. That's all you get from a tour: cash.

Schoenberger: How about money?

Lennon: I am doing alright. I am rich in England, and medium well-off in America. 'Cause a lot of money is stuck in England.

Schoenberger: And you can't get it over?

Lennon: 'Til 1977. And the pound might be worth 2 pfennigs by then. So, we'll see what happens. You might suddenly see me touring in 1977 . . . very enthusiastically . . .

Schoenberger: Why can't you get it in before 1977?

Lennon: Because there is some mad law. The English don't allow any money out of the country if they can help it. And they always tell me to invest in this and that.

Schoenberger: Do you?

Lennon: No.

Schoenberger: So where do you keep the money you have?

Lennon: It's just in a bank. I never invested anything.

Schoenberger: You can see the amount?

Lennon: I never look at it. It never changes. They give you an interest now and then. The only things you can invest in are like big fascist things. Like South African gold mines. All those things that don't . . . I couldn't bother with having shares and all that. It's quite enough to get a chance without watching the shares on Wall Street or in England. I said: Give me a list of things I can invest in that don't involve exploiting people. And they couldn't come up with anything. And I am not that fanatical like Joan Baez or not brave enough to [refuse to] pay taxes. I just pay them and I know they buy bonds with them. I just can't deal with it. Especially in England I can't deal with it. So, I just leave it in the bank. And it either goes up with the market or goes down with the market. And that's it.

Schoenberger: How about the oldies album? Why did you do all the oldies?

Lennon: I started out doing these in '73 with Phil Spector. I just came off *Mind Games*, which to me was like an interim record between being a manic political lunatic to back to being a musician again. And *Mind Games* is like the cross between them. I was really playing mind games, mind games is what it was. I had enough of this trying to be deep and think . . . "Why can't I have some fun??" And my idea of fun with music was to sing. Sing anything. And whenever I sang in a studio, when I wasn't singing my own deep and personal songs—it was singing rock 'n' roll, which I started out to do.

So I thought: I know what to do. I'll make a rock 'n' roll album of all the songs I'm always singing in the studio between takes. And I don't even wanna be the producer. I'll do it with Phil Spector. 'Cause I've worked with him before. It took me three weeks to talk him into the fact that he could produce it . . . and it wasn't gonna be co-production like "Imagine" and other things, where I never let go of the control. I just said, "You're gonna do it. I just wanna be [Spector-produced artist] Ronnie Spector, or the Chiffons, or whoever it is. And I'll just sit there and sing. I'm not even gonna come in until you got it on the tape. I'm not gonna check anything—the bass drum, or the drums like I want it. . . . It's gonna be like you want it. And I'll just do singing." And it was great at first that there he was, being the Phil Spector that I never allowed him to be. In complete control of 28 guys playing live. And to me it was . . . for a lot of us who hadn't been there originally it was like seeing the Spector sessions of the early '60s, which none of us saw. And he was fantastic.

But it got madder and madder, and it ended up breaking down, just falling apart . . . everybody was drunk, except for about two people, actually. It was just a drunken madhouse. And he ended up with the tapes. And I couldn't get hold of them. He had them locked in his house. And I found out he'd secretly paid for the sessions, through Warner Brothers or something. I didn't know anything about it, because all my sessions are just paid for by EMI or Capitol, and I never even think about it. And now not only the session's collapsed, but I haven't gotten any tapes. . . . The having fun fell into having no fun. Then I was hanging around L.A. for months and months, waiting for him to come out of his hole. All these stories came out: He's had an accident, he's dying. . . . You never know what to believe, 'cause he lives an incredibly surreal life, in his own head. You call him . . . or he won't turn up for a session. And instead of saying he doesn't feel like going he'd say something like, "The studio's being burned down." First I'd be accepting all this, then I started checking up . . . and there was nothing wrong with the studio . . .

Anyway, it was really bummy. So I ended up hanging around L.A., waiting for him to come out. Sometimes I got annoyed. Then I said, "I can't be annoyed. I'm crazy, he's crazy. He's crazier than me, that's all. Maybe this is the way it's supposed to"—any rationalization. Then I got fed up. And I got fed up being drunk, and I got depressed. I never leave tapes in the studio. There is no unreleased work. It was driving me crazy. Then I decided—I was getting drunk with Harry Nilsson a lot—and one drunken morning I said, "Why don't we do some work instead? Instead of just getting into trouble?? My name gets in the paper, you never get mentioned . . . and I get all the problems. I am the one with the immigration problems. So let's do something constructive." "Constructive" turned out to [be], "OK, let's make an album of Harry." And that was fine by me. I didn't want to make an album by me, I wasn't in the mood. So, we ended up doing it. Halfway through I sobered up. Cause I had this idea—if we all lived together: Ringo, Harry Nilsson, Klaus Voorman[n]—somehow Keith Moon got in on it. This is my brilliant idea, to have us all live together and work together. And we'd all be in tune. But it was a madhouse.

And halfway through I realized that we were committed, and this wasn't my album, and somebody was paying RCA, and we'd better get on with it. And Harry, after the first session, comes to me, and he's got no throat, no voice, whatsoever. I say, "What's going on?" And he's got no voice. I don't know if it was psychological or what. It was a bit of that. There I've got this great singer with no voice, and a house full of drunken lunatics. So, I suddenly got sober in the middle of it. I'm responsible, I'm the producer, man! I'd better straighten out. So I straightened out. And I got to be the one that was straight, and they were all looking at me like that. . . . I soon got to be the odd man out. I ended up locking myself in the bedroom, trying to keep away. So we finished that one, and then I went back and started *Walls and Bridges*. I was straight as a die by then. Just seeing other people drunk is enough to straighten out.

The day before we started *Walls and Bridges* some deal was made, and Phil sent me the tapes back, of the rock 'n' roll stuff. We'd cut about eight tracks. In eight months!! I couldn't deal with him then; I finished *Walls and Bridges*. And then I started playing the eight tracks—I didn't even wanna hear them. Only about four of them were savable, the rest of them were . . . miles out of tune . . . just mad. You couldn't use them, 28 guys playing out of tune!! I just salvaged what there was of them. And I was getting depressed. What can I do? Make an EP? They don't have EPs in America. Put them out one by one? I wasn't sure enough of their quality that they were gonna be singles. Some of them were alright, but I didn't feel confident about them.

So I recorded 10 more in five days and stuck it all together—and that is it. It started out to be fun and ended up ... it ended up to be fun. The 5-day sessions were great fun. We just did two or three a night and we didn't get all into it. We all just rocked, relaxed. It started out fun, became hell, and ended up fun. There was so much buildup. Waiting for this great record. Of Lennon and Spector. And I nearly for the first time didn't put it out. But then I let people hear it; people who had not been involved. And the record company who hadn't been involved, they never heard of it. And they said, "It's alright. We like it." And friends liked it. They said it's alright; it ain't bad. Actually they liked some of it. And that's the story, folks . . .

Schoenberger: And right now, about your plans? '75?

Lennon: Stay alive in '75. That's my motto. I don't know. I just feel pretty alright. '74 was just hell. Just a drag. '74 lasted about three years. . . . A little bit of it tailed into '75. But I just feel good now, I'm writing well. So I'm happy.

Schoenberger: How do you do it? Do you write when you are in the mood? Is your mind always thinking about writing?

Lennon: I'm always at it. The best stuff usually comes out on impulse. Or inspiration. And I hardly have to think about it. But I am always writing. In the back of my head, or if somebody says something, I'm storing it away—a line, or an idea. There is never a moment when I'm not writing, almost. Although I don't think I'm writing. There's [not] a specific time when I just sit down and write.

Schoenberger: Do you have a lot of songs stored away, or ready?

Lennon: I never have a lot left over. I have some left over that I occasionally forget, and then remember them, and just use bits of them.

Schoenberger: How do you write the lyrics?

Lennon: I just scribble on a bit of paper, you know. And then leave it in a sort of pile. And when it begins to be more interesting, I venture on to the typewriter and type it out. And the typewriter adds things, too. I change it as I type it. It's usually the third draft when I get to the typewriter. Depending on how easy it came. If it just all came it's just like "write it and type it." But if it's a general song, I'll type it a few more times. But the final version is never until we've recorded it. I always change a word or two, at the last minute.

Schoenberger: You have the lyrics first, and then the music?

Lennon: Usually. It's better. I like that. The music is sort of easy. I sometimes envy Elton John. Bernie Taupin sends him a big stack of words, and he writes all the songs in five days. I could do that. But I am too egocentric to use other people's words. That's the problem. So it's my own fault. I still like black music, disco music . . . "Shame, Shame, Shame" or "Rock Your Baby," I'd give my eyetooth to have written that.

But I never could. I am too literal to write "Rock Your Baby." I wish I could. I'm too intellectual, even though I'm not really an intellectual. I feel as though I am a writer, really. And the music is easy. The music is just all over the place.

Schoenberger: How about you as a father? How old is your son [Julian] now?

Lennon: He is 11 now.

Schoenberger: All I know is that you took him to Disneyworld . . . right?

Lennon: Yeah, that was hell. Disneyland was better, the first time, in L.A., I took him there. Because I went with a gang, and there were a few of us who were flying a little. But Disneyworld—I was there on the most crowded day of the year, around Christmas or something. Seeing him is good. What we do is irrelevant. I went through a period of, "What are we gonna do?" and all that crap. It doesn't really matter. As long as he's around. Cause I don't see him that often.

Schoenberger: How is it for an 11-year-old boy to have John Lennon as a father?

Lennon: It must be hell.

Schoenberger: Does he talk about that to you?

Lennon: No, because he is a Beatle fan. I mean, what do you expect?? I think he likes Paul better than me. . . . I have the funny feeling he wishes Paul was his Dad. But unfortunately he got me. . . . It must be hard to be son of anybody. He is a bright kid and he's into music. I didn't encourage him, but he's already got a band in school. But they sing rock 'n' roll songs, 'cause their teacher is my age. So he teaches them "Long Tall Sally" and a couple of Beatles numbers. He likes Barry White and he likes Gilbert O' Sullivan. He likes Queen, though I haven't heard them yet. He turns me on to music.

I call him and he says, "Have you heard Queen?" and I say "No, what is it?" I've heard of them. I've seen the guy . . . the one who looks like Hitler playing a piano. . . . Sparks? I've seen Sparks on American TV. So I call him and say, "Have you seen Sparks? Hitler on the piano?" and he says, "No. They are alright. But have you seen Queen?" and I say "What's

Queen?" and then he tells me. His age group is hipper to music . . . at 11 I was aware of music, but not too much.

Schoenberger: How is it when you walk around in New York? I guess, you are not walking around with a body guard like a lot of other people?

Lennon: Are you kidding? It's not 1965, it's '75. People just see me. And occasionally just bother me a bit. But the most they ask for is an autograph. I don't care, I sign an autograph. Sometimes the taxi drivers, if they are young, get a little bit. . . . And I say, "Yes, it is me. Keep your eye on the road." But apart from that it's no hassle. In general I just walk around. I love it. People just say, "Oh, it's him," or, "It isn't him," but they don't jump on me. Because I'm not in the prime of my career, or whatever they call it. I am not Elton. He can get around, but it's pretty hard.

Schoenberger: What about simpler days, like in Hamburg?

Lennon: You know what I have written—carved—on a church in Hamburg? "John loves Cyn." That was my first going out with her at that time. A church that overlooks . . . just outside the Reeperbahn. [*A street in Hamburg, and an area known for its nightlife. —Ed.*] But out right in town, and it's got a big green tower, that you can walk up in. And we all carved our names on there. You can have a look. There will be John + Cyn, [original Beatles bassist] Stu [Sutcliffe] + [German photographer and artist] Astrid [Kirchherr], Paul + . . . what the hell was the girl at that time?

Schoenberger: Were they all English girls?

Lennon: Except for Astrid with Stu. I think Stu and Astrid is up there . . . but I know John + Cyn is. We stuck our names up there with whoever we were hanging on then. I didn't go out with a German girl. I ended up with an American, I never saw her again.

Schoenberger: Did you ever meet Elvis?

Lennon: Once, yeah. It's an interesting story. We were terrified. He is our idol. We went to meet him, all the gang this day. We went in and he was sitting in front of a TV. We were in the middle of a tour, '65 or something. He had this TV, I remember. He had an amplifier and a bass plugged into it. And watching with no sound on the TV. And playing bass and singing, and we were sort of singing along. But we were really just watching him. I always thought of it from our point of view; I never thought of it from his. And years later I heard from a friend, who is friendly with his ex-wife, that he was terrified too: a) 'cause we were the new thing and b) what was gonna happen. And that he had been prancing around for hours in preparation, thinking of what to say. And we worshipped him.

It's a strange story . . . I just remember sitting there and him playing the bass. And me thinking "It's Elvis! It's Elvis!" It's actually Elvis. He looked great then, no weight on him. He looked good. And he was shy a bit. I'd like to see him in Vegas 'cause that's where he's supposed to be at home. But I'd be embarrassed if they said, "And there in the audience is John Lennon." I'd hate it. I'm dying to see him.

Schoenberger: Tell me about your therapy with [Arthur] Janov.

Lennon: Part of it was not to self-control yourself, in any way. That included anything so I would just eat and eat and eat. And it was all very well for the mind, but for the body it was terrible. But the idea was, "Well, I am an artist, not a model, so fuck it. I wonder who I try to please . . .?" It was me I was trying to please, I found out; too late, after I'd got about 5 million pounds. And I wore the same clothes for two years. I had two things: a jumpsuit—not a fashionable one; one you get to do the plumbing in. I had two of them. And that's all I wore for almost two years. In the middle of the Janov thing I got fat as hell. I was living on chocolate and Dr. Pepper. . . . I mean, Janov was an idiot, but he was not bad. His therapy was good. It was just he was a pain in the neck. So I got big, and I wore the same clothes. . . . I got used to it. I didn't feel terrible about it, but I didn't enjoy it. I was a slob.

Schoenberger: Your sex life? Did it change while you were at it? Did you get conscious of being ugly?

Lennon: No, because I was in the therapy with Yoko, and we both were as fat as hell. And in the dark it feels great. We both would roll around. . . .

It's when you wanna go somewhere else, or when someone else sees you that you are conscious of it. Sometimes I don't like dressing up. And I don't dress up for months, or almost a year. Just wear a T-shirt and jeans. And someday I just get an urge to get dressed. And then you can't wear anything—nothing looks good, nothing . . . you always look like an asshole.

Schoenberger: Did you go shopping?

Lennon: I wouldn't do it. I wouldn't buy anything. 'Til the weight was gone. George is a lucky one. He eats like a pig—and nothing happens. Makes me mad. Ringo gets fat as a pig. I wasn't a fat kid. I just got fat through greed. Ringo was a fat kid, so he always had problems. I got fat when we got rich and famous. And he didn't, he watched it.

Schoenberger: How did you keep your sanity when you got rich and famous?

Lennon: I didn't. I was born crazy, so it wasn't that unreal. It was just like a dream. Like being *Alice in Wonderland.*

Schoenberger: Is it the same thing when you look back now?

Lennon: Yeah. This is a dream, right now. I am sort of aware, but it's sort of unreal, being here.

Schoenberger: For me, being with you, suddenly it's not "John Lennon," but a person, a man . . .

Lennon: I am a guy, yeah. That is true. But how do you know unless you see somebody? I am just some guy who did . . . whatever. Always see me as me. I was always me, all the way through it. . . . I love motels 'cause there is no reception area. I like hotels too. But I like motels as well. Just invisible places where you check in with a credit card, in the middle of the night, anywhere. Some guys in taxis now, old guys, they recognize the voice is English, but they don't recognize me. They don't know who the hell I am. They say, "Oh, you're English! I was over there in the war . . ." And they go on and on . . . and tell me amazing life stories. . . . They ask, "what do you do?" and I say, "I'm a musician," and they say, "Are you doing alright?" "Yeah, I am . . ."

LENNON ON . . .

Ringo Starr's Solo Success

"I'm most happy—I guess we all are, in a way—for Ringo's success, because the other three of us. . . . It always went around that Ringo was dumb, but he ain't dumb. But he didn't have much of a writing ability and he wasn't known for writing his own material, and there was a bit of a worry that . . . you know, although he can make movies and he does make movies and he's good at it, but how is his recording career gonna be? [*Pauses, then laughs.*] And in general, it's probably better than mine, actually. So he's doing all right. And I'm happy about that."

—from interview with Tom Snyder, broadcast on *Tomorrow*, NBC (US), April 25, 1975

LENNON ON . . .

"How Do You Sleep?"

"Two things I regretted. One, that there was so much talk about Paul [McCartney] that they missed the song; it was a good track. And I should've kept me mouth shut. Not on the song [but about McCartney]; it could've been about anybody. When you look at 'em back . . . Dylan said it about his stuff, that he found that most of it's about him. I wrote a sort of 'Son of "How Do You Sleep?"' on *Walls and Bridges* . . . 'Steel and Glass,' which I thought was about a few people, but then I'm realizing, 'Oh, it's me *again*?' So it's not about Paul. It's about me. I'm really attacking myself. But I regret the association. . . . But he lived through it. The only thing that matters is how he and I feel about those things and not what the writer or the commentator thinks about it. Him and me are OK, so I don't care what they say."

—from interview with Bob Harris, broadcast on *The Old Grey Whistle Test*, BBC (UK), April 18, 1975

LENNON ON . . .

Manager Brian Epstein

"Epstein fronted for the Beatles, and he played a great part at whatever he did. He was theatrical, that was for sure, and he believed in us. But he certainly didn't package us the way they say he packaged us. He was good at his job, to an extent. He wasn't the greatest businessman. But you have to look at this: If he was such a great packager, so clever at packaging products, whatever happened to Gerry and the Pacemakers, Cilla Black, and all the other packages? Where are they? Where are those packages? Only one package survived, the original package."

—from interview with Lisa Robinson, published in *Hit Parader* (US), December 1975

LENNON ON . . .

His Silence

"If you think of us next time, remember, our silence is a silence of love and not of indifference. Remember, we are writing in the sky instead of on paper—that's our song. Lift your eyes and look up in the sky. There's our message. Lift your eyes again and look around you, and you will see that you are walking in the sky, which extends to the ground. We are all part of the sky, more so than of the ground. Remember, we love you."

—from full-page ad with the headline A LOVE LETTER FROM JOHN AND YOKO TO PEOPLE WHO ASK US WHAT, WHEN, AND WHY, published in the *New York Times*, May 27, 1979

THE REAL JOHN LENNON

Barbara Graustark | Circa August 1980 |
Published September 29, 1980, *Newsweek* (US)

John Lennon lived in seclusion for about five years, raising his son and leaving business matters to Ono, before going public again in the latter half of 1980. He began giving interviews in late summer and then, on November 17, he and Ono released *Double Fantasy*. The album—the first from Lennon in nearly six years—spent eight weeks at the top of the charts and gave birth to three major hits: "Watching the Wheels," which chronicled the ex-Beatle's life over the previous half decade; and "Woman" and "(Just Like) Starting Over," both about his revitalized relationship with Ono.

Approximately three months before the album's release, the couple spoke with *Newsweek's* Barbara Graustark about a wide range of subjects, including Lennon's years out of the public eye and his desire to resume his career as his fortieth birthday approached. As the conversation ended, he described the inner peace he had finally achieved. —Ed.

In the nine years since the Beatles broke up, John Lennon, their most brilliant and controversial member, has had a turbulent coming of age. After a flurry of post-Beatle albums of wildly uneven quality, a four-year fight with the Immigration Service to stay in the United States, a fifteen-month separation from his wife, Yoko Ono, and the birth of their son, Sean, Lennon disappeared from public view in 1975. Now, on the eve of his 40th birthday, he is reemerging with the most eagerly awaited album of the year. Called "Double Fantasy," it is a "Scenes From a Marriage" in fourteen songs—seven by Lennon, seven by Ono. Wide-ranging in style—from the rockin' boogie of Lennon's "(Just Like) Starting Over" to Ono's gospel-tinged "Hard Times Are Over," from his starry-eyed "Beautiful Boy [(Darling Boy)]" to her acid-tongued rock-disco "Kiss, Kiss, Kiss"—the forthcoming album is full of unaffected gusto and is likely to appeal to the broadest tastes.

A few years ago, the couple switched roles: Lennon became a "house-husband," baby-sitting and baking bread, while Ono became the family's business manager. Their real-estate holdings are extensive—five cooperatives in Manhattan's legendary Dakota apartment house, half a dozen residences scattered from Palm Beach, Fla., to a mountain retreat in upstate New York, and four dairy farms.

Recently, Lennon and Ono sat down with NEWSWEEK's Barbara Graustark for his first major interview in five years. Whippet-thin in Levis and work shirt, smoking French cigarettes and nibbling sushi, the ex-Beatle talked expansively about himself, showing no sign of the inner demons that once haunted his songs:

GRAUSTARK: *Why did you go underground in 1975? Were you tired of making music—or of the business itself?*

LENNON: It was a bit of both. I'd been under contract since I was 22 and I was always "supposed to." I was supposed to write a hundred songs by Friday, supposed to have a single out by Saturday, supposed to do this or that. I became an artist because I cherished freedom—I couldn't fit into a classroom or office. Freedom was the plus for all the minuses of being an oddball! But suddenly I was obliged to a record company, obliged to the media, obliged to the public. It wasn't free at all!

I've withdrawn many times—part of me is a monk, and part a performing flea! The fear in the music business is that you don't exist if you're not at Xenon with Andy Warhol. As I found out, life doesn't end when you stop subscribing to Billboard.

Q. *Why five years?*

A. If you know your history, it took us a long time to have a live baby. [*Ono suffered a miscarriage in November 1968. —Ed.*] And I wanted to give five solid years to Sean. I hadn't seen Julian, my first son [by his ex-wife Cynthia], grow up at all, and now there's a 17-year-old man on the phone talkin' about motorbikes.

I'm an avid reader, mainly history, archeology and anthropology. In other cultures, children don't leave the mother's back until 2. I think most schools are prisons—a child's thing is wide open and to narrow it down and make him compete in the classroom is a joke. I sent Sean to kindergarten. When I realized I was sending him there to get rid of him, I let him come home. . . . If I don't give him attention at 5, then I'm gonna have to give him double doses of it in his teen-age years. It's owed.

Q. *Paul McCartney's theory is that you became a recluse because you'd done everything—but be yourself.*

A. What the hell does that mean? Paul didn't know what I was doing—he was as curious as everybody else. It's ten years since I really communicated with him. I know as much about him as he does about me, which is zilch. About two years ago, he turned up at the door. I said, "Look, do you mind ringin' first? I've just had a hard day with the baby. I'm worn out and you're walkin' in with a damn guitar!"

Q. *Give me a typical day in the life of John and Yoko.*

A. Yoko became the breadwinner, taking care of bankers and deals. And I became the housewife. It was like one of those reversal comedies! I'd say [*mincingly*], "Well, how was it at the office today, dear? Do you want a cocktail? I didn't get your slippers, and your shirts aren't back from the laundry." To all housewives, I say I now understand what you're screaming about. My life was built around Sean's meals. Am I limiting his diet too much? [The Lennons maintain a "macrobiotic" life-style, eschewing dairy products, liquor and meat.] Is *she* gonna talk business when she comes home from work? I'm a rich housewife—but it still involves caring.

Q. *Yoko, why did you decide to take over as business manager?*

ONO: There's a song by John on the album called "Clean-up Time"—and it really was that for us. Being connected to Apple [the Beatles' corporation] and all the lawyers and managers who had a piece of us, we weren't financially independent—we didn't even know how much money we had. We still don't! Now we are selling our shares [25 per cent] of Apple stock to free our energy for other things. People advised us to invest in stocks and oil but we didn't believe in it. You have to invest in things you love. Like cows, which are sacred animals in India. Buying houses was a practical decision—John was starting to feel stuck in the Dakota and we get bothered in hotels. Each house that we've bought was chosen because it was a landmark that needed restoring.

Q. *John, how hard was it not to be doing something musical?*

LENNON: At first, it was very hard. But musically my mind was just a clutter. It was apparent in "Walls and Bridges" [his 1974 solo album], which was the work of a semisick craftsman. There was no inspiration, and it gave off an aura of misery. I couldn't hear the music for the noise in my own head. By turning away, I began to hear it again. It's like Newton, who never would have conceived of what the apple falling meant had he not been daydreaming under a tree. That's what I'm living for . . . the joy of having the apple fall on my head once every five years.

Q. *Did you just stop listening to music?*

A. I listened mostly to classical or Muzak. I'm not interested in other people's work—only so much as it affects me. I have the great honor of never having been to Studio 54 and I've never been to any rock clubs. It's like asking Picasso, has he been to the museum lately?

Q. *Why did you decide to record again?*

A. Because *this* housewife would like to have a career for a bit! On Oct. 9, I'll be 40 and Sean will be five and I can afford to say, "Daddy does something else as well." He's not accustomed to it—in five years I hardly picked up a guitar. Last Christmas our neighbors showed him "Yellow Submarine" and he came running in, saying, "Daddy, you were singing . . . were you a Beatle?" I said, "Well—yes, right."

Q. *Why did you collaborate with Yoko on this LP?*

A. It's like a play—we wrote the play and we're acting in it. It's John and Yoko—you can take it or leave it . . . otherwise [*laughing*], it's cows and cheese, my dear! Being with Yoko makes me whole. I don't want to sing if she's not there. We're like spiritual advisers. When I first got out of the Beatles, I thought, "Oh great. I don't have to listen to Paul and Ringo and George." But it's boring yodeling by yourself in a studio. I don't need all that space anymore.

Q. *You've come a long way from the man who wrote, at 23, "Women should be obscene rather than heard." How did this happen?*

A. I was a working-class macho guy who was used to being served and Yoko didn't buy that. From the day I met her, she demanded equal time, equal space, equal rights. I said, "Don't expect me to change in any way. Don't impinge on my space." She answered, "Then I can't be here. Because there *is* no space where you are. Everything revolves around you and I can't breathe in that atmosphere." I'm thankful to her for the education.

Q. *People have blamed Yoko for wrenching you away from the band and destroying the Beatles. How did it really end?*

A. I was always waiting for a reason to get out of the Beatles from the day I filmed "How I Won the War" [in 1966]. I just didn't have the guts to do it. The seed was planted when the Beatles stopped touring and I couldn't deal with not being onstage. But I was too frightened to step out of the palace. That's what killed Presley. The king is always killed by his courtiers. He is overfed, overindulged, overdrunk to keep him tied to his throne. Most people in the position never wake up. Yoko showed me what it was to be Elvis Beatle, and to be surrounded by sycophant slaves only interested in keeping the situation as it was—a kind of death. And that's how the Beatles ended—not because she "split" the Beatles, but because she said to me, "You've got no clothes on."

Q. *How do you look back on your political radicalism in the early '70s?*

A. That radicalism was phony, really, because it was out of guilt. I'd always felt guilty that I made money, so I had to give it away or lose it. I don't mean I was a hypocrite—when I believe, I believe right down to the roots. But being a chameleon I became whoever I was with. When you stop and think, what the hell was I doing fighting the American Government just because Jerry Rubin couldn't get what he always wanted—a nice, cushy job?

Q. *Do you ever yearn for the good old days?*

A. Nah! Whatever made the Beatles the Beatles also made the '60s the '60s, and anybody who thinks that if John and Paul got together with George and Ringo, "The Beatles" would exist, is out of their skulls. The Beatles gave everything they had to give—and more. The four guys who used to be that group can never ever be that group again even if they wanted to be. What if Paul and I got together? It would be boring. Whether George or Ringo joined in is irrelevant because Paul and I created the music, OK? There are many Beatle tracks that I would redo—they were never the way *I* wanted them to be. But going back to the Beatles would be like going back to school. . . . I was never one for reunions. It's all over.

Q. *Of all the new songs, only "I'm Losing You" seems to harbor the famous Lennon demons. How did you come to write it?*

A. It came out of an overwhelming feeling of loss that went right back to the womb. One night, I couldn't get through to Yoko on the telephone and I felt *completely* disconnected. . . . I think that's what the last five years were all about—to reestablish me for meself. The actual moment of awareness when I remembered who I was came in a room in Hong Kong because Yoko had sent me around the world to be by meself. I hadn't done anything by meself since I was 20. I didn't know how to check into a hotel . . . if someone reads this, they'll think, "These bloody pop stars!" They don't understand the pain of being a freak. . . . Whenever I got nervous about it, I took a bath, and in Hong Kong I'd had about 40 baths. I was looking out over the bay when something rang a bell. It was the recognition—my God! This relaxed person is me from way back. *He* knew how to do things. It doesn't rely on any adulation or hit record. Wow! So I called Yoko and said, "Guess who? It's me!"

I wandered around Hong Kong at dawn, alone, and it was a thrill. It was rediscovering a feeling that I once had as a youngster walking the mountains of Scotland with an auntie. The heather, the mist . . . I thought—aha! *This* is the feeling that makes you write or paint. . . . It was with me all my life! And that's why I'm free of the Beatles—because I took time to discover that I was John Lennon before the Beatles and will be after the Beatles and so be it.

LENNON ON . . .

Moving On

"If the Beatles or the '60s had a message, it was to learn to swim. Period. And once you learn to swim, swim. The people who are hung up on the Beatles and the '60s dream missed the whole point when the Beatles and the '60s *became* the point. Carrying the Beatles or the '60s dream around all your life is like carrying the Second World War and Glenn Miller around. That's not to say you can't enjoy Glenn Miller or the Beatles, but to live in that dream is the twilight zone. It's not living now. It's an illusion."

—from interview with David Sheff, September 1980, published in
Playboy (US), January 1981

LENNON ON . . .

Returning to His Musical Roots

"All through the taping of 'Starting Over,' I was calling what I was doing 'Elvis Orbison': 'I want you I need only the lonely.' I'm a born-again rocker, I feel that refreshed, and I'm going right back to my roots. It's like Dylan doing *Nashville Skyline*, except I don't have any Nashville, you know, being from Liverpool. So I go back to the records I know—Elvis and Roy Orbison and Gene Vincent and Jerry Lee Lewis. I occasionally get ripped off into Walruses or 'Revolution 9,' but my far-out side has been completely encompassed by Yoko."

—from interview with Jonathan Cott, New York, December 5, 1980, published in
Rolling Stone (US), January 22, 1981

LENNON ON . . .

Interpretations of His Music

"I've had tongue in cheek all along. 'I Am the Walrus,' all of them had tongue in cheek. Just because other people see depths of whatever in it. What does it really mean, 'I am the eggman'? It could have been a pudding basin for all I care. It's just tongue in cheek. . . . It [interpretation of the lyrics] gets to be *stupid*. That's why I started, from the 'Mother' album [*John Lennon/Plastic Ono Band*] onwards, trying to shave off all imagery, pretentions of poetry, illusions of grandeur, à la Dylan, Dylanesque. I didn't want any of that. Just say what it is, simple English, make it rhyme, and put a backbeat on it and express yourself as simply and straightforward as possible."

—from interview with Andy Peebles, BBC Radio, December 6, 1980

JOHN LENNON: THE MAN, THE MEMORY

**Dave Sholin | December 8, 1980, the Dakota (Lennon's home), New York |
Broadcast December 14, 1980, RKO Radio Network (US)**

On December 8, 1980, after a session with *Rolling Stone* photographer Annie Leibovitz, John Lennon and Yoko Ono talked at length in their New York City apartment with DJ Dave Sholin, from San Francisco's KFRC. After the interview, which was to be syndicated via the RKO Radio Network, Sholin and his team gave Lennon a lift to his recording studio and flew home to California.

"We had a great buzz of what a tremendous day it was," the DJ recalled in a 2010 interview. "And I get in the car [back in San Francisco], turn on KFRC, and hear Bill Lee playing Beatles songs, which, at that time of night for KFRC, if you know what Bill was doing, we were playing Gap Band, all kinds of stuff. We weren't playing the Beatles at that time of night. So I thought something was up. I said, 'This is strange.' And then I hear other stations playing Beatles songs, go back to hear Bill, and he does the announcement of what had happened. So you go from being about as high as you can possibly be in an incredible day to about as low as you can be in a matter of seconds. It was one of those moments that, even thirty years later, it still hits you hard."

Though other Q&As have been erroneously touted as Lennon's last, Sholin's interview—which has not previously appeared in print—turned out to be the last one the ex-Beatle would ever give. As such, the artist's comments about his work and life—and especially about his plans for the 1980s and his own mortality—took on new meaning.

RKO's producers edited out the DJ's questions and inserted his newly recorded voice-overs; they also added music that tied into Lennon and Ono's remarks as well as a summary of the horrible events that followed the conversation by only a few hours. Here's the resulting program, just as it aired a mere six days after Lennon's death. —Ed.

[*Snippet from John Lennon's "Imagine" plays.*]

Dave Sholin: John Lennon, the Man, the Memory. Dedicated to Yoko Ono. December 8, 1980. The dream is over. John Lennon is dead. John Lennon, the idol of millions, devoted husband of Yoko Ono and father to Sean Ono Lennon, was brutally gunned down in front of the Dakota, his New York apartment house. The suspect in custody, a twenty-five-year-old man from Hawaii who seemed to pattern his life after Lennon's and admitted to the vicious killing without hesitation or remorse. Mark Chapman spent hours outside the Dakota apartment building waiting for Lennon. And according to the security guard and New York City Police, fired at the man whose music moved millions as he walked from his limousine to the entryway of the Dakota.

Detective James Sullivan: Mr. Chapman came up behind him and called to him—"Mr. Lennon!"—as he arrived at that doorway. And then in a combat stance, he fired. He emptied the Charter Arms .38 caliber gun that he had with him and shot John Lennon.

Sholin: New York City chief of detectives James Sullivan says Chapman dropped his gun after the shooting, waiting to be apprehended as John Lennon was fatally wounded.

Nina [bystander]: I was passing the Dakota. I saw John and Yoko come out of the limousine.

Sholin: A woman identified only as Nina was outside the Dakota at the time of the shooting.

Nina: They walked out of the limousine. They walked up the path into the gate. And just about when I was approaching the corner, I heard shots, loud shots. They were ear-deafening. And I stood there for a minute, and then I walked across the street. There were two joggers there. They stopped, also. They asked me, "Did you hear those shots?" And I said,

"Yes." I said, "I don't know what happened." Then they said that John and Yoko went into the building.

Sholin: Lennon was rushed to nearby Roosevelt Hospital with Yoko Ono at his side. She was shocked. She couldn't believe it, and she begged police to tell her it wasn't true, that it hadn't happened. But by the time Lennon arrived at the Roosevelt emergency room, the world Yoko Ono knew came crashing down with a sudden and violent finality as the official statement was made.

Hospital Spokesman: John Lennon was brought to the emergency room shortly before 11 PM. He was dead on arrival.

Sholin: John Lennon had dreamed during life of a world united by love. Perhaps we've never come closer than in the hours after the death of John Lennon. Anyone who came through the '60s and '70s with their eyes and ears open couldn't help but be touched by the profound musical and sociological impact of John Lennon. In a lot of ways he defined and shaped our culture, and certainly he commented on it. You didn't have to know all of John Lennon's lyrics or every event in his life to mourn his passing. All you had to do was feel for Lennon from the heart. And from the flow of tears and the swell of music following his shooting, it was obvious how close to the heart Lennon had come to all of us.

Just a few hours before the dark event that would turn the Dakota apartments into the scene of a horrible killing as New York City itself turned dark, along with [scriptwriter] Laurie Kaye, [KFRC engineer] Ron Hummel, and Warner Brothers' [promotion director] Bert Keane, I sat and talked with John and Yoko for almost three hours for the only radio interview granted following the release of their new album, *Double Fantasy*. In that amount of time, I know we all felt like we had made two good friends.

I'm Dave Sholin. What follows, then: the interview that we all congratulated ourselves on and felt better about than any other. We only hope that in some small way, it serves as a tribute to a great man and as a comfort to his grieving widow.

We began talking with Yoko Ono alone, a person that John Lennon said changed his life. In the past five years, their role reversal led to a business life for Yoko and a househusbandship for John. And throughout their enduring relationship, Yoko Ono was John Lennon's stabilizing force and guiding light. That was the sentiment behind "[(Just Like)] Starting Over," from *Double Fantasy*.

[*Lennon's "(Just Like) Starting Over" plays.*]

Sholin: [*Voice-over.*] No matter what the couple had been through, it was time for an outstretched hand, and lots of love.

Yoko Ono: In "Starting Over," that's what John is saying, though it's a song that's written to me. But . . . I mean, it's to his woman, but in fact he is addressing it to all women. And I think it's beautiful. And so each time when I hear this song I feel like choking up again. . . . [The] '80s is probably gonna be—and I'm very optimistic about that—we're gonna start a dialogue all over again, which will be beautiful.

John Lennon: The Beatles had the top five numbers at one time, right? So I can never get more than I've ever had in that respect. I'm not saying I could never have five numbers at once 'cause that's wishing meself bad luck. But let's face the reality: I've had the boyhood thing of being the Elvis and getting my own spot on the show. I want to be with my best friend. My best friend, my wife. Who could ask for anything more? I'd sooner do something else together than not work together, and I think that comes across in the work now. And we feel like this is just the start now, you see. *Double Fantasy*'s our . . . we feel like this is our first album. I know we've worked together before; we even made albums together before. But we feel like this is the first album. I feel like nothin' happened before today.

[*Lennon's "Watching the Wheels" plays.*]

Ono: He was in Bermuda, relaxing with Sean, and I was here working, taking care of the business. I mean, I would have joined them if I liked that sort of thing but—not only that, I was busy—but I don't really enjoy being in a warm place. [*Laughs.*] I like New York. And then, we were having conversations on the phone every day. So he would call and say,

"How's this?" Or he would say, "Are you tired? Do you mind if I just sing you one?"

And it was so funny because, you know, we felt obligated, of course, to listen to each other's songs. And when we have a song that we want to let the other person hear, we're so dying . . . I'll be saying, "Would you mind, John? Are you tired?" "Not another one," you know. That way. Because it's hard, you know. It's hard to listen to somebody else's song. But in a way, because we both liked each other's songs in this album particularly, it worked out very well.

Lennon: [*Shouting.*] I don't know what came over me all of a sudden, love! I didn't know what came over me! I was possessed by this rock 'n' roll devil, you know! [*Softer, serious.*] But partly because, suddenly, I got the songs.

Ono: Even now, you know, those things just come to you.

Lennon: We just suddenly had, if you pardon the expression, diarrhea of creativity. In fact, we went in the studio and cut about twenty-two tracks and cut it down to fourteen to make the dialogue. They were all dialogue songs, meaning that we were writing as if it was a play and we were two characters in it. But it's real life but not real as well, because on a song or a record it can't be real.

I mean, we could've taken it a step further and made this record so maybe she would be called Ziggy Stardust and I would be called Tommy, and then you would call it a rock opera. But we always worked from our own selves as near as we could. So the album, the work we did on this thing, is really a play, but we're using ourselves as the characters. And what we sing about in the record and the songs are real diaries of how we feel. But also it's always not really, really real, because it's a song and it's on a record, and you project it in a different way.

Ono: It was bigger than both of us in a sense. I mean, we didn't try to be together, and also we're still not trying to be together or anything like that. It just seems like a very functional relationship. And this time, when we were going to make *Double Fantasy*, because we haven't been working together as artists for such a long time, we were both very scared. I thought we were going to start fighting like a dog and a cat, really fighting over remix or whatever. So I was depressed about it and John felt that too, probably. And when we went in the studio, we found that somehow, we were ticking and starting to work together in a very inspired way. And we couldn't believe it.

It was really, truly a dialogue in a sense that I would make one song and sing it to him over the phone, and then he'd react to that in a way and then he would write another song. And vice versa—he'd write a song, and I'd say, "Oh, all right, that's how he feels. OK, how about this?" [*Laughs.*] It was really interesting.

Lennon: We had discussed going back in the studio, but I didn't have the material. But I wasn't worried about it because I hadn't done it for a long time. "Maybe if I switch into that there'll be something there." But it just sort of came. And I called her, 'cause I was in Bermuda with Sean, and she was here in New York. And I called her, and I said, "Well, look, we were talking about recording. It must have triggered something off here because I'm getting all this stuff."

And I started singing it to her down the phone or playing a cassette, and she would call back two hours later and say, "When you sang that, 'Losing You' . . ." She'd come back with "Moving On" or something. And then I'd say, "Oh, OK, 'Moving On.'" And then I'd be swimming or doing anything and then suddenly something else would come, like "Starting Over." I'd say, "Hey, well, look, this is what happened."

And it started working, coming out like that. So I couldn't wait to get back and start. I suddenly had all this material after not really trying but not not trying either for five years. I'd been so locked in the home environment and completely switched my way of thinking that I didn't really think about music at all. My guitar was sort of hung up behind the bed, literally. I don't think I took it down in five years.

Ono: Both of us were very nervous, but at the same time we were so excited with the songs. We knew they were gonna be good, and we had twenty-two songs. It was very hard for us to choose for the first album. And we decided that we should put songs like "Losing You" and "Moving On" in, though some people might think they're sort of negative. But we tried to make sure that the whole tone of the album would be on a positive side. That's very important. But to throw that [arguably negative material] in was very important to show that people go through that, too. Like a catharsis . . . that people go through that with us and see what happens, and then, in the end, hard times are over for a while, maybe. We wanted to show a real picture, not just all pretty, you know.

Lennon: It inspired me completely. As soon as she would sing something to me, or play the cassette down the phone, within ten or fifteen minutes, whether I wanted to work or not, if you call it work, I would suddenly get this song coming to me. And I always felt that the best songs were ones that came to you rather than. . . . I do have the ability, you know, if you asked me to write a song for a movie or something and they say, "It's about this," I can sit down and sort of make a song. I wouldn't be thrilled with it, but I can make a song like that. I find it difficult to do that, but I can do it. I call it craftsmanship. I've had enough years at it to sort of put something together. But I never enjoyed that.

I like it to be inspirational, from the spirit. And being with Sean and switching off from the business sort of allowed that channel to be free for a bit. You know, it wasn't always on. It was switched off, and when I sort of switched it on again, zap, all this stuff came through. So now, well, we did enough material for the next album almost, and we're already talking about the third album. So we're full of [*shouts in deep voice*] vim and vigor!

Ono: It was very strange. Just when we finished stringing the songs together for the album, and we're saying, "Ah, it's over, we're finished" and in the next room somebody was saying, "Quick, quick, come over here 'cause 'Starting Over' is playing." So we just rushed to that room and we heard it for the first time and that "ting, ting, ting" [sound]. By the way, that "ting, ting" is sort of a bell for wishes. And if you make a wish and you hear that "ting, ting, ting," your wish will come true. So it sounded so good, and we just felt we did it.

[*Snippet from Lennon and Ono's "(Just Like) Starting Over" plays.*]

"Starting Over," "Woman," "Watching the Wheels" . . . those three songs, especially "Watching the Wheels," even now when I hear it, and this is after remixing and, I mean, I heard it over a hundred times really, but it really makes me choke up. You know why? Because "Watching the Wheels" is a song that sums up what he was doing this past five years. And I went through with him in a way. And it was very hard for him, because people were very suspicious about it. Like, "What are you doing now?" "I'm not doing anything." "Well, when is your next album coming?" That sort of thing.

And even now, when he declares that he's a househusband. I mean, there's an aspect of it that. . . when it was on the news, a newscaster who's a guy . . . it was definitely very embarrassing. [The newscaster said] "He's now a househusband, so he claims." [Clears throat.] That kind of thing. [Laughs.] And his [the newscaster's] face was changing. And I think it's a very courageous thing to do. And a lot of people were saying, "Oh, this album is just full of love songs. What's that?" But he knows all that aspect.

It's very easy for him to do a macho song. [Sings.] Just another rocker. [Speaking again.] And say whip the women or kick them out of the room or whatever, and get drunk . . . with the boys. I mean, that image is so prevalent in the rock world, and it's so easy to keep that up. But at the time that that is the macho image, to come out and say "I'm a househusband, and here I am with a son, and I still love my wife," which is . . . people get embarrassed, you know. "What is *that?*" You know? I think that's a very courageous thing to do.

[*Lennon's "Cleanup Time" plays.*]

Sholin: [*Voice-over.*] In 1975 John Lennon and Yoko were blessed with the child they'd wanted so badly—their son, Sean Ono Lennon.

Lennon: He was born on October the ninth, which I was, so we're almost like twins. The funny thing is, if he doesn't see me a few days or if I'm really, really busy and just sort of get a glimpse of him, or if I'm feeling depressed without him even seeing me, he sort of picks up on it, and he starts getting that way.

So it's like I can no longer afford to have artistic depressions, which usually produced a miserable song, but it was something I could use. So if I start going really deep, sort of wallowing in a depression so I kind of enjoy it as best I can, he'll start coming down with stuff, so I'm sort of obligated to keep up. But sometimes I can't because something'll make me depressed, and there's no way I can deal with it. And then sure as hell, he'll get a cold or trap his finger in the door or something will happen. So now I have more reason to stay healthy and bright. I can no longer wallow in it and say, "Well, this is how artists are supposed to be, I suppose. Write the blues, you know . . ."

Sholin: [*Voice-over.*] John told us he didn't want to repeat his macho mistakes of the past. He wanted to be a true father to Sean, an around-the-clock daddy.

Lennon: A boy was really programmed to go in the army. That was about it, you know. And you had to be tough, and you're not supposed to cry, and you're not supposed to show emotion. And I know Americans show more emotion and are more open than English people. But it's pretty similar over here. There's that Calvinist, Protestant, Anglo-Saxon ethic, which is don't touch, don't react, don't feel. And I think that's what screwed us all up, and I think it's time for a change.

Sholin: [*Voice-over.*] Lennon obviously realized that he could never be called a typical father; his fame and wealth made that label absurd. But the love in John Lennon's heart for Sean, and the desire that love created to spend as much time as possible with his boy, led to some deep thinking on raising a child.

Lennon: I took the time . . . any famous star . . . and I'm not going to name any names, but many of them have had problems with their kids, either killing themselves or in various ways. I don't buy that bit about quality over quantity. You know, like an hour a week of intense rolling in the hay together is better than twenty minutes every day of you being bitchy and just being yourself around him. So I don't try and be the God Almighty kind of figure that never . . . is always smiling and just this wonderful father.

Nobody knows about children, that's the thing. . . . You look in the books—there's no real experts. Everybody's got a different opinion. You learn by default in a way. I made a lot of mistakes already, but what can you do? I think it's better for him to see me as I am. If I'm grumpy, I'm grumpy. If I'm not, I'm not. If I want to play, I play. If I don't, I don't. I don't kowtow to him. I'm straight with him as I can be.

Yes, I can afford to take the time, but anybody with a working wife might be able to afford to take the time if they've not got a working wife because they're poor and they both have to work. But I know lots of dads who aren't working that hard, who are just sitting in an office all day anyway to avoid life. They're sitting behind desks, and they're doing nothing, just shoveling paper, right, waiting for lunchtime to get a cocktail. But I don't buy that "My career is so important that I'll deal with the kids later" bit, which I already did with my first marriage and my first child.

I kind of regret it. My other son by my first marriage is seventeen. I don't remember seeing him as a child. It didn't even enter . . . like most guys of twenty-four, twenty-five, they're too intent on their career, really.

Yoko was a poor artist when I met her, OK, and living in not the best conditions, and she had a child, and the child went wherever she went, you see. She didn't treat her first child like I treated mine.

Ono: I took her onstage.

Lennon: She took her onstage. . . . And she would take her when they were making movies. 'Cause I saw before we got together . . . I've seen her work and the way she worked. And Kyoko was running around all over the place. And there are many artistically inclined people that have worked like that in the past. Not since the '60s, but in the '30s and many other times. So even if I was poor, it's the state of mind I'm in. I would work out some way for him to be around us somehow. I would have chosen my career to suit that.

You don't have to be rich to love your kids. I learned a lot from the child because they're not hypocrites, and they're not phony. They know when you're . . . I mean, he knows already. Anybody with a child that's spent any moments with them, you know, and it's good for you, I think, because one does tend to fool oneself, and the kids don't buy it.

Ono: You were saying, remember, that he wants to be a daddy when he's older?

Lennon: Oh, yeah. Because I hadn't been in the studio for five years or whatever, so he's used to me being around all the time, 'cause it's a pleasure for me to hang around the house. I was always a homebody. I think a lot of musicians are. You write and you play in the house, anyway. Or when I was wanting to be a painter when I was younger, I was always in the house. Or write poetry, it was always in the house.

But I started to work, and he started seeing a bit less of me. I've let him come to the studio, but it was a bit boring [for him]. He was excited, but long story short: at the end of the session that was going on, I'd got on a night schedule where I'd be coming in when he'd be getting up. So he'd see me at breakfast, but I'd be different. I was a sort of shredded . . . "Aha, OK"—like that. Then we were sort of lying down on the bed together, maybe watching some cartoon or whatever, and he just sat up and said, "You know what I want to be when I grow up?" And I said, "No, what's that?" He looked me right in the eye: "Just a daddy." [*Ono laughs.*]

I thought, *Mmm-hmm.* And I said, "You mean you don't like it that I'm working now, right, and going out a lot?" He says, "Right." I said, "Well, I'll tell you something, Sean. It makes me happy to do the music, and I might have more fun with you if I'm happier, right?" And he said, "Mmm-hmm." That was the end of that. I think I was BSing him, but he caught me off guard there because . . . "just a daddy."

Sholin: [*Voice-over.*] If being a daddy to his and Yoko's child was the ultimate fantasy for John Lennon, then so was the outcome of their latest studio work together.

Lennon: When you go to late [at night], you think, *Wow, great. This is great, we've done it.* And then the next time you hear it, [you think,] *Well, she's not quite what I was thinking of, it's not right, it's not right.*

So I would go yea and nay on it all the time. But I think basically we thought if people will listen to it for what it is and not listen to it with preconceived ideas of how it ought to be or as compared to something else, then if people could listen to it just as if it wasn't even John and Yoko, just that it came over the radio. And you accepted it or not accepted it as you hear it, not as you expect to hear John Lennon, or expect to hear Yoko Ono, or expect to hear an ex-Beatle, or expect to hear whatever. Or having read some good review or a bad review. Forget about that. *Just get it on the radio,* I thought, and it'll be all right.

Ono: The way I looked at it was probably, it's an album that's not gonna do too well. But in the end, you know, maybe like two years later or something, people will say, "Ah, that was good." Because I knew that the theme was good, I knew the dialogue was important, et cetera. And each song was all right, you know. So I had a feeling that even if it takes a long time, people would know about it. But I didn't think it was gonna be that instant, you know?

Sholin: [*Voice-over.*] The instant acceptance of *Double Fantasy* comes from the positive message of the album and the sincerity of the loving thoughts John and Yoko put into it. John felt the emotional honesty they put across and the musical dialogue opened themselves up to the public.

Lennon: Even as I put it in my last incarnation, "Everybody's Got Something to Hide Except Me and My Monkey." It means really that one cannot be absolutely oneself in public, because the fact that you're in public makes you . . . you have to have some kind of defense, or whatever it is. But we always tried, whether from *Two Virgins* through *Imagine,* through anything we've done together, the films we made together, we always tried to get as near to the uncensored, as it were, for what we are. Not to project an image of something that we're not.

Because having been in that sort of pop business so long—I'd tried to retain myself throughout it but obviously not always being successful at that—it was most uncomfortable when I didn't feel I was being myself. You know, when I would have to smile when I didn't want to smile, and it became like being a politician, you know. And what I really got through this five years is: I'm not running for office. I like to be liked. I don't like to offend people. I would like to be a happy, contented person. I don't want to have to sell my soul again, as it were, to have a hit record. I've discovered that I can live without it. It'd make it happier for me, but I'm not gonna come back in and try to create a persona who would not be myself.

Sholin: [*Voice-over.*] Until he could be himself in his music, John Lennon wouldn't head back in the studio.

Lennon: It's like the channels on the radio were jammed, you know? I was not getting clear signals. And after ten or fifteen, almost twenty years of being under contract, and having to produce two albums a year in the early days and a single every three months, regardless of what the hell else you were doing. Or what your family life was like, or what your personal life was like. Nothing counted; you just have to get those songs out. And Paul and I turned out a lot of songs in those days. And it was easier because it was the beginning of our business . . . you know, relationship and career. Paul and I developed in public, as it were. We had a little rehearsal in private, but mainly we developed our abilities in public.

But then it got to be format. And not the pleasure that it was. And that's when I felt that I'd lost myself. Not that I was on purpose being a hypocrite or a phony, but it took something away from what I set out to do. I started out to do rock 'n' roll because I absolutely liked doing it. So that's why I ended up doin' a track like "Starting Over." It's kinda tongue-in-cheek. You know it's "w-e-e-e-e-l-l-l-l-l, w-e-e-e-e-l-l-l-l-l." It's sort of à la Elvis and that, and I hope people accept it like that. I think it's a serious piece of work, but it's also tongue-in-cheek, you know?

I mean, I went right back to me roots. All the time we were doin' it, I was callin' it Elvis Orbison, you know? And it's not going back to being Beatle John in the '60s, it's being John Lennon, whose life was changed completely by hearing American rock 'n' roll on the radio as a child. And that's the part of me that's coming out again, and that's why I'm enjoying this time. I'm not trying to compete with my old self, or compete with the young new-wave kids, or anything like that, that are comin' on. I'm not competing with anything. I'm trying to go back and enjoy it, as I enjoyed it originally.

[*Snippet from the Beatles' "Rock and Roll Music" plays.*]

Sholin: [*Voice-over.*] Lennon's inspiration has always been rock 'n' roll and, for at least the last twelve years, Yoko Ono. Before Yoko, there was another important relationship for Lennon.

Lennon: As I was saying to someone the other day, there's only two artists I've ever worked with for more than one night's stand, as it were. That's Paul McCartney and Yoko Ono. I think that's a pretty damned good choice.

Because, in the history of the Beatles, Paul met me the first day I did "Be-Bop-a-Lula" live onstage, OK? And a mutual friend brought him to see my group, called the Quarrymen. And we met, and we talked after the show, and I saw he had talent. And he was playing guitar backstage, and doin' "Twenty-Flight Rock" by Eddie Cochran. And I turned around to him right then on the first meeting and said, "Do you wanna join the group?" And he went, "Hmm, hmm . . ." And I think he said yes the next day, as I recall it. Now, George came through Paul, and Ringo came through George, although of course I had a say in where they came from, but the only person I actually picked as my partner—who I recognized had talent, and I could get on with—was Paul.

Now, twelve or however many years later I met Yoko, I had the same feeling. It was a different feel, but I had the same feeling. So I think as a talent scout I've done pretty damn well.

Sholin: [*Voice-over.*] But John wasn't exactly acting as a talent scout when he first met Yoko Ono.

Lennon: It was 1966, and I got a call from a guy called John Dunbar, who used to be married to [singer] Marianne Faithfull—you know, everybody's connected. And he had a gallery in London called Indica Gallery, an art gallery. And I used to go there occasionally to see whatever art show was on, you see? And he said, "Oh, I've got this . . .

there's this fantastic Japanese girl coming from New York, and she's gonna do this other thing but she's also gonna put on an exhibition at my gallery. And it's gonna be this big event. Something about black bags!" And I thought, *Oooh, orgies!* you know. These artists, they're all ravers, you know? It was in the days of happenings and paint and all that stuff, right? So I go right down there, you know, for the opening. Goody, goody! You know? Lennon goes down to see what's happening.

I get down there, and it's the night before the opening. I thought there was going to be a big party, and an opening and the whole bit, you know? I didn't wanna get involved. I wanted to watch, you know? I get there, and it's all white and quiet, and there's just these strange things all on display, like an apple on a stand for two hundred pounds—when the pound was worth eight dollars or whatever. And there's hammers, saying HAMMER A NAIL IN. All this very peculiar stuff. And a ladder with a painting on the sky . . . or it looked like a blank canvas on the ceiling with a spyglass hanging from it.

So I'm lookin' 'round, and there doesn't seem to be many people. There's a couple of people downstairs. And I didn't know who was who. So I get up the ladder, and I look through this spyglass, and it said, YES. And I took that as a personal, positive message, because most of the avant-garde artists of that period were all negative. Like, break a piano with an ax; it was mainly male—I'm looking at the female here—it was mainly male art, and it was all destructive, and nay, nay, nay, nay, nay, you know? But here was this little crazy message on the ceiling.

And then the guy introduced me to her. And she didn't know who the hell I was. She had no idea. She was living in a different environment altogether. And I was sayin', "Well, this is a good con, isn't it? Apples at two hundred pounds and hammer a nail. Who's gonna buy this?" You know? I didn't know what concept art was, which in a nutshell is the idea is more important than the object. So that's why you won't see many rich concept artists around, because you can't really, you know . . . like the guy that wraps up . . . what's the guy that wraps up the—

Laurie Kaye [KFRC scriptwriter]: Christo.

Lennon: Christo wraps up things. He doesn't expect you to buy the canvas. What he's doing is selling you this idea, whatever it is he's projecting. It was the same kind of thing, but I hadn't come across it before. How do you sell a nail and a hammer? So anyway, the gallery owner was all fussin' 'round, saying, "Is he gonna buy something?" And she's ignoring me. So he introduced us, and I said, "Well, where's the event?" You know, "Where's the happening?" 'Cause I'd seen the bag. So she just takes a card out and gives it to me, and it just says, BREATHE. So I said [*breathes heavily*], "You mean that?" She said, "You got it." [*Ono laughs.*] I said, "Uh-huh, all right." I'm beginning to catch on here. So, and then I see this hammer, this thing hanging—

Ono: I just remember his nose. . . . He did it exactly like that.

Lennon: Well, you know, what else are you gonna do? That was the big event. I mean, all the way from New York for that? So I see the hammer hanging on the thing with a few nails. And I said, "Well, can I at least hammer a nail in? You know, I've come all the way from the suburbs for this." And she says, "No!"

Ono: [*Laughs.*] 'Cause it's before the opening, and I wanted everything to be right, you know?

Lennon: It was before the opening, and she didn't want the thing messed up. So anyway, the gallery owner has a little word with her. And she comes over to me, and she says, "All right." No smiling or anything. Because, you know how she is, she doesn't . . . she's not runnin' for office—she never was, so . . . she looks at me, and she says, "You give me five shillings. You give me five shillings, and you can hammer a nail in." So I looked at her and said, "I'll give you an imaginary five shillings and hammer an imaginary nail in, OK?"

And that's when we connected really, and we looked at each other like . . . you know that sort of . . . something went off. Well, I didn't see her again for a few weeks. We went to a Claes Oldenburg [American sculptor] opening. . . . I went with Paul, and I don't know who she was with. But I got separated from Paul, and I felt this sort of vibe behind me. And I looked 'round, and there she was. And we're both very shy, believe it or not. And I don't know what I said. We said something.

We didn't really get together until eighteen months later. We didn't make love till two years. You think we're rock 'n' rollers, you know, all the life that people lead. And it's all right coming on with somebody [when] you know that it's not going to go anywhere. The one-night stand and groupies and that. But with a real relationship. . . . I was so paranoid and it was eighteen months or a year before we even got near to each other physically, as it were. 'Cause I didn't know how to treat somebody—a real woman. I only knew how to treat groupies, really.

[*Lennon's "Out the Blue" plays.*]

Sholin: [*Voice-over.*] The relationship developed, and in spite of the ups and downs, John and Yoko came through the '70s together.

Ono: I think both of us in our own way and together really stood against it in a way and said, "OK, well, try to destroy us." We couldn't just be destroyed that way, you know. And we managed it, we feel.

Lennon: It was quite a long trip. But we've been together now longer than the Beatles. You know that?

Ono: That is interesting, isn't it?

Lennon: People always think in terms of, "John and Yoko just got together, and the Beatles split." But we've been together longer than the Beatles.

Ono: I don't feel that we're role models. Because I think each person has his or her own karma and their needs are different, in each person. And when we were separated and John was doing his thing in L.A. and I was doing my things here and all that, we weren't saying, "Do like what we're doing." When we didn't have a child, we weren't saying, "Well, look, you shouldn't have a child." It's the same thing now. For us, this is what happened, you know? I'm not even saying this is the best for us. I don't know what is best or what should be, but this is what happened, and we did our best, and we're just surviving, you know.

Sholin: [*Voice-over.*] John Lennon believed in Yoko and her love like nothing else in the world. He says she saved his life and taught what a real relationship was and how deep feelings can really be. Yoko learned from John as well.

Ono: Before I got together with him, I was a macho woman. I was really . . . I was going my way, kind of. If I was with somebody, I would not really face his problems. "Leave me alone about it," you know. "I have my own problems." And when I got together with John, because he's a strong guy, I had to face his problems, too. And I realized that in this society, men do have their problems, too. Like he came from Liverpool or he was not in the right class or [his] auntie telling him that he has to be a veterinarian or something. That sort of thing. They go through hell. So I realized that men do have problems as well. And that was a very good education for me.

Sholin: [*Voice-over.*] Lennon had his education, too—what he calls his "lost weekend" in Los Angeles—an eighteen-month separation from Yoko at her request that brought out some of his most painful and self-destructive music and memories.

[*Lennon's "Whatever Gets You Thru the Night" plays.*]

Lennon: The worst was being separated from Yoko and realizing that I really, really needed to be with her, wanted to be with her, and could not literally survive without her, as a functioning human being. I just went to pieces. And I didn't [previously] realize that I needed her so much.

[*Lennon's "Dear Yoko" plays, followed by his "#9 Dream."*]

Sholin: [*Voice-over.*] The haunting "#9 Dream" came from John Lennon's L.A. bachelor period.

Lennon: I was haunted, all right, because I realized that I needed her more than she needed me, and I always thought the boot was on the other foot, you know? And that's as honest as I can get. And the image is always . . . 'cause the pop star . . . and Burt Reynolds said it, and God bless him: the women have always kicked him out. And Yoko kicked me out. I didn't go off on a "I'm gonna be a rock 'n' roll bachelor." She literally said, "Get out." And I said, "Oh, OK, OK, I'm going." You know, I was going to be a bachelor, free . . . I'd been married all me life, you know? I'd been married before Yoko, and I immediately married Yoko, so I'd never been a bachelor since I was twenty or something. So I thought *Whooo-hoo, hah, hah!* It was God-awful. [*Ono laughs.*]

And the other thing I want to say about Burt Reynolds . . . Barbara Walters asked him, "What do you want to be remembered as?" and he said, "The best father that ever was." And I thought, *Thank God!* I'd begun to feel maybe I'm the only father that's interested in relating. And is it gonna become, "Oh, John Lennon's now sellin' this family business"? And, "He's been through peace and love, and now he's comin' on like Daddy" and all that.

And I'm only talking about it because that's what I've done, and that's how I feel. And admitting that it is . . . I'm more feminist now than I was when I sang, "Woman Is the Nigger [of the World]." I was intellectually a feminist then; but now I feel at least I've put my body where my mouth was. And tried to really live up to my own preachings, as it were. And to see somebody like Burt Reynolds—who is the world's number-one male star, over all the pop stars worldwide—to have the guts to say he wants to be known as a father, I thought, *Oh, great. I'm not gonna be alone on this one.*

Sholin: [*Voice-over.*] But Lennon was alone in Los Angeles during parts of 1973 and 1974. The events that ate away at his and Yoko's relationship proved temporarily too much in control.

Ono: When we got together . . . and of course there was an element of being really crazy about each other. So that was all right. But when his macho side was sort of coming out here and there, I was saying, "What is this?" And coupled with [the fact that] the world was against me. . . . So I mean, the whole world is behind this macho guy. What's this? And I was really getting sort of upset about it. So by the time . . . it was 1973, was it? I just felt like saying to John, "Well, look, why don't you just go to L.A. and have fun? Leave me alone." You know. And I just wanted to think straight. 'Cause I couldn't think straight anymore with all that going on.

So then when we came back together again, I think that he really tried hard in a way to make it work. And all the things that he did since then, I just can't help . . . I started to have just a great respect for him. I didn't know that this guy can do this, you know. I knew that he could do other things. I mean, he's talented, you know, and all that. But this I didn't believe that he could do. One is to just leave the whole business to me. Just give me carte blanche. You need a lot of courage to do that. "Here's a blank check, take care of it," you know. And in fact he gave me . . . it was a symbolic gesture, but he gave me a blank check, just signed it, and I had it framed. Great.

And also he felt that he should take care of Sean. But that was not for me in a way. I think he wanted that experience. And I think that a lot of people, a lot of guys, secretly want to stay at home. That suits their temperament or whatever. Or they want to cook, but they're sort of shy about it. There are a lot of guys like that. And I think he enjoyed cooking. Basically he likes to stay at home, and he doesn't like to do business. Now, I never did business either, but I prefer doing business to staying at home—let's put it that way—or taking care of a child. I just can't do it, manage it. So it's just an individual difference. But it worked out very well, because by that time the world made it so difficult for me that the only area that I can channel my energies into was this family business. So I thought, *All right, let's do that.*

Sholin: [*Voice-over.*] Then, as in 1968, the year he and Yoko brought out their *Two Virgins* album, he felt the pressures of the press, which tended to criticize harshly whenever Lennon did something outrageous. Even in his experimental music on *Two Virgins* with Yoko.

Lennon: I used to have a place where I worked in the house again, upstairs in my first incarnation with my other wife and kid. And I used to make kinda freaky music at home. And you would hear it coming through on things like "Tomorrow Never Knows" on *Revolver*, or "Rain" and some little backwards things. But I never made that the whole track.

[*Snippet from the Beatles' "Tomorrow Never Knows" plays.*]

Ono: Well, you had sort of freaky stuff on cassettes . . .

Lennon: But at home I'd make far freakier stuff, you know? I would take the sort of most usable [material] and add it to the Beatles, or to my tracks of the Beatles, like "I Am the Walrus" or "Strawberry Fields," whatever. Fiddled around a bit, or put loops or something funny. But at home I was really far out. And I had a kinda little studio, which was really just a lot of tape recorders. And we made *Two Virgins* that way.

She came over for a date, as it were. And I didn't know what to do, and she didn't know what to do. I didn't know what to do with her, so I said, "You wanna go upstairs and play with the tapes?" [*Ono laughs.*] So . . . 'cause we didn't know what to do, we did play with the tapes all night, and we made *Two Virgins*. And I was showin' her all me different tape recordings, and how I made the funny sounds . . .

Ono: You were running around—

Lennon: I was runnin' around pushing buttons and playin' the mellotron, and she started into her Yoko Ono stuff, which is now stuff you hear on [songs by the] B-52s or Lene Lovich and all that stuff. She started doin' this "Oooooh, ohh, ow" and all that. And I thought, *This is great!* And I was goin' "Bloobulb, bloblub" on the tapes, and she was goin' "Owww, ohhh!" And we made a tape all night, and in the morning we made love, as the sun came up. But we'd made this album's worth of sound together, without consciously setting out to make something. And that was the first togetherness.

And we shot the cover ourselves, privately. We got somebody to set the camera up. Took the shot, and put out *Two Virgins*. And that was the start of the whole shebang.

Sholin: [*Voice-over.*] It took Lennon five months to get the other Beatles to approve the *Two Virgins* album cover. The stark, unflattering nude self-portrait was turned down by the record company, and the album was distributed independently. John mimics the public outcry of 1968 against him and Yoko.

Lennon: "What are they doing? This Japanese witch has made him crazy, and he's gone bananas." But all she did was take the bananas part of me out of the closet more, you know, that had been inhibited by the other part. It was a complete relief to meet somebody else who was as far out as I was, you know? That was the real thing. [*Ono laughs.*]

Now we'd like to have a commercial success, but when we made *Two Virgins*, we weren't worried about commercial. . . . We just wanted to put out a statement of where it was at, we wanted to share the thing.

Ono: Naively.

Lennon: No, not naively at all, because some people accepted it and a lot of people didn't.

Ono: That's true, yeah.

Lennon: But the thing had an effect. The fact that an Elvis Presley would take his clothes off and expose . . . now we had other shots for that cover, which made us look a lot more sexy and attractive. Believe me, you know. You know, if you pose a certain way and you just do it like this. And there were a couple more shots that later came out in a calendar with the *Live Peace in Toronto* album, where we look a little more attractive as a couple in a star kinda way. But [for *Two Virgins*] we deliberately chose the one where we were standing there in all our glory, like a little flab 'round the waist, the legs a little . . . you know, nothing pretty about it.

We wanted to say, "We met. We're in love. We wanna share it." And it was a kind of statement, as well, of an awakening for me, too, you know? "This Beatle thing that you've heard all about? This is how I am, really." You know? "This is me, naked, with the woman I love. You wanna share it?" And people did and people didn't. But now you can't get it for two hundred bucks, *Two Virgins*, right? So that's the way it goes.

[*The Beatles' "The Ballad of John and Yoko" plays.*]

Sholin: [*Voice-over.*] In 1968 Yoko was the one influencing John with her far-out artistic and creative concepts. John says he wishes he'd been more open to many of them.

Lennon: Some of the ideas that she wanted both of us to do then . . . I must say, I was more square then than I am now, in a way . . . that I wished we'd done because now other people have done them because. . . . And I would say, "No, I'm not gonna do that! Are you kiddin'? I'm not doin' that." I would start reserving, you know? "I don't wanna do that. We're in enough trouble as it is, you know. Let's not do that!"

Ono: And also, I started to feel guilty because, for instance, he wrote a song called "Power to the People," which is a very powerful song, and then my "Open Your Box" was on the B-side, and of course that was banned in America. And that sort of thing started to happen. So I felt that maybe I was doing a disfavor to him, in a way because, well, you know, he could be number one all the time, but now because he's involved with somebody a bit radical or this and that, that he's getting that . . . well, if you ban the B-side, you're banning the single. That sort of thing. And I was starting to feel guilty a bit. But on the other hand, well, we did a lot of interesting things. We were having fun, as well. It was exciting. "Woman Is the Nigger of the World"—

Lennon: That was banned, "Woman Is the Nigger of the World," because of the word *nigger*. Now, I had *Ebony* and *Jet* [magazines] both say they are not offended, and we went down there with Dick Gregory, just in case there were any questions there. And the statement "Woman is the nigger of the world" was made by Yoko in 1967 or '8 to an English woman's magazine called *Nova*, which was a kind of *Vogue*. And she was on the cover and the title was WOMAN IS THE NIGGER OF THE WORLD. I immediately stole the title and wrote a song. It didn't come [out] until '71. [*Actually 1972. —Ed.*] And there was all this hullabaloo about the word *nigger*, but the hullabaloo was from the white community, you know, not from the black community. 'Cause they understood where it was comin' from.

Ono: 'Cause they don't think that they're niggers, and that's why they didn't care. But the whites basically thought, *Well, niggers. Well, that's their word . . .*

Lennon: She came from a background of classical music, studyin' piano at five, and all the things that rich kids do, you know? And [Austrian classical composers Arnold] Schoenberg and [Anton] Webern she'd studied at Sarah Lawrence and all that. I didn't know any of that stuff. And she was turning me on to it. Even [German playwright and director] Bertolt Brecht. I knew when we did *Some Time in New York City*, to me we were doin' a newspaper. So one would rush it out into print, you see? So there were mistakes, say, a little harmony wasn't perfect. We didn't go back and perfect every note. We just "printed" it out, you know, and sometimes there's words missing or something like that.

And it was later that she said, "Well, you know what we did there?" I said, "No. We got into a lotta trouble, that's all I know! And the harmony's funny or something, you know." 'Cause we had—her idea, again—she had Chairman Mao and Richard Nixon dancing naked on the cover. It wasn't really their bodies; we just stuck their heads on 'em. Well, the record company stuck a label on it in the supermarkets, and you couldn't even get it off when you went home, you know? And there was no genitals, nothing, on it.

But anyway, she and I started getting down about that record, saying it was a mistake, even though we tried to say something about women, and we tried to say something about love and peace or whatever . . . the war. We got into so much trouble. So she then took me to see Richard Foreman's production of the *Threepenny Opera* of Bertolt Brecht, which . . . I don't know when it was originally out, in the '20s or the '30s. [*It debuted in 1928. —Ed.*] And I said, "Oh, I see. So we're not alone," you know? [*Ono laughs.*] I don't know what happened to Brecht when he first put that out, but it was the same idea—meaning, you know, to make a statement on the society right now, right away and no BS. Just say it, you know? "I think this is wrong, that's right. This is my opinion."

[*Snippets from Lennon's "Woman Is the Nigger of the World" and "Power to the People" play.*]

Sholin: [*Voice-over.*] John Lennon and Yoko Ono were always willing to take a stand with their music, especially as the '60s ended and the new decade dawned.

Lennon: Communicate is the thing. It's that need to communicate. Politics was in the air in those days. C'mon. I mean, you couldn't avoid it, right? And being artists, when we get into something we get *into* it, you know what I mean? We wanted to be right down on the front lines. As we always said to everybody—with flowers, but still right down there. We want to go all the way with it. And I think we did go all the way with it, too, you know? [*Laughs.*] Our intentions were good.

[*Snippet from Lennon's "Give Peace a Chance" plays.*]

Ono: Love is the only thing that is going to change the society. In that sense, I think love is a very powerful political weapon as well. And I think that if we go on like this, we have a choice of becoming used by the capitalist society in the sense that we'll all become components of the capitalist society and finally be replaced by the computers, or we'll just stand up and have a human renaissance. Just say, "We're human again. We do want to reach each other and hold each other and become human again."

Sholin: [*Voice-over.*] Good intentions to Lennon meant not just exposing injustices or inequalities but the most important message of all—spreading love.

[*Lennon's "Love" plays, followed by the Beatles' "The Word."*]

Lennon: It sort of dawned on me that love was the answer when I was younger. On the Beatles' *Rubber Soul* album, the first expression of it was a song called "The Word": "The word is love / In the good and the bad books that I have read . . . " "The word is love" seemed like the underlying theme to the universe or to everything that was worthwhile, got down to this love, love, love thing. And it was the struggle to love, be loved, and express that. You know, there's something about love that's fantastic. Even though I'm not always a loving person, I wanna be that, I wanna be as loving as possible.

[*Snippet from the Beatles' "All You Need Is Love" plays.*]

Lennon: Or in the Christian sense, as Christ-like as possible. In the Hindu sense, as Gandhi-esque as possible. And we always approached it . . . and when I met her, even though we were from two different schools of thought, as it were, we found that that was the common denominator. That's why we became the "love and peace" couple. Because before I met her she was protesting against war in a black bag in Trafalgar Square. And when we met, and we discussed what we wanted to do together, what we wanted to do was carry on—me in my love, love, love, and her in her peace, peace, peace. Put it together and that's how we came out with the bed-in. Because I couldn't go down as John Lennon and lie in a bag in Trafalgar Square, because I might get attacked [in] those days. It was dangerous—it was dangerous for her even as an individual protest. So we developed this thing of how to express what we both believe in together the best we can.

Sholin: [*Voice-over.*] Times have changed, though, and the world caught up with John and Yoko and what they were trying to do both musically and politically.

Lennon: This time they're ready for us, man. We can go on and do our stuff without even steppin' . . . without even changing a thing. We could go on, right back. And I dug out the old records we'd made; I dug out the B-52s. And I talked to my assistant, who'd tried to turn me on to them eighteen months before, but I said, "No, I'm not into the music now." I didn't want to hear anything. He was trying to play me Pretenders and Madness and all that stuff, and I didn't want to listen to it. And I said, "Get me some more of this! What's goin' on out there?" He brought all this kooky—whatever you wanna call it—stuff in, and we looked at each other and we thought, *Ha ha! They've finally caught up to what we were trying to do all the time,* which is another form of expression.

And we thought, *This time, surely, they're gonna understand it.* And here we are doin' it—again. It's not that much different from what we did . . . if you take the Plastic Ono Band albums—which are title-less—I call mine *Mother* for reference—it had "Mother" and "God" and a couple of tracks like that on—and her album [*Yoko Ono/Plastic Ono Band*], which was the same cover but a kinda reverse trick. The first track on her thing is called "Why?" You play that and you play something modern now, and see if we weren't on the right track in 1969 and not . . . right on, we were.

Ono: Even now, I have this thing about, "Oh, if Yoko is on the album, she's gonna be the freak so let's not buy the album." So I was very worried for John's sake.

Lennon: I sat her down and said, "Listen." She doesn't like listening. She likes to either do, or do something else. But I held her in the chair and said, "Listen to this [B-52s song] "Rock Lobster"! Listen to this stuff!

Ono: So what I did was in this album I'm not really freaking out so much. Even in "Moving On," when I do that end a little bit, just sort of modestly. I was worried: again, maybe some record-industry people will say, "Oh, Yoko is doing her freak number," and that might kill his chance again, so I was very careful this time.

Lennon: But I wouldn't have done it if we hadn't done it together. That was the point, which . . . your insecurity makes you say that, but the fact is if I couldn't have worked with her, I wouldn't have bothered. I wouldn't enjoy just putting an album out by myself, having to do this by myself, having to go to the studio by myself.

Because . . . even though I was in a group, I've had that kind of game before. I didn't want to work with another guy even. The fact of a man and wife working together and presenting ourselves as man and wife. Not as a sexual object male or her even separately as a sexual object female that sings love songs and is available to the audience. It's not that. We're presenting ourselves as a couple, and to work with your best friend is a joy. And I don't intend to stop it. If we hadn't had the success we'd had with this record, I would have been quite happy because I know I can live without it.

Sholin: [*Voice-over.*] *Double Fantasy*, the album that brought John and Yoko together in the studio for the first time in years, was truly a fantasy come true for both of them. But surprisingly, the album's title had more basic roots.

Lennon: I was takin' Sean and the nanny and the family—except for Mother, who was here selling cows—in Bermuda to the botanical gardens for lunch to the Italian restaurant, 'cause I could get espresso and Sean could get some junk food. And I was just walking in, and I looked down and in the botanical garden [*phone rings*]—we're in the office, folks, that's why it's buzzin'—it said FREESIA DOUBLE FANTASY and it was some flowers. And I just thought, Double Fantasy—*that's a great title!* 'Cause it has so many meanings that you couldn't even begin to think what it means, so it means everything you can think of. I mean, it's a double couple. It's real life but it's still a fantasy, because it's now in plastic and in photograph. And it's fantastic! [*Ono laughs.*] And it just sort of seemed to be perfect for a title of the album. And there's two of us. And it just sort of says it all somehow—without really saying anything, it says everything. And it's a flower, actually.

Ono: And also, in the ten years, we learned that John has his own fantasy and I have mine, too, you know? And that's all right, you see? We don't have to unify our thoughts totally. I mean, there's an overall plan that we have, or a dream that we have, which we share, you know? But then we come from a totally different background—I mean, in the sense of men and women. And that's fine. So we are showing the difference of the fantasies, too.

Sholin: [*Voice-over.*] *Double Fantasy* is reality, too. John said the songs ring true not just for him and Yoko but for any couple with its share of problems.

Lennon: We're not presenting ourselves as the perfect couple, because we don't want to get into that bag either, right? Because we're trying to present what it is—a relationship that lots of other people are having, but they're maybe not songwriters and they don't express it that way. And the letters we're getting back are from couples, apart from the kids who just like it as music. The main excitement is the letters from people who are married with kids, or not necessarily married but relating together, and realizing that we're not sellin' ourselves as the perfect couple. We have our problems. We've had our problems. No doubt, we'll have problems. But, you know, we're trying. We wanna stay together, we wanna be a family. And that's the kind of level we're relating to. I am not aiming at sixteen-year-olds. If they can dig it, please dig it. But when I was singing and writing this and working with her, I was visualizing all the people of my age group, from the '60s—

Ono: [*Laughs.*] That's true.

Lennon: —being in their thirties and forties now, just like me. And having wives and children, and having gone through everything together. I'm singing to them. I hope the young kids like it as well, but I'm really talking to the people that grew up with me. And saying, "Here I am now. How are you? How's *your* relationship goin'? Did you get through it all? Wasn't the '70s a drag, you know? Here we are. Well, let's try and make the '80s good, you know?" 'Cause it's still up to us to make what we can of it. It's not out of our control. I still believe in love, peace; I still believe in positive thinking, when I can do it. I'm not always positive, but when I am, I try and project it.

Ono: But overall we're getting more and more positive, aren't we? Because somehow . . .

Lennon: Because we survived! That's the thing. You have to give thanks to God, or whatever it is up there, the fact that we all survived. We all survived Vietnam, or Watergate, or the tremendous upheaval of the whole world that's changed. . . . We were the hip ones in the '60s, but the world is not like the '60s. The whole map's changed. And we're goin' into an unknown future, but we're still all here. While there's life, there's hope.

Sholin: [*Voice-over.*] "While there's life, there's hope." That was John Lennon's message before his own life was tragically taken just a few hours later. Lennon's last few years had been filled with love and hope and a beautiful, positive approach to everything he did. And nobody was more eager to point out the difference from his past work than Lennon himself, using "Starting Over" as the classic example of his outlook for the '80s.

Lennon: The beginning of *Mother*, the Plastic Ono album, you hear this litany "bong!" Very slow church bell, which is like a death knell. "I don't believe in, I don't believe in," and the Freudian things about mother and father, and that was a kind of negative/positive. I was tryin' to make a positive out of a negative, but it was heavy going. And the reason this one goes "ting, ting, ting" is to show that I've come through. And whoever's listening must've come through, or they wouldn't be here. Because I always considered my work one piece, whether it be with Beatles, David Bowie, Elton John, Yoko Ono . . . and I consider that my work won't be finished until I'm dead and buried, and I hope that's a long, long time. So to me it's part of one whole piece of work from the time I became public to now. And that's the connecting point between that, and the '80s is like we got a new chance, you know?"

[Snippet from Lennon's "(Just Like) Starting Over" plays.]

Sholin: [*Voice-over.*] Along with a new chance and the promise the '80s bring, John and Yoko felt the time was right for human honesty in relationships.

Ono: Now I know both sides. It's better to know both sides, because I ran into situations where I was really penniless and I had to sort of scrounge around and all that. That was interesting, too. It was an interesting experience. They were both interesting. But I had to really understand about woman's problems in a sense . . . well, in a sense I bypassed that because of my background and because after that I was being an artist here and everything. And I bypassed that until I met John and realized what women are going through. So it was a very good education in a way.

Sholin: [*Voice-over.*] Sexual struggles only hurt our chances for coming together as loving men and women, [Lennon believed]. In other words, we'd built up too many barriers between male and female.

Lennon: Well, isn't it time we destroyed it because where has it gotten us after all these thousands of years? Are we still gonna be clubbing each other to death? Do I have to arm wrestle you to have a relationship with you as another male? Do I have to seduce her or come on with her, that I'm gonna lay her because she's a female, or come on as some sexual. . . . Can we not have a relationship on some other level besides that same old stuff all the time? I mean, it's kids' stuff, man; it's really kids' stuff. And I don't wanna go through life pretendin' to be James Dean or Marlon Brando, you know? In a movie—not in real life, even—in a movie version of them.

Ono: And in the name of freedom, people wanted to not have dialogue with each other, but just wanted to hang around being single. I'm not promoting marriage or anything like that. I'm just talking about marriage of the soul, the mind, exchange of spirit and soul, which you can have with women or men. And it would be nice because, after all, the society is created by men and women and propagation is the basis of the society still. So it's nice to have a dialogue between two sexes.

[Lennon's "Mind Games" plays.]

Sholin: [*Voice-over.*] Back in the early days of John and Yoko, the love that went into their music was perhaps not as obvious as it is today. John relates this to the craziness of the times.

Lennon: Not only the fact that we got together and, boom, it was like an explosion, but there was also the Beatle thing about us getting together and whether they split because of us or not or whatever the reason—all that stuff. The Beatles were splittin', the Beatles were arguin', John and Yoko was getting together. The anti-Vietnam crusades were going on all over. And we were involved in so many things, and we were puttin' out so much work, and we were making movies, making public appearances, performing at shows and all, and traveling the world, and doing all that. So there was no time to reflect. There was only time to put out immediate impressions of what was happening.

Ono: But we were really honest about it. You can say that maybe we were naive or something, but still we were very honest about it, about everything we did, you know?

Lennon: That's why I referred to "the word is love" on *Rubber Soul* straight through to "All You Need Is Love" to "Give Peace a Chance" to "imagine there's no countries . . . imagine no war," in other words, to right to this moment now. This album doesn't say "imagine the whole world like that," because I've said that in a way. What I'm saying now is, "Now let's put the spotlight on the two of us and show how we're trying to imagine there's no wars. To live that love and peace, rather than sing about it only."

[*Lennon's "Oh Yoko" plays.*]

Ono: I mean, everybody knows what love is. It's not something that you can explain, but it's a very strong energy and power.

Lennon: Well, I tried to define it in my own way: "Love is real, real is love" [a line in Lennon's song "Love"]. And it's a very simple lyric, or even simplistic—I don't know which way it would go—but what can you call it? You can say, "Love is like a flower" . . .

Ono: It's like saying, "What is air?" And you say, "H_2O." It doesn't mean anything.

Lennon: It's whatever it is when it feels good is love, and the other one is not love, you know?

[*Snippet from Lennon's "Love" plays.*]

Sholin: [*Voice-over.*] That's the message John and Yoko have for their listeners in *Double Fantasy*. Thanks to the years of experimentation and discovery, they found the answer lies in a loving relationship.

Lennon: I'm forty. I wanna talk to the people my age. I'm happy if the young people like it, and I'm happy if the old people like it. I'm talkin' to guys and gals that have been through what we went through, together—the '60s group that has survived. Survived the war, the drugs, the politics, the violence on the street—the whole shebang. That we've survived it, and we're here. And I'm talkin' to them. And the "Woman" song is to Yoko, but it's to all women. And because my role in society—or any artist or poet's role—is to try and express what we all feel. Not to tell people how to feel, not as a preacher, not as a leader, but as a reflection of us all. And it's like that's the job of the artist in society, not to . . .

They're not some alienated being living on the outskirts of town. It's fine to live on the outskirts of town, but artists must reflect what we all are. That's what it's about—artists, or poets, or whatever you want to call it. And that's what I'm tryin' to express on behalf of all the men to all the women, through my own feelings about women—when it dawned on me, "God! It *is* the other half of the sky," as the late, great Chairman MacDougal said, right? [*An apparent reference to an old Chinese proverb, also attributed to Chairman Mao. —Ed.*] I mean, they are the other half of the sky, and without them there is nothing. And without us there's nothing. There's only the two together creates children, creates society. So what's all this BS about, you know, women are this and men are that? We're all human, man. We're all human. And I am tryin' to say it to Yoko, but to all women, you know? On behalf of all men, in a way. If that's takin' it too much on meself, I feel that artists are that—they're a reflection of society—mirrors.

[*Lennon's "Woman" plays, followed by the Beatles' "It's Only Love."*]

Sholin: [*Voice-over.*] John says Yoko led him to enlightening realizations about love and human relationships. He also wasn't above lifting her ideas for some of their heaviest musical concepts—like "Imagine."

[*Snippet from Lennon's "Imagine" plays.*]

Lennon: "Imagine" was a straight lift out of her book *Grapefruit*. There are pieces in there saying, "Imagine this, imagine that," but . . . so I didn't give her credit. . . . Hmm. Tra-la-la-la-la.

Ono: You dedicated the album to me instead.

Lennon: So I dedicated the album to her—which is a cop-out. But, you know . . . I was only as honest as I could be then, you see? You can only be what you think . . . as best you can at the time. But the point of the song, right, is . . . because people kept saying, "What are you doin'? What are you doin' in the bed-in? What are you doing in *Two Virgins*? What are you doin' together? What are you doin'? What are you doin'?" That was where we first came out with "All we're sayin' is give peace a chance." [It] literally came out of my mouth as a spoken word to a reporter. [*Snippet from Lennon's "Give Peace a Chance" plays.*] After being asked millions and millions of times, "What are you doin'?" "Well, all I'm sayin' is give peace a chance." Not that I have the answer, or I've got a new format for society, 'cause I don't, and I don't believe anybody else has. "Show me the plan" as "Revolution" said. [*Snippet from the Beatles' "Revolution 1" plays.*] The Beatles' "Revolution," my "Revolution" song, said, "Show me the plan." Before we knock all the buildings down. [*Snippet from Lennon's "Give Peace a Chance" plays.*]

"Imagine" is the same thing; you hit it right on the head. It's just "*Imagine* if there were no countries." Not no places where we each had our little spot. But imagine . . . there was a time, you know, when you didn't have to have a passport to go from country to country. What kind of world are we creating? Really! It used to be you go around, you know? What is this game that somehow this is America and then just across the field is Canada and that you have to have all kinds of papers and pictures and stamps and passports and . . . the concept of imagining no country, imagining no religion, not imagining no god—although you're entitled to do that, too—imagine no denominations, imagining that we revere Jesus Christ, Muhammad, Krishna, [Tibetan Buddhist master] Milarepa, equally. We don't have to worship either one that we don't have to, but imagine there's no Catholic/Protestant. No Jew/Christian. That we allow it all—freedom of religion for *real*. For real.

[*Lennon's "Imagine" plays.*]

Ono: It's very important for some women that we get equal rights and things like that, but I think we go beyond that. And for some people it's a big step that we're gonna be in. But I think that we are people, first of all. And there are many things that we don't know about human beings. I don't know either, but there's an immense possibility. I think our rights and our freedoms and our powers go beyond those systems, and we shouldn't limit ourselves to that. So in a way, instead of fighting for that, we can trust in ourselves and rely on our own power, which is immense. Each person is like a total universe, and we are very powerful people. So we should realize that, rather than to try to fight and get something outside of ourselves. We always had . . . there's a human-race dream, you know? Like, we always wanted to fly, so now we have planes, you know? And the next dream is probably wanting to be peaceful . . .

Lennon: Well, the other great dream of mankind, one was to fly—which might've taken us a long time, but it took somebody to imagine it first.

Ono: Yes, kept imagining—

Lennon: The second was [to] reach the moon, right?

Ono: Yes, which we reached.

Lennon: Which we reached. Now, sure, it was an American in an American rocket, because that was the way history was at that time. But mankind reached the moon, because they said, "One giant step for mankind." It was for all of us we went to the moon.

Ono: We were always saying, like, wanting the moon . . .

Lennon: But nowadays even football players are doin' it, right? Which we were doing then, which is projecting the future in a positive way. Now people are saying, "You're naive, you're dumb, you're stupid." OK, it might've hurt us on a personal level to be called names, but what we were doing . . . you can call it magic, meditation, projection of goal—which businesspeople do, they have courses on it. The footballers do it. They pray, they meditate before the game. They visualize themselves winning. [Tennis star] Billie Jean King visualizes every move on the court. What we were doing, we were early pioneers of that movement, which is to project a future in which we can have goals which we can reach. Right? People project their own future.

So what we wanted to do was say, "Let's imagine a nice future." She's right, the males like even Aldous Huxley and George Orwell, who produced 1984 . . . you look into Orwell's life, it was all torture and this, that, and the other, and he was brought up in a certain environment in a male-dominated society full of Marxist stuff about Spain, and they were all from the '30s . . . whatever, that period when they had those dreams of socialism answering everything. Right? And their dreams fell to dust after the war. And then they wrote these books projecting this horrific Big Brother, monsters controlled by robots. And even now, I think these people that project the space fantasies are projecting war in space continually, with women in miniskirts, available sexual objects, and the men with super-macho John Wayne guns on their hips.

I'm sayin' it's time for the people to get hip to that, man. Because they're projecting our future. Do we want our children to be out in space, or our grandchildren fighting—maybe not Russians but Venusians in space? You see? If it works for a football player and a tennis player, it can work for all of us. We have to project a positive future. I mean, I think that's what Christ and Muhammad and those people were saying in their way in their time for their society.

Sholin: [*Voice-over.*] That was perhaps John Lennon's heaviest point— that without a positive outlook, humanity can't survive. That's what he and Yoko wanted to project: people have an all-important power inside themselves, and it's time to use it, not necessarily politically but lovingly as well.

Ono: Politicians rely on the fact that people are not thinking. And if each person, all of us, would really be centered and really start thinking for ourselves, then they don't have a chance. Because we're like really very powerful gods and goddesses, you know?

Lennon: In retrospect, if I was trying to say that same thing again, I would say the people have the power. I don't mean power of the gun. They have the power to make and create the society they want. We all created this together; it wasn't a few kings or a few generals. We might have invested the power in a Napoleon, or the Germans might've been hypnotized by Hitler. Does that make the Germans different from the rest of the human race? No way! You know it coulda happened anywhere. It just happened there at that moment in time. OK?

And also the world—we do breathe in and we breathe out. So you go to the left, you go to the right. In the long term it's meaningless. Even since I was conscious of politics, it was the right in the '50s, the left in the '60s, and sort of nothing in the '70s, and it's going to the right. If everybody's gonna panic and just react to an illusionary right wing that's gonna kill everybody, well, that's what you're gonna get. I believe that it doesn't have to be like that just 'cause the guy has a right-wing [view] or supposedly has a different political view than other people.

Now, personally, I've never voted in me life. How d'ya like that? There's a Beatles book that was handed out in the 1964 tour, a book of photographs, and on the top of it, it shows this young John Lennon in his usual big-mouth way sayin', "No phony politician's ever gonna get through to me." Well, I take the "phony politician" out, because I don't think all politicians are phony. I won't categorize even politicians now, because I've learned a lot since I was twenty-three.

But I don't think politics is the only answer, you see? I think this idea that we elect these leaders and then expect them to do miracles for us. . . . Now, Kennedy is a big dream for everybody because he didn't live to fulfill or let us down. It's not to negate what Kennedy was and what he means to people, but the reality is, had he lived, how do you know how well he would've done at the time? Right? Or how the war would've gone and how everything would've gone? So investing leaders with supernatural powers—whether they be pop stars, politicians, or movie stars or football heroes—it don't work, it just doesn't work. Because we put them up on the pedestal and then immediately want to knock them off.

So Reagan's gonna go in there. All the so-called rightists are all gonna be waitin' for him to do what they want. And when he doesn't because it's impossible, because the presidency is such a vast, awe-inspiring position for any man to be in, and it means a lot more than some local right/left group, that he cannot possibly fulfill the dreams of the right wing, the same way as Carter or Kennedy could never have fulfilled the dreams of the left wing. It is too much invested in one man, one group, and I don't believe in that.

[*Lennon's "Only People" plays.*]

Sholin: [*Voice-over.*] Just like everyone has power within themselves, John and Yoko realized they carry an outside power as well, because of who they are and what they had accomplished.

Ono: We are fully aware of our power, whatever that is, and we nurture it, and we try to be very careful about our own life because of that. And also try to communicate and, you know, communicate as much as we can with that power, you know? But all of you do, in a way . . . so, in degrees, and that's what you should use and that's what it means: to communicate and to tell each other, reassure each other, that we are here together.

Lennon: People are believing in projecting their own power, visualizing goals, visualizing positiveness, and doing these things that are changing the world. It all takes time. You see, I think the bit about the '60s . . . we were all full of hope, and then everybody got depressed and the '70s were terrible . . . that attitude that everybody has, that the '60s was therefore negated for being naive and dumb and the '70s is really where it's at—which means, you know, putting makeup on and dancing in the disco—which was fine for the '70s . . . but I don't negate the '60s. I don't negate the '70s.

The seeds that were planted in the '60s—and possibly they were planted generations before—but the seed . . . whatever happened in the '60s, the flowering of that is in the feminist, feminization of society. The meditation, the positive learning that people are doing in all walks of life . . . that is a direct result of the opening up of the '60s.

Now, maybe in the '60s we were naive, and like children everybody went back to their room and said [*imitates voice of young child*], "Well, we didn't get a wonderful world of just flowers and peace and happy chocolate, and it wasn't just pretty and beautiful all the time." And that's what everybody did: "We didn't get everything we wanted." Just like babies. And everybody went back to their rooms and sulked. "And we're just gonna play rock 'n' roll and not do anything else. We're gonna stay in our rooms, and the world is a nasty, horrible place 'cause it didn't give us everything we cried for." Right?

Cryin' for it wasn't enough. The thing the '60s did was show us the *possibility* and the responsibility that we all had. It wasn't the answer. It just gave us a glimpse of the possibility, and in the '70s everybody's gone, "Nya, nya, nya, nya." And possibly in the '80s maybe everybody'll say, "Well, OK, let's project the positive side of life again," you know? The world's been goin' on a long time, right? It's probably gonna go on a long time.

Ono: But also, the '60s was sort of really going out and communicating and expanding, but in the '70s, people think that nothing happened. But in a way, we went back inside us. There's a lot of very interesting, magical psychic things that happened, you know, people got tuned into. And so, with the '60s expansion and '70s knowledge, I think the '80s is gonna be another step up, you know? It'll be beautiful, you know?

Sholin: [*Voice-over.*] Do things become more beautiful or easier to understand as Yoko and John find themselves growing older? How about emotions over the years?

Lennon: You don't get so emotionally up and down when you're older. Because when you're younger, your genes are different or your hormones are different. So it absolutely has to express different. You can become mellower without becoming rigid. I'm still open to anything. I still believe almost in anything until it's disproven. I don't have any set pattern. I don't have any set answers. I'm as open as ever, but just . . . my hormones don't work the same, that's all.

Ono: The thing is, young people in love and they're tender. . . . I mean, go back to "I Want to Hold Your Hand." They're very mellow songs, what are you talking about? You know? And we're talking about starting over. We're talking about falling in love again, to each other, you know? And that's the most beautiful, young, fresh thing to do. Nobody in the menopausal age can do that. So this conventional idea that if people are talking about love that means that they're out of the game, you know . . . and people who are talking about, "I wanna kick your pants," or whatever, you know . . .

Lennon: [*Sings to the tune of "I Want to Hold Your Hand."*] I want to kick your pants . . .

Ono: —or something like that or some violent song is "Right on, youth!" or something is a totally wrong idea.

[*Lennon's "Remember" plays.*]

Sholin: [*Voice-over.*] What about the idea that every individual feels the need to join some kind of movement or group? Is that a wrong idea?

Lennon: There's that part of us all, including meself, that wants to belong to some group. I don't mean a rock group, but a group in society, because it makes you feel secure when times are hard, or there seems to be a threat of war, or a threat of monetary crisis. And the media, with help from the public and the politicians, hype it up that it's the end of the world, or the end of America, or the end of financial empire, or whatever it is. And everybody gets insecure and wants to belong to a group, including me.

You know, I was always wanting to belong to something, even though I always wanted to be the rebel on the outside, part of me always wanted to be part of it. And it's an insecurity. I'm not sayin' that anybody who's become a born-again Christian or a born-again whatever the other groups are . . . but, in general, to me it looks like a sign of insecurity because I recognize it in myself—that when I do go through that terrible insecurity of the world is collapsing or going crazy, it doesn't make sense anymore, [I think,] *Wouldn't it be easier if I was just along with these people—this few hundred or few thousand that all think the same way?* And it makes life easier like that.

People realize that it's not the end of the world, the apocalypse is not gonna happen, no matter what some person might threaten us with. Those people have been wavin' those END OF THE WORLD [signs] . . . I remember those END OF THE WORLD IS NIGH cartoons when I was twelve, you know? My whole generation, our whole generation, was brought up with the H-bomb. I remember [British philosopher and social critic] Bertrand Russell and all the H-bomb . . . the reason we were rock 'n' rollers, apparently, in the '50s was 'cause the bomb might go off any minute. I mean, I don't think that's gonna happen. I really don't think it's gonna happen.

[*The Beatles' "In My Life" plays.*]

Sholin: [*Voice-over.*] For people who lived through the '60s and '70s, the death of John Lennon felt like the end of the world. But with his extremely positive way of projecting the future—his future with Yoko and Sean and our future as human beings on Earth—it's doubtful that John Lennon would have wanted his death to be regarded as any kind of end.

As fans of Lennon gathered outside the Dakota apartments following John's death and sang his songs to remember him, Yoko Ono asked through a spokesperson that the crowds go home. Yoko said there would be no funeral but that since John had loved and prayed for the human race, everyone should please pray the same way for him. Yoko asked for a ten-minute silent vigil, a tribute to John Lennon, a man the world loved.

John Lennon cared deeply about his family, humanity, and the music that originally inspired him. Just like people are coming together in the '80s, John said music is, too. All different styles from all the past years, and he loved it all, especially rock 'n' roll's golden greats.

[*Lennon's recording of Gene Vincent's "Be-Bop-a-Lula" plays.*]

Lennon: If the oldies but goldies come on, it's one of my favorites. If I hear "Be-Bop-a-Lula," I can hear it over and over again. Every time it comes on, I switch up the thing. I have the record still. If I hear Elvis . . . I heard him sing "I Want You, I Need You, I Love You" the other day. I mean, I was just in *heaven.* Of course, I was going back to my youth and remembering the dates and what was going on when I heard that music.

Ono: Music is just a format, and we're adding many different formats, and that's interesting. But new wave is gonna be old one day, too, and very soon. It'll be old hat. The minute it's out there and it's number one, that means that it's old hat, you know? And I think it's nice to discover all different forms of music, and that's nice.

Lennon: Bruce Springsteen's "Hungry Heart"—which I think is a great record—is to me the same kind of period sound as "Starting Over." I think the Cars' "Touch and Go" is right out of the '50s. [*Sings.*] "Uh, uh, oh . . ." That new wave, a lot of it is '50s stuff. But with the '80s styling, and that's what I think "Starting Over" is: it's a '50s song made with an '80s approach.

Ono: Look, music form never dies and that goes right back to Chopin or Beethoven or Bach. They're as fresh as ever. And so whatever form you use is fine. However you feel then and it's appropriate to your emotion, that's what you should use.

Lennon: I never believed that you can like rock *or* disco. I loved disco right from word scratch. And all those complaints about it being all the same is exactly what I heard about Little Richard and Fats Domino. They [listeners] couldn't tell the difference because the backing was always the same, the saxophones. But you could select from Fats Domino which are the best tracks. [Little Richard's] "Lucille" as opposed to someone that we can't even remember, right, with the same kind of rhythm. Also, now disco is part of the music scene. It's integrated into the whole. It's affected country and western, it's affected pop, it's affected the ballads. It is now part of the music. New wave will be exactly the same. It's another wave that joins the ocean of music.

Sholin: [*Voice-over.*] Lennon said he and Yoko were eager to jump into that ocean of music in the '80s. He said the same was true of his other musical partners years ago.

Lennon: I mean, that was the thing about the Beatles: they never stuck to one style. They never just did blues or just rock. We loved all music. We did "In My Life," "Anna" on the early things, and lots of ballady things, you know? My image was more rocky, you know? But if you look down those Beatle tracks, I'm right there with all the sentimental . . . just the same as Paul or anybody else. I loved that music just as much.

Sholin: [*Voice-over.*] But Beatles aside, John Lennon wanted to make music, and he wanted to make music with Yoko Ono, the woman he loved and called his best friend.

Ono: After he came back from Bermuda, the first night when he came back from Bermuda, I took him to a restaurant and we had a nice dinner, and we felt so good because after about a month of separation and just feeling a bit tipsy—we'd had a little wine and everything—and coming home, but we had to come home a bit early because of Sean. "Oh, well, we should go home before twelve." That sort of thing. And that sounded like Cinderella to me, you know? And it was a beautiful night, early summer, and the carriage was going in Central Park, and you hear all these sort of carriage sounds and everything. It almost made me feel like it was not this era. It could be any era. So it was a very romantic feeling, and coming back, and the gate was still open at the Dakota. We just strolled in, and I just went to the piano. And I just started writing the whole thing. So good, that's how it was.

[*Ono's "I'm Your Angel" plays.*]

Sholin: [*Voice-over.*] Lennon was filled with creativity and inspiration to make music, he said in his last interview, and then to perform.

Lennon: I'm so hungry for makin' records because of the way I feel. I wanna make some more records before I tour. So I'd like to make at least one more album before actually making that final decision of calling those very expensive session musicians and takin' them on the road, you know? But when I went in there, I had no intention of going live, because I've noticed a lot of people like the Clash don't do any personal appearances hardly anymore, and they just make a video and a record. And so part of me was thinking, *Well, all right.* But when we were playing in that studio . . . and then, I don't know whether it was Tony [Levin], the bass player, or the drummer . . . after we'd done "Starting Over," he said, "Can we do this again? I mean, let's take it on the road!" And that was the first time it came: I thought, *My God, this would be fun, wouldn't it?* And if we can do it in the way we've done the album, which is have fun, enjoy the music, enjoy the performance, be accepted as John and Yoko, then I'd be happy to go out there.

Sholin: [*Voice-over.*] But John Lennon won't have a chance to go out there, as he wanted to do with Yoko and the band. Instead, there will be no stage, no concert, and no more music other than the tracks left over from the *Double Fantasy* sessions. For John Lennon, there will be no more earthly existence. But to say he is dead is wrong. His spirit, his love, his music, his power . . . none of these are gone or forgotten.

For Yoko Ono, who will have to be the strongest of all, the void created by the passing of John Lennon will be the hardest to bear. If Yoko can fill that emptiness with beautiful memories of a love shared and a life lived together, then perhaps the pain in her heart will be eased. We all hope so.

A great man is gone, but a great love survives.

[*Lennon's "(Just Like) Starting Over" plays. Then, following closing credits, Lennon's "Nobody Told Me" plays.*]

ABOUT THE PARTICIPANTS

Tariq Ali, an activist, essayist, novelist, and filmmaker who lives in London, is a member of the editorial committee of the *New Left Review* and a contributor to such publications as the *Guardian* and the *London Review of Books*. He is the author of many books, including *The Duel*, *The Obama Syndrome*, and *The Islamic Quintet*, a set of five historical novels.

Tallulah Bankhead, who died in 1968, was an American stage and screen actress.

Robin Blackburn, a British historian, is a former editor of and longtime contributor to the *New Left Review*. Currently a professor at England's University of Essex, he spent nearly a decade as distinguished visiting professor of historical studies at the New School in New York.

Dick Cavett, a three-time Emmy Award winner, was a prominent figure in American television for five decades, beginning in the 1960s. A one-time talent coordinator and writer for Johnny Carson's *Tonight Show*, he went on to host his own critically acclaimed talk shows, which appeared in the United States at various times on ABC, CBS, PBS, and several other networks.

Bob Cross attended England's Keele University and accompanied Maurice Hindle on his visit to John Lennon's home. Hindle lost touch with Cross after leaving Keele, and nothing is known of his postcollege activities.

Dennis Elsas, one of the most popular voices in New York radio, spent more than twenty-five years as a disc jockey at WNEW-FM, the area's leading progressive rock radio station, where he interviewed such musicians as Pete Townshend, Mick Jagger, and Paul McCartney. He currently hosts shows on WFUV-FM, which serves the New York metropolitan area, and Sirius XM Satellite Radio's Classic Vinyl channel (26). In 2010 he created *Rock 'n' Roll Never Forgets*, a live multimedia show that features clips from his radio programs and reminiscences about his on-air interviews with leading rock and folk artists. Audio excerpts from many of those conversations are available at denniselsas.com.

Joe Garagiola, who died in 2016, was a catcher for four American Major League Baseball teams who went on to become a popular television announcer and host. He appeared regularly on *Today* from 1967 to 1973 and from 1990 to 1992 and also guest-hosted *The Tonight Show*.

Barbara Graustark has been an editor at the *New York Times* since 1993. Previously, she served as articles editor of *Metropolitan Home* and, before that, as a business reporter at *Newsweek*, where she covered lifestyle topics and pop music. She coauthored *Strawberry Fields Forever: John Lennon Remembered* and wrote, produced, and directed the 1984 documentary *Yoko Ono: Then & Now*.

Pete Hamill spent close to forty years writing for the *New York Post*, the *New York Daily News*, the *Village Voice*, and *Newsday*, and he served time as editor of the *Post* and editor in chief of the *Daily News*. He has contributed to a wide range of magazines, including *Esquire*, the *New Yorker*, *Playboy*, and *Rolling Stone*, and he won a Grammy Award for his liner notes to Bob Dylan's *Blood on the Tracks*. He has published about a dozen novels and nearly as many nonfiction books, including the 1995 memoir *A Drinking Life*.

Maurice Hindle was born and grew up in Warwickshire, England. He has taught literature and drama at several English universities, but principally at the Open University. Among his publications are the Penguin Classics editions of *Frankenstein* and *Dracula* and a scholarly edition of Daniel Defoe's *Colonel Jacque*. He authored *Shakespeare on Film*, and his current work in progress is *Singing His Heart and Speaking His Mind: The Songworld of John Lennon*.

Doreen Kelso, who was known to listeners simply as Doreen, was one of the most popular personalities at Wellington, New Zealand's, 2ZB, the radio station where she worked for thirty-two years. Kelso, a native of Australia, died in 2003.

Rosemary Leary, who died in 2002 at age sixty-six, was the fourth of Timothy Leary's five wives. She married him in 1967, fled the country with him after he escaped from prison in 1970, and spent twenty-three years in hiding. They separated in 1971 and divorced in 1976.

Dr. Timothy Leary, who died in 1996 at age seventy-five, was a psychologist and writer who became one of the leading countercultural figures of the 1960s as an advocate of LSD and other psychedelic drugs. Leary, who had a PhD from the University of California at Berkeley, worked as a professor at Harvard University, where he conducted LSD research until the school terminated his contract. He authored or coauthored nearly two dozen books.

Shirley MacLaine, the American actress, has appeared in dozens of films, including *The Apartment, Irma La Douce,* and *Terms of Endearment,* and has been featured on such TV shows as *Downton Abbey.* The winner of six Academy and Golden Globe Awards, she has authored several autobiographical books.

Fred Robbins, who died in 1992 at age seventy-three, was a longtime media personality, first in Baltimore and then in New York. He hosted a jazz radio program as well as TV variety and quiz shows, and interviewed celebrities for CNN and many magazines. The eulogy he delivered for jazz great Louis Armstrong, a longtime friend, was subsequently entered into the *Congressional Record.*

Jerry Rubin was a leading countercultural figure in America in the late 1960s who became friends with John Lennon and Yoko Ono. A founding member of the Youth International Party (a.k.a. the Yippies), he authored several books, including *Do It!* In an apparent major turnabout, he became a Wall Street stockbroker in 1980. He also organized networking parties in Manhattan that thousands of entrepreneurs and young executives attended. He was fifty-six when he was hit by a car and killed while jaywalking in Los Angeles in 1994.

Frances Schoenberger, who moved from Germany to the United States in 1969, has reported from Hollywood on stars and films for many years and has interviewed such celebrities as Clint Eastwood, David Bowie, Brad Pitt, and Arnold Schwarzenegger. She is a member of the Hollywood Foreign Press Association and sits on the selection committee for the Golden Globes. She is the author of a German-language memoir called *Barefoot in Hollywood: My Life Amid the Stars.*

Dave Sholin, who was the national music director of the now-defunct RKO Radio Network, has been Top 40 editor of the music industry trade publication *Gavin*, vice president of promotion at Island Records and Capitol Records, and senior director at EMI Collective. Today, in addition to hosting an afternoon radio show on central Oregon country station KSJJ-FM and working as a voiceover talent, he is involved in music promotion and marketing, overseeing strategic partnerships for Digital Music Universe, and curating boomermusicupdate.com. He also serves as executive producer for the Americana music channels the Train and Cowboys, Singers & Poets on Accuradio.com.

Howard Smith, who died in 2014 at age seventy-seven, was a journalist, broadcaster, and film director. He wrote a column for the *Village Voice* for more than twenty years and also contributed to such publications as *Playboy* and the *New York Times*. In 1972 Smith produced and directed the Oscar-winning documentary film *Marjoe*, about evangelist Marjoe Gortner. The organizers of the Smith Tapes Project—a multifaceted publishing effort involving more than a hundred of his interviews with such luminaries as Jim Morrison, Janis Joplin, Jerry Garcia, Andy Warhol, John Lennon, and Yoko Ono—released a limited-edition box set that earned a Grammy nomination in 2014. It is available from thesmithtapes. com, which also offers all five of Smith's conversations with Lennon and Ono in a CD set called *I'm Not the Beatles.*

Daniel Wiles, a 1970 graduate of England's Keele University, became a producer and director. He has directed episodes of *Book Four* and *6 O'Clock Show* as well as a 2011 BBC documentary called *Frank Skinner on George Formby.*

ABOUT THE EDITOR

Jeff Burger edited *Leonard Cohen on Leonard Cohen: Interviews and Encounters* (2014) and *Springsteen on Springsteen: Interviews, Speeches, and Encounters* (2013), both published in North America by Chicago Review Press. He has been a writer and editor for more than four decades and has covered popular music throughout his journalism career.

His reviews, essays, and reportage on that and many other subjects have appeared in more than seventy-five magazines, newspapers, and books, including *All Music Guide, Barron's, Circus, Creem, Family Circle, Gentlemen's Quarterly, High Fidelity,* the *Los Angeles Times, Melody Maker, No Depression,* and *Reader's Digest.* He has published interviews with many leading musicians, including Tommy James, Billy Joel, Foreigner's Mick Jones, Roger McGuinn, the Righteous Brothers, Bruce Springsteen, the members of Steely Dan, and Tom Waits; and with such public figures as F. Lee Bailey, Sir Richard Branson, James Carville, Suze Orman, Sydney Pollack, Cliff Robertson, and Wolfman Jack.

Burger has been editor of several periodicals, including *Phoenix* magazine in Arizona, and he spent fourteen years in senior positions at *Medical Economics,* America's leading business magazine for doctors. A former consulting editor at Time Inc., he currently serves as editor of *Business Jet Traveler,* which was named one of the country's best business magazines in 2011, 2013, and 2016 in the American Society of Business Publication Editors' Azbee Awards competition.

Burger—whose website, byjeffburger.com, collects more than forty years' worth of his music reviews and commentary—lives in Ridgewood, New Jersey. His wife, Madeleine Beresford, is a preschool director and teacher, and a puppeteer. The couple have a son, Andre, and a daughter, Myriam.

CREDITS

I gratefully acknowledge the help of everyone who gave permission for material to appear in this book. I have made every reasonable effort to contact copyright holders. If an error or omission has been made, please bring it to the attention of the publisher.

Radio interview with Doreen Kelso, June 21, 1964. Copyright ©1964. Broadcast date unknown, 2ZB (Wellington, New Zealand). Printed by permission of New Zealand Ministry for Culture and Heritage.

Interview with Fred Robbins, October 29, 1966. Copyright © 1966. Broadcast on *Assignment: Hollywood*, syndicated (US). Printed by permission of Lorelei Robbins.

TV interview with Joe Garagiola, May 14, 1968. Copyright © 1968. Broadcast May 14, 1968, *The Tonight Show*, NBC. Printed by permission of *The Tonight Show*.

Excerpts from conversation with Maurice Hindle, Daniel Wiles, and Bob Cross, December 2, 1968. Copyright © 1968 by Hard Rock Cafe International (USA), Inc. Brief excerpts originally published in *Unit*, January 1969. Printed by permission of HardRock.com/lennontapes.

Conversation with Timothy and Rosemary Leary, May 29, 1969. Copyright © 2012 by the Futique Trust. Published at timothylearyarchives.org. Reprinted by permission of the Futique Trust.

Interviews with Howard Smith, December 17, 1969, and January 23, 1972. Copyright © 1969, 1972. Broadcast on WABC-FM and WPLJ-FM (New York), December 1969 and January 23, 1972. Printed by permission of Ezra Bookstein/The Smith Tapes.

Conversation with Tariq Ali and Robin Blackburn, January 21, 1971. Copyright © 1970. Edited excerpts published March 8, 1971 in the *Red Mole*. Printed by permission of Tariq Ali.

INDEX